W9-CSZ-898

SOUL EATER

ATSUSHI OHKUBO

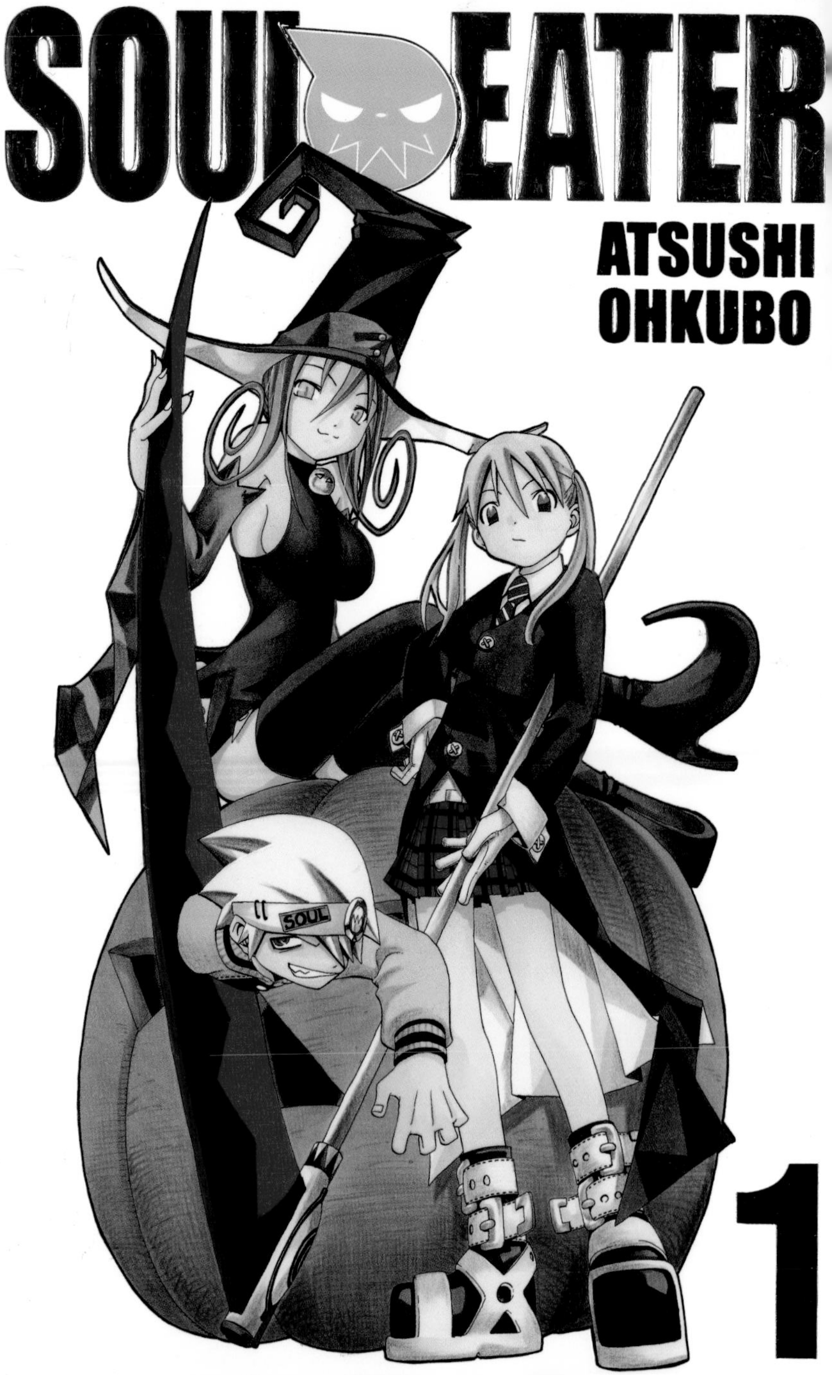
SOUL

1

SOUL EATER

1

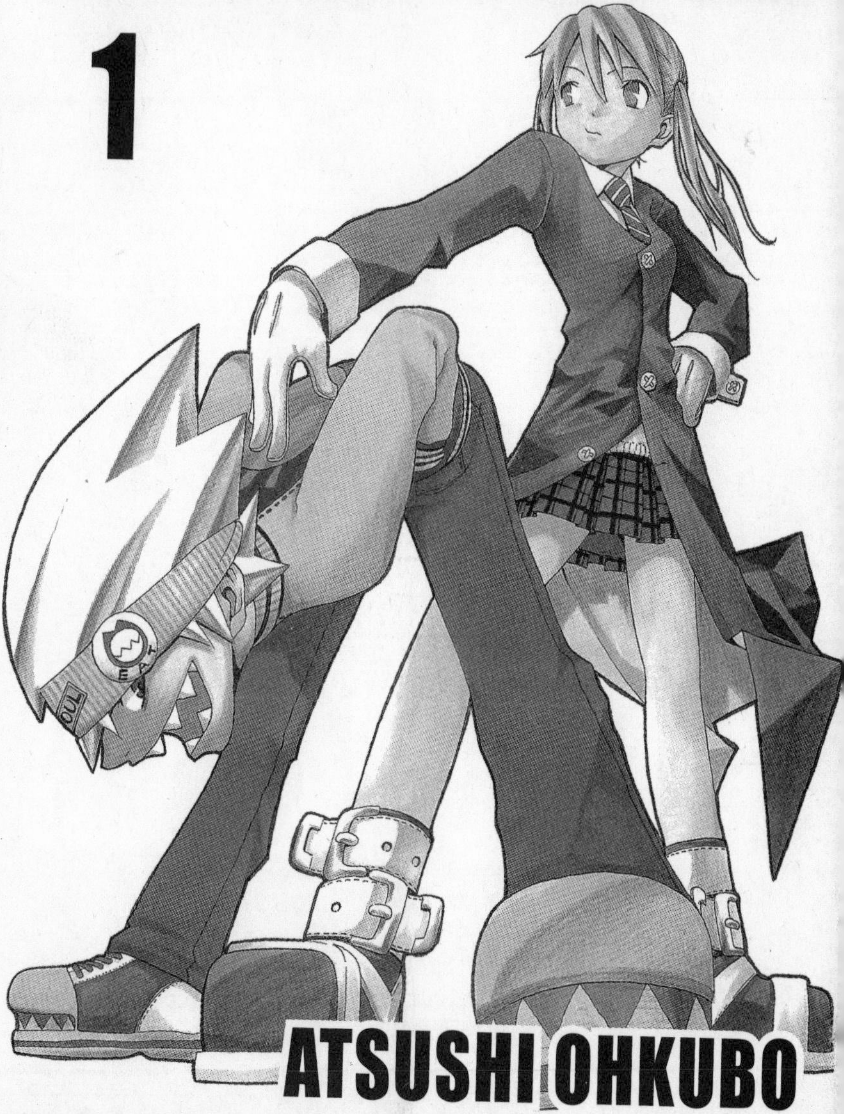

ATSUSHI OHKUBO

SOUL EATER

vol. 1
by ATSUSHI OHKUBO

Listen to the Beat of the SOUL

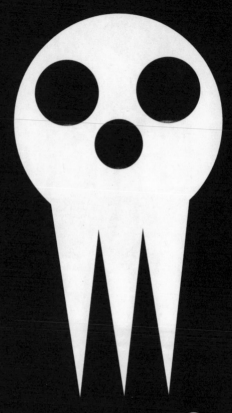

CONTENTS

PROLOGUE 1: SOUL EATER

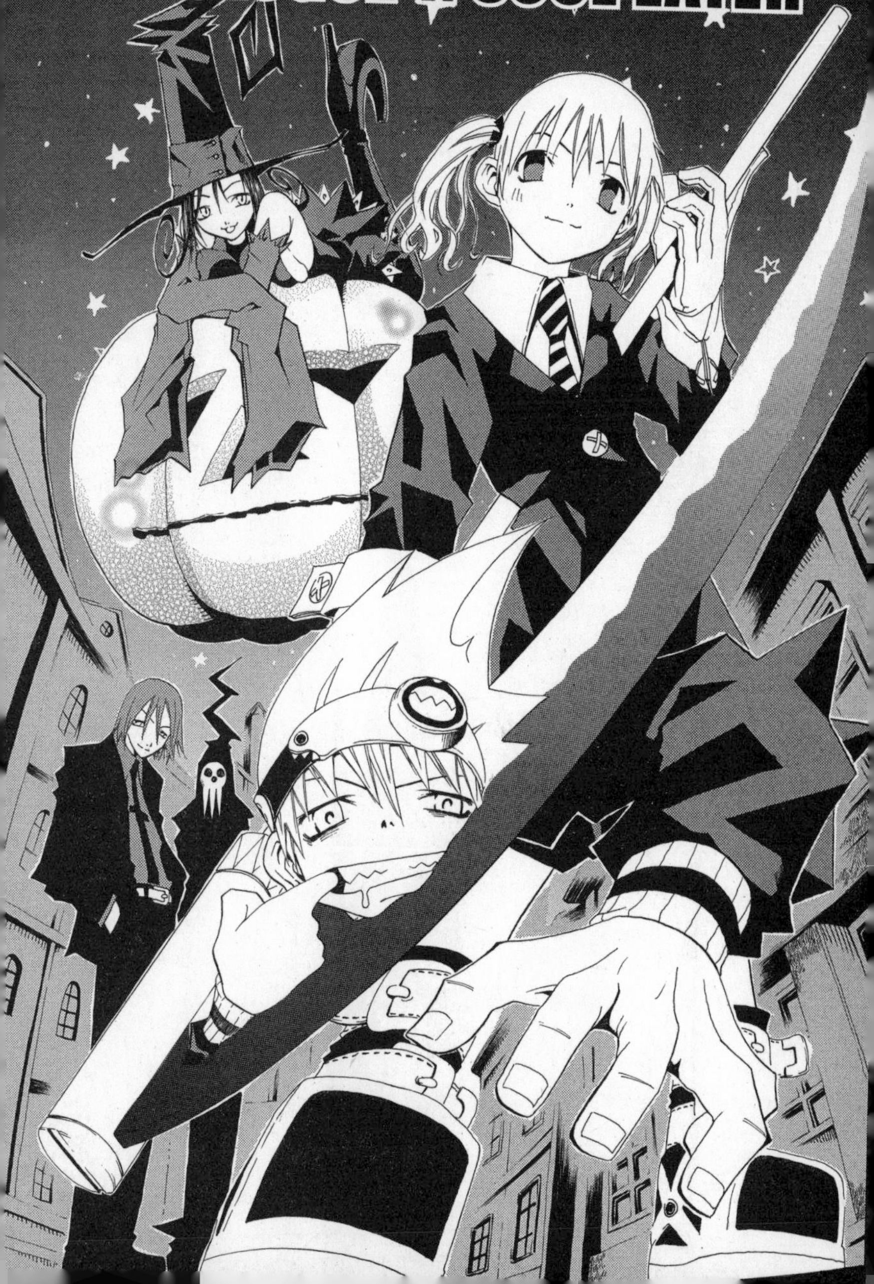

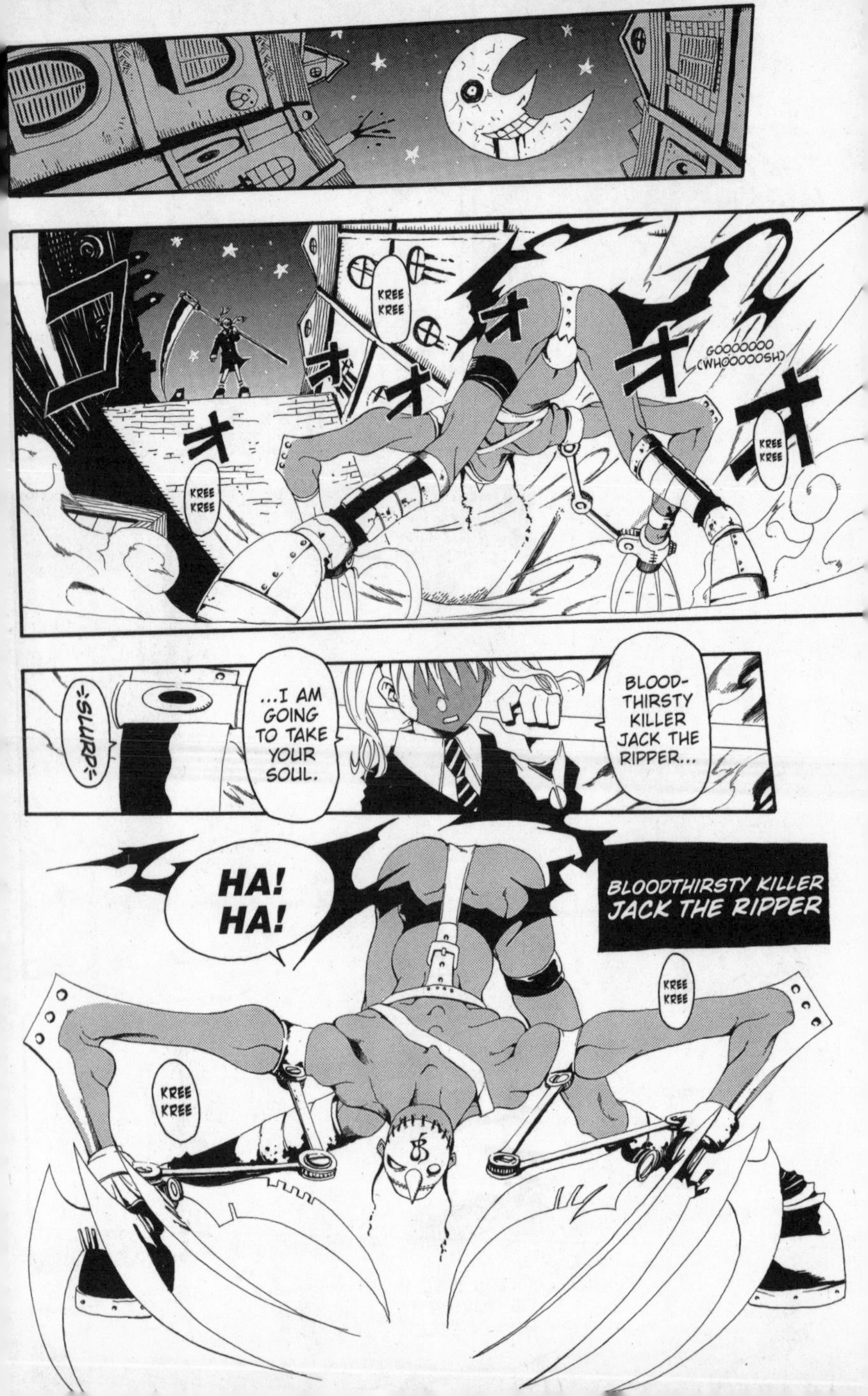
GOOOOOOO (WHOOOOOSH)
KREE KREE
KREE KREE
KREE KREE
BLOOD-THIRSTY KILLER JACK THE RIPPER...
...I AM GOING TO TAKE YOUR SOUL.
-SLURP-
BLOODTHIRSTY KILLER JACK THE RIPPER
KREE KREE
HA! HA!
KREE KREE

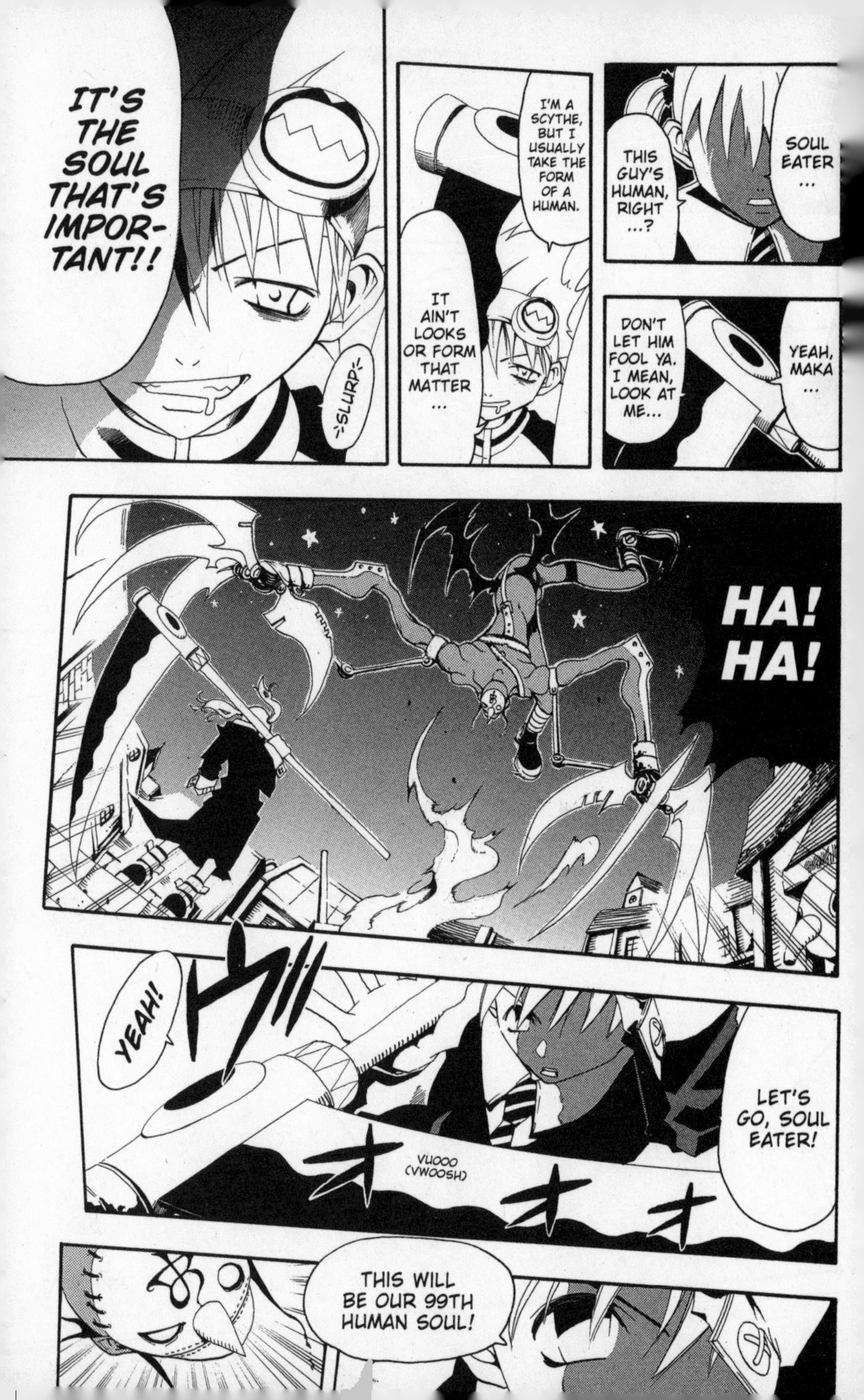
SOUL EATER...
THIS GUY'S HUMAN, RIGHT...?
YEAH, MAKA...
DON'T LET HIM FOOL YA. I MEAN, LOOK AT ME...
I'M A SCYTHE, BUT I USUALLY TAKE THE FORM OF A HUMAN.
IT AIN'T LOOKS OR FORM THAT MATTER...
-SLURP-
IT'S THE SOUL THAT'S IMPORTANT!!
HA! HA!
LET'S GO, SOUL EATER!
VUOOO (VWOOSH)
YEAH!
THIS WILL BE OUR 99TH HUMAN SOUL!

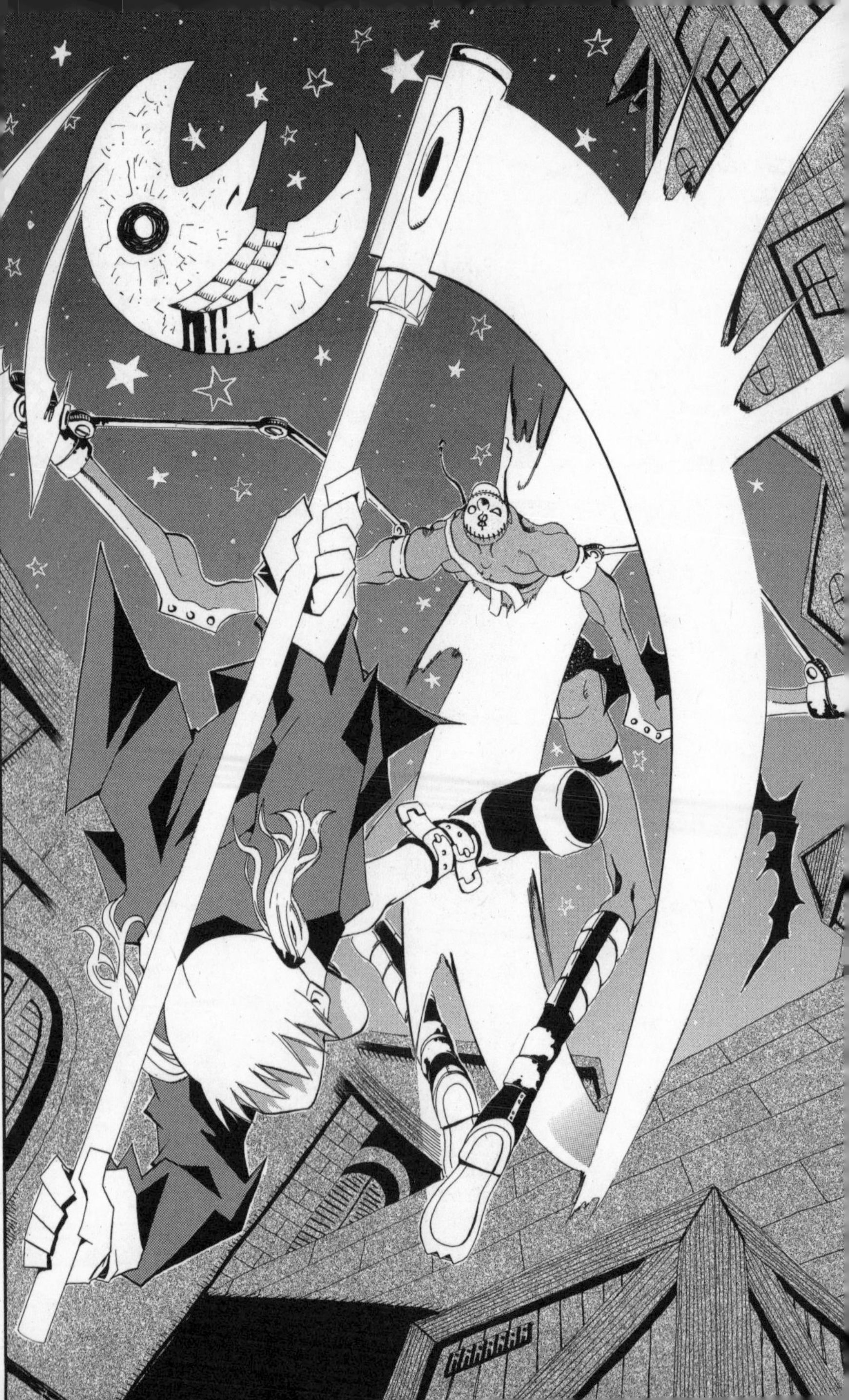

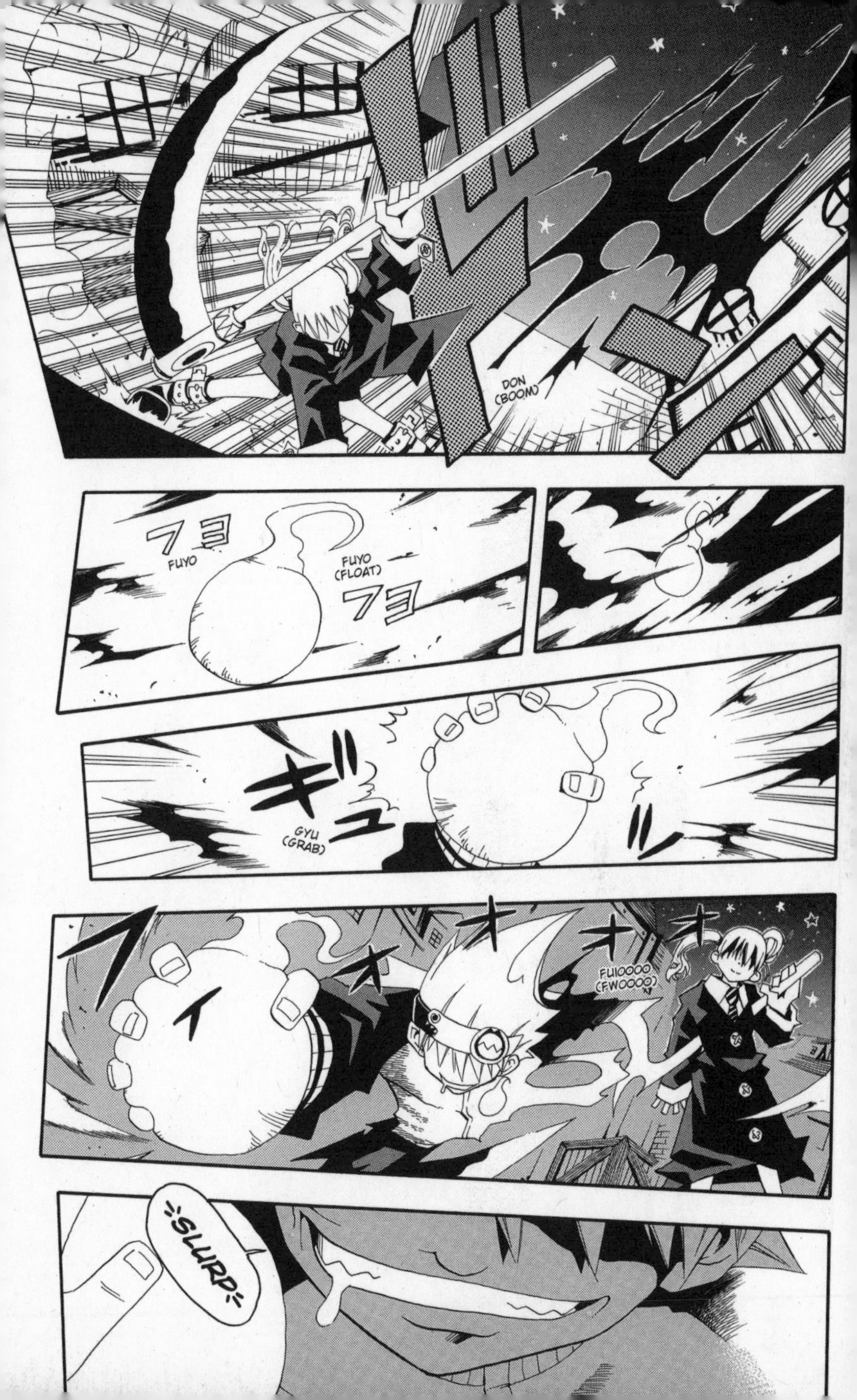
DON
(BOOM)
フヨ
FUYO
FUYO
(FLOAT)
フヨ
ギュ
GYU
(GRAB)
FUIOOOO
(FWOOOO)
SLURP

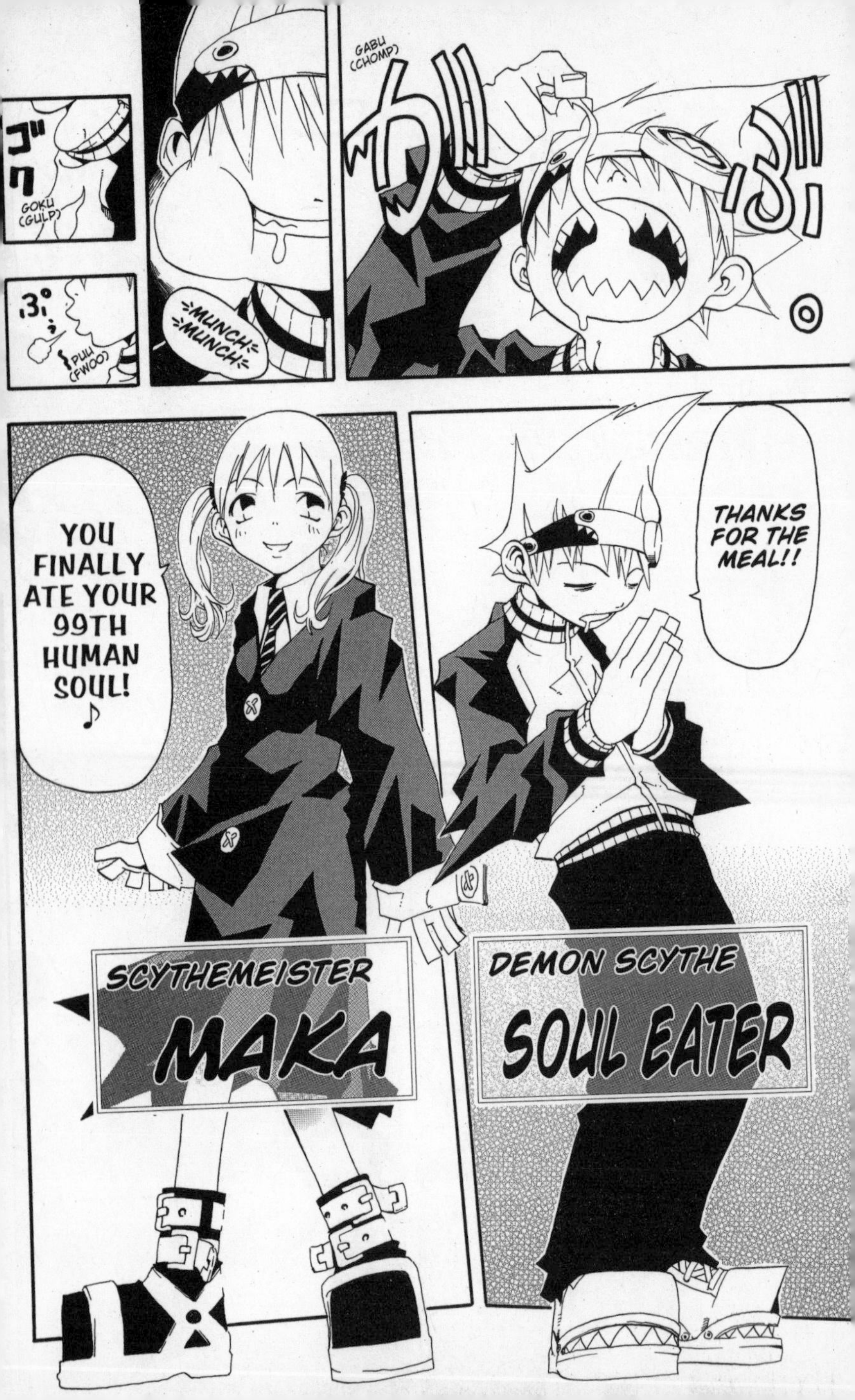
GABU (CHOMP)
MUNCH MUNCH
ゴク
GOKU (GULP)
PUU (FWOO)
THANKS FOR THE MEAL!!
DEMON SCYTHE
SOUL EATER
YOU FINALLY ATE YOUR 99TH HUMAN SOUL! ♪
SCYTHEMEISTER
MAKA

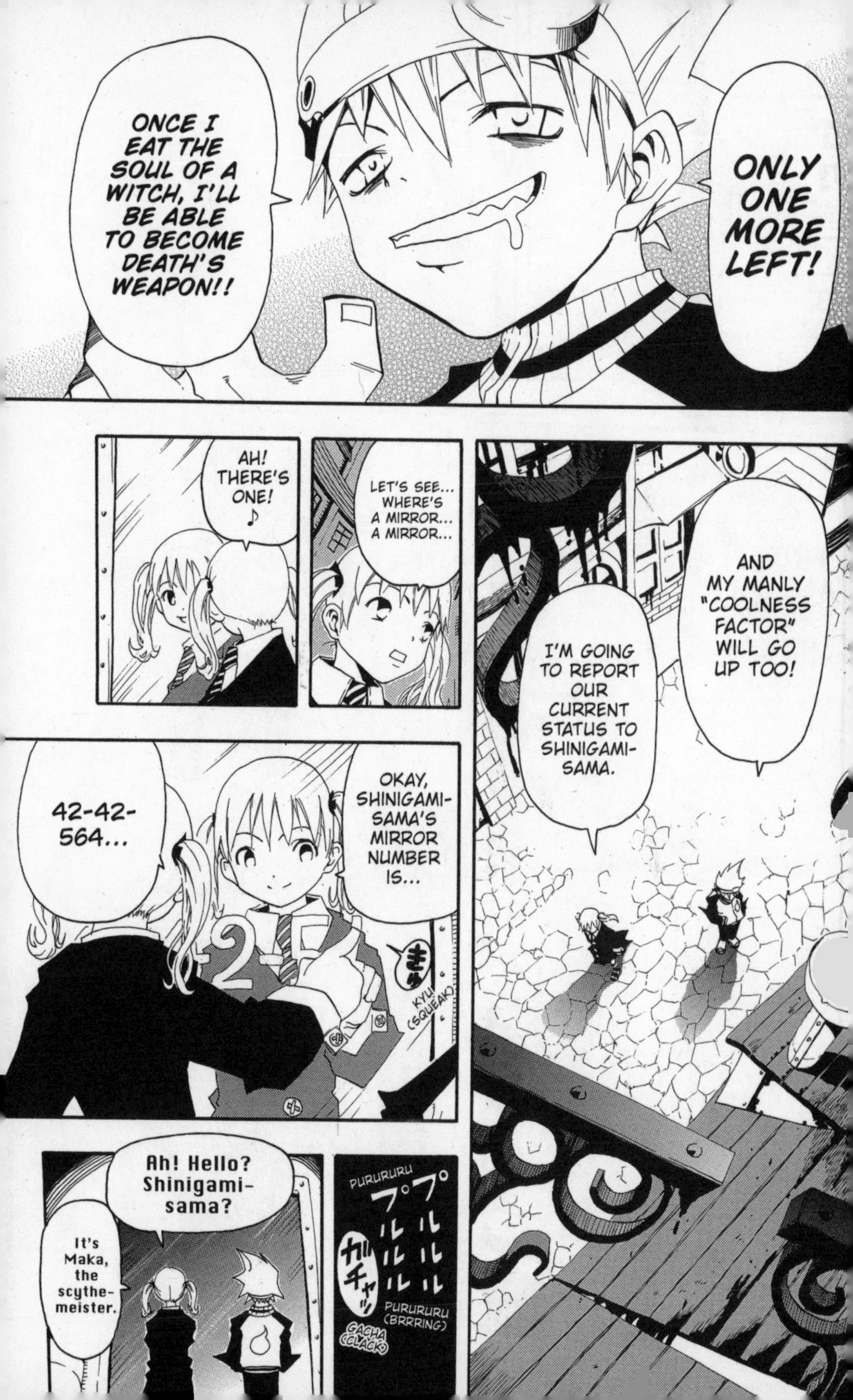
ONLY ONE MORE LEFT!
ONCE I EAT THE SOUL OF A WITCH, I'LL BE ABLE TO BECOME DEATH'S WEAPON!!
AND MY MANLY "COOLNESS FACTOR" WILL GO UP TOO!
I'M GOING TO REPORT OUR CURRENT STATUS TO SHINIGAMI-SAMA.
LET'S SEE... WHERE'S A MIRROR... A MIRROR...
AH! THERE'S ONE! ♪
OKAY, SHINIGAMI-SAMA'S MIRROR NUMBER IS...
KYU (SQUEAK)
42-42-564...
PURURURU
PURURURU (BRRRING)
GACHA (CLACK)
Ah! Hello? Shinigami-sama?
It's Maka, the scythe-meister.

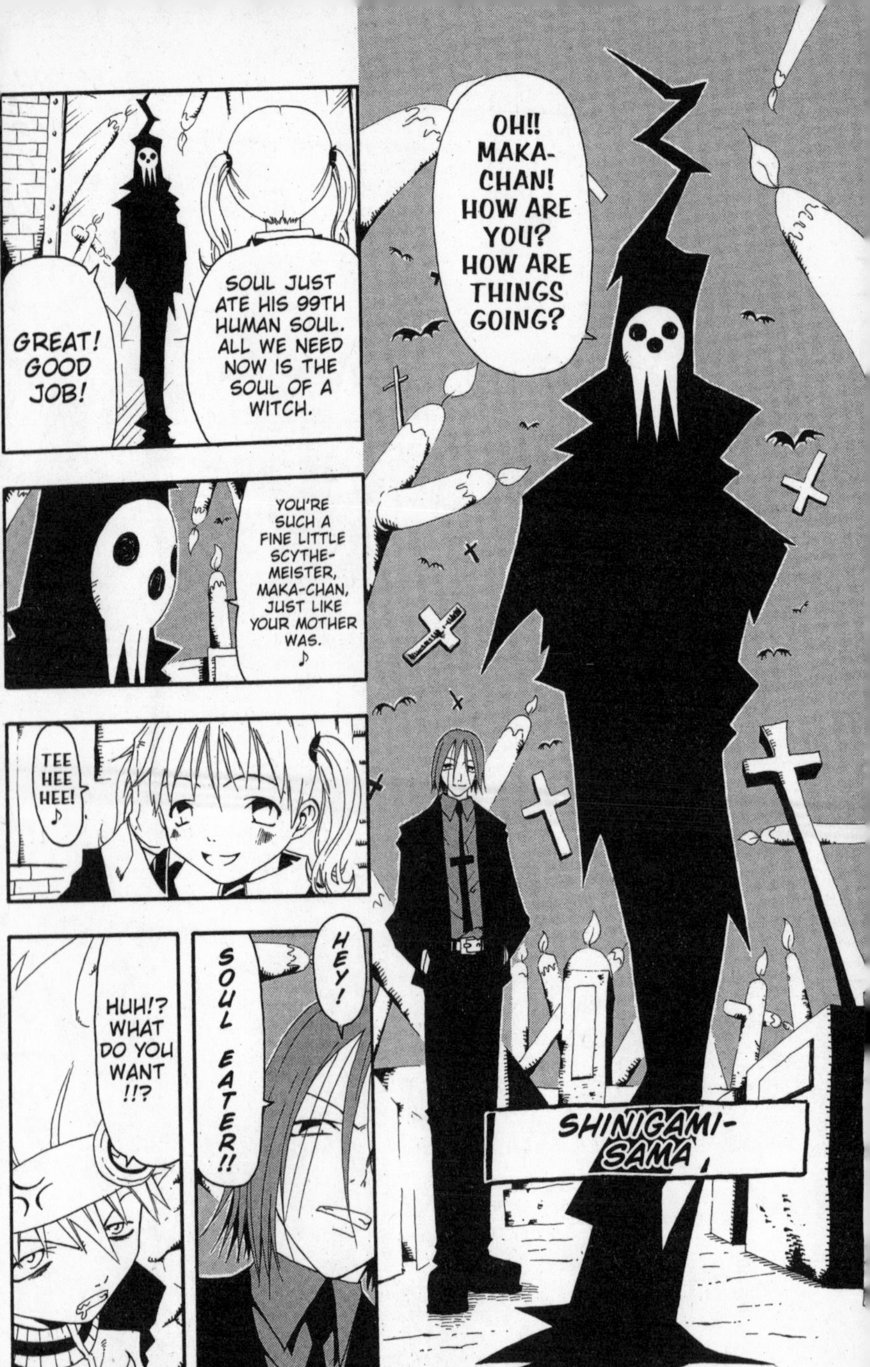
OH!! MAKA-CHAN! HOW ARE YOU? HOW ARE THINGS GOING?
SHINIGAMI-SAMA
SOUL JUST ATE HIS 99TH HUMAN SOUL. ALL WE NEED NOW IS THE SOUL OF A WITCH.
GREAT! GOOD JOB!
YOU'RE SUCH A FINE LITTLE SCYTHE-MEISTER, MAKA-CHAN, JUST LIKE YOUR MOTHER WAS. ♪
TEE HEE HEE! ♪
HEY!
SOUL EATER!!
HUH!? WHAT DO YOU WANT!!?

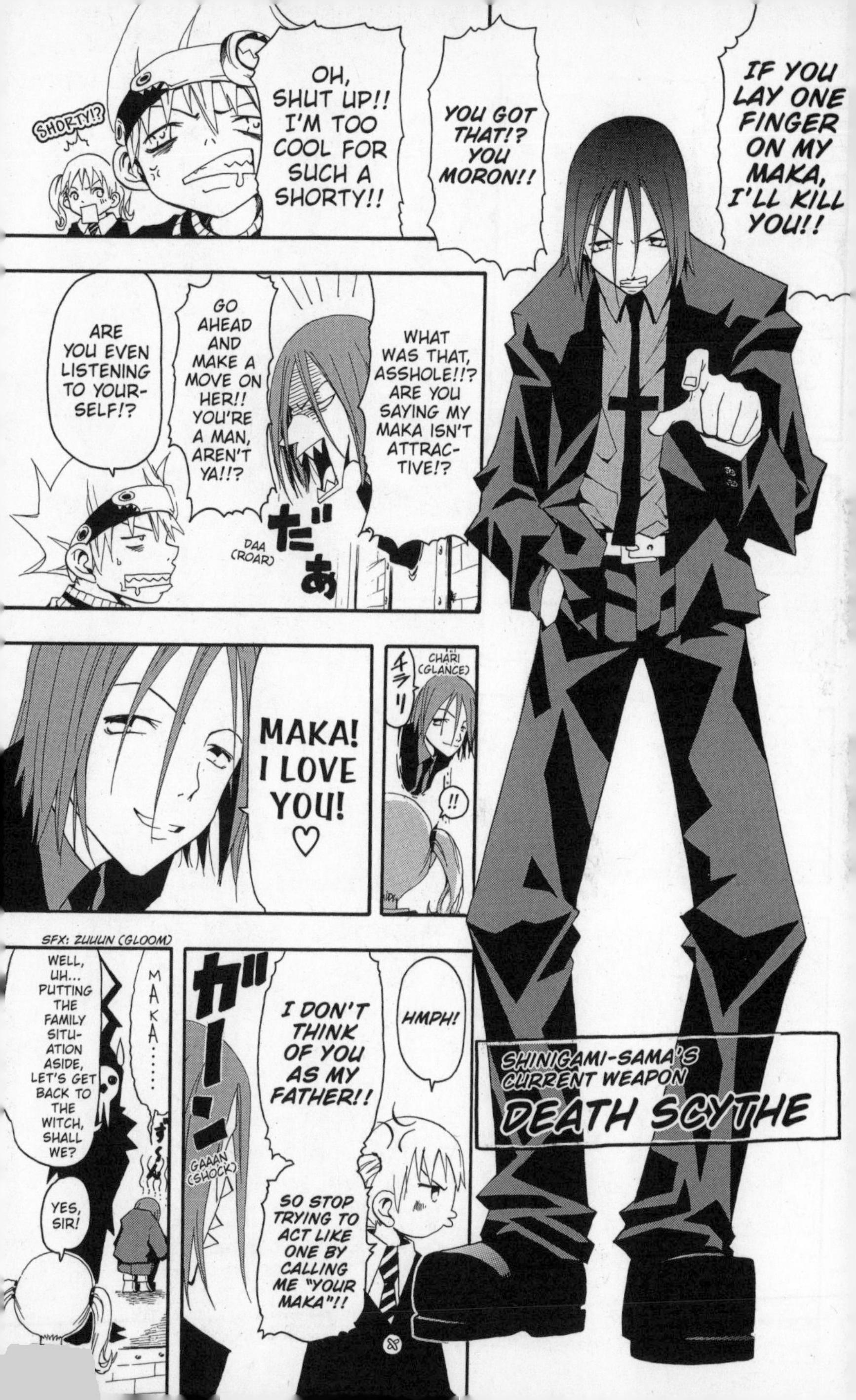
IF YOU LAY ONE FINGER ON MY MAKA, I'LL KILL YOU!!
YOU GOT THAT!? YOU MORON!!
SHINIGAMI-SAMA'S CURRENT WEAPON
DEATH SCYTHE
OH, SHUT UP!! I'M TOO COOL FOR SUCH A SHORTY!!
SHORTY!?
WHAT WAS THAT, ASSHOLE!!? ARE YOU SAYING MY MAKA ISN'T ATTRACTIVE!?
GO AHEAD AND MAKE A MOVE ON HER!! YOU'RE A MAN, AREN'T YA!!?
ARE YOU EVEN LISTENING TO YOURSELF!?
DAA (ROAR)
CHARI (GLANCE)
!!
MAKA! I LOVE YOU! ♡
HMPH!
I DON'T THINK OF YOU AS MY FATHER!!
SO STOP TRYING TO ACT LIKE ONE BY CALLING ME "YOUR MAKA"!!
GAAAN (SHOCK)
SFX: ZUUUN (GLOOM)
WELL, UH... PUTTING THE FAMILY SITUATION ASIDE, LET'S GET BACK TO THE WITCH, SHALL WE?
MAKA......
YES, SIR!

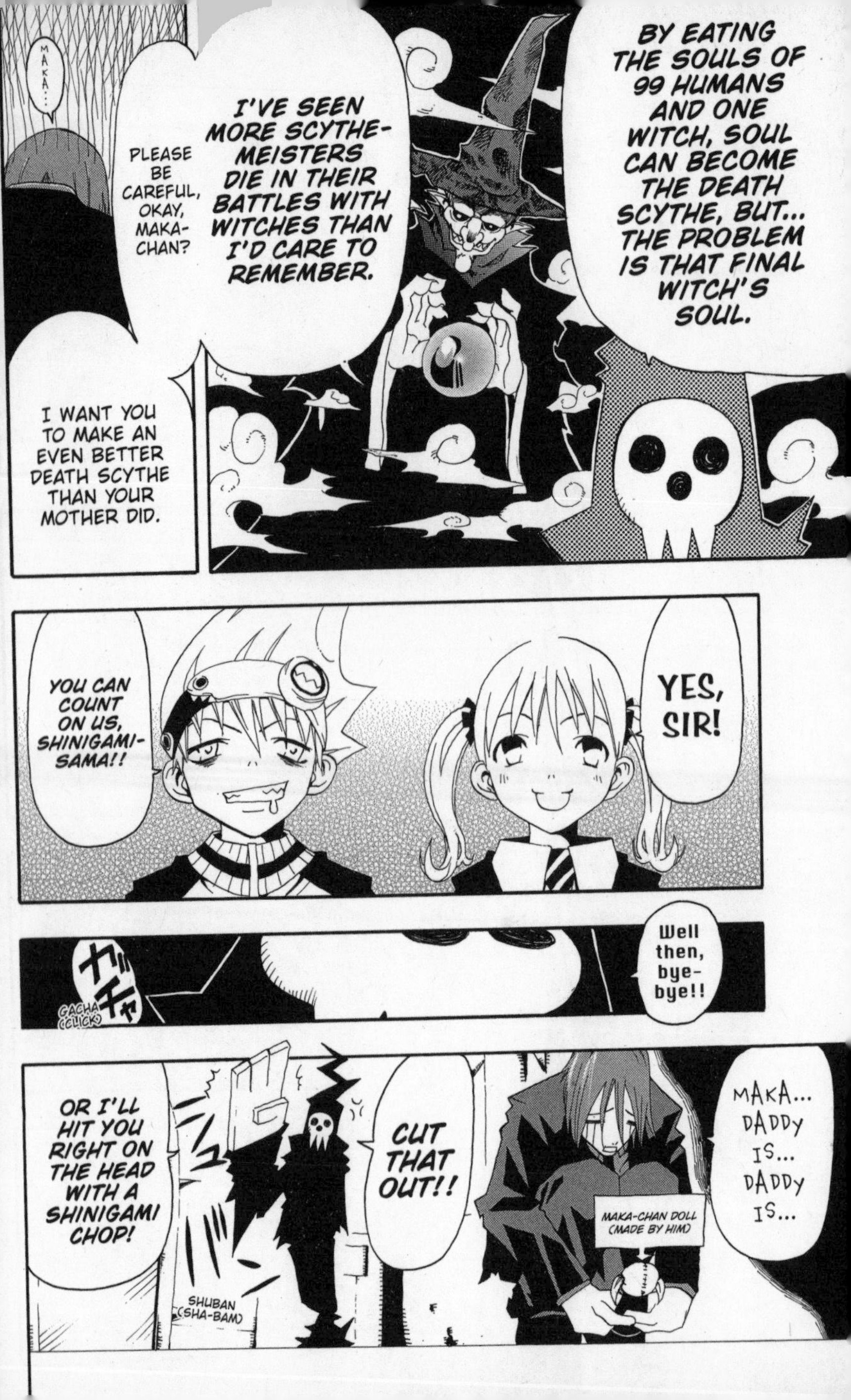
BY EATING THE SOULS OF 99 HUMANS AND ONE WITCH, SOUL CAN BECOME THE DEATH SCYTHE, BUT... THE PROBLEM IS THAT FINAL WITCH'S SOUL.
I'VE SEEN MORE SCYTHE-MEISTERS DIE IN THEIR BATTLES WITH WITCHES THAN I'D CARE TO REMEMBER.
PLEASE BE CAREFUL, OKAY, MAKA-CHAN?
MAKA...
I WANT YOU TO MAKE AN EVEN BETTER DEATH SCYTHE THAN YOUR MOTHER DID.
YES, SIR!
YOU CAN COUNT ON US, SHINIGAMI-SAMA!!
Well then, bye-bye!!
GACHA (CLICK)
MAKA... DADDY IS... DADDY IS...
MAKA-CHAN DOLL (MADE BY HIM)
CUT THAT OUT!!
OR I'LL HIT YOU RIGHT ON THE HEAD WITH A SHINIGAMI CHOP!
SHUBAN (SHA-BAM)

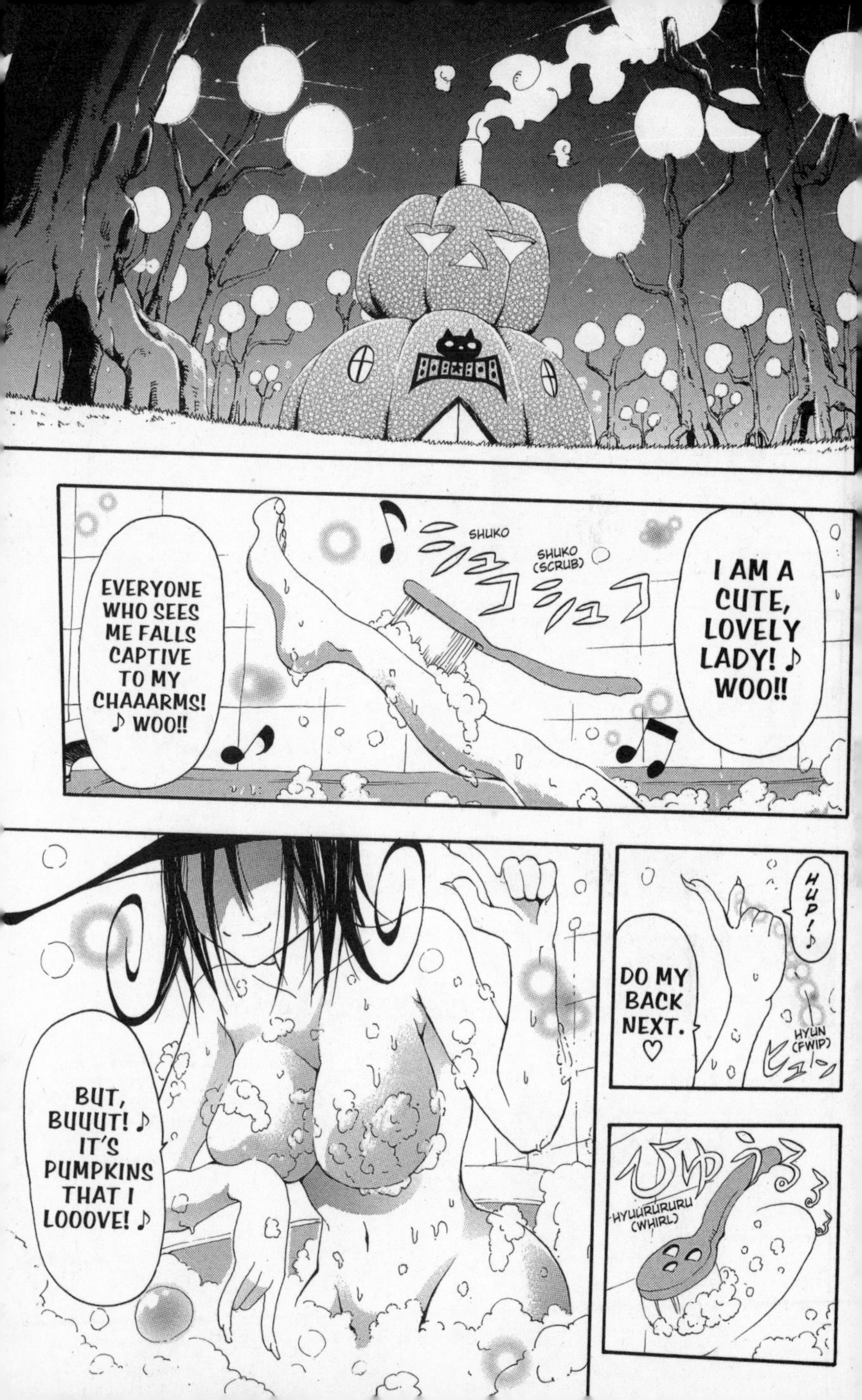
I AM A CUTE, LOVELY LADY! ♪ WOO!!
SHUKO
SHUKO (SCRUB)
EVERYONE WHO SEES ME FALLS CAPTIVE TO MY CHAAARMS! ♪ WOO!!
HUP! ♪
DO MY BACK NEXT. ♡
HYUN (FWIP)
HYUURURURU (WHIRL)
BUT, BUUUT! ♪ IT'S PUMPKINS THAT I LOOOVE! ♪

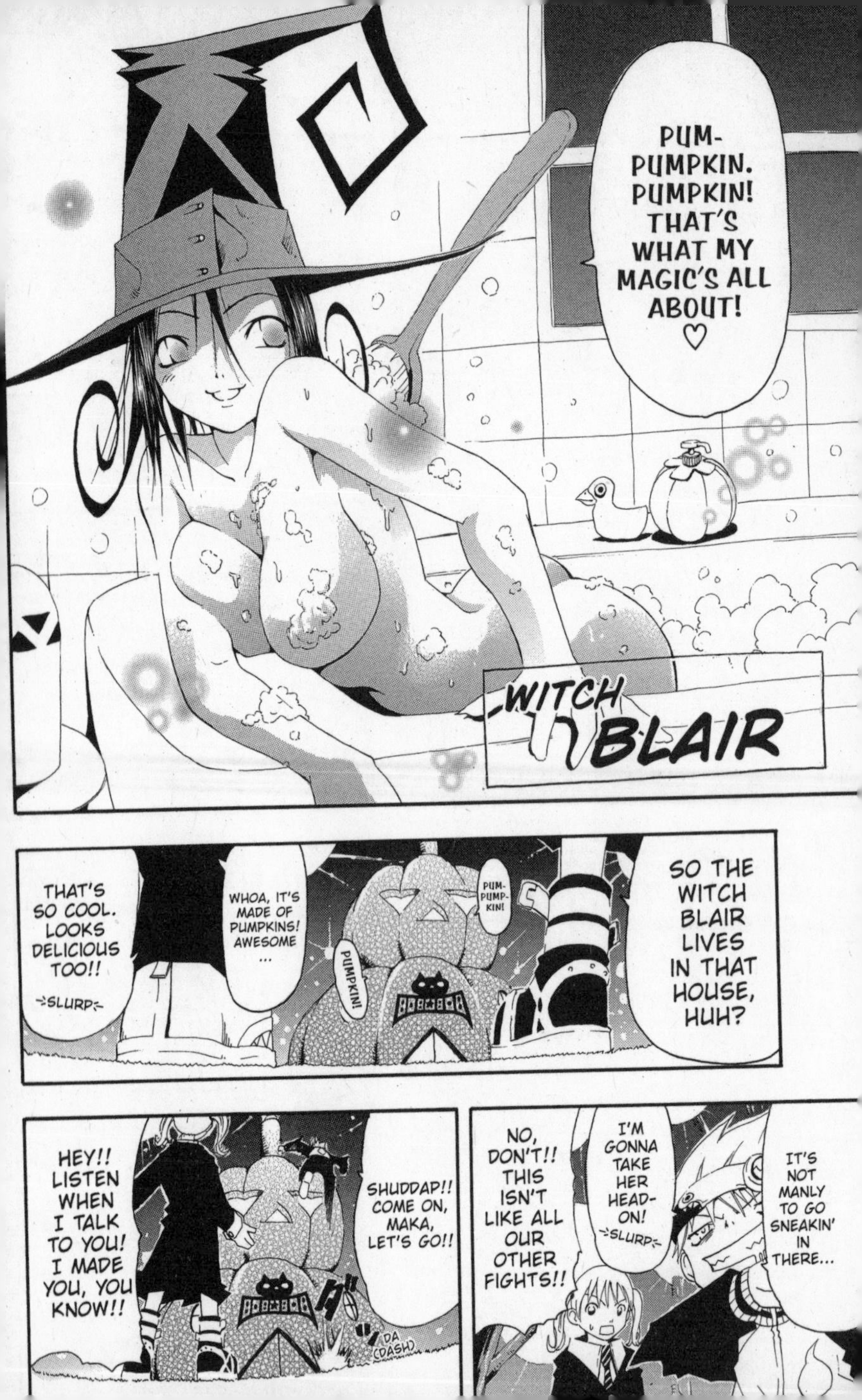
PUM-PUMPKIN. PUMPKIN! THAT'S WHAT MY MAGIC'S ALL ABOUT! ♡
WITCH BLAIR
SO THE WITCH BLAIR LIVES IN THAT HOUSE, HUH?
PUM-PUMP-KIN!
PUMPKIN!
WHOA, IT'S MADE OF PUMPKINS! AWESOME ...
THAT'S SO COOL. LOOKS DELICIOUS TOO!!
SLURP
IT'S NOT MANLY TO GO SNEAKIN' IN THERE...
I'M GONNA TAKE HER HEAD-ON!
SLURP
NO, DON'T!! THIS ISN'T LIKE ALL OUR OTHER FIGHTS!!
SHUDDAP!! COME ON, MAKA, LET'S GO!!
DA (DASH)
HEY!! LISTEN WHEN I TALK TO YOU! I MADE YOU, YOU KNOW!!

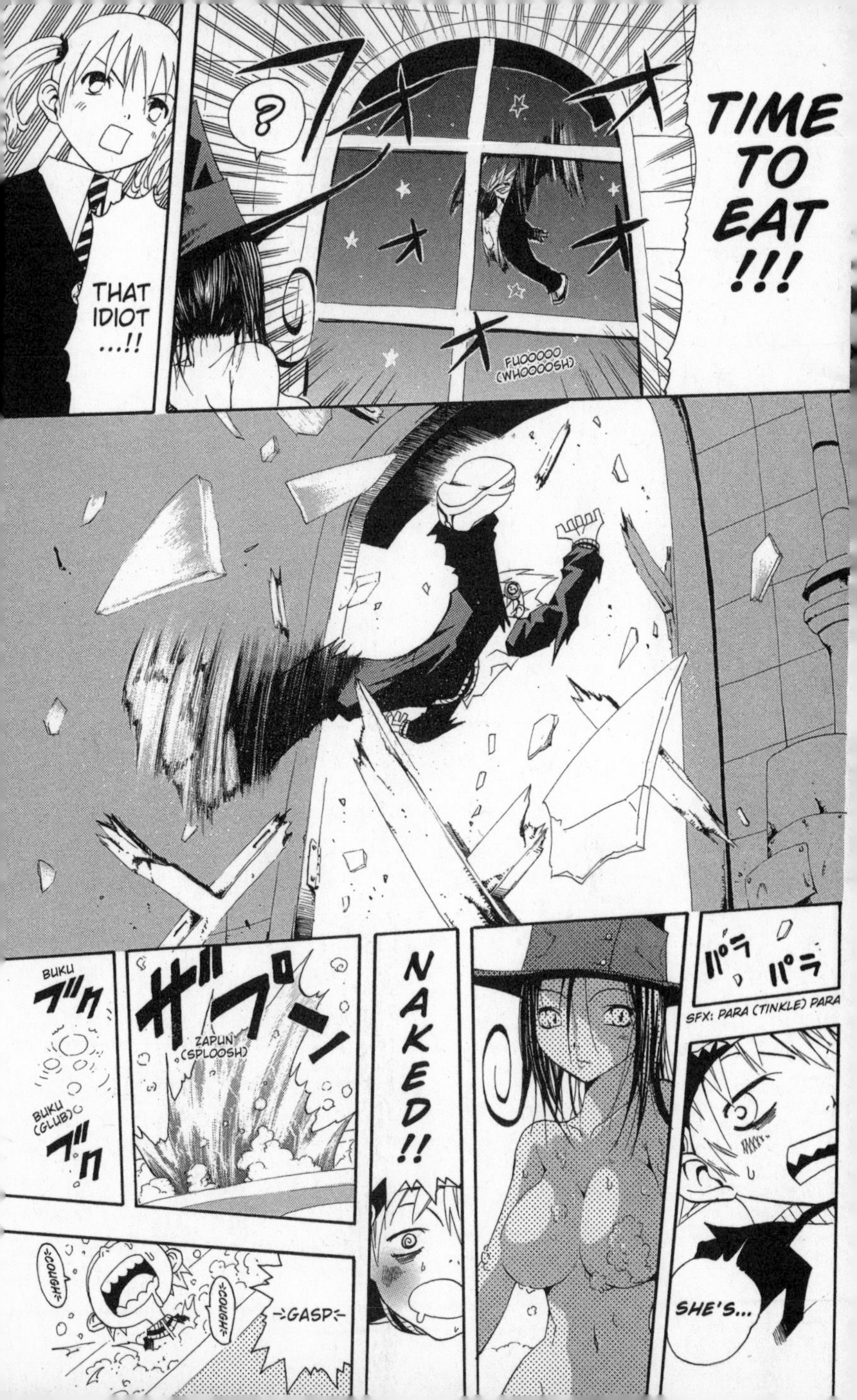
TIME TO EAT!!!
?
FUOOOOO (WHOOOOSH)
THAT IDIOT ...!!
パラ パラ
SFX: PARA (TINKLE) PARA
SHE'S...
NAKED!!
GASP
ザプーン
ZAPUN (SPLOOSH)
ブク
BUKU
ブク
BUKU (GLUB)
COUGH
COUGH

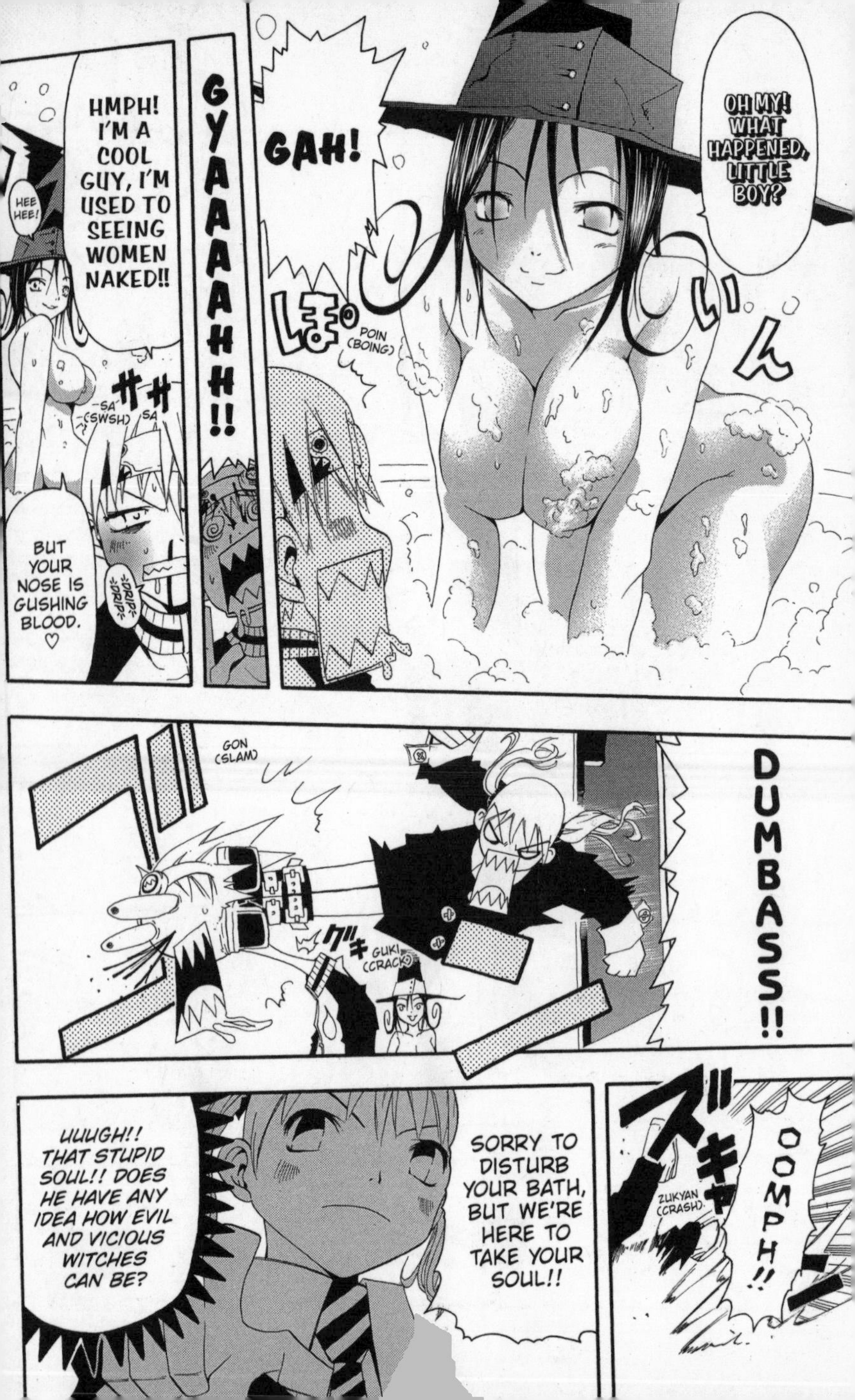
OH MY! WHAT HAPPENED, LITTLE BOY?
GAH!
POIN (BOING)
GYAAAAAHH!!
HEE HEE!
HMPH! I'M A COOL GUY, I'M USED TO SEEING WOMEN NAKED!!
SA SA (SWSH)
BUT YOUR NOSE IS GUSHING BLOOD. ♡
DRIP DRIP
DUMBASS!!
GON (SLAM)
GUKI (CRACK)
OOMPH!!
ZUKYAN (CRASH)
SORRY TO DISTURB YOUR BATH, BUT WE'RE HERE TO TAKE YOUR SOUL!!
UUUGH!! THAT STUPID SOUL!! DOES HE HAVE ANY IDEA HOW EVIL AND VICIOUS WITCHES CAN BE?

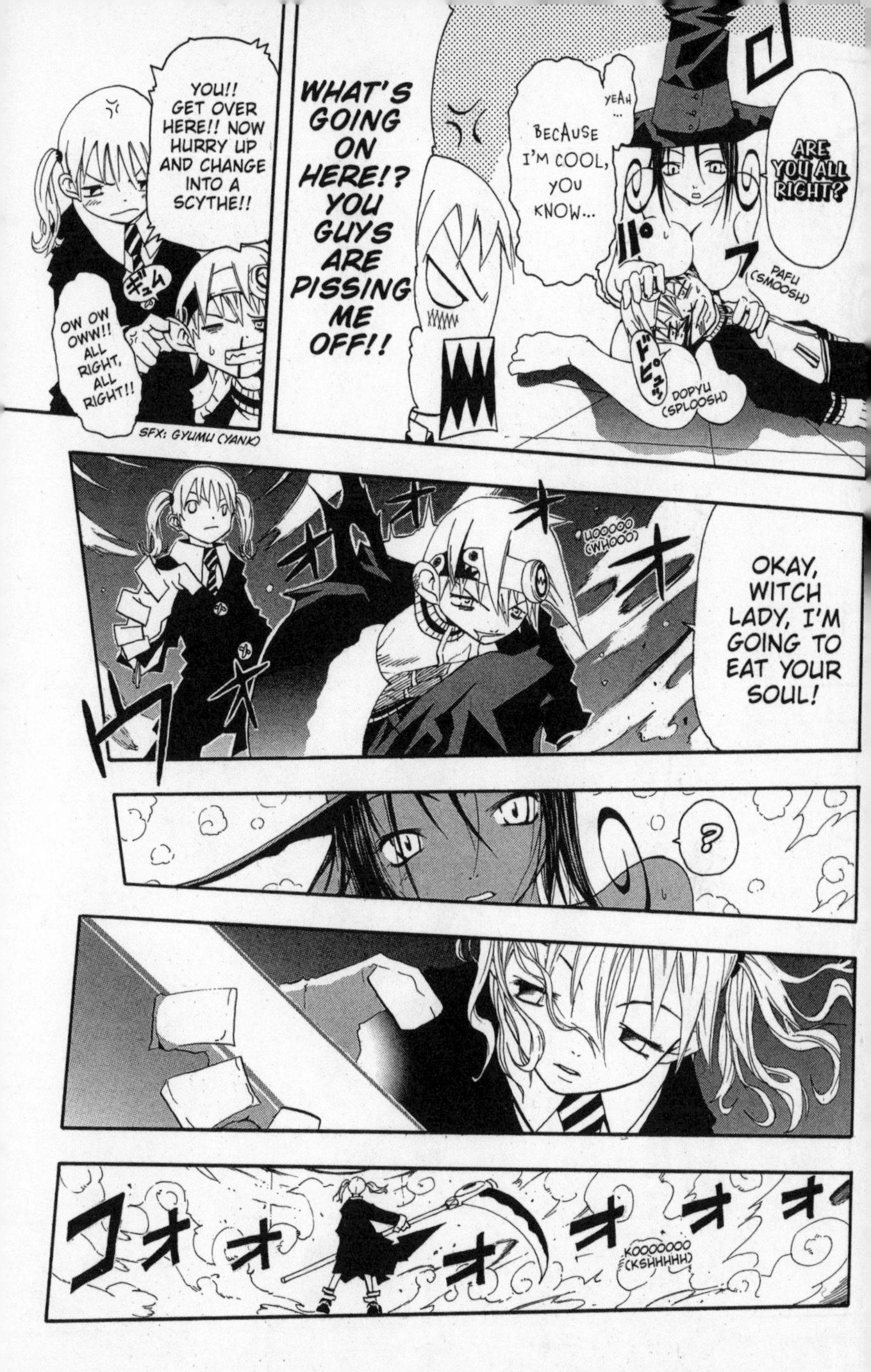
ARE YOU ALL RIGHT?
YEAH... BECAUSE I'M COOL, YOU KNOW...
PAFU (SMOOSH)
DOPYU (SPLOOSH)
WHAT'S GOING ON HERE!? YOU GUYS ARE PISSING ME OFF!!
YOU!! GET OVER HERE!! NOW HURRY UP AND CHANGE INTO A SCYTHE!!
OW OW OWW!! ALL RIGHT, ALL RIGHT!!
SFX: GYUMU (YANK)
OKAY, WITCH LADY, I'M GOING TO EAT YOUR SOUL!
HOOOOO (WHOOO)
?
KOOOOOOO (KSHHHHH)

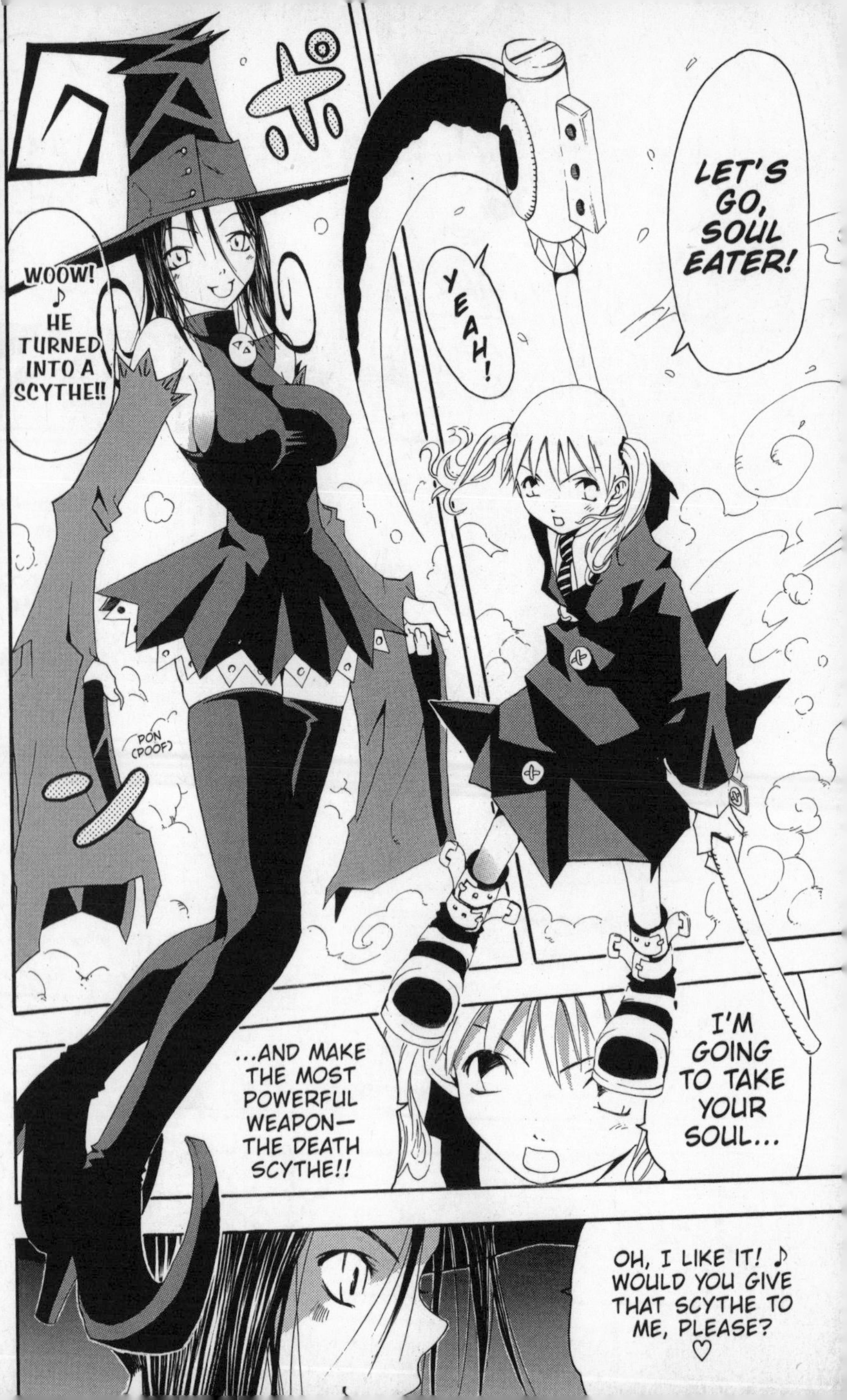
LET'S GO, SOUL EATER!
YEAH!
WOOW! ♪ HE TURNED INTO A SCYTHE!!
PON (POOF)
I'M GOING TO TAKE YOUR SOUL...
...AND MAKE THE MOST POWERFUL WEAPON— THE DEATH SCYTHE!!
OH, I LIKE IT! ♪ WOULD YOU GIVE THAT SCYTHE TO ME, PLEASE? ♡

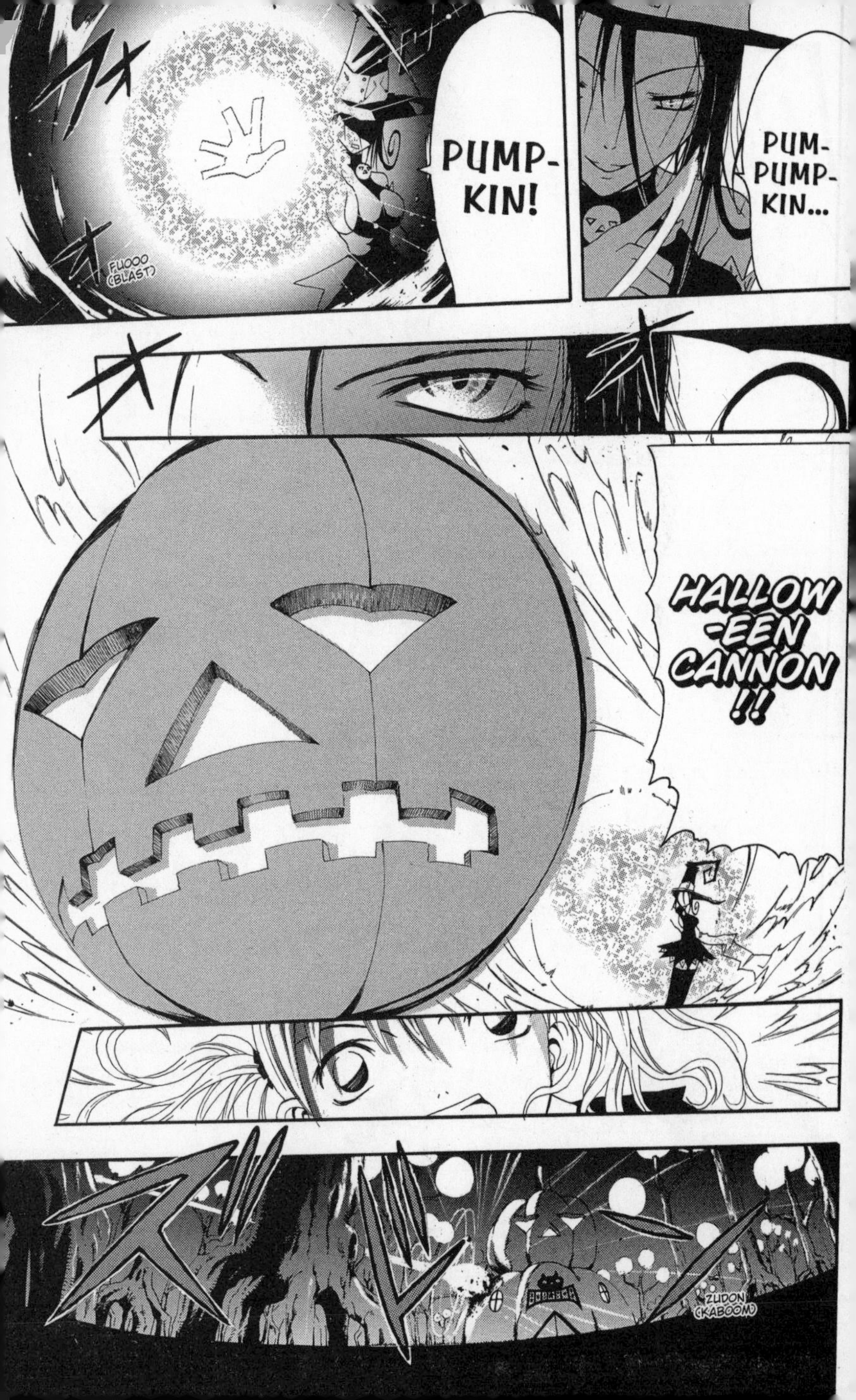
PUM-PUMP-KIN...
PUMP-KIN!
FUOOO (BLAST)
HALLOW-EEN CANNON!!
ZUDON (KABOOM)

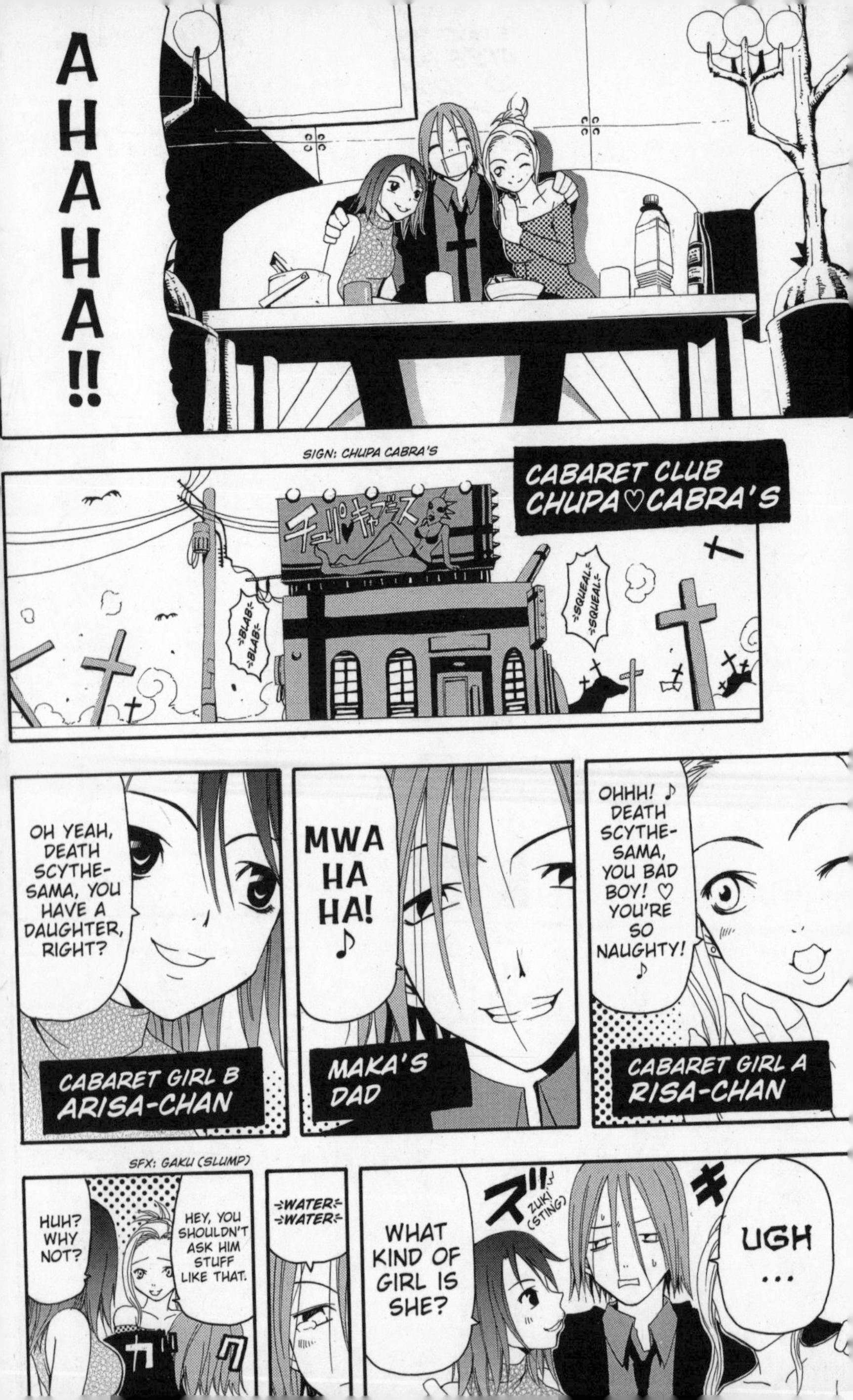
AHAHAHA!!
SIGN: CHUPA CABRA'S
CABARET CLUB CHUPA♡CABRA'S
SQUEAL SQUEAL
BLAB BLAB
OHHH! ♪ DEATH SCYTHE-SAMA, YOU BAD BOY! ♡ YOU'RE SO NAUGHTY! ♪
CABARET GIRL A RISA-CHAN
MWA HA HA! ♪
MAKA'S DAD
OH YEAH, DEATH SCYTHE-SAMA, YOU HAVE A DAUGHTER, RIGHT?
CABARET GIRL B ARISA-CHAN
SFX: GAKU (SLUMP)
UGH ...
ZUKI! (STING)
WHAT KIND OF GIRL IS SHE?
WATER WATER
HEY, YOU SHOULDN'T ASK HIM STUFF LIKE THAT.
HUH? WHY NOT?

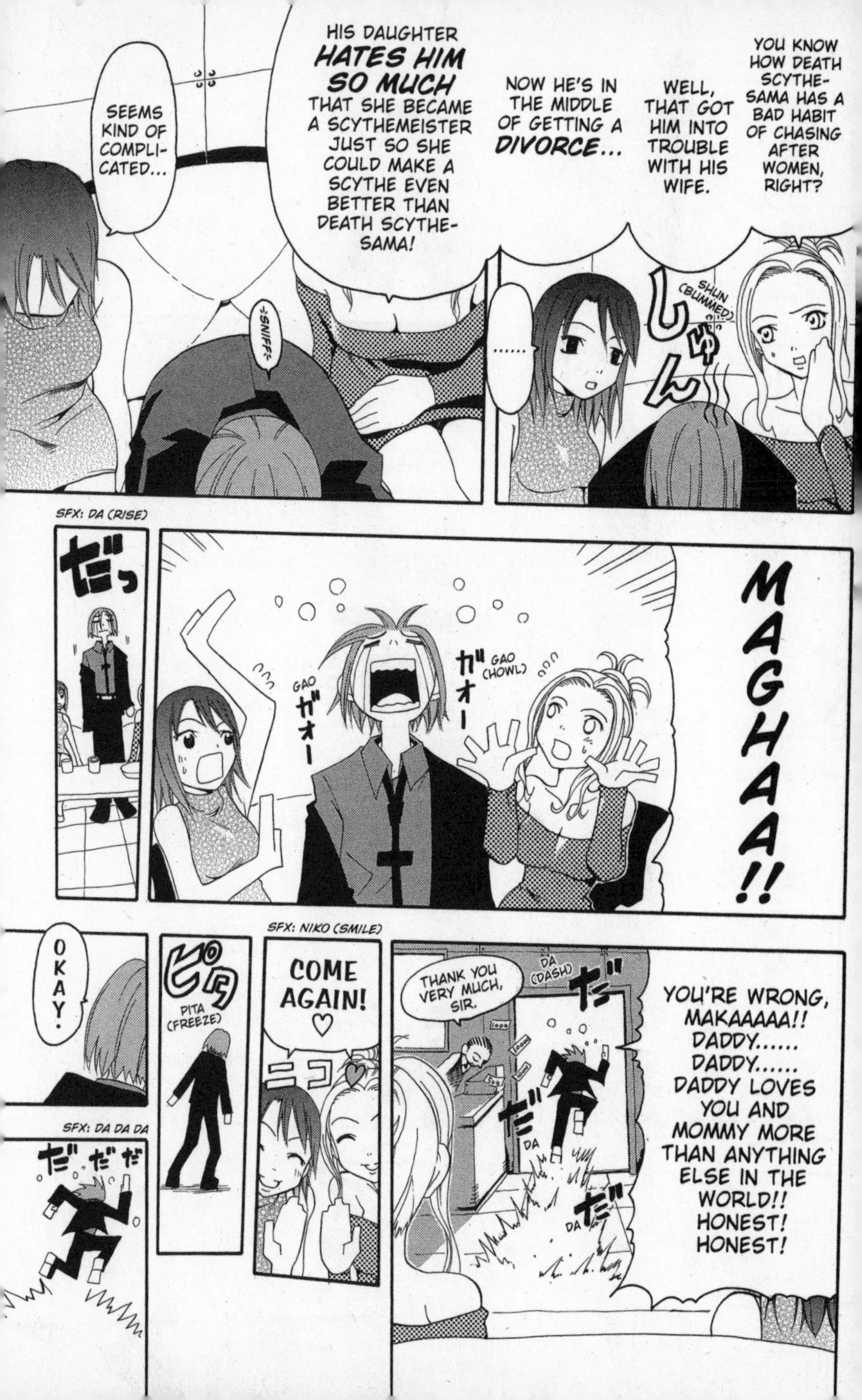
YOU KNOW HOW DEATH SCYTHE-SAMA HAS A BAD HABIT OF CHASING AFTER WOMEN, RIGHT?
WELL, THAT GOT HIM INTO TROUBLE WITH HIS WIFE.
NOW HE'S IN THE MIDDLE OF GETTING A DIVORCE...
SHUN (BUMMED)
......
HIS DAUGHTER HATES HIM SO MUCH THAT SHE BECAME A SCYTHEMEISTER JUST SO SHE COULD MAKE A SCYTHE EVEN BETTER THAN DEATH SCYTHE-SAMA!
SNIFF
SEEMS KIND OF COMPLICATED...
MAGHAAA!!
GAO (HOWL)
GAO
SFX: DA (RISE)
YOU'RE WRONG, MAKAAAAA!! DADDY...... DADDY...... DADDY LOVES YOU AND MOMMY MORE THAN ANYTHING ELSE IN THE WORLD!! HONEST! HONEST!
DA (DASH)
THANK YOU VERY MUCH, SIR.
DA
DA
SFX: NIKO (SMILE)
COME AGAIN! ♡
PITA (FREEZE)
OKAY.
SFX: DA DA DA

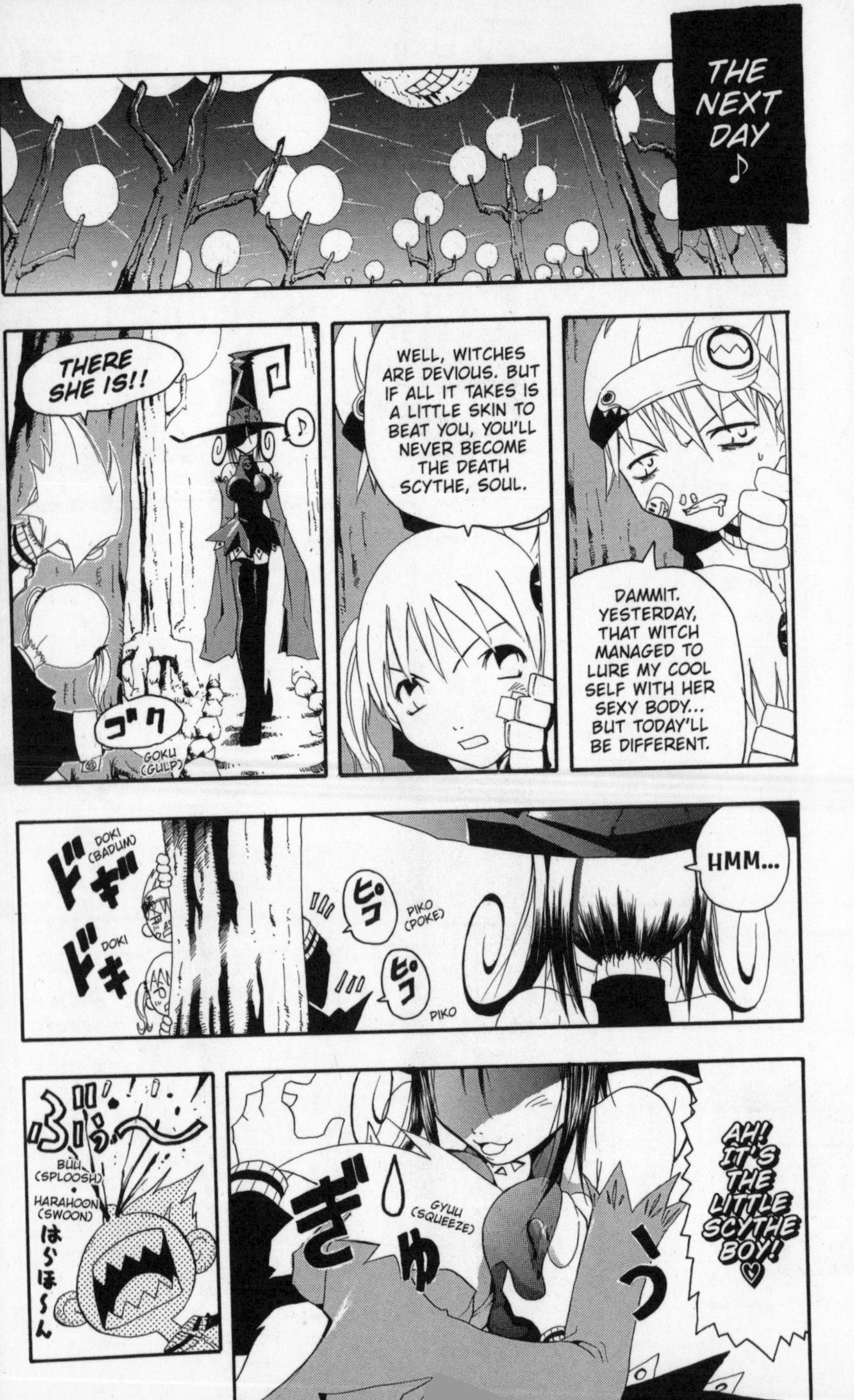
THE NEXT DAY ♪
DAMMIT. YESTERDAY, THAT WITCH MANAGED TO LURE MY COOL SELF WITH HER SEXY BODY... BUT TODAY'LL BE DIFFERENT.
WELL, WITCHES ARE DEVIOUS. BUT IF ALL IT TAKES IS A LITTLE SKIN TO BEAT YOU, YOU'LL NEVER BECOME THE DEATH SCYTHE, SOUL.
THERE SHE IS!!
♪
ゴク
GOKU (GULP)
HMM...
ピコ
PIKO (POKE)
ピコ
PIKO
ドキ
DOKI (BADUM)
ドキ
DOKI
AH! IT'S THE LITTLE SCYTHE BOY! ♡
ぎゅっ
GYUU (SQUEEZE)
BUU (SPLOOSH) • HARAHOON (SWOON)
はらほ～ん

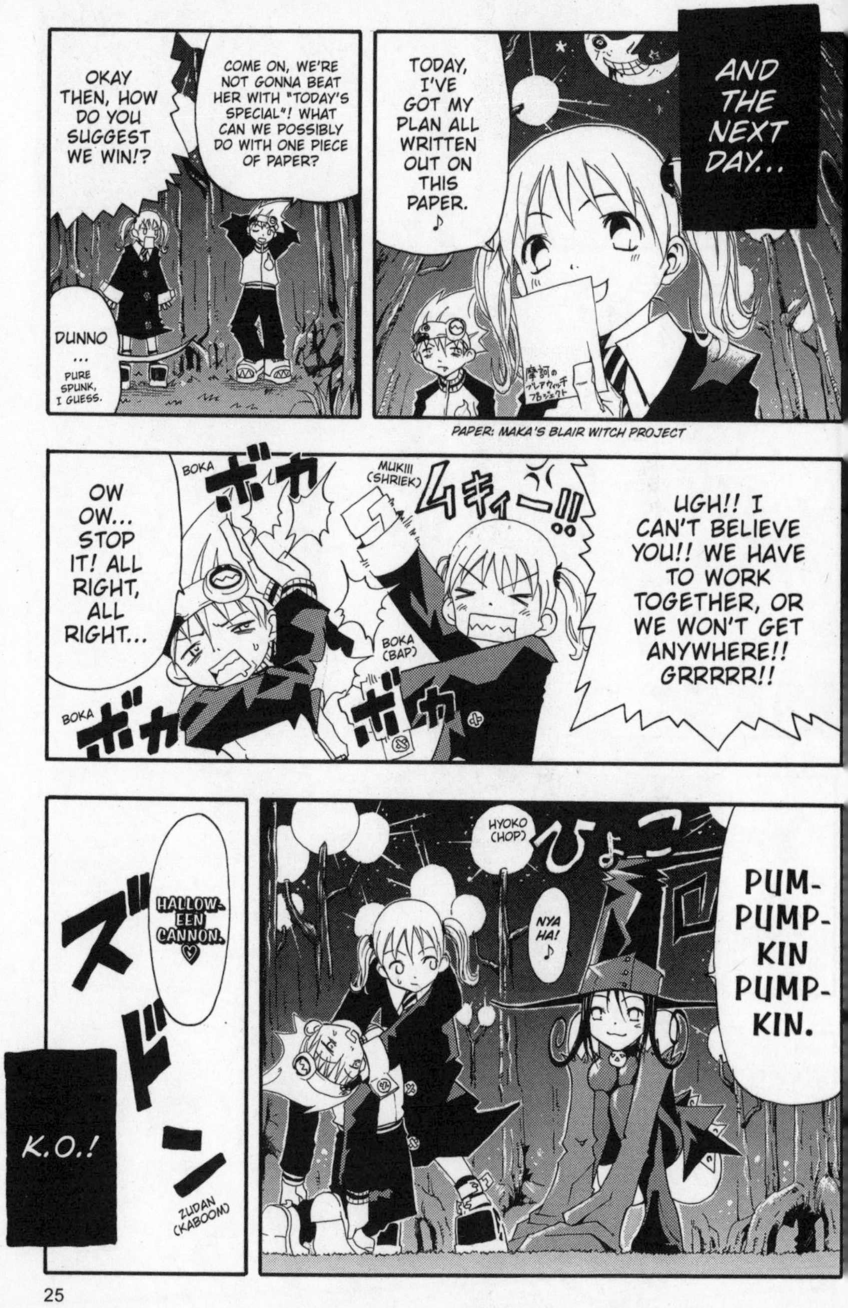
AND THE NEXT DAY...
TODAY, I'VE GOT MY PLAN ALL WRITTEN OUT ON THIS PAPER. ♪
摩訶のブレアウィッチプロジェクト
COME ON, WE'RE NOT GONNA BEAT HER WITH "TODAY'S SPECIAL"! WHAT CAN WE POSSIBLY DO WITH ONE PIECE OF PAPER?
OKAY THEN, HOW DO YOU SUGGEST WE WIN!?
DUNNO ...
PURE SPUNK, I GUESS.
PAPER: MAKA'S BLAIR WITCH PROJECT
UGH!! I CAN'T BELIEVE YOU!! WE HAVE TO WORK TOGETHER, OR WE WON'T GET ANYWHERE!! GRRRRR!!
ムキィー!!
MUKIII (SHRIEK)
ボカ
BOKA
OW OW... STOP IT! ALL RIGHT, ALL RIGHT...
ボカ
BOKA (BAP)
ボカ
BOKA
PUM-PUMP-KIN PUMP-KIN.
ひょこ
HYOKO (HOP)
NYA HA! ♪
HALLOW-EEN CANNON. ♡
ズドーン
ZUDAN (KABOOM)
K.O.!

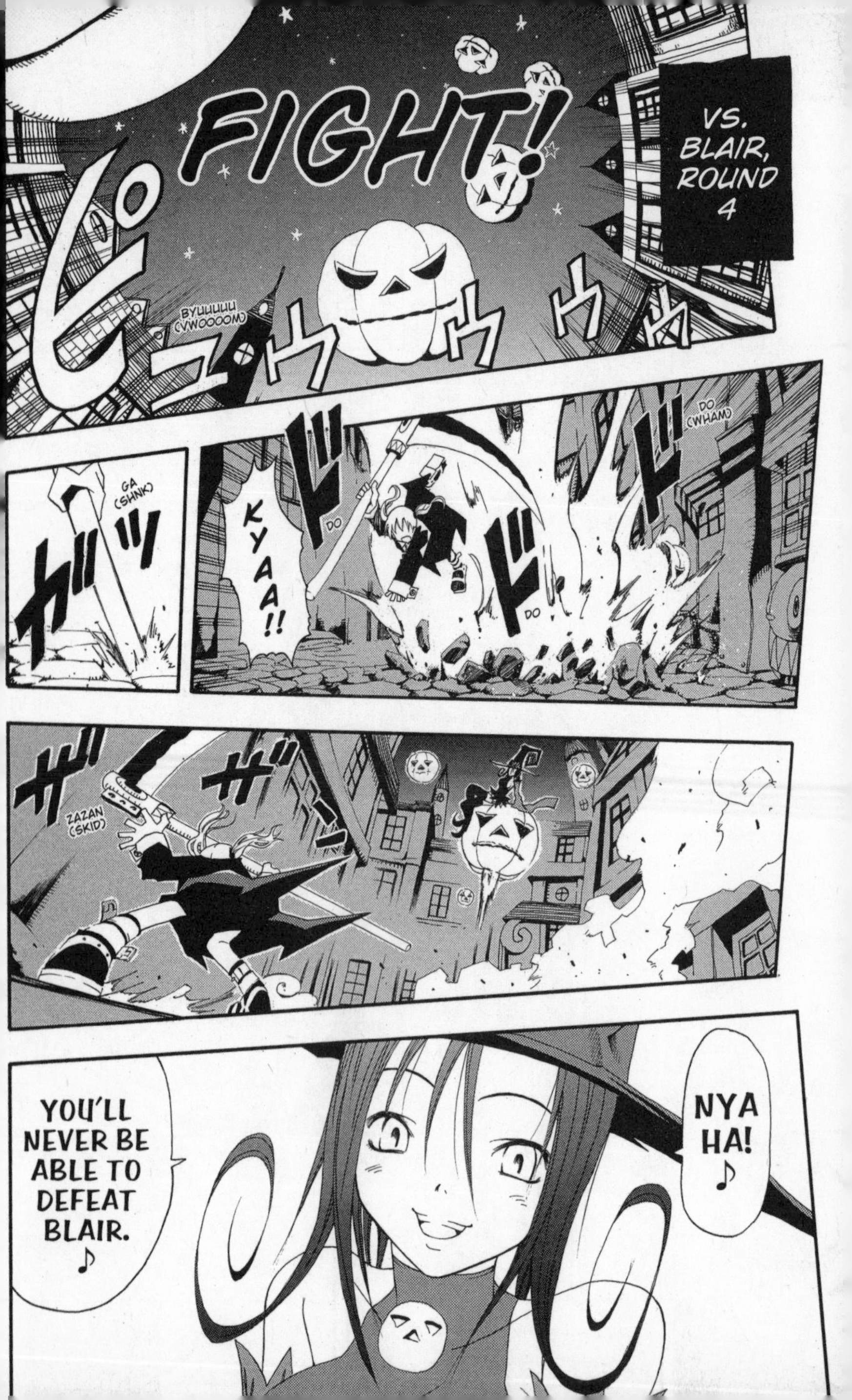
VS. BLAIR, ROUND 4
FIGHT!
BYUUUUU (VWOOOOM)
DO (WHAM)
DO
KYAAA!!
DO
GA (SHNK)
ZAZAN (SKID)
NYA HA! ♪
YOU'LL NEVER BE ABLE TO DEFEAT BLAIR. ♪

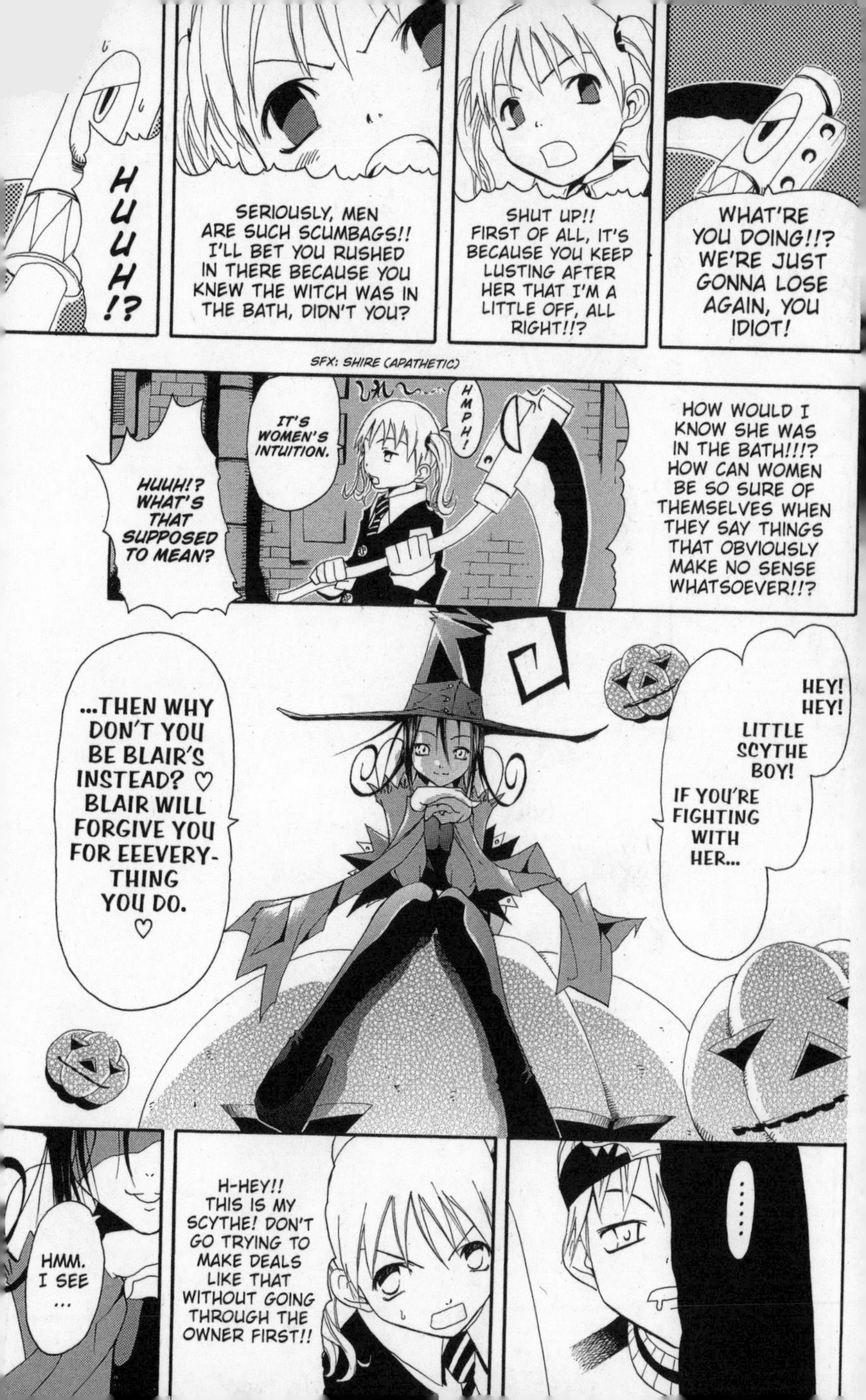

WHAT'RE YOU DOING!!? WE'RE JUST GONNA LOSE AGAIN, YOU IDIOT!
SHUT UP!! FIRST OF ALL, IT'S BECAUSE YOU KEEP LUSTING AFTER HER THAT I'M A LITTLE OFF, ALL RIGHT!!?
SERIOUSLY, MEN ARE SUCH SCUMBAGS!! I'LL BET YOU RUSHED IN THERE BECAUSE YOU KNEW THE WITCH WAS IN THE BATH, DIDN'T YOU?
HUUH!?
SFX: SHIRE (APATHETIC)
HOW WOULD I KNOW SHE WAS IN THE BATH!!!? HOW CAN WOMEN BE SO SURE OF THEMSELVES WHEN THEY SAY THINGS THAT OBVIOUSLY MAKE NO SENSE WHATSOEVER!!?
HMPH!
IT'S WOMEN'S INTUITION.
HUUH!? WHAT'S THAT SUPPOSED TO MEAN?
HEY! HEY! LITTLE SCYTHE BOY!
IF YOU'RE FIGHTING WITH HER...
...THEN WHY DON'T YOU BE BLAIR'S INSTEAD? ♡ BLAIR WILL FORGIVE YOU FOR EEEVERYTHING YOU DO. ♡
......
H-HEY!! THIS IS MY SCYTHE! DON'T GO TRYING TO MAKE DEALS LIKE THAT WITHOUT GOING THROUGH THE OWNER FIRST!!
HMM. I SEE ...

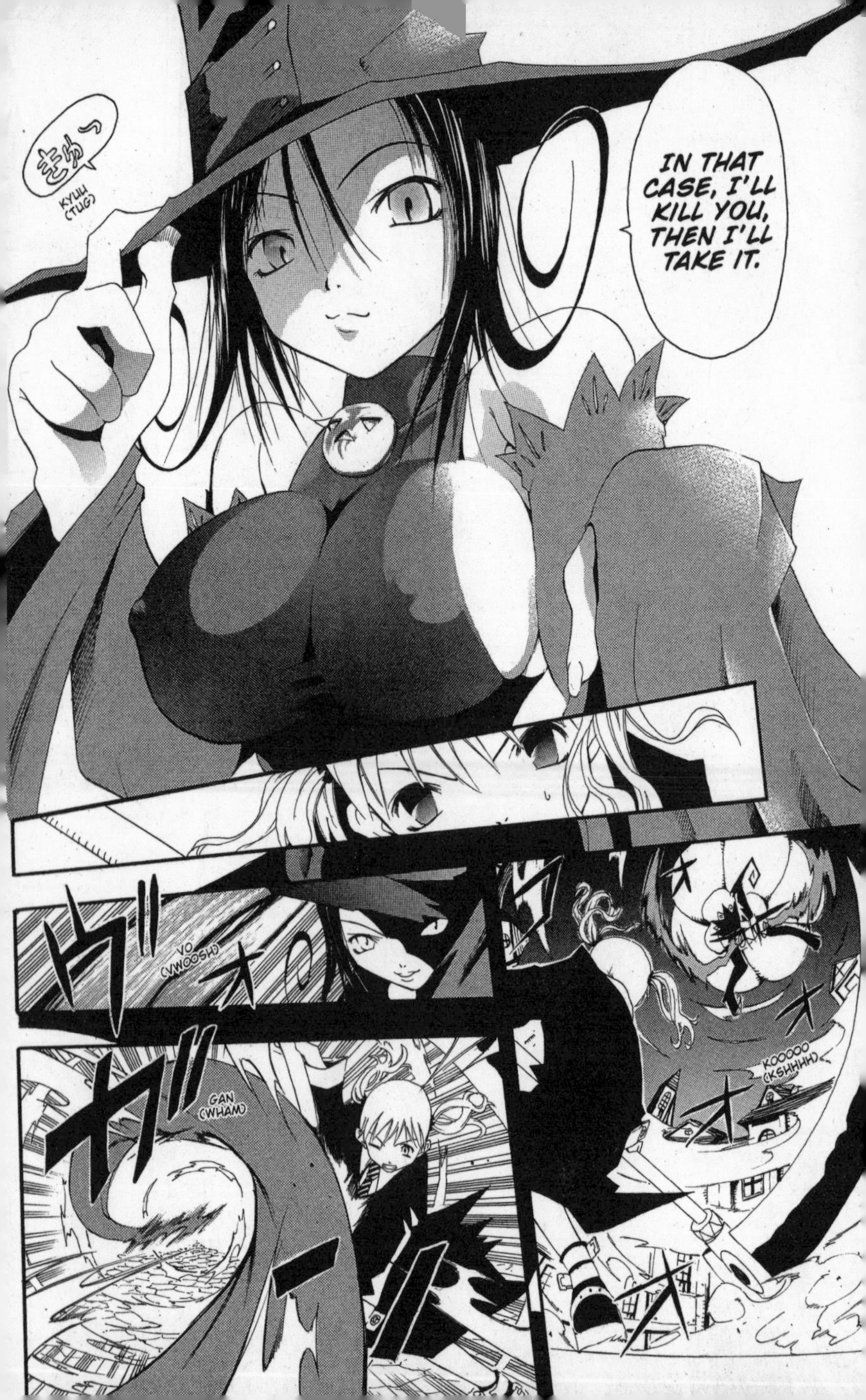
IN THAT CASE, I'LL KILL YOU, THEN I'LL TAKE IT.
きゅっ
KYUU (TUG)
KOOOOO (KSHHHH)
VO (VWOOSH)
GAN (WHAM)

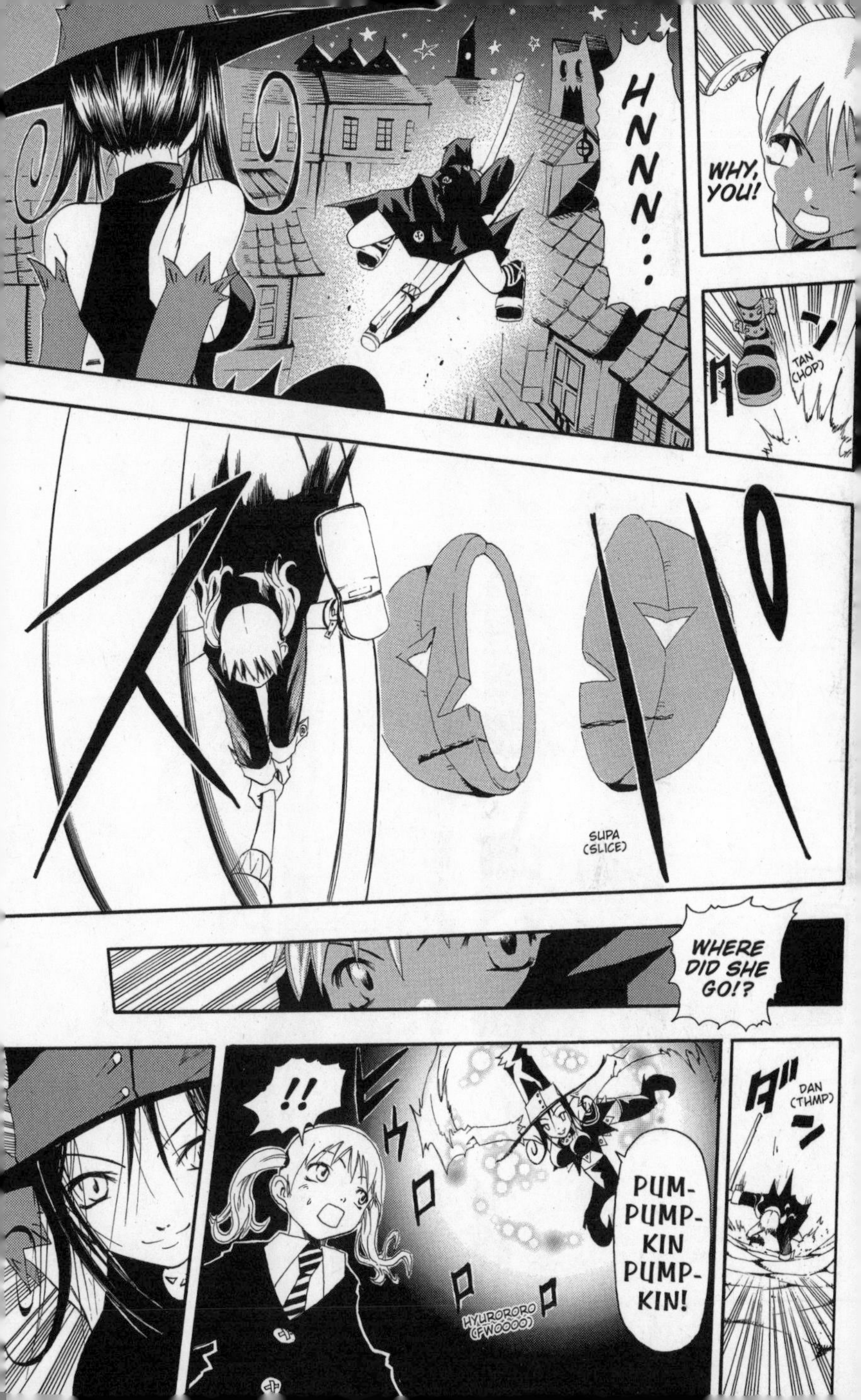
WHY, YOU!
TAN (CHOP)
HNNN...
SUPA (SLICE)
WHERE DID SHE GO!?
DAN (THMP)
!!
PUM-PUMP-KIN PUMP-KIN!
HYURORORO (FWOOOO)

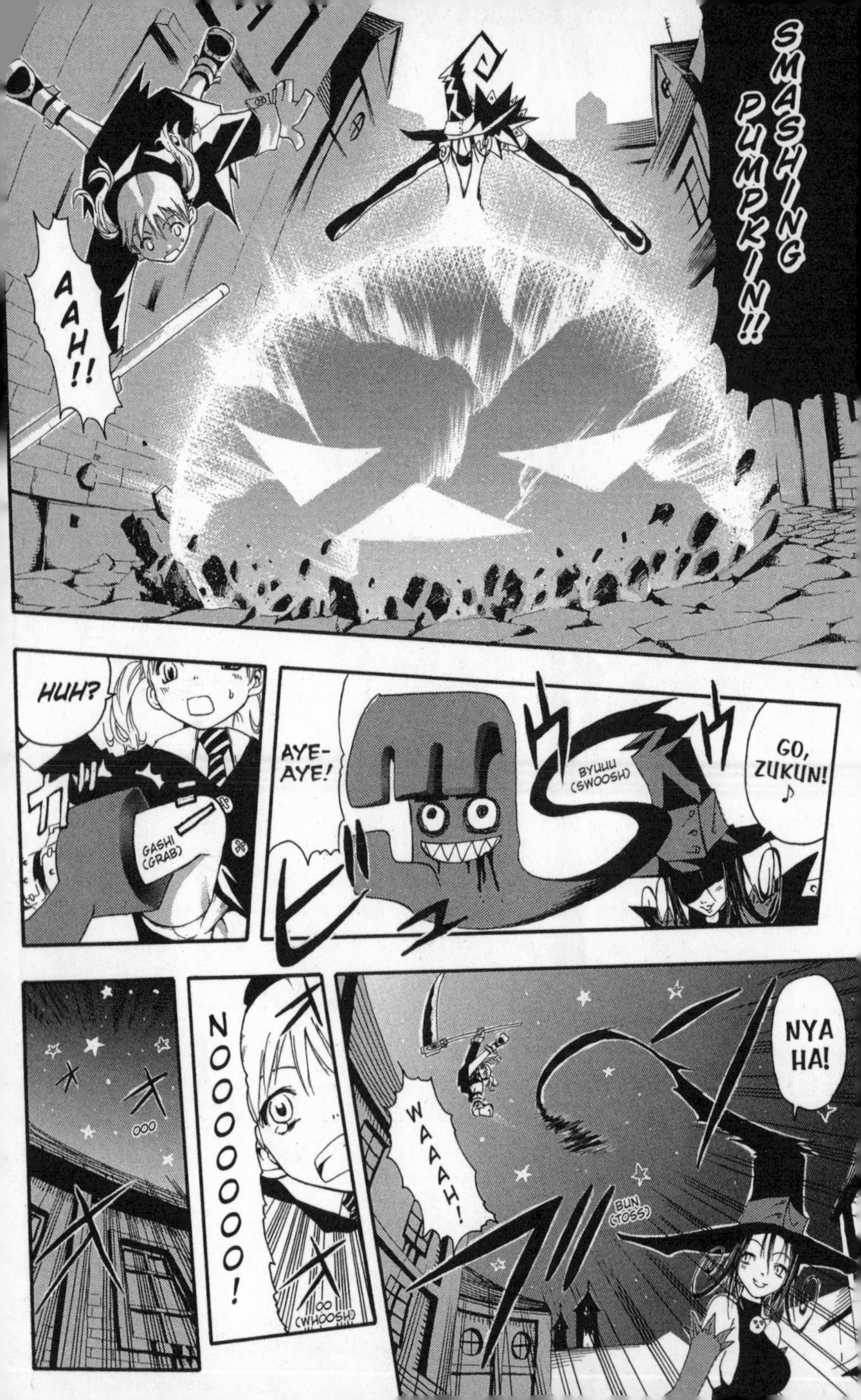
SMASHING PUMPKIN!!
AAH!!
GO, ZUKUN! ♪
BYUUU (SWOOSH)
AYE-AYE!
HUH?
GASHI (GRAB)
NYA HA!
BUN (TOSS)
WAAAAH!
NOOOOOOOO!
OO (WHOOSH)
OOO

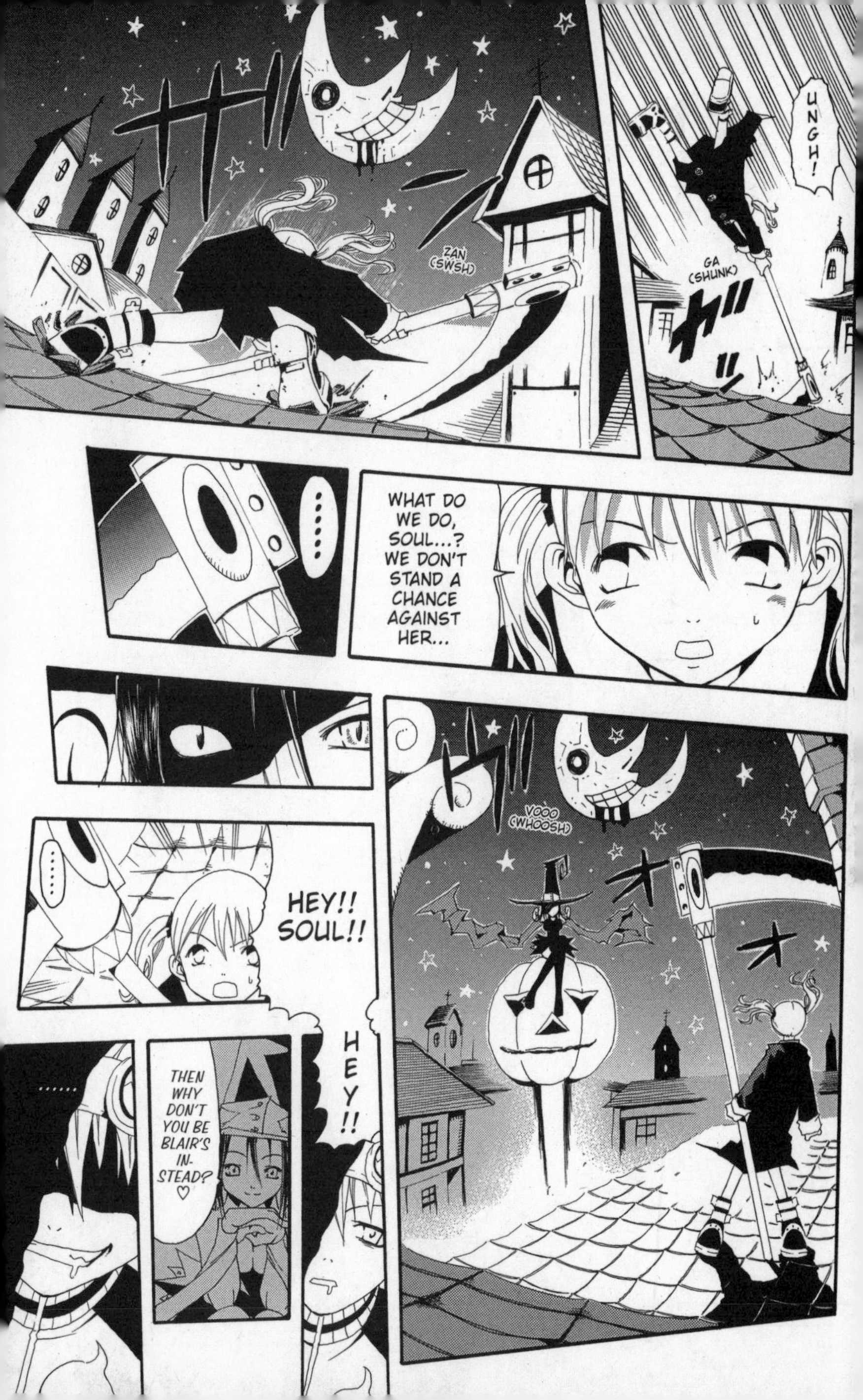
UNGH!
GA (SHUNK)
ZAN (SWSH)
WHAT DO WE DO, SOUL...? WE DON'T STAND A CHANCE AGAINST HER...
......
VOOO (WHOOSH)
......
HEY!! SOUL!!
HEY!!
THEN WHY DON'T YOU BE BLAIR'S IN-STEAD? ♡
......

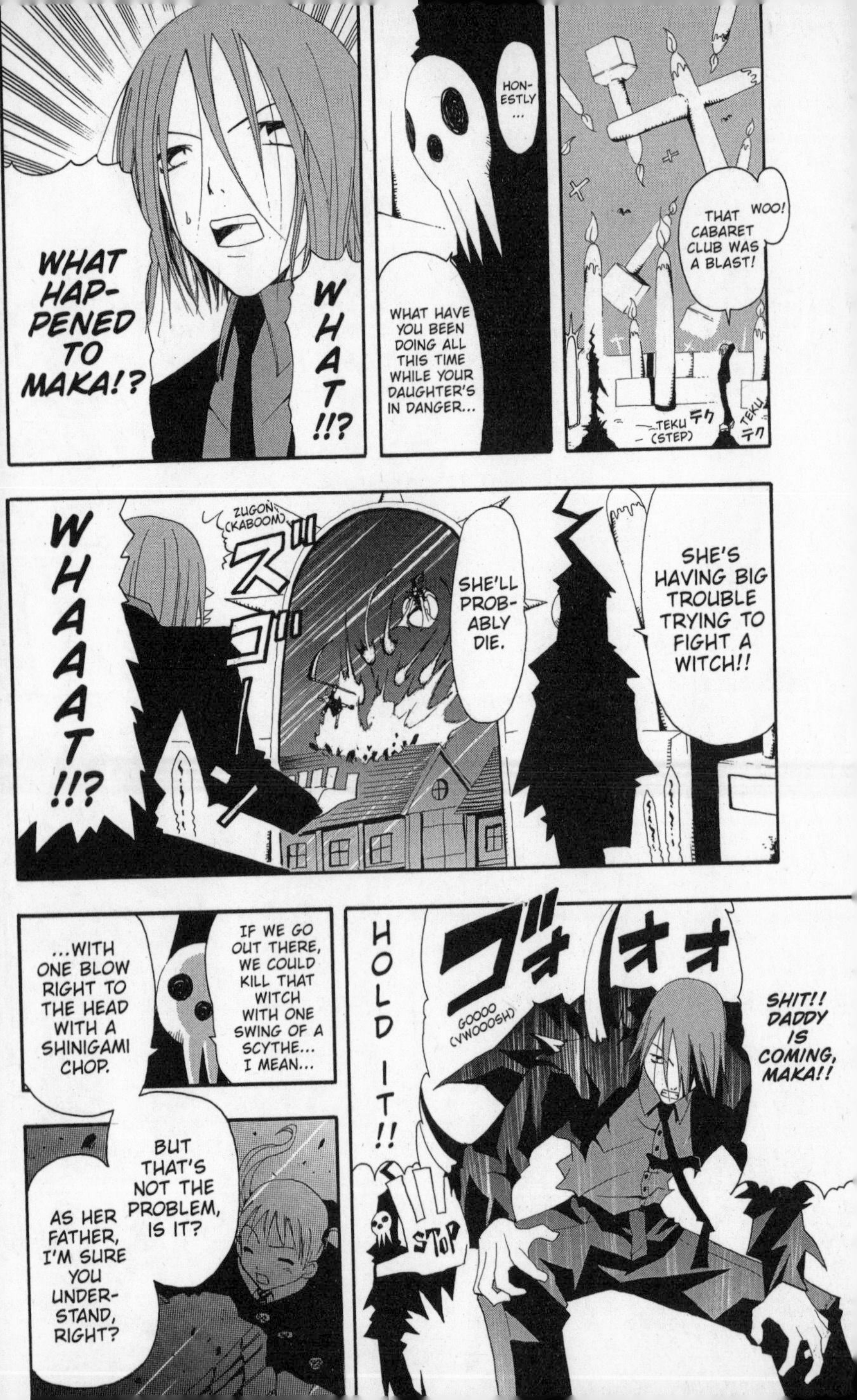
THAT CABARET CLUB WAS A BLAST! WOO!
TEKU テク (STEP)
TEKU テク
HON-ESTLY...
WHAT HAVE YOU BEEN DOING ALL THIS TIME WHILE YOUR DAUGHTER'S IN DANGER...
WHAT!!?
WHAT HAP-PENED TO MAKA!?
SHE'S HAVING BIG TROUBLE TRYING TO FIGHT A WITCH!!
SHE'LL PROB-ABLY DIE.
ZUGON (KABOOM) ズゴ
WHAAAAT!!?
SHIT!! DADDY IS COMING, MAKA!!
ゴォオオ GOOOO (VWOOOSH)
HOLD IT!!
STOP
IF WE GO OUT THERE, WE COULD KILL THAT WITCH WITH ONE SWING OF A SCYTHE... I MEAN...
...WITH ONE BLOW RIGHT TO THE HEAD WITH A SHINIGAMI CHOP.
BUT THAT'S NOT THE PROBLEM, IS IT?
AS HER FATHER, I'M SURE YOU UNDER-STAND, RIGHT?

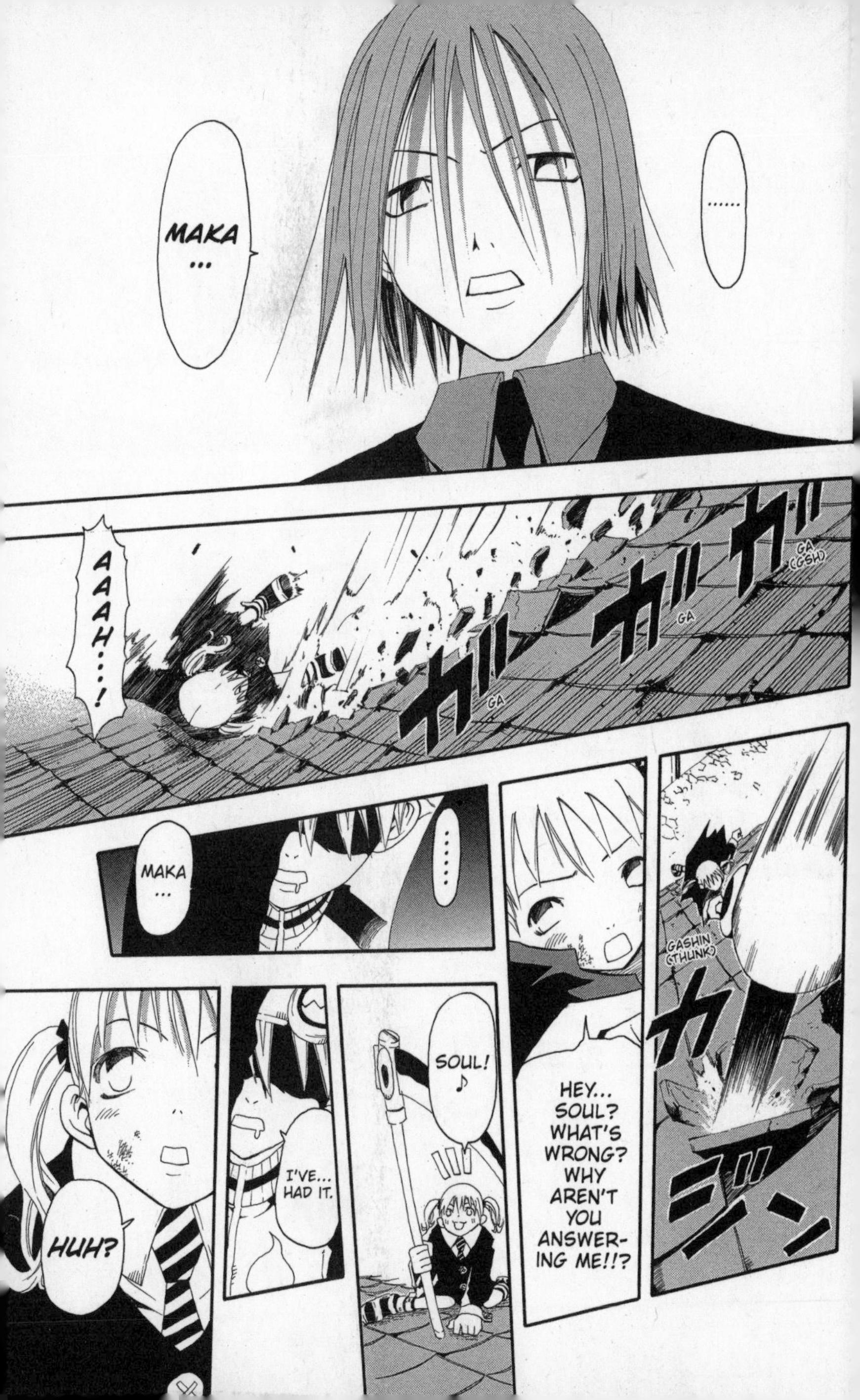

......
MAKA ...
GA (GSH)
GA
GA
AAAAH...!
GASHIN (THUNK)
HEY... SOUL? WHAT'S WRONG? WHY AREN'T YOU ANSWERING ME!!?
......
MAKA ...
SOUL! ♪
I'VE... HAD IT.
HUH?

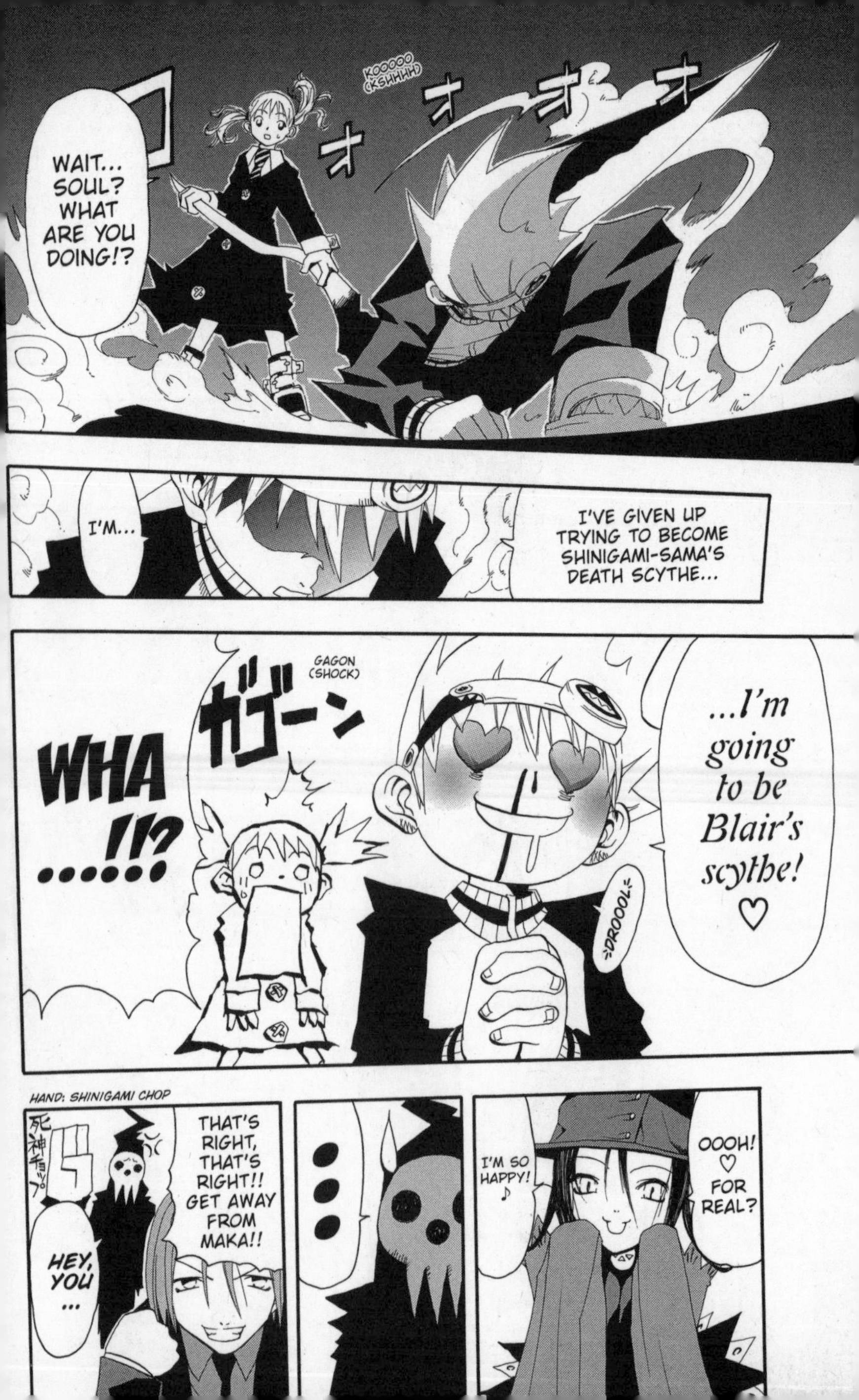
KOOOOO (KSHHHH)
WAIT... SOUL? WHAT ARE YOU DOING!?
I'VE GIVEN UP TRYING TO BECOME SHINIGAMI-SAMA'S DEATH SCYTHE...
I'M...
...I'm going to be Blair's scythe! ♡
DROOOL
GAGON (SHOCK)
WHA......!!?
HAND: SHINIGAMI CHOP
OOOH! ♡ FOR REAL?
I'M SO HAPPY! ♪
• • •
THAT'S RIGHT, THAT'S RIGHT!! GET AWAY FROM MAKA!!
死神チョップ
HEY, YOU ...

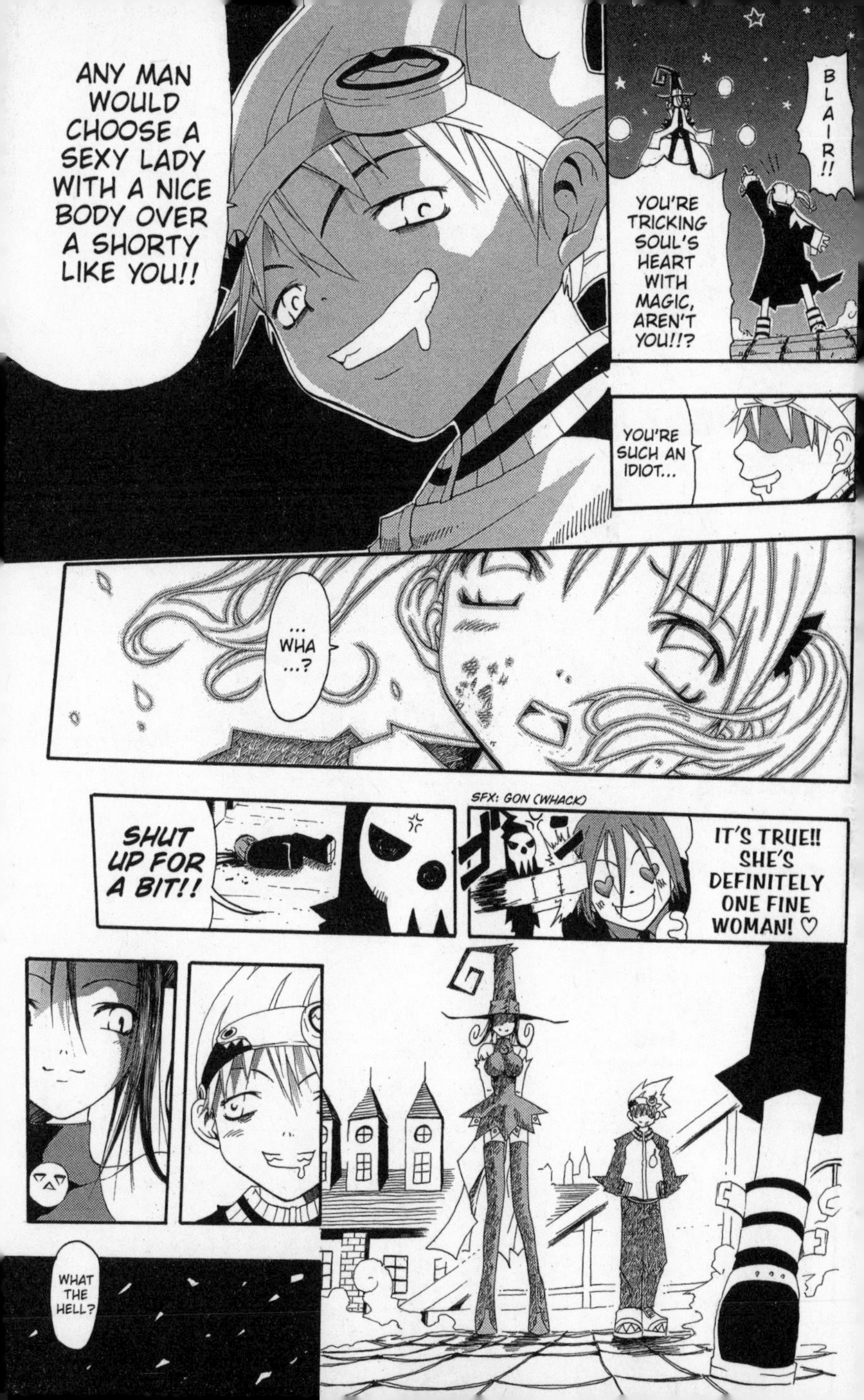
BLAIR!!
YOU'RE TRICKING SOUL'S HEART WITH MAGIC, AREN'T YOU!!?
YOU'RE SUCH AN IDIOT...
ANY MAN WOULD CHOOSE A SEXY LADY WITH A NICE BODY OVER A SHORTY LIKE YOU!!
... WHA ...?
IT'S TRUE!! SHE'S DEFINITELY ONE FINE WOMAN! ♡
SFX: GON (WHACK)
SHUT UP FOR A BIT!!
WHAT THE HELL?

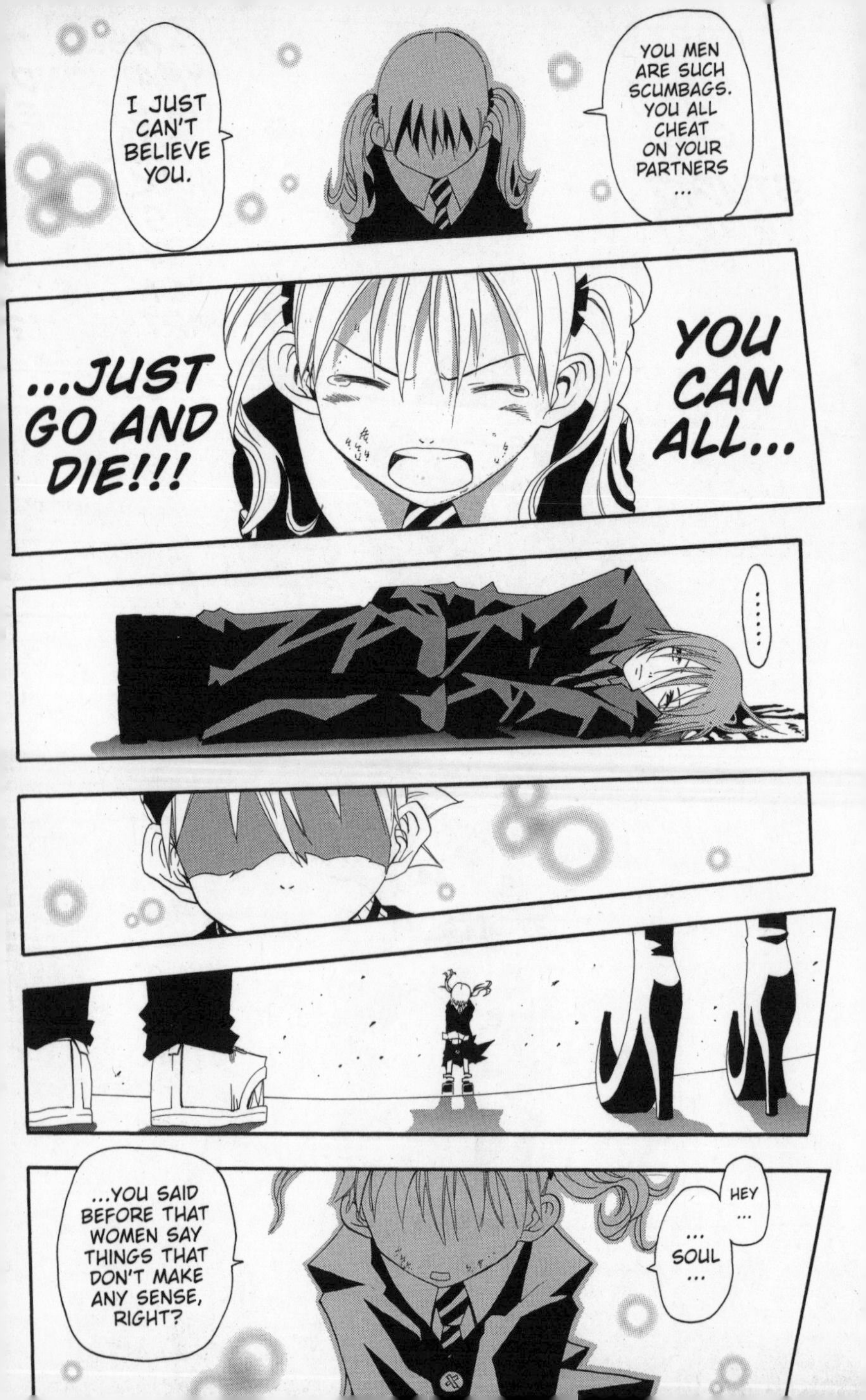
YOU MEN ARE SUCH SCUMBAGS. YOU ALL CHEAT ON YOUR PARTNERS ...
I JUST CAN'T BELIEVE YOU.
YOU CAN ALL...
...JUST GO AND DIE!!!
......
HEY ... ... SOUL ...
...YOU SAID BEFORE THAT WOMEN SAY THINGS THAT DON'T MAKE ANY SENSE, RIGHT?

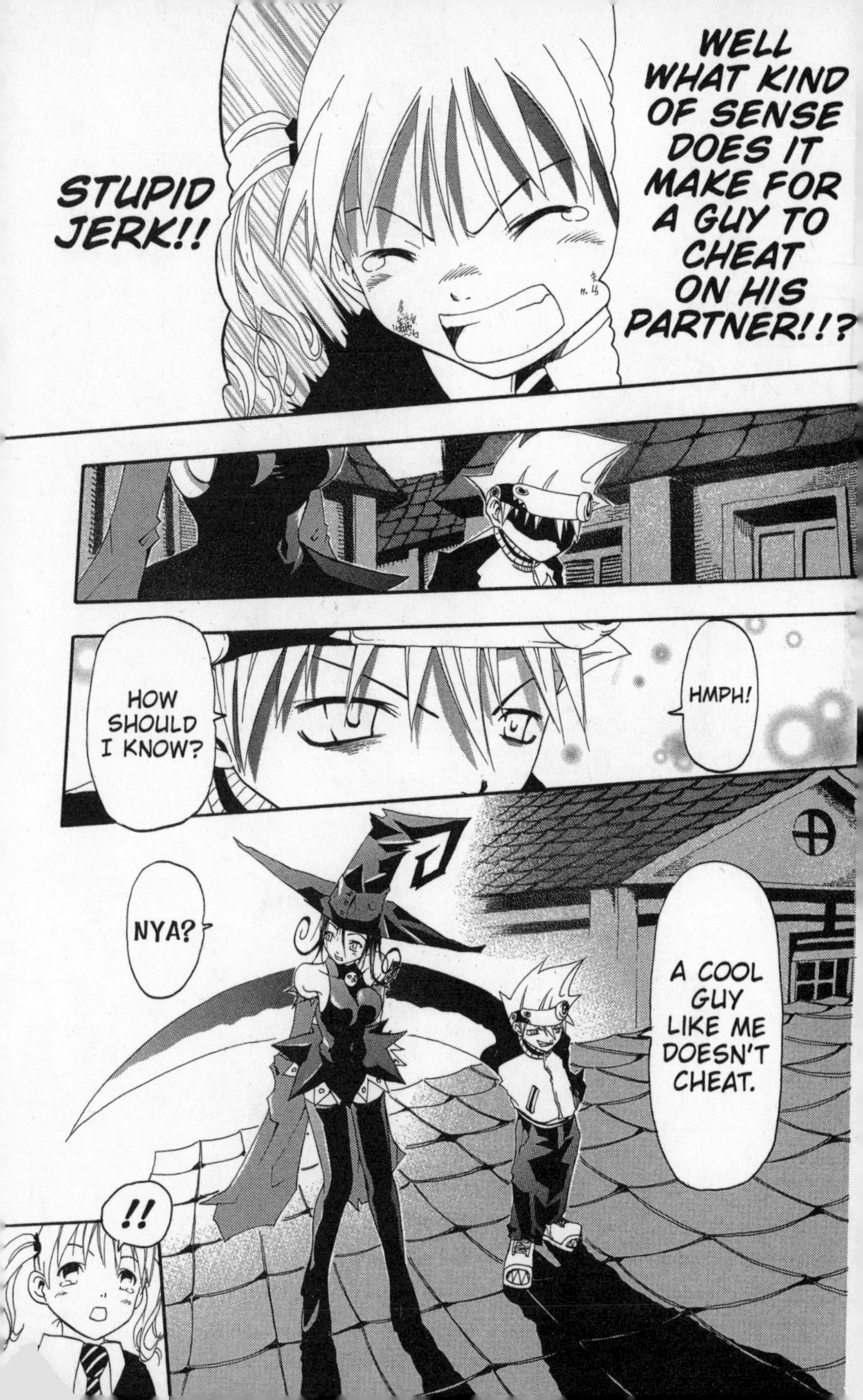
WELL WHAT KIND OF SENSE DOES IT MAKE FOR A GUY TO CHEAT ON HIS PARTNER!!?
STUPID JERK!!
HMPH!
HOW SHOULD I KNOW?
A COOL GUY LIKE ME DOESN'T CHEAT.
NYA?
!!

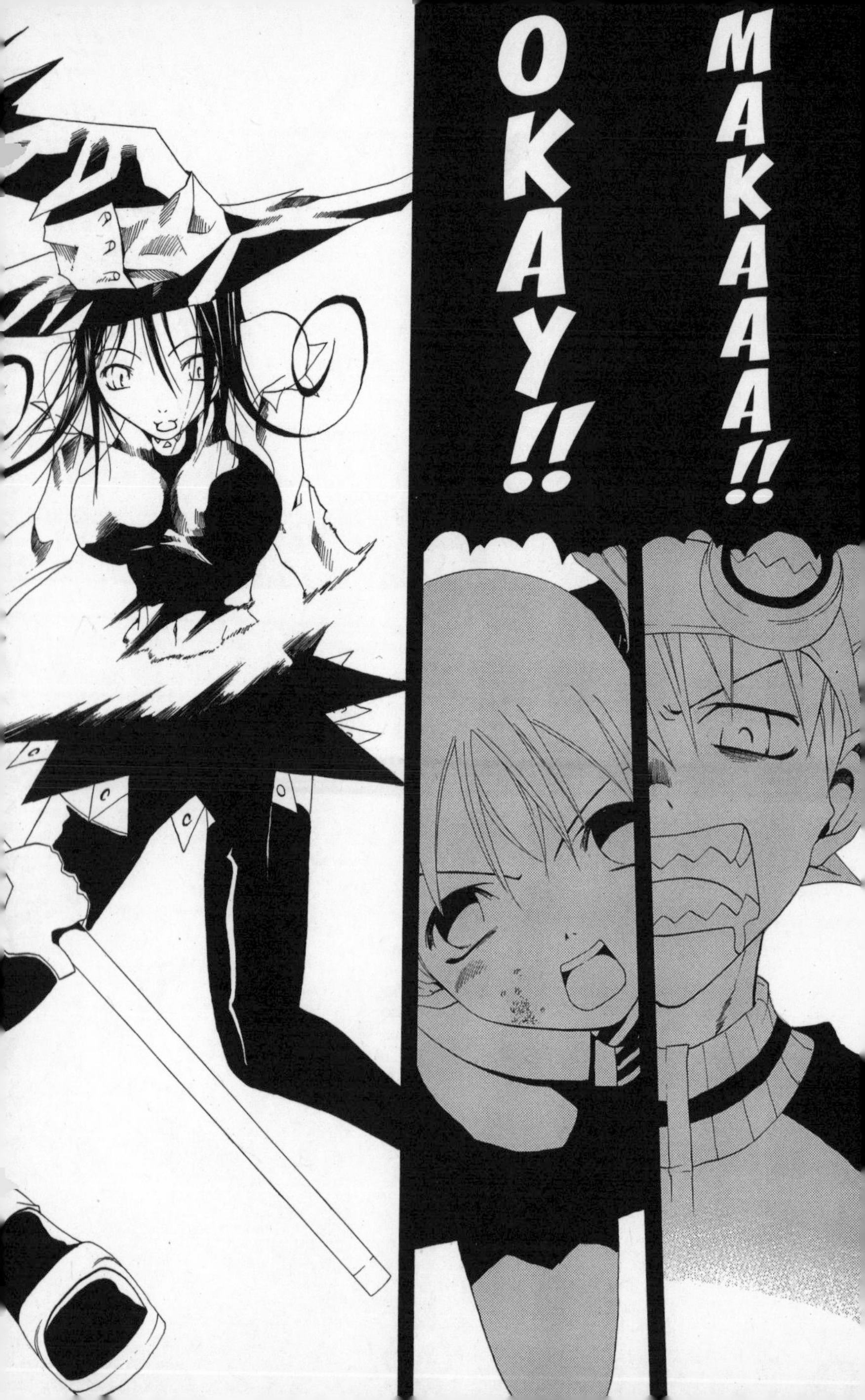
MAKAAAA!!
OKAY!!

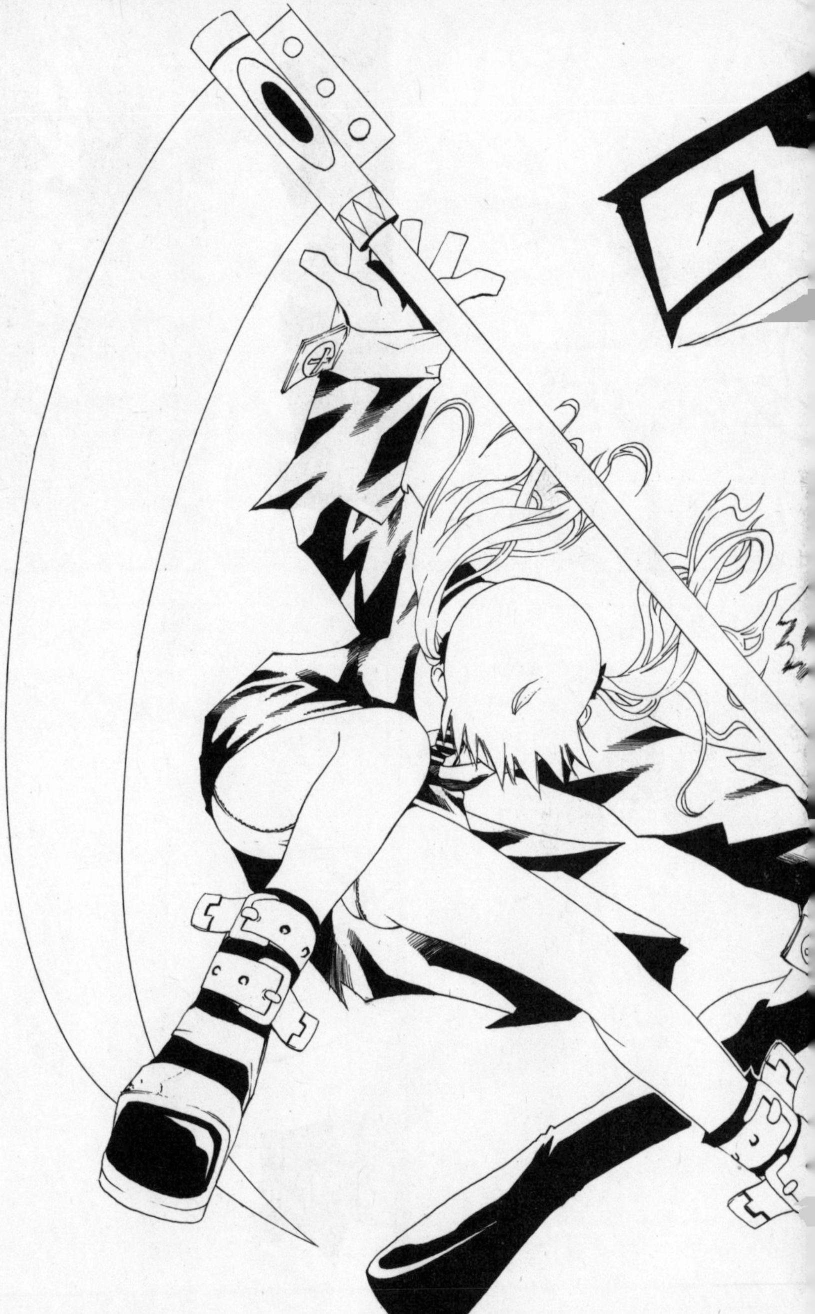

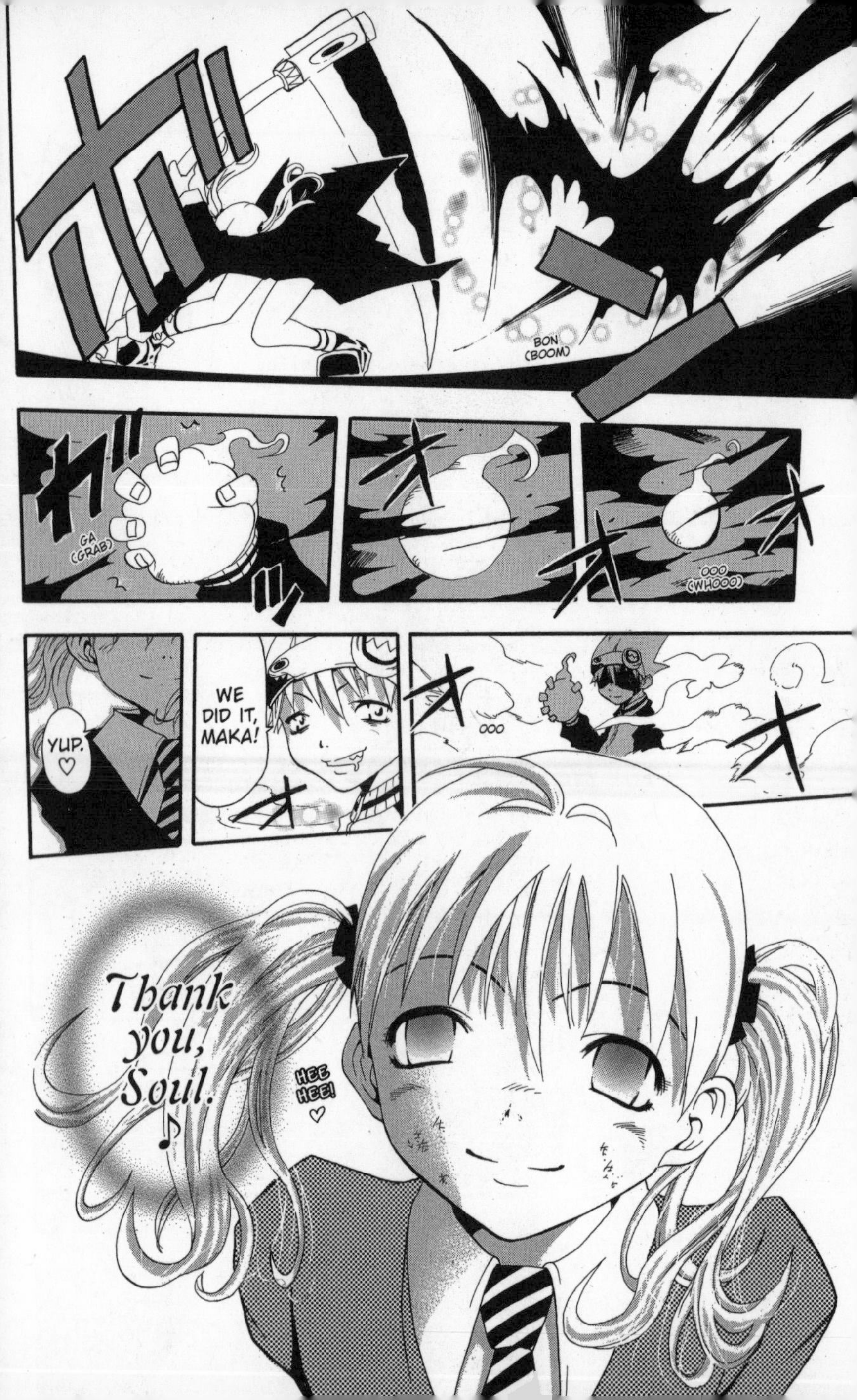
BON (BOOM)
OOO (WHOOO)
GA (GRAB)
OOO
WE DID IT, MAKA!
YUP. ♡
Thank you, Soul. ♪
HEE HEE! ♡

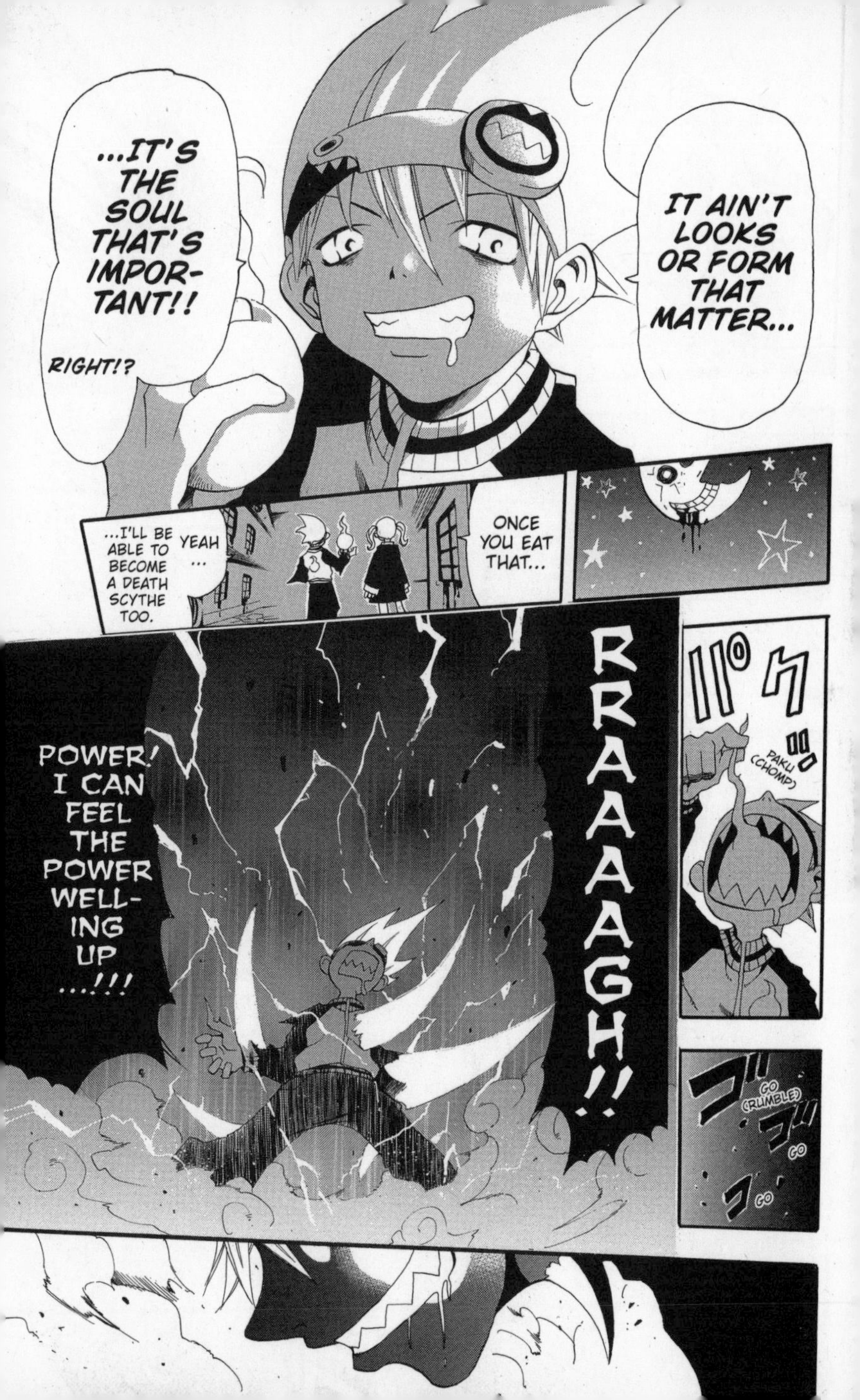
IT AIN'T LOOKS OR FORM THAT MATTER...
...IT'S THE SOUL THAT'S IMPOR-TANT!!
RIGHT!?
ONCE YOU EAT THAT...
YEAH...
...I'LL BE ABLE TO BECOME A DEATH SCYTHE TOO.
パク
PAKU (CHOMP)
GO (RUMBLE)
GO
GO
RRAAAAGH!!
POWER! I CAN FEEL THE POWER WELL-ING UP...!!!

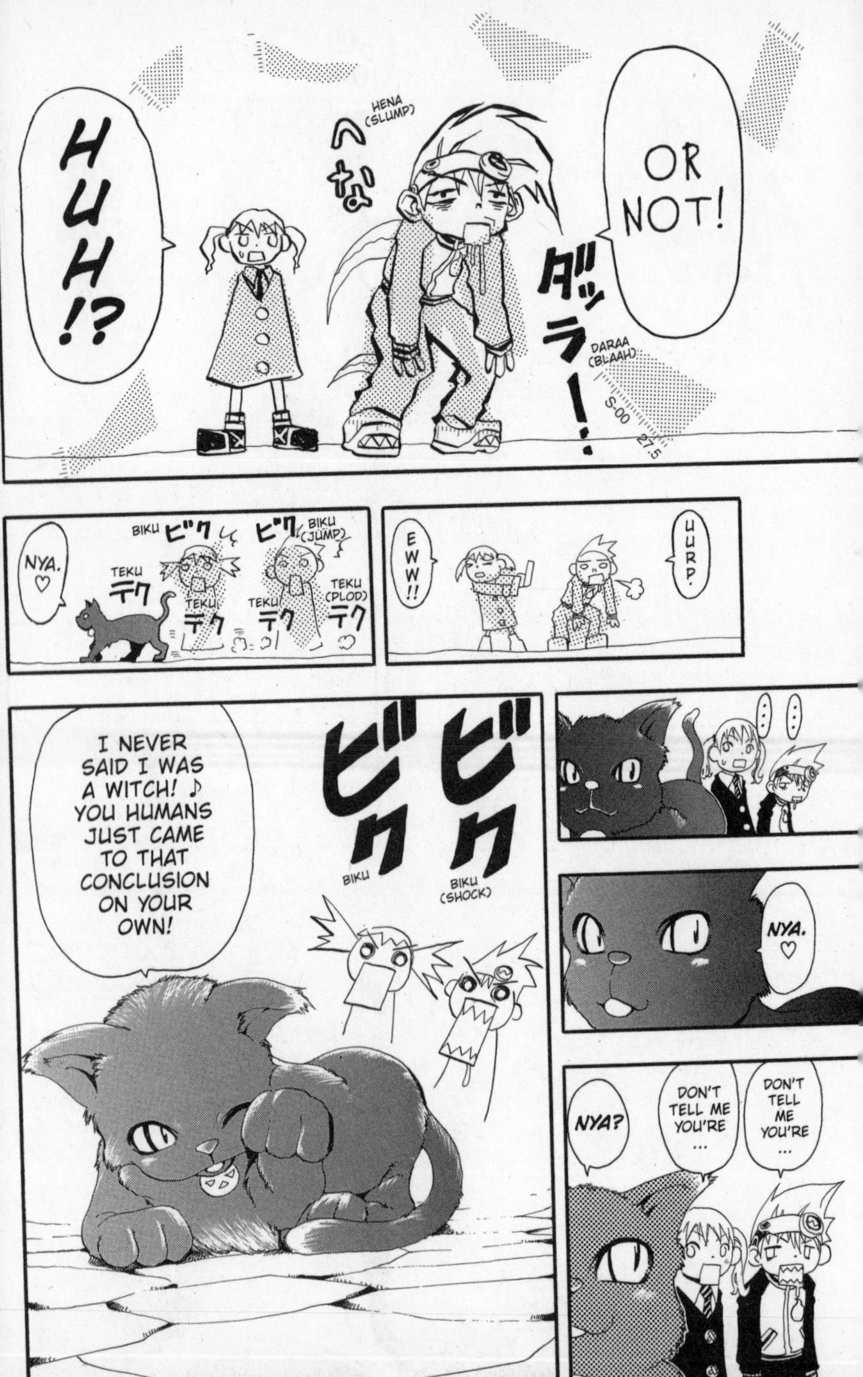
OR NOT!
ダッラー!!
DARAA (BLAAH)
S-00 27.5
へな
HENA (SLUMP)
HUH!?
UURP.
EWW!!
ビク
BIKU (JUMP)
ビク
BIKU
テク
TEKU (PLOD)
テク
TEKU
テク
TEKU
テク
TEKU
NYA. ♡
...
...
NYA. ♡
DON'T TELL ME YOU'RE ...
DON'T TELL ME YOU'RE ...
NYA?
ビク
BIKU (SHOCK)
ビク
BIKU
I NEVER SAID I WAS A WITCH! ♪ YOU HUMANS JUST CAME TO THAT CONCLUSION ON YOUR OWN!

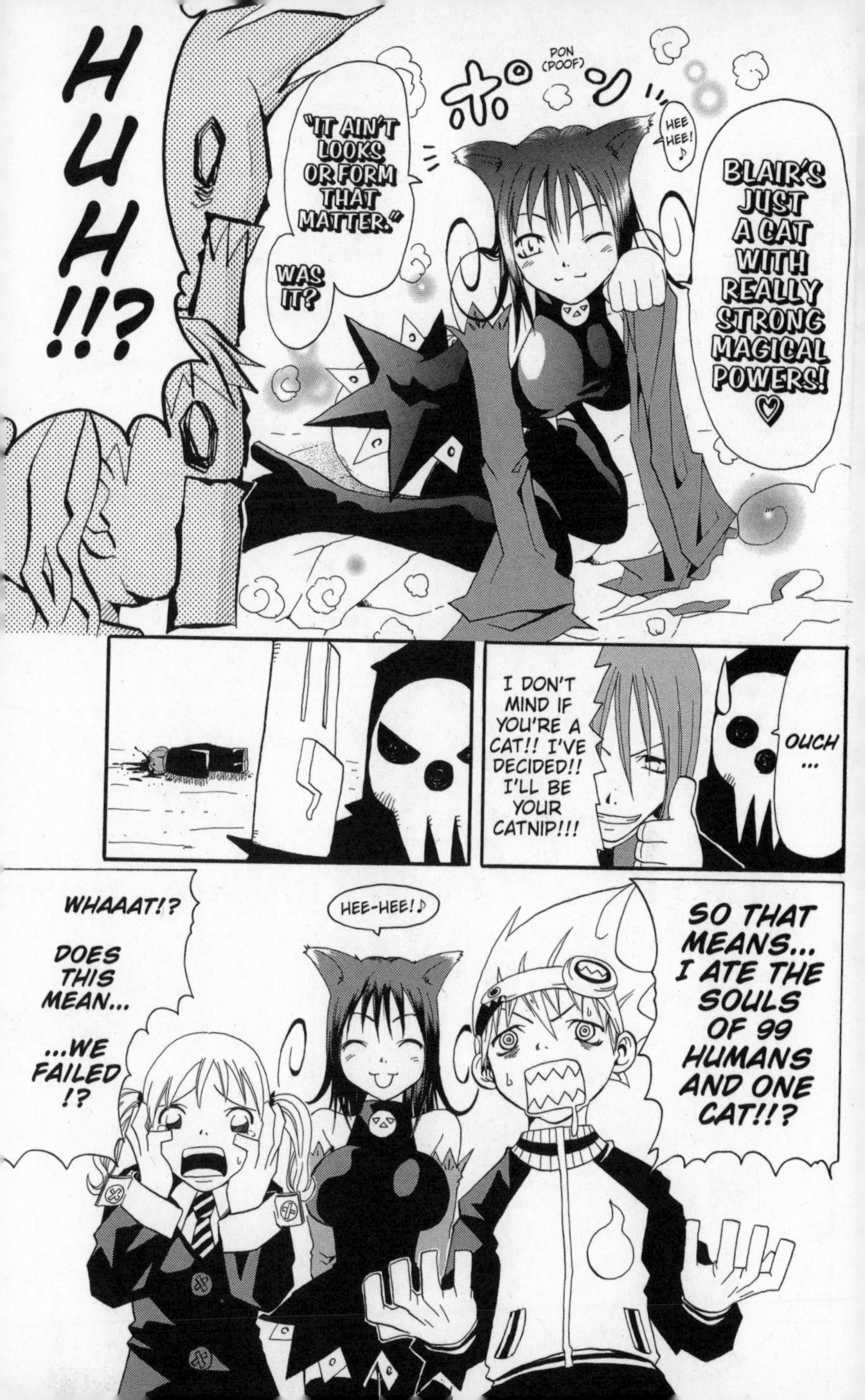
PON (POOF)
HEE HEE! ♪
BLAIR'S JUST A CAT WITH REALLY STRONG MAGICAL POWERS! ♡
"IT AIN'T LOOKS OR FORM THAT MATTER."
WAS IT?
HUH!!?
OUCH ...
I DON'T MIND IF YOU'RE A CAT!! I'VE DECIDED!! I'LL BE YOUR CATNIP!!!
SO THAT MEANS... I ATE THE SOULS OF 99 HUMANS AND ONE CAT!!?
HEE-HEE!♪
WHAAAT!?
DOES THIS MEAN...
...WE FAILED!?

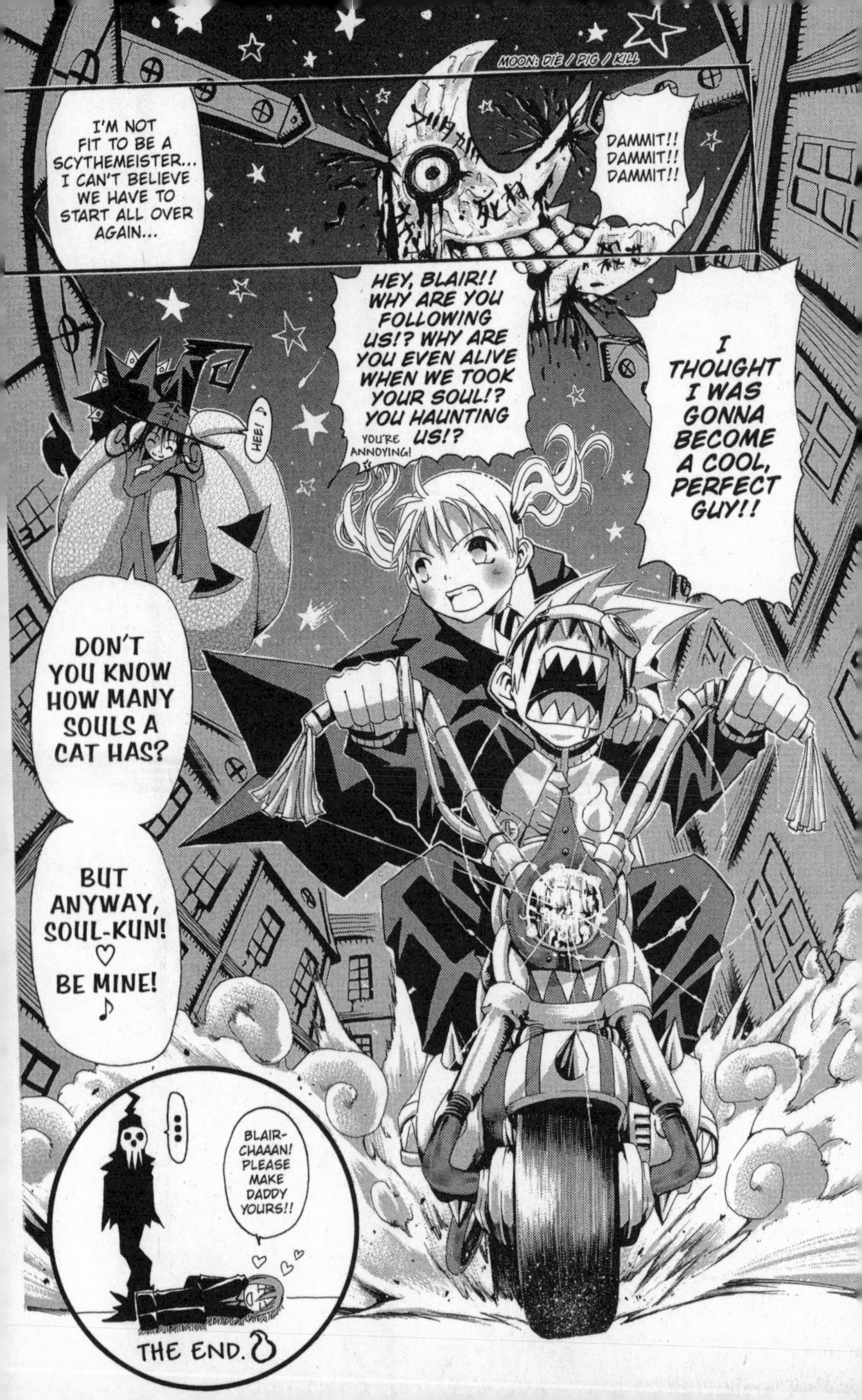
MOON: DIE / PIG / KILL
DAMMIT!! DAMMIT!! DAMMIT!!
I'M NOT FIT TO BE A SCYTHEMEISTER... I CAN'T BELIEVE WE HAVE TO START ALL OVER AGAIN...
I THOUGHT I WAS GONNA BECOME A COOL, PERFECT GUY!!
HEY, BLAIR!! WHY ARE YOU FOLLOWING US!? WHY ARE YOU EVEN ALIVE WHEN WE TOOK YOUR SOUL!? YOU HAUNTING US!?
YOU'RE ANNOYING!
HEE! ♪
DON'T YOU KNOW HOW MANY SOULS A CAT HAS?
BUT ANYWAY, SOUL-KUN! ♡ BE MINE! ♪
BLAIR-CHAAAN! PLEASE MAKE DADDY YOURS!!
...
THE END.

SOUL EATER

PROLOGUE 2: BLACK ☆ STAR

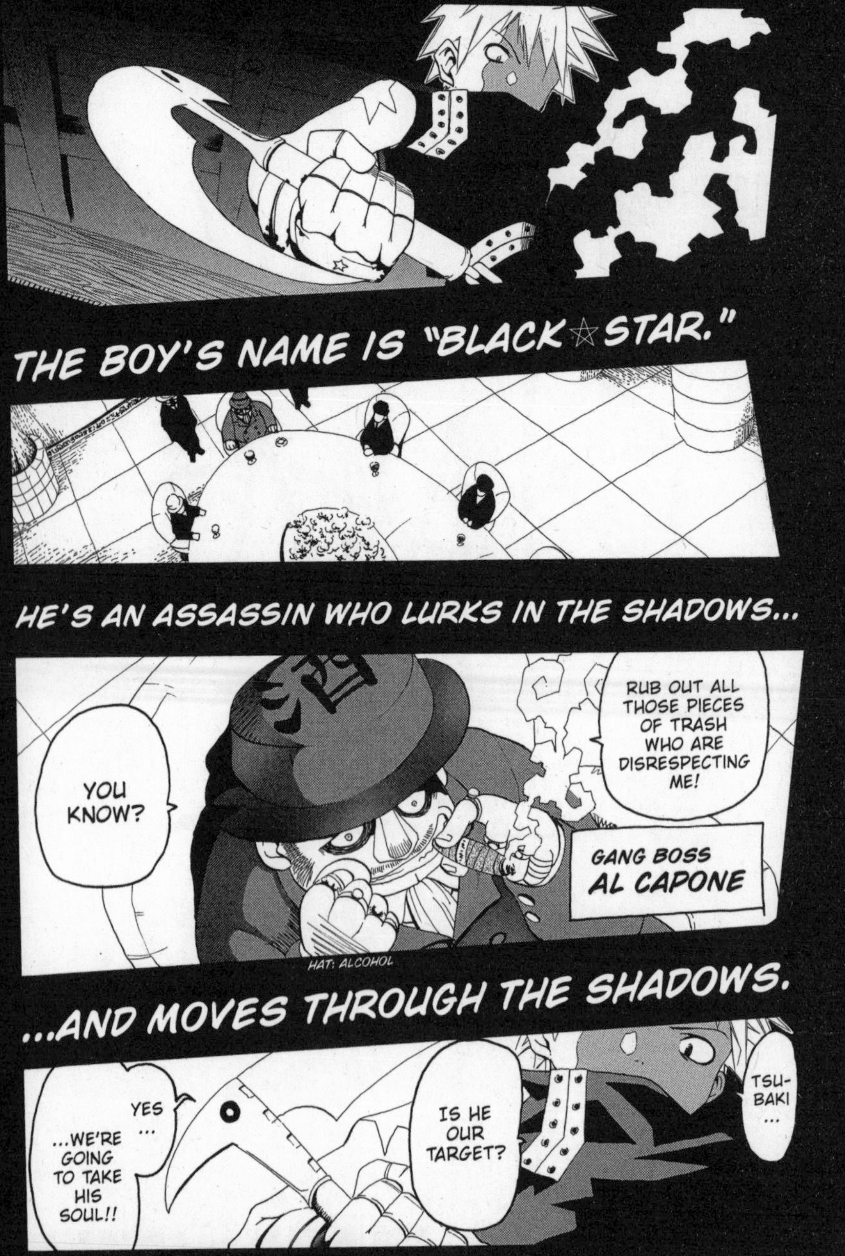
THE BOY'S NAME IS "BLACK☆STAR."
HE'S AN ASSASSIN WHO LURKS IN THE SHADOWS...
RUB OUT ALL THOSE PIECES OF TRASH WHO ARE DISRESPECTING ME!
GANG BOSS AL CAPONE
YOU KNOW?
HAT: ALCOHOL
...AND MOVES THROUGH THE SHADOWS.
TSU-BAKI...
IS HE OUR TARGET?
YES...
...WE'RE GOING TO TAKE HIS SOUL!!

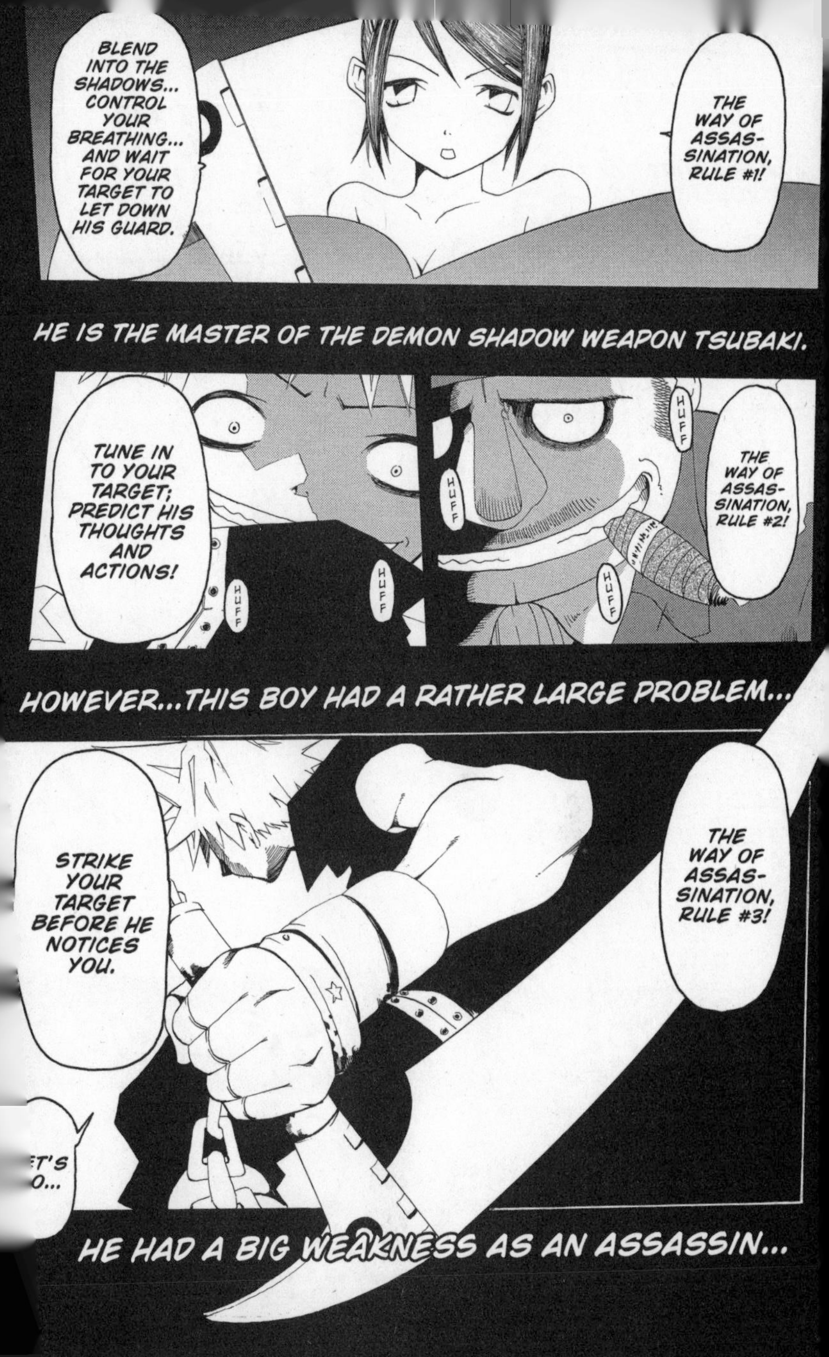
THE WAY OF ASSASSINATION, RULE #1!
BLEND INTO THE SHADOWS... CONTROL YOUR BREATHING... AND WAIT FOR YOUR TARGET TO LET DOWN HIS GUARD.
HE IS THE MASTER OF THE DEMON SHADOW WEAPON TSUBAKI.
THE WAY OF ASSASSINATION, RULE #2!
HUFF
HUFF
HUFF
HUFF
HUFF
TUNE IN TO YOUR TARGET; PREDICT HIS THOUGHTS AND ACTIONS!
HOWEVER...THIS BOY HAD A RATHER LARGE PROBLEM...
THE WAY OF ASSASSINATION, RULE #3!
STRIKE YOUR TARGET BEFORE HE NOTICES YOU.
HE HAD A BIG WEAKNESS AS AN ASSASSIN...

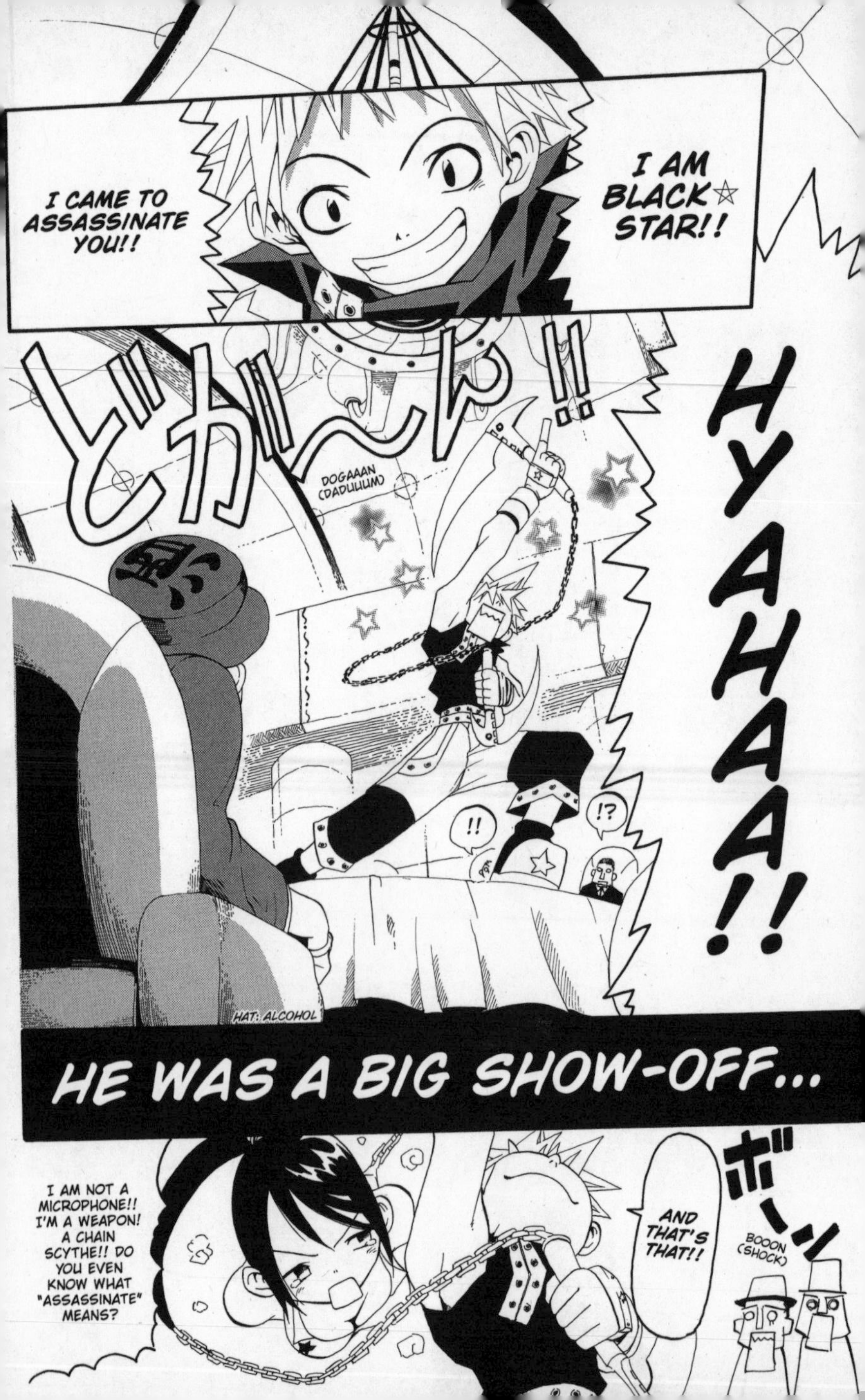
I AM BLACK☆STAR!!
I CAME TO ASSASSINATE YOU!!
HYAHAA!!
どが〜ん!!
DOGAAAN (DADUUUM)
!?
!!
HAT: ALCOHOL
HE WAS A BIG SHOW-OFF...
ボーッ
BOOON (SHOCK)
AND THAT'S THAT!!
I AM NOT A MICROPHONE!! I'M A WEAPON! A CHAIN SCYTHE!! DO YOU EVEN KNOW WHAT "ASSASSINATE" MEANS?

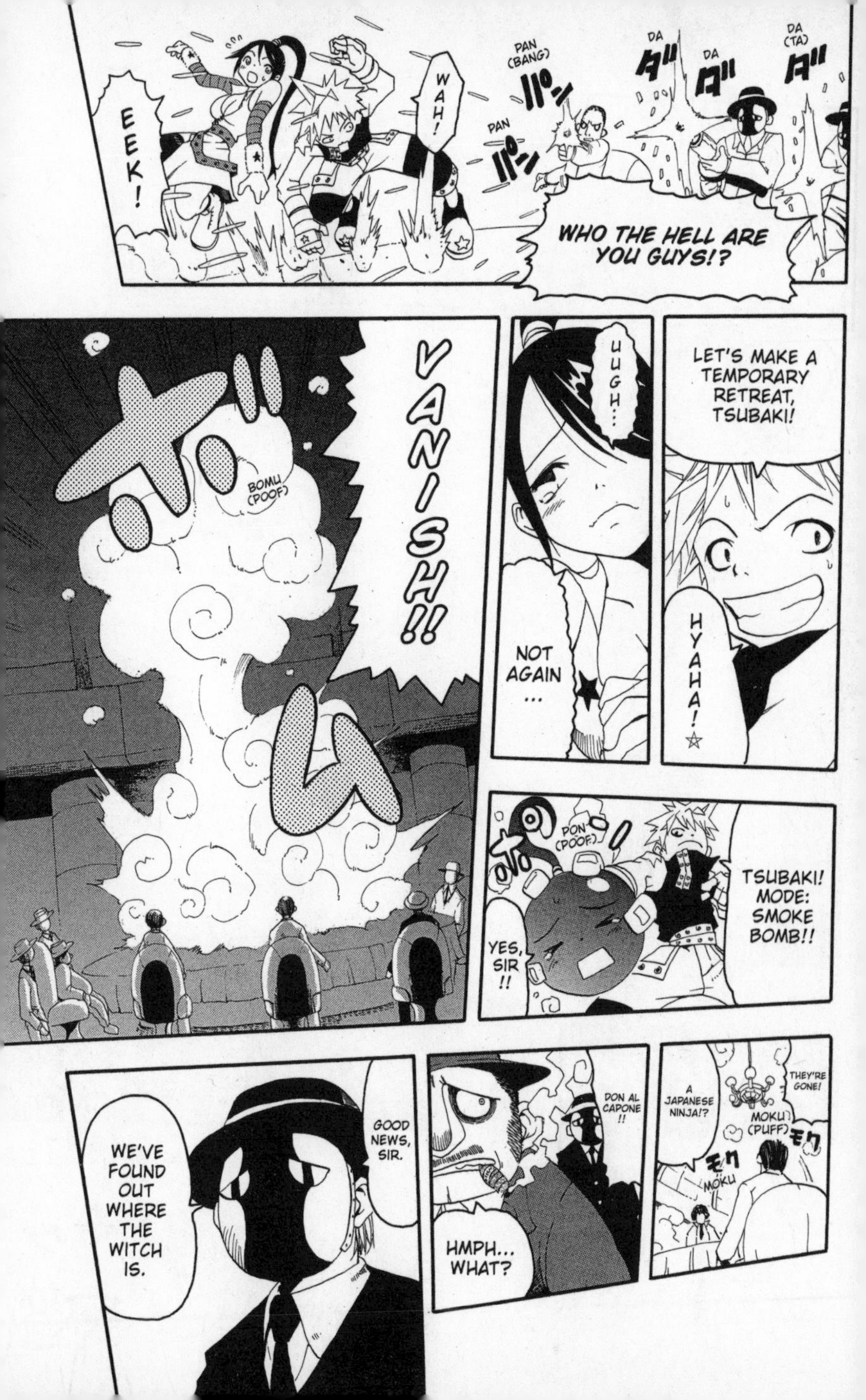

DA (TA)
DA
DA
PAN (BANG)
PAN
WAH!
WHO THE HELL ARE YOU GUYS!?
EEK!
LET'S MAKE A TEMPORARY RETREAT, TSUBAKI!
HYAHA!☆
UUGH...
NOT AGAIN...
TSUBAKI! MODE: SMOKE BOMB!!
PON (POOF)
YES, SIR!!
VANISH!!
BOMU (POOF)
THEY'RE GONE!
A JAPANESE NINJA!?
MOKU (PUFF)
MOKU
DON AL CAPONE!!
HMPH... WHAT?
GOOD NEWS, SIR.
WE'VE FOUND OUT WHERE THE WITCH IS.

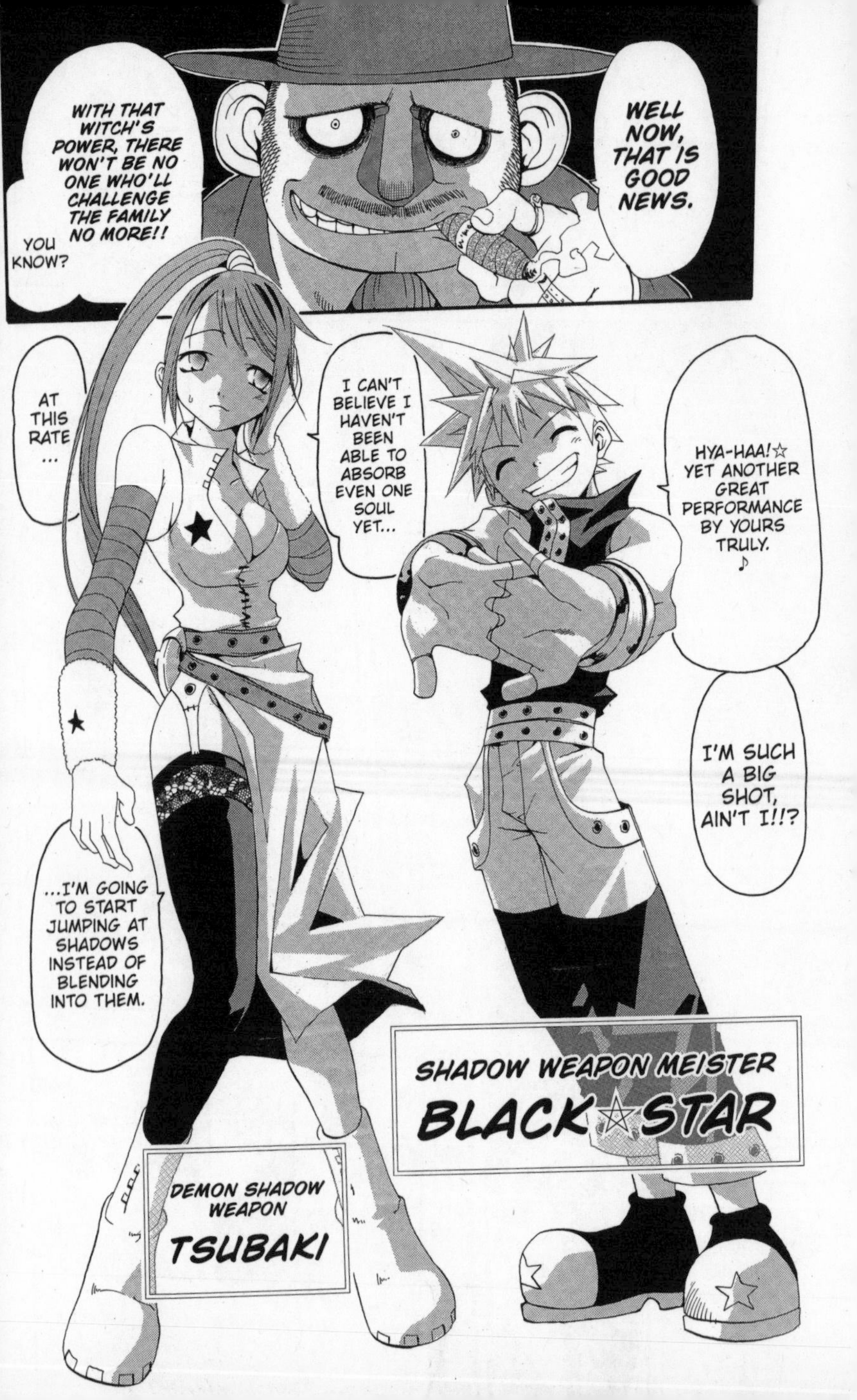
WELL NOW, THAT IS GOOD NEWS.
WITH THAT WITCH'S POWER, THERE WON'T BE NO ONE WHO'LL CHALLENGE THE FAMILY NO MORE!!
YOU KNOW?
HYA-HAA!☆ YET ANOTHER GREAT PERFORMANCE BY YOURS TRULY. ♪
I'M SUCH A BIG SHOT, AIN'T I!!?
SHADOW WEAPON MEISTER
BLACK☆STAR
I CAN'T BELIEVE I HAVEN'T BEEN ABLE TO ABSORB EVEN ONE SOUL YET...
AT THIS RATE...
...I'M GOING TO START JUMPING AT SHADOWS INSTEAD OF BLENDING INTO THEM.
DEMON SHADOW WEAPON
TSUBAKI

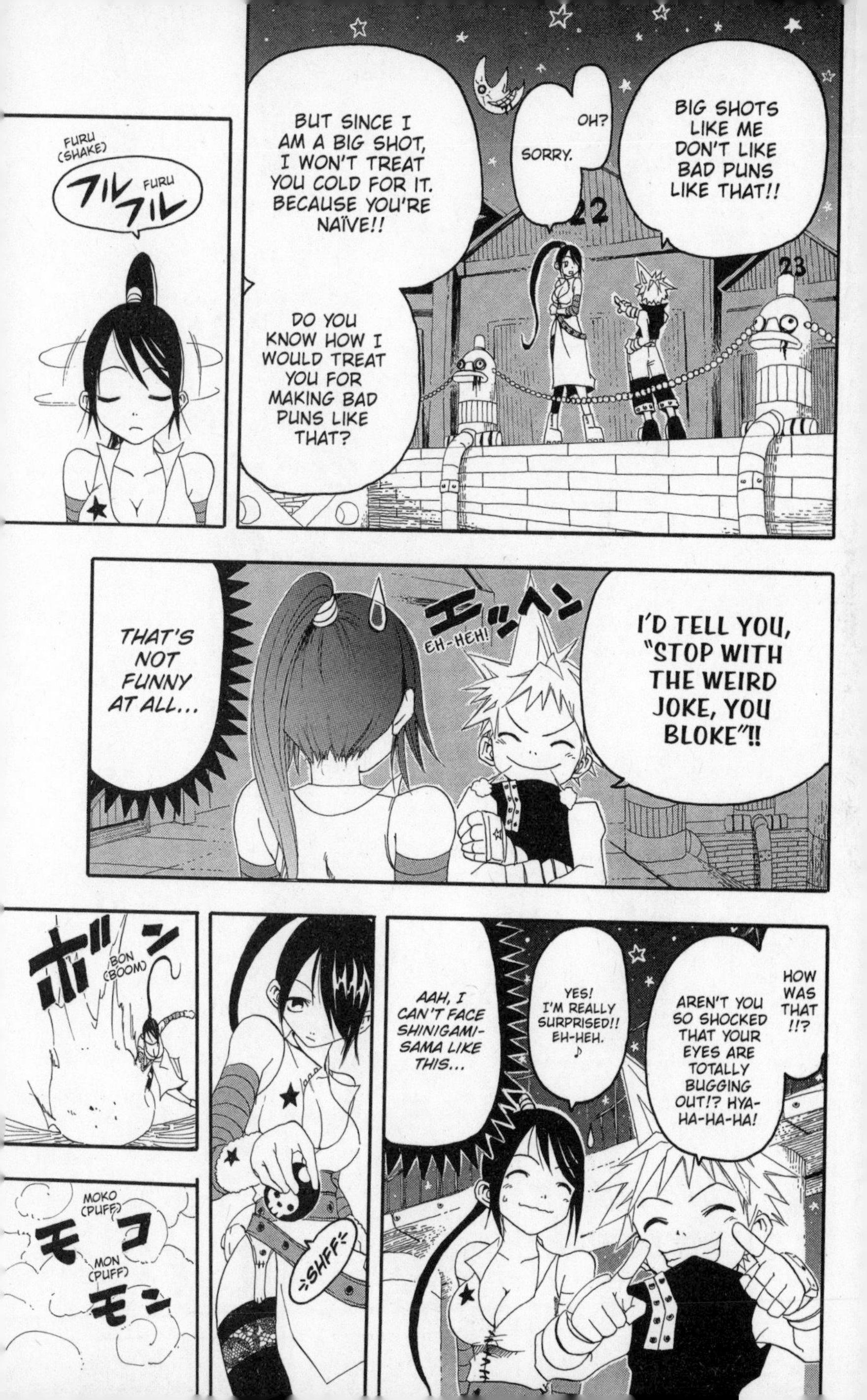
BIG SHOTS LIKE ME DON'T LIKE BAD PUNS LIKE THAT!!
OH? SORRY.
BUT SINCE I AM A BIG SHOT, I WON'T TREAT YOU COLD FOR IT. BECAUSE YOU'RE NAÏVE!!
DO YOU KNOW HOW I WOULD TREAT YOU FOR MAKING BAD PUNS LIKE THAT?
22
23
フルフル
FURU (SHAKE) FURU
I'D TELL YOU, "STOP WITH THE WEIRD JOKE, YOU BLOKE"!!
エッヘン
EH-HEH!
THAT'S NOT FUNNY AT ALL...
HOW WAS THAT!!?
AREN'T YOU SO SHOCKED THAT YOUR EYES ARE TOTALLY BUGGING OUT!? HYA-HA-HA-HA!
YES! I'M REALLY SURPRISED!! EH-HEH. ♪
AAH, I CAN'T FACE SHINIGAMI-SAMA LIKE THIS...
SHFF
ボン
BON (BOOM)
モコ
MOKO (PUFF)
モン
MON (PUFF)

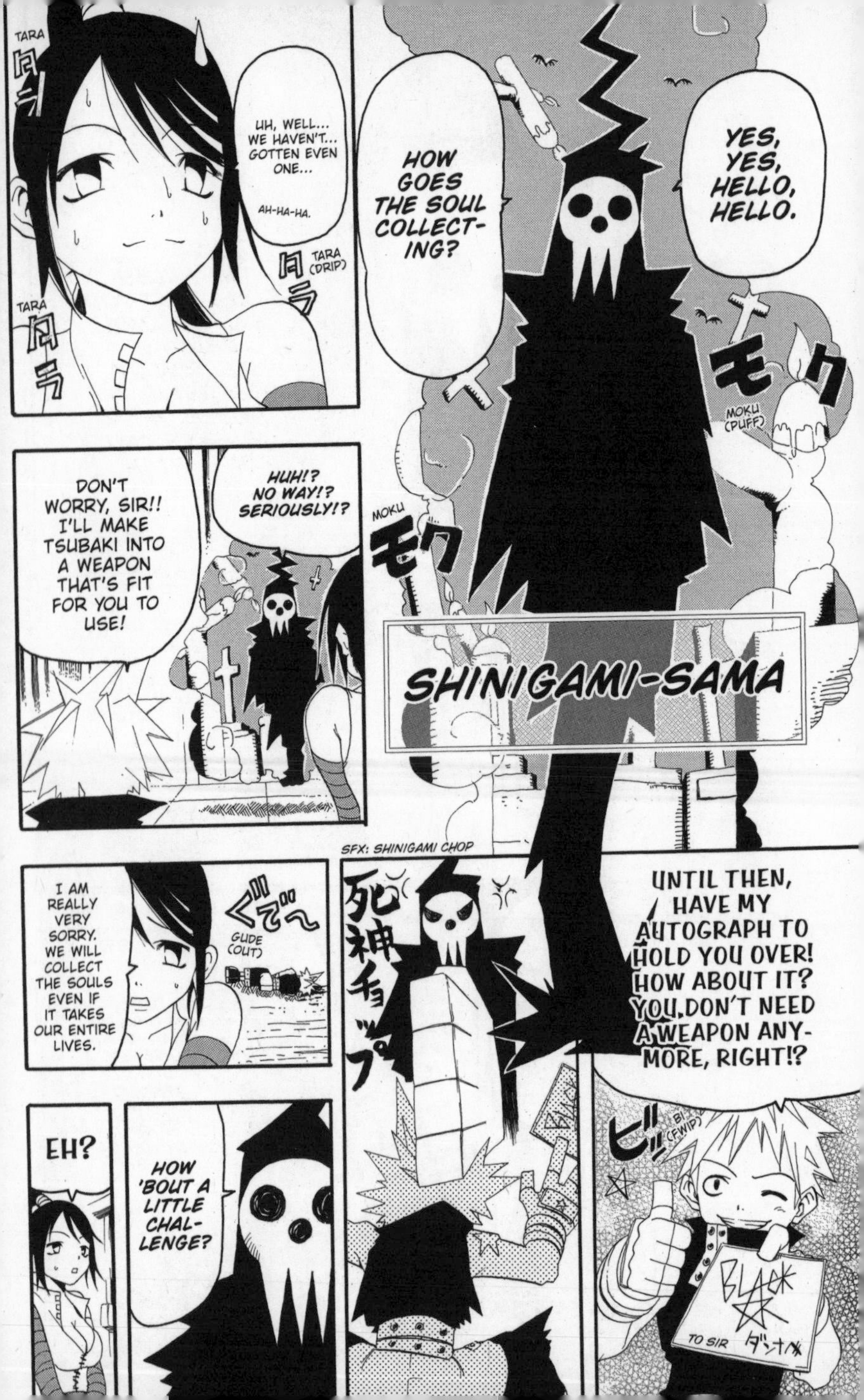
YES, YES, HELLO, HELLO.
HOW GOES THE SOUL COLLECT-ING?
MOKU (PUFF)
モク
MOKU
モク
SHINIGAMI-SAMA
UH, WELL... WE HAVEN'T... GOTTEN EVEN ONE...
AH-HA-HA.
TARA (DRIP)
タラ
TARA
タラ
TARA
タラ
HUH!? NO WAY!? SERIOUSLY!?
DON'T WORRY, SIR!! I'LL MAKE TSUBAKI INTO A WEAPON THAT'S FIT FOR YOU TO USE!
UNTIL THEN, HAVE MY AUTOGRAPH TO HOLD YOU OVER! HOW ABOUT IT? YOU DON'T NEED A WEAPON ANY-MORE, RIGHT!?
ビッ
BI (FWIP)
TO SIR
SFX: SHINIGAMI CHOP
死神チョップ
ぐでぇ
GUDE (OUT)
I AM REALLY VERY SORRY. WE WILL COLLECT THE SOULS EVEN IF IT TAKES OUR ENTIRE LIVES.
HOW 'BOUT A LITTLE CHAL-LENGE?
EH?

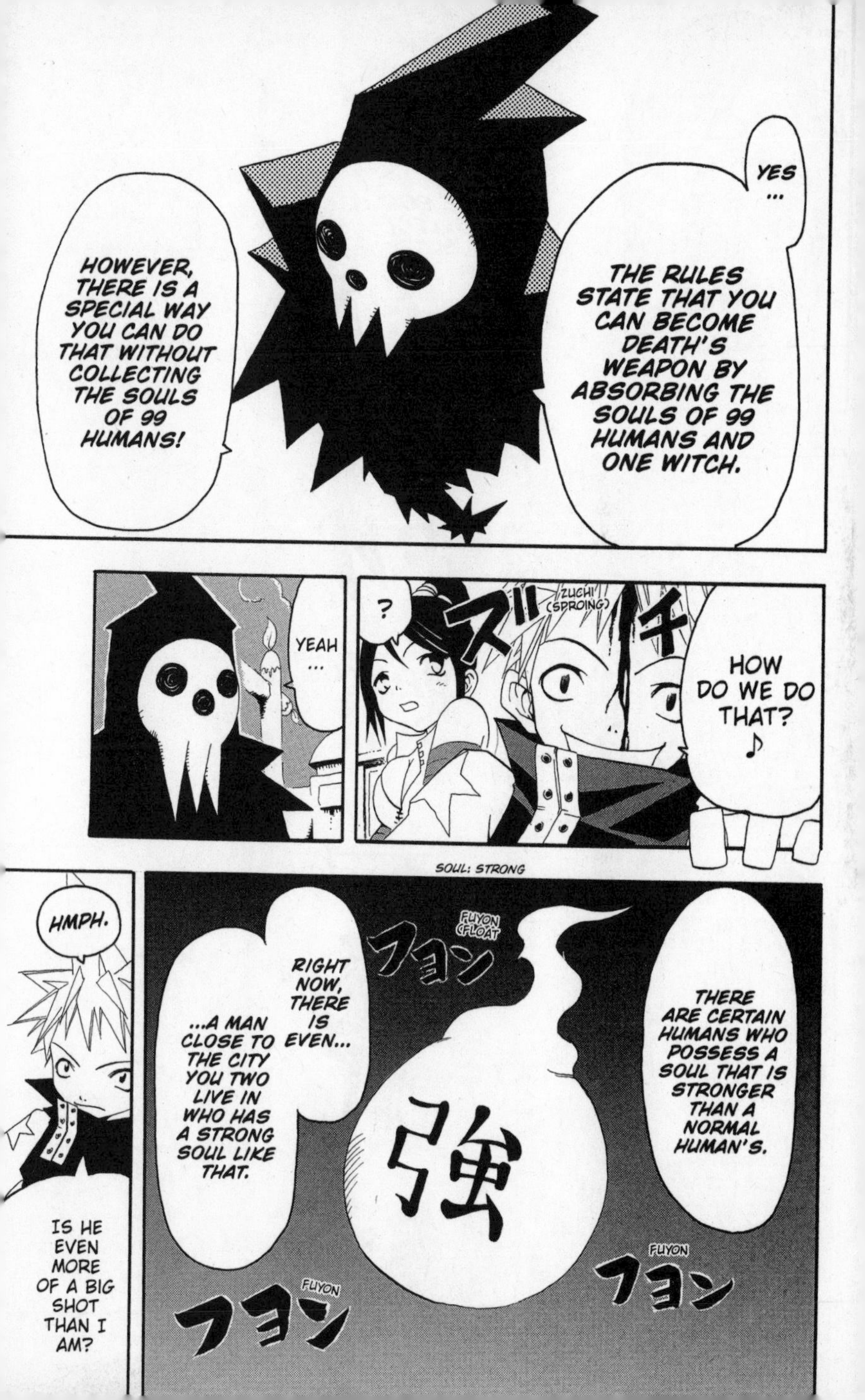
YES...
THE RULES STATE THAT YOU CAN BECOME DEATH'S WEAPON BY ABSORBING THE SOULS OF 99 HUMANS AND ONE WITCH.
HOWEVER, THERE IS A SPECIAL WAY YOU CAN DO THAT WITHOUT COLLECTING THE SOULS OF 99 HUMANS!
HOW DO WE DO THAT? ♪
ZUCHI (SPROING)
?
YEAH...
SOUL: STRONG
THERE ARE CERTAIN HUMANS WHO POSSESS A SOUL THAT IS STRONGER THAN A NORMAL HUMAN'S.
FUYON (FLOAT)
RIGHT NOW, THERE IS EVEN...
...A MAN CLOSE TO THE CITY YOU TWO LIVE IN WHO HAS A STRONG SOUL LIKE THAT.
FUYON
FUYON
HMPH.
IS HE EVEN MORE OF A BIG SHOT THAN I AM?

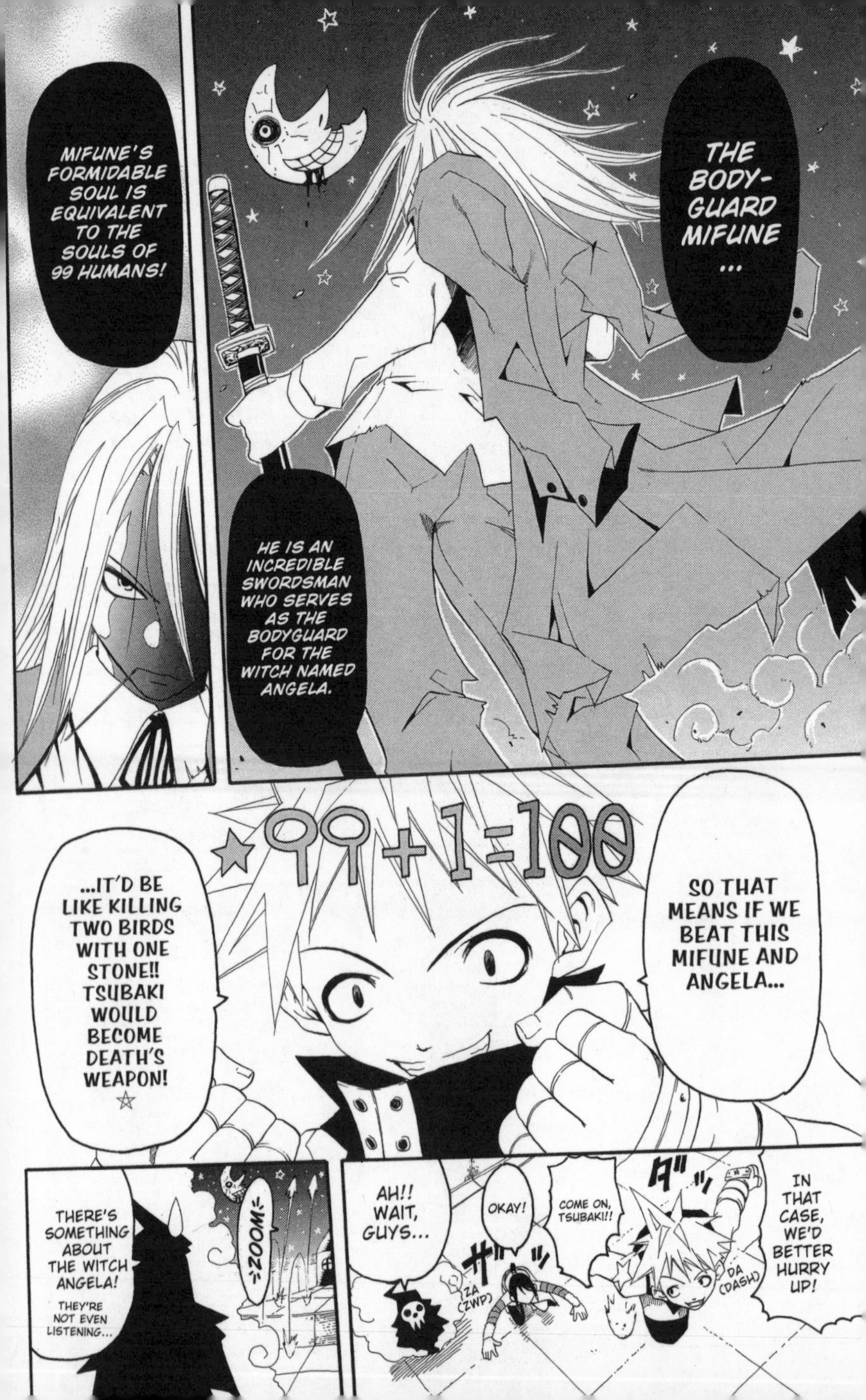
THE BODY-GUARD MIFUNE ...
HE IS AN INCREDIBLE SWORDSMAN WHO SERVES AS THE BODYGUARD FOR THE WITCH NAMED ANGELA.
MIFUNE'S FORMIDABLE SOUL IS EQUIVALENT TO THE SOULS OF 99 HUMANS!
SO THAT MEANS IF WE BEAT THIS MIFUNE AND ANGELA...
99 + 1 = 100
...IT'D BE LIKE KILLING TWO BIRDS WITH ONE STONE!! TSUBAKI WOULD BECOME DEATH'S WEAPON!
IN THAT CASE, WE'D BETTER HURRY UP!
DA (DASH)
COME ON, TSUBAKI!!
OKAY!
ZA (ZWP)
AH!! WAIT, GUYS...
ZOOM
THERE'S SOMETHING ABOUT THE WITCH ANGELA!
THEY'RE NOT EVEN LISTENING...

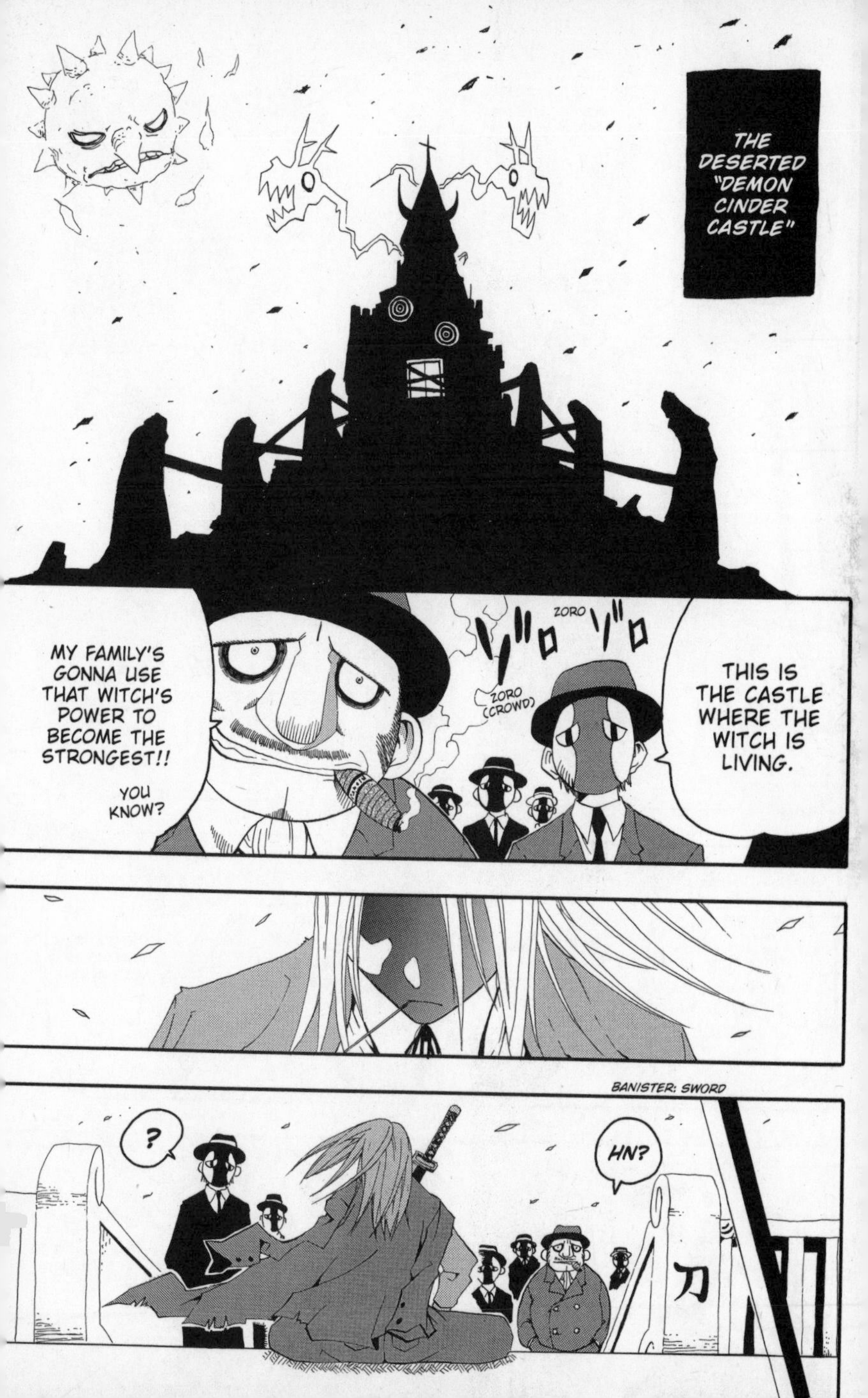
THE DESERTED "DEMON CINDER CASTLE"
THIS IS THE CASTLE WHERE THE WITCH IS LIVING.
ゾロゾロ
ZORO
ZORO (CROWD)
MY FAMILY'S GONNA USE THAT WITCH'S POWER TO BECOME THE STRONGEST!!
YOU KNOW?
BANISTER: SWORD
HN?
?
刀

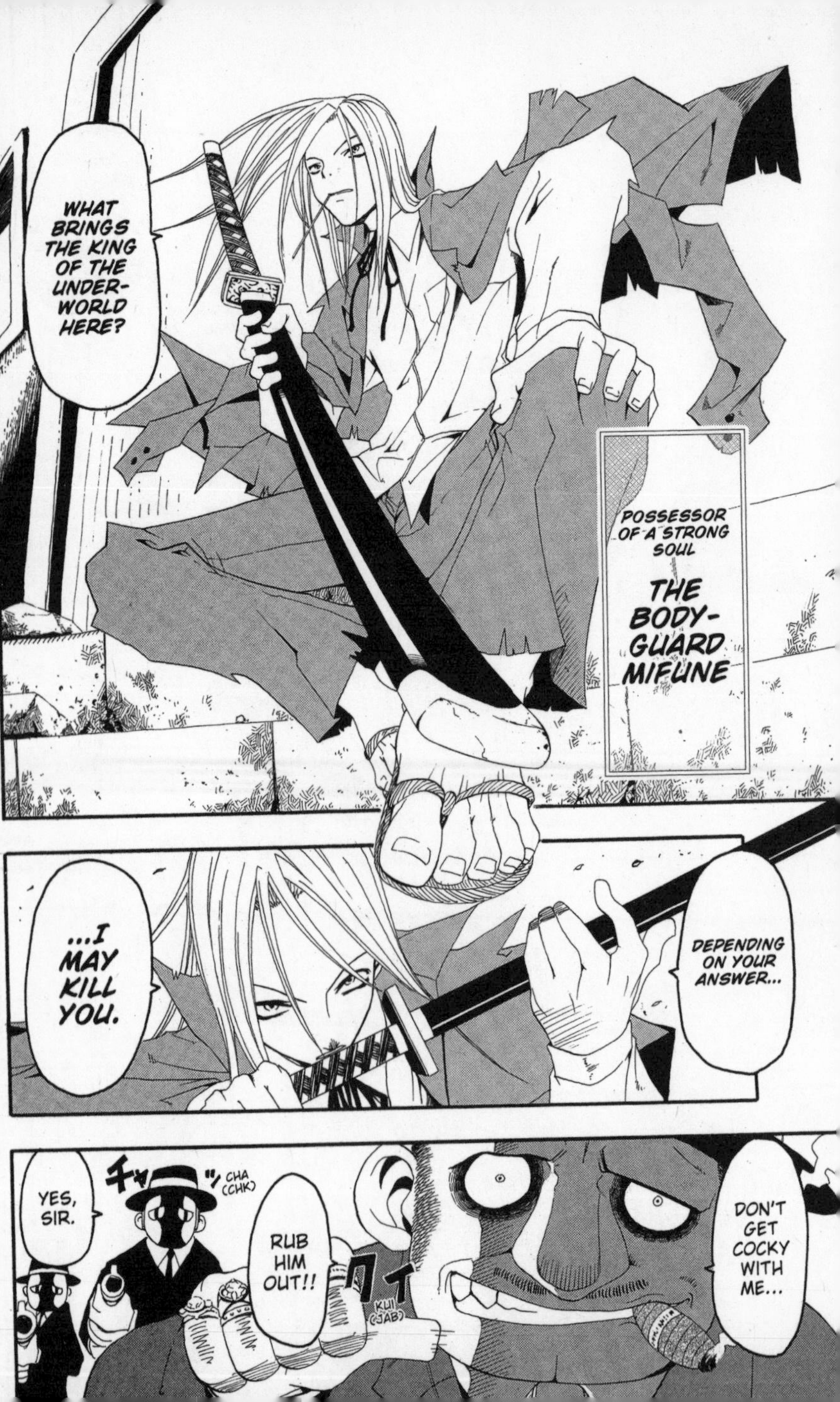
WHAT BRINGS THE KING OF THE UNDER-WORLD HERE?
POSSESSOR OF A STRONG SOUL
THE BODY-GUARD MIFUNE
DEPENDING ON YOUR ANSWER...
...I MAY KILL YOU.
DON'T GET COCKY WITH ME...
KUI (JAB)
RUB HIM OUT!!
CHA (CHK)
YES, SIR.

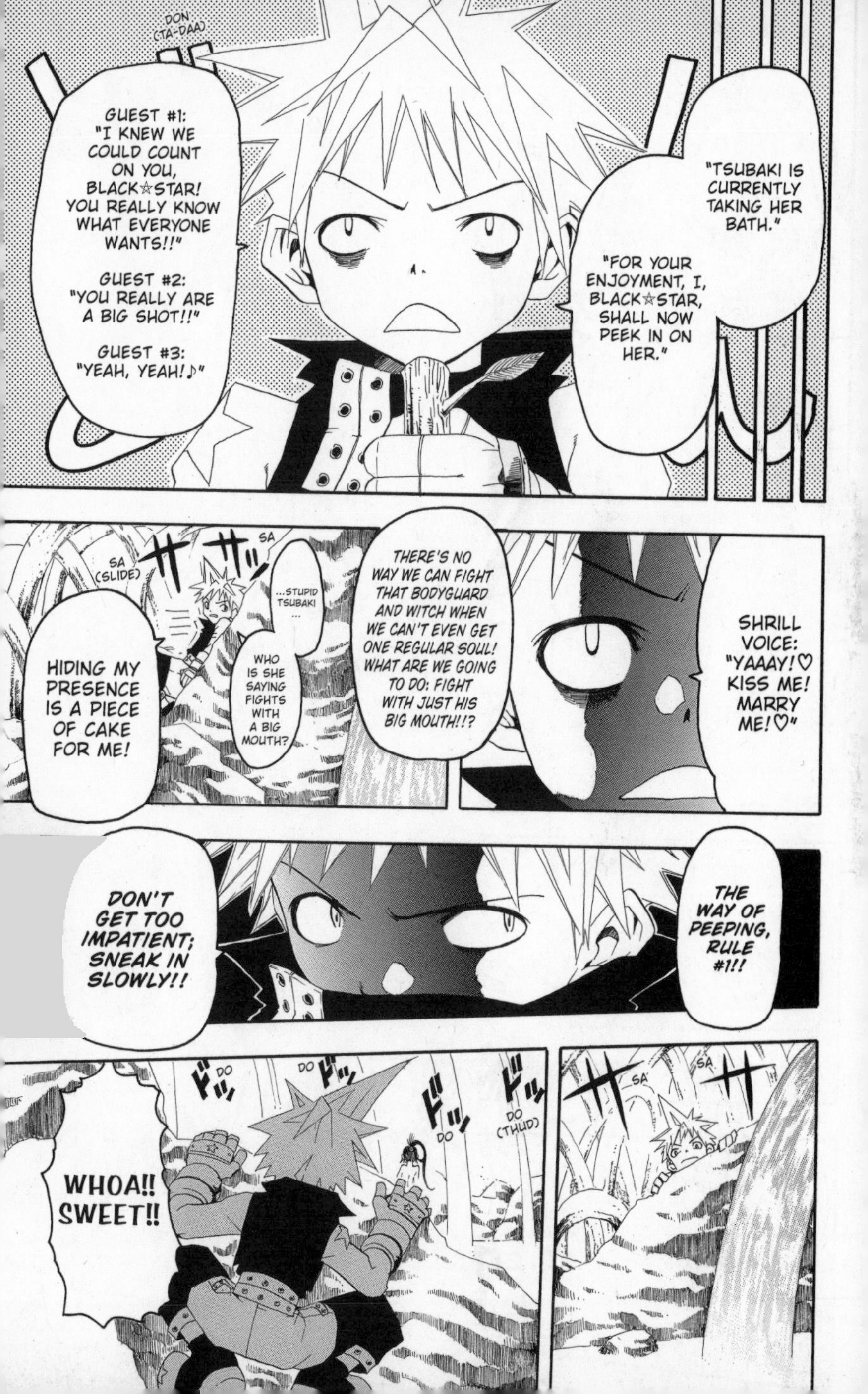
DON (TA-DAA)
"TSUBAKI IS CURRENTLY TAKING HER BATH."
"FOR YOUR ENJOYMENT, I, BLACK☆STAR, SHALL NOW PEEK IN ON HER."
GUEST #1: "I KNEW WE COULD COUNT ON YOU, BLACK☆STAR! YOU REALLY KNOW WHAT EVERYONE WANTS!!"
GUEST #2: "YOU REALLY ARE A BIG SHOT!!"
GUEST #3: "YEAH, YEAH!♪"
SHRILL VOICE: "YAAAY!♡ KISS ME! MARRY ME!♡"
SA
SA (SLIDE)
THERE'S NO WAY WE CAN FIGHT THAT BODYGUARD AND WITCH WHEN WE CAN'T EVEN GET ONE REGULAR SOUL! WHAT ARE WE GOING TO DO: FIGHT WITH JUST HIS BIG MOUTH!!?
...STUPID TSUBAKI ...
WHO IS SHE SAYING FIGHTS WITH A BIG MOUTH?
HIDING MY PRESENCE IS A PIECE OF CAKE FOR ME!
THE WAY OF PEEPING, RULE #1!!
DON'T GET TOO IMPATIENT; SNEAK IN SLOWLY!!
SA
SA
DO (THUD)
DO
DO
DO
WHOA!! SWEET!!

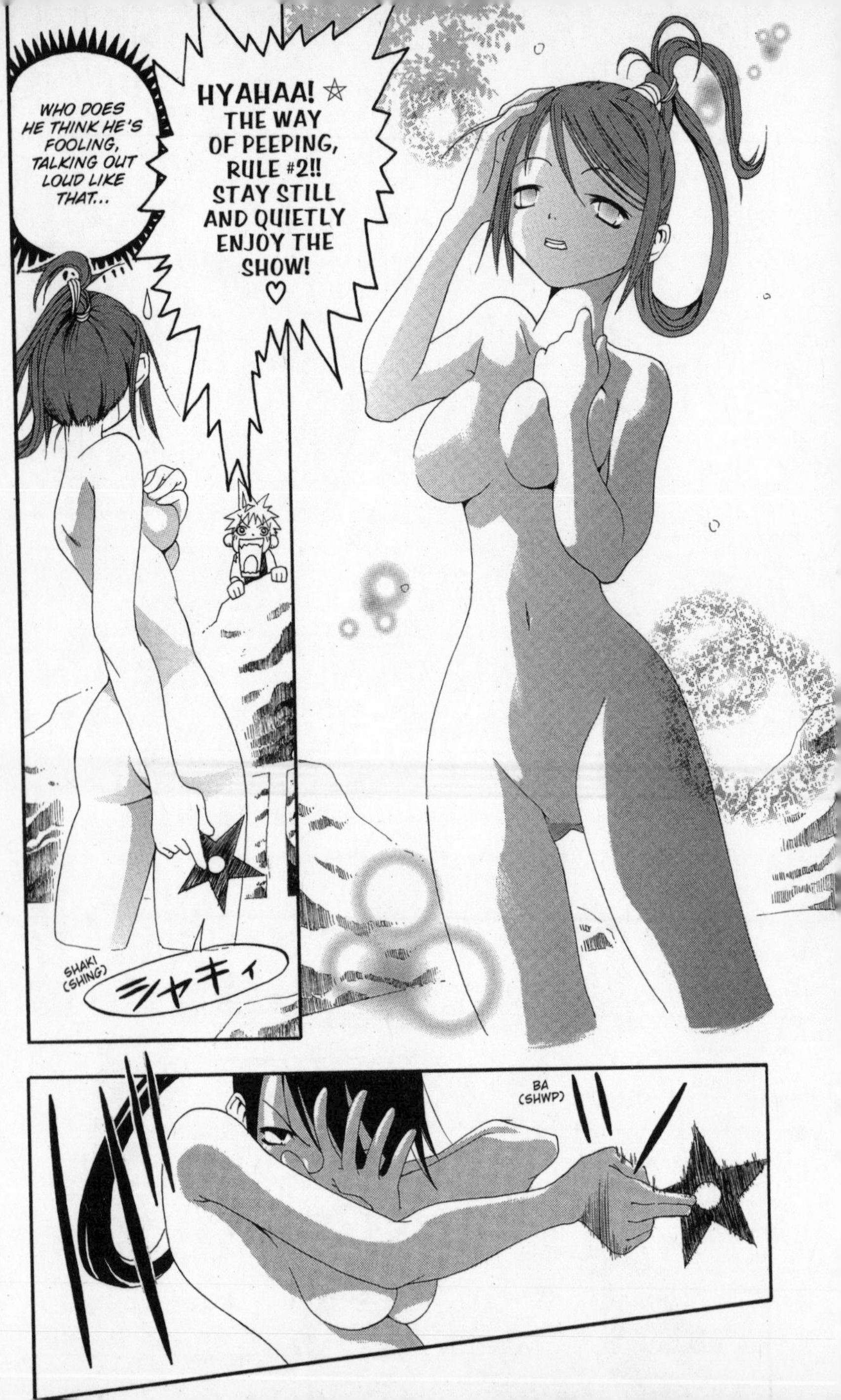
HYAHAA! ☆ THE WAY OF PEEPING, RULE #2!! STAY STILL AND QUIETLY ENJOY THE SHOW! ♡
WHO DOES HE THINK HE'S FOOLING, TALKING OUT LOUD LIKE THAT...
シャキィ
SHAKI (SHING)
BA (SHWP)

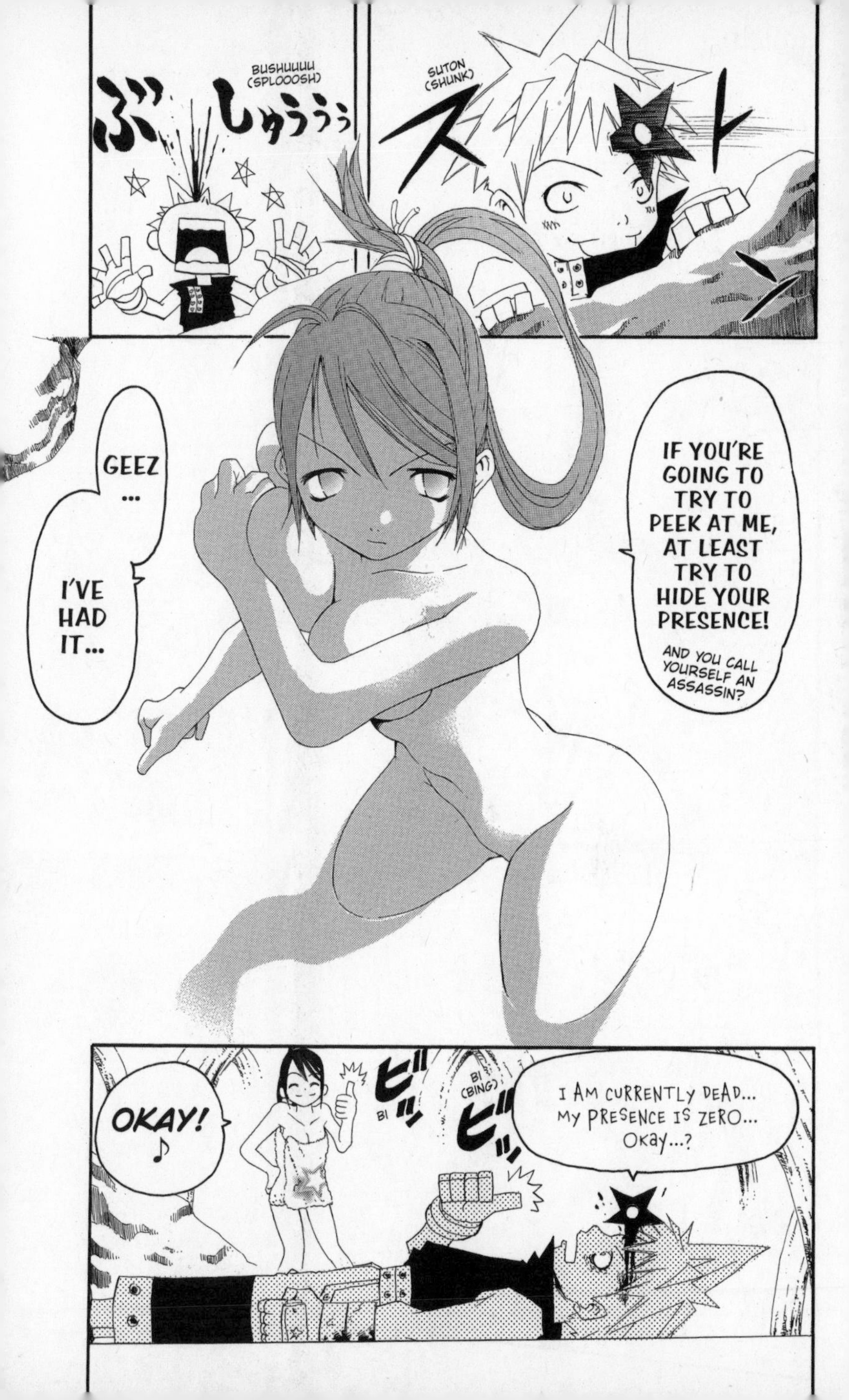
SUTON (SHUNK)
BUSHUUUU (SPLOOOSH)
IF YOU'RE GOING TO TRY TO PEEK AT ME, AT LEAST TRY TO HIDE YOUR PRESENCE!
AND YOU CALL YOURSELF AN ASSASSIN?
GEEZ ...
I'VE HAD IT...
I AM CURRENTLY DEAD... MY PRESENCE IS ZERO... OKAY...?
BI (BING)
BI
OKAY! ♪

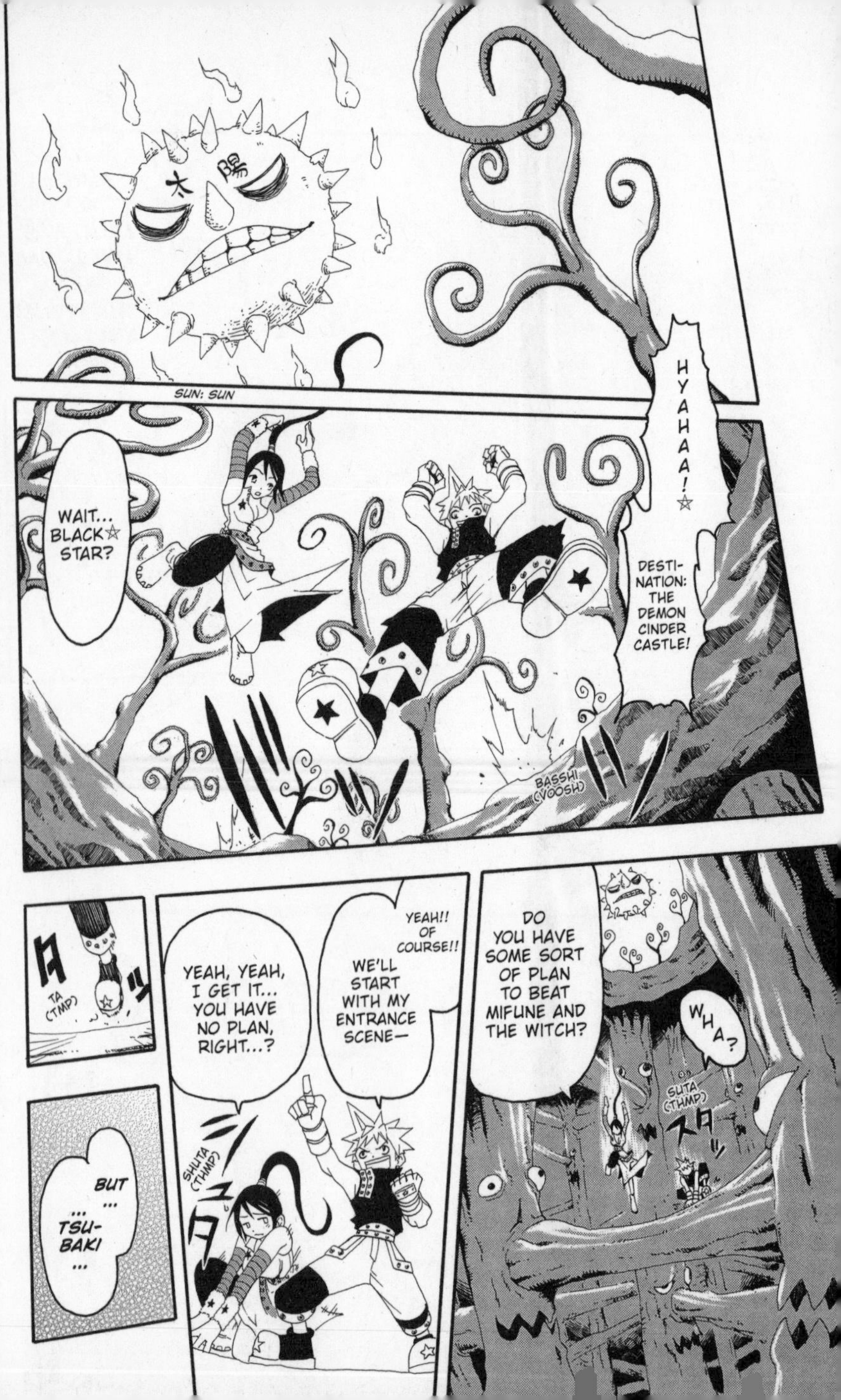
SUN: SUN
HYAHAA!☆
DESTI-NATION: THE DEMON CINDER CASTLE!
BASSHI (VOOSH)
WAIT... BLACK☆ STAR?
DO YOU HAVE SOME SORT OF PLAN TO BEAT MIFUNE AND THE WITCH?
WHA?
SUTA (THMP)
YEAH!! OF COURSE!!
WE'LL START WITH MY ENTRANCE SCENE—
YEAH, YEAH, I GET IT... YOU HAVE NO PLAN, RIGHT...?
SHUTA (THMP)
TA (TMP)
BUT ... TSU-BAKI ...

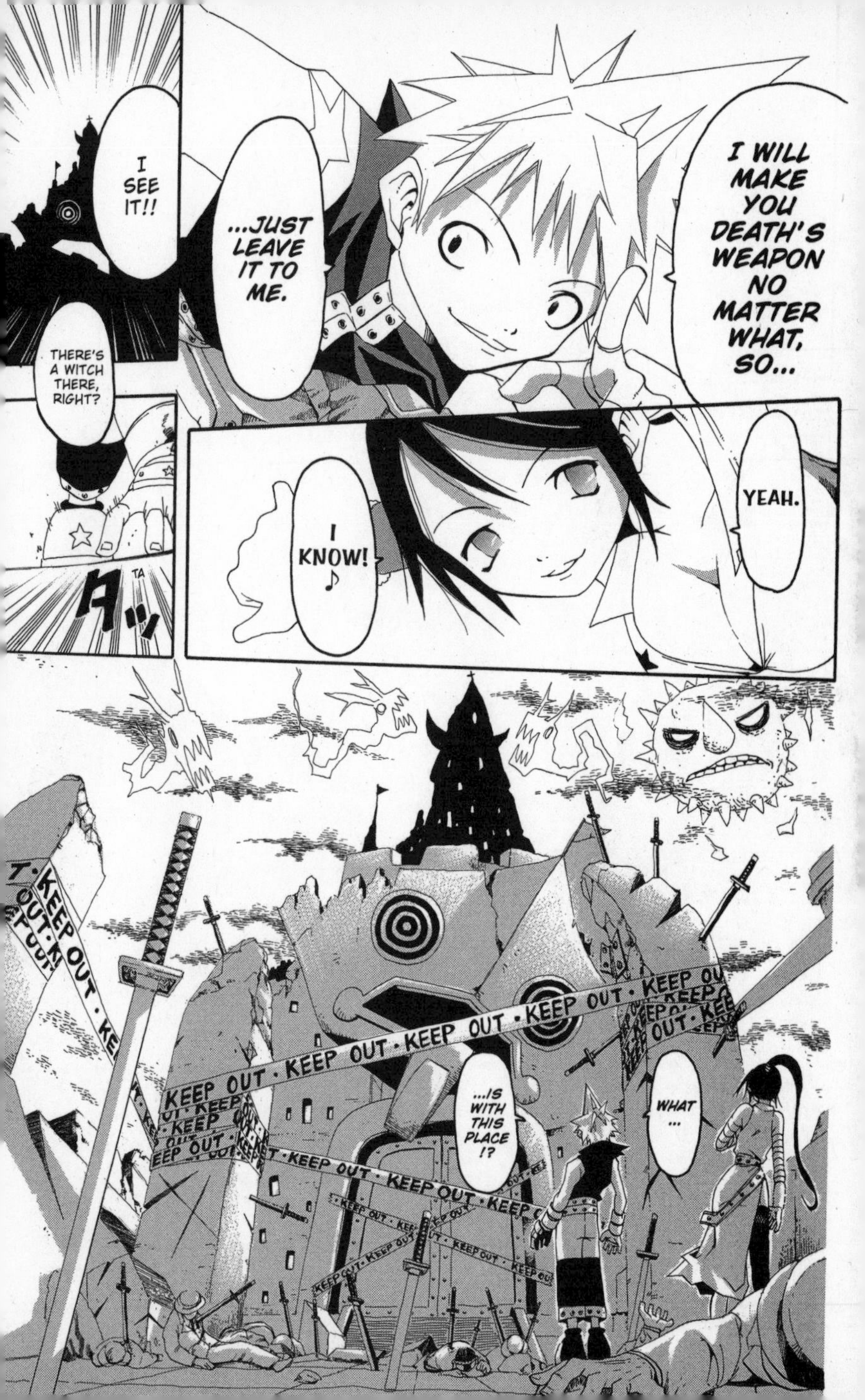
I WILL MAKE YOU DEATH'S WEAPON NO MATTER WHAT, SO...
...JUST LEAVE IT TO ME.
YEAH.
I KNOW! ♪
I SEE IT!!
THERE'S A WITCH THERE, RIGHT?
TA
KEEP OUT · KEEP OUT · KEEP OUT · KEEP OUT
WHAT ...
...IS WITH THIS PLACE !?

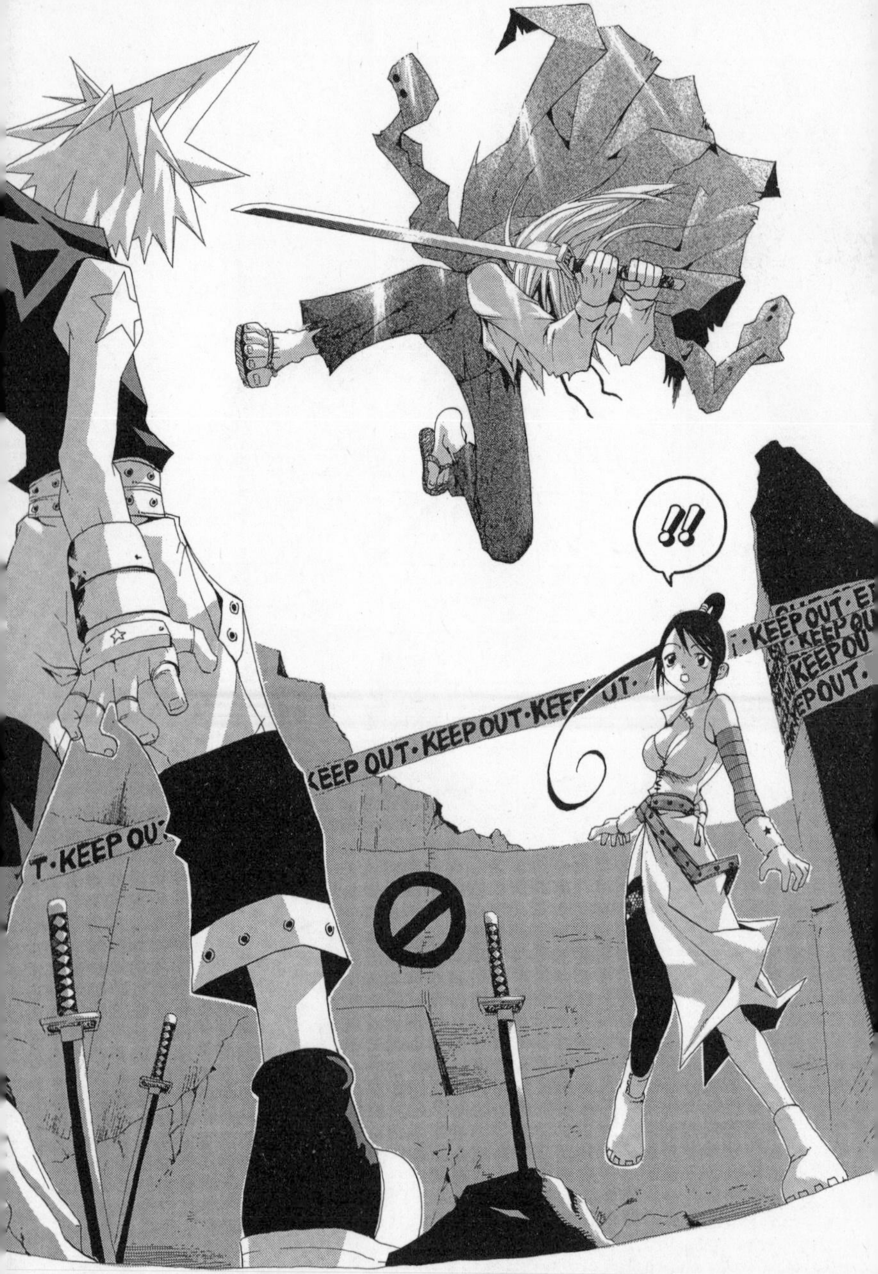
!!
KEEP OUT·KEEP OUT·
T·KEEP OUT

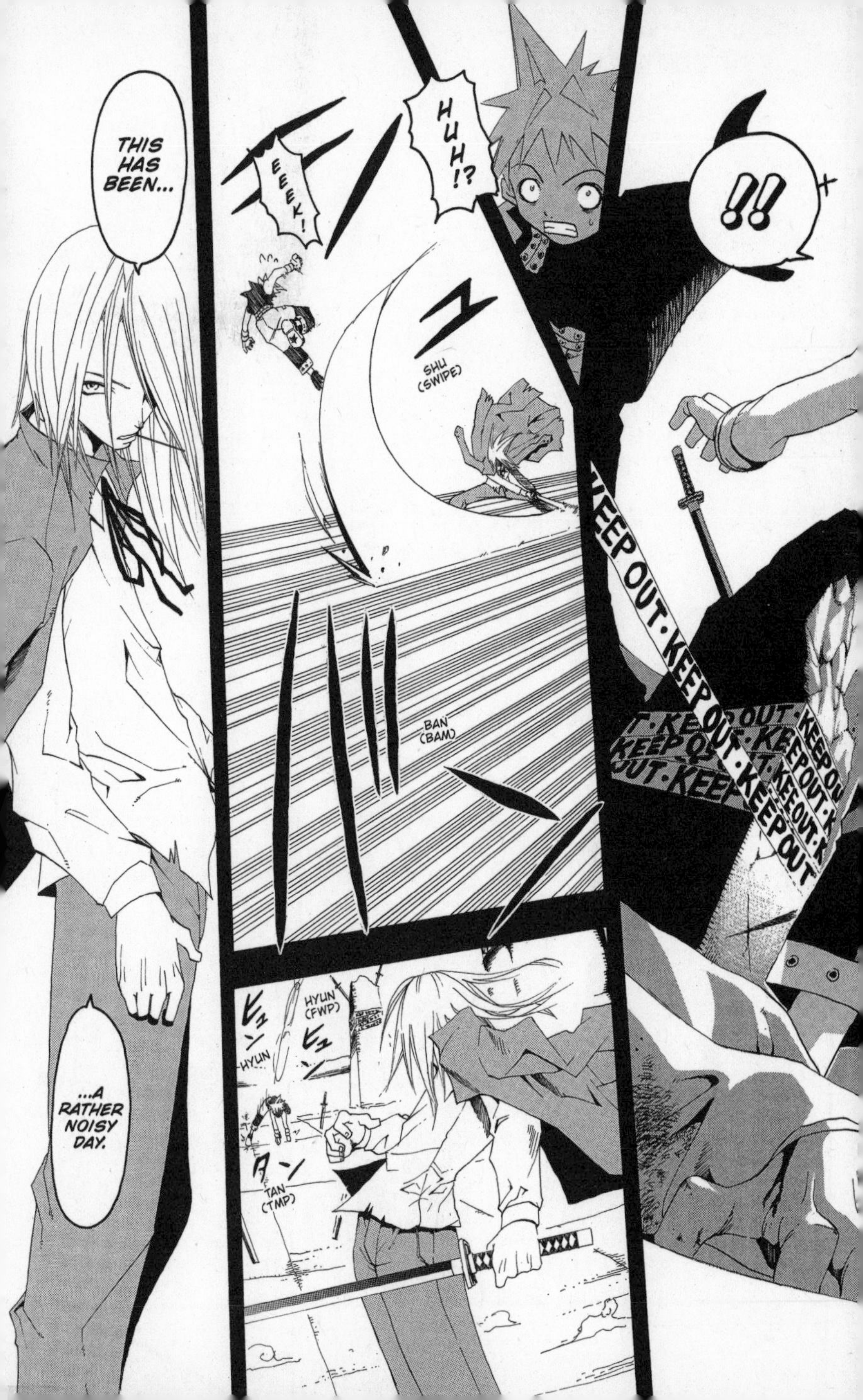

!!
KEEP OUT · KEEP OUT
HUH!?
EEEEK!
SHU (SWIPE)
BAN (BAM)
HYUN (FWP)
HYUN
TAN (TMP)
THIS HAS BEEN...
...A RATHER NOISY DAY.

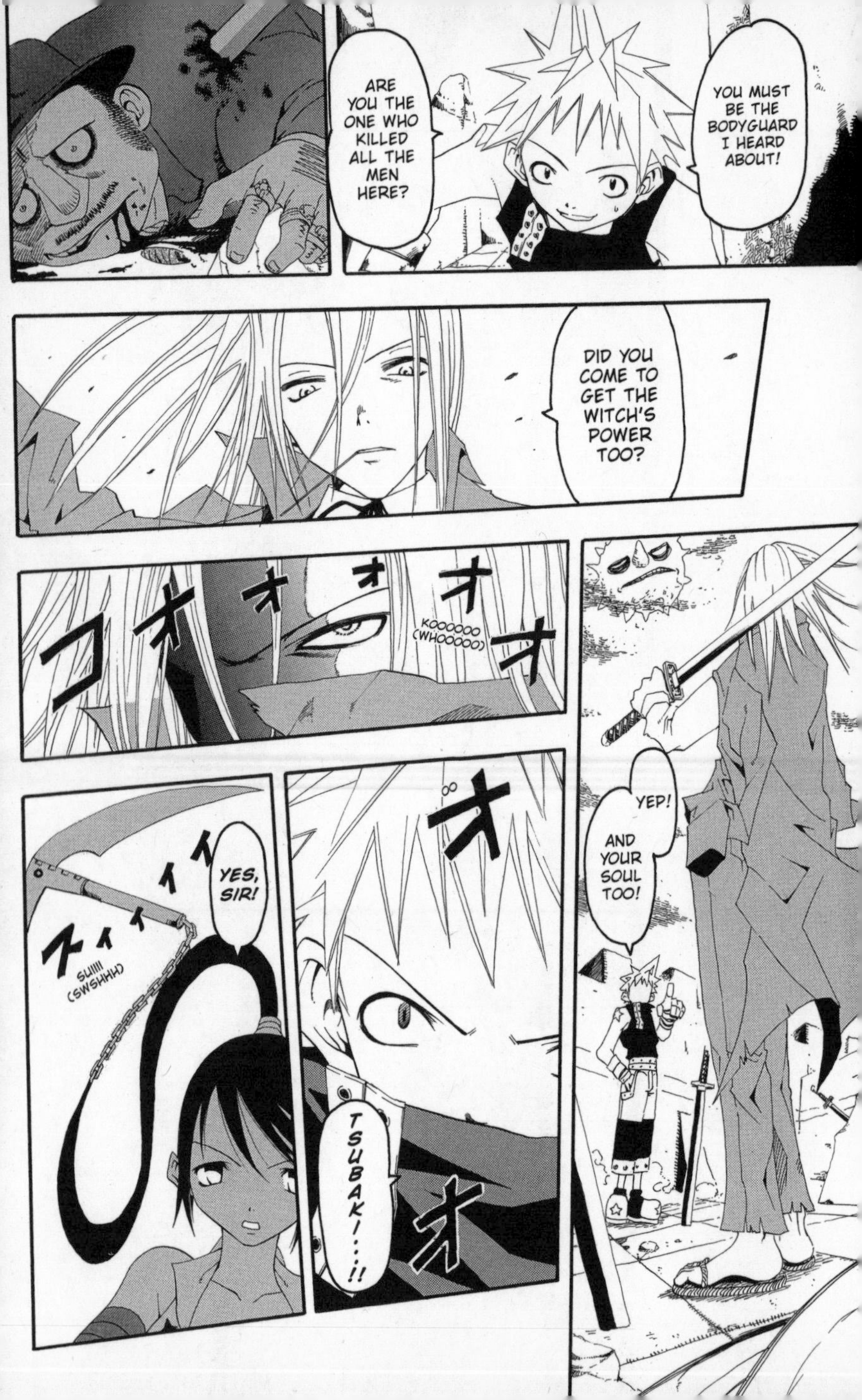
YOU MUST BE THE BODYGUARD I HEARD ABOUT!
ARE YOU THE ONE WHO KILLED ALL THE MEN HERE?
DID YOU COME TO GET THE WITCH'S POWER TOO?
YEP!
AND YOUR SOUL TOO!
コォォォォオ
KOOOOOO (WHOOOOO)
オ
TSUBAKI...!!
YES, SIR!
スィィィ
SUIIII (SWSHHH)

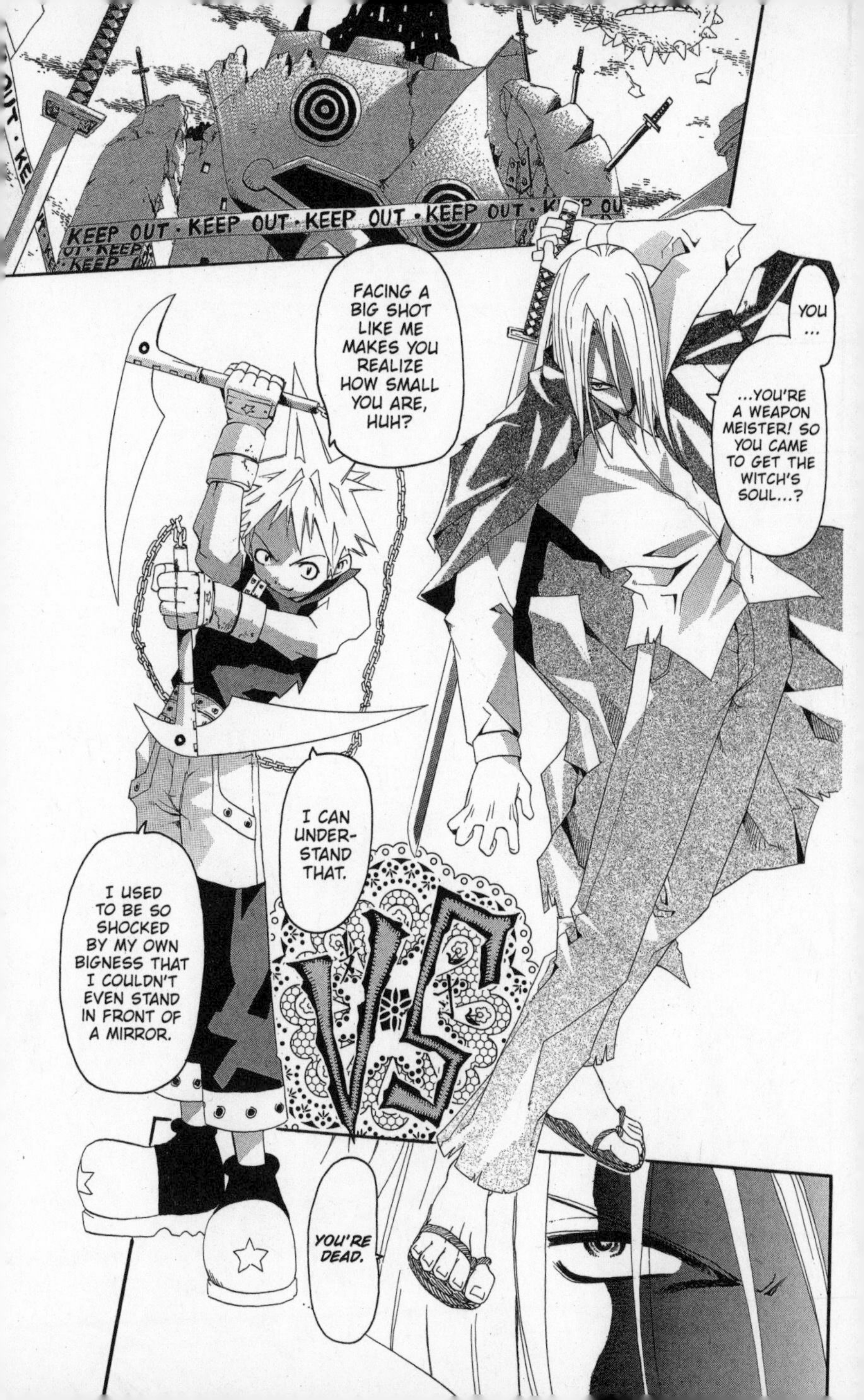
KEEP OUT · KEEP OUT · KEEP OUT · KEEP OU
YOU ...
...YOU'RE A WEAPON MEISTER! SO YOU CAME TO GET THE WITCH'S SOUL...?
FACING A BIG SHOT LIKE ME MAKES YOU REALIZE HOW SMALL YOU ARE, HUH?
I CAN UNDER-STAND THAT.
I USED TO BE SO SHOCKED BY MY OWN BIGNESS THAT I COULDN'T EVEN STAND IN FRONT OF A MIRROR.
VS
YOU'RE DEAD.

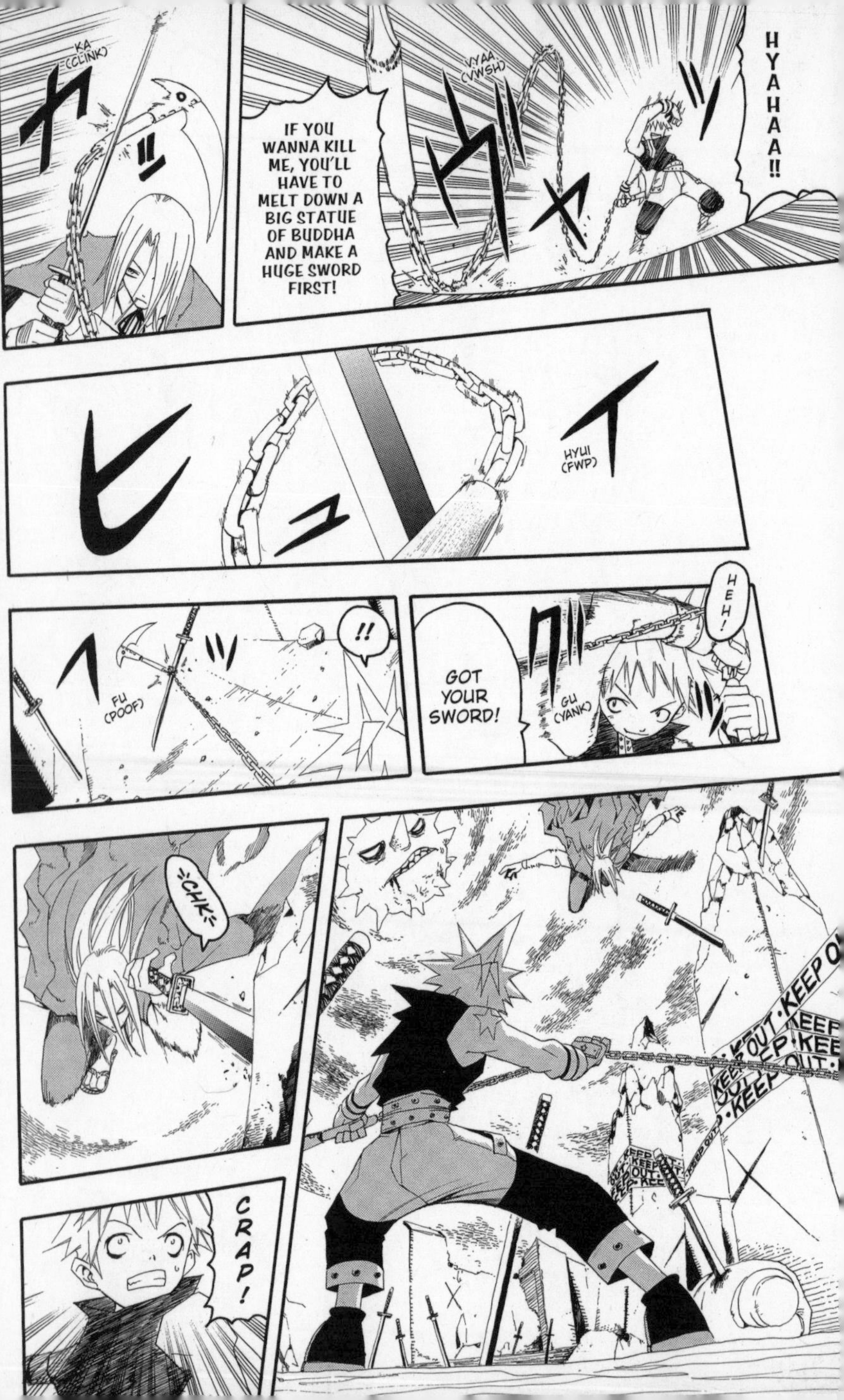
HYAHAA!!
VYAA (VWSH)
IF YOU WANNA KILL ME, YOU'LL HAVE TO MELT DOWN A BIG STATUE OF BUDDHA AND MAKE A HUGE SWORD FIRST!
KA (CLINK)
HYUI (FWP)
HEH!
GU (YANK)
GOT YOUR SWORD!
!!
FU (POOF)
CHK
CRAP!

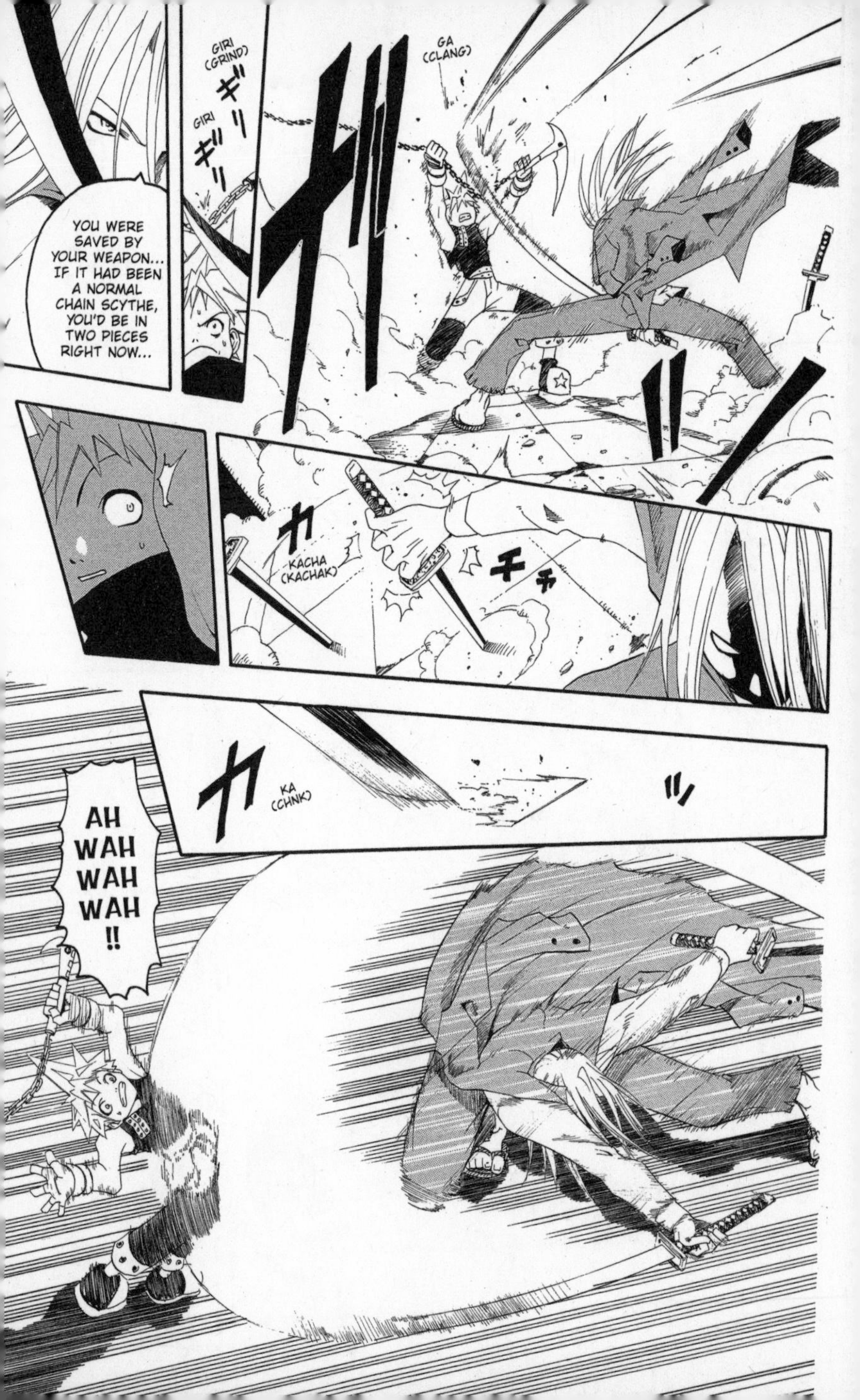
GA (CLANG)
GIRI (GRIND)
ギリ
GIRI
ギリ
YOU WERE SAVED BY YOUR WEAPON... IF IT HAD BEEN A NORMAL CHAIN SCYTHE, YOU'D BE IN TWO PIECES RIGHT NOW...
KACHA (KACHAK)
KA (CHNK)
AH WAH WAH WAH!!

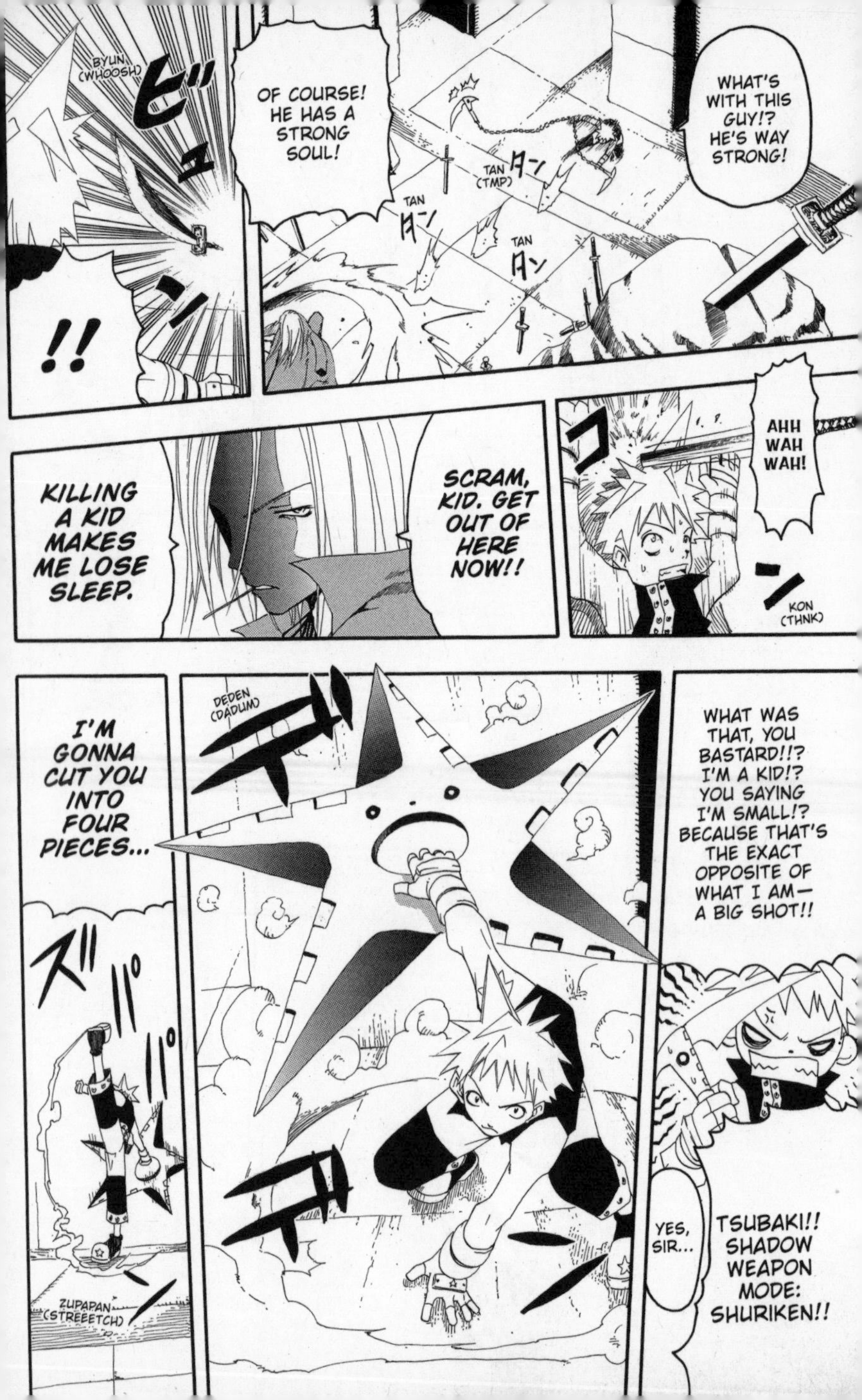
WHAT'S WITH THIS GUY!? HE'S WAY STRONG!
TAN (TMP)
TAN
TAN
OF COURSE! HE HAS A STRONG SOUL!
BYUN (WHOOSH)
!!
AHH WAH WAH!
KON (THNK)
SCRAM, KID. GET OUT OF HERE NOW!!
KILLING A KID MAKES ME LOSE SLEEP.
WHAT WAS THAT, YOU BASTARD!!? I'M A KID!? YOU SAYING I'M SMALL!? BECAUSE THAT'S THE EXACT OPPOSITE OF WHAT I AM— A BIG SHOT!!
TSUBAKI!! SHADOW WEAPON MODE: SHURIKEN!!
YES, SIR...
DEDEN (DADUM)
I'M GONNA CUT YOU INTO FOUR PIECES...
ZUPAPAN (STREEETCH)

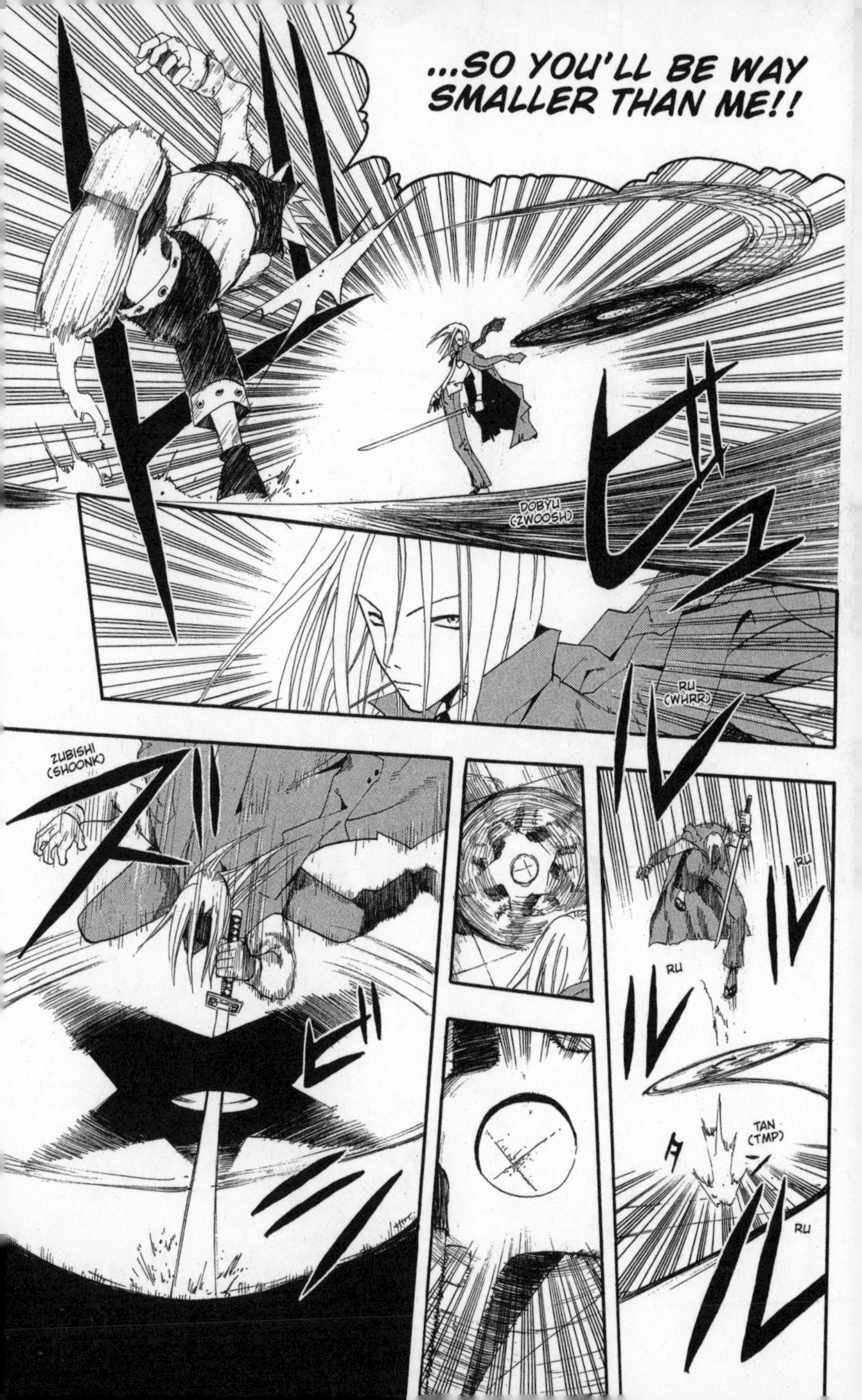
...SO YOU'LL BE WAY SMALLER THAN ME!!
DOBYU (ZWOOSH)
RU (WHRR)
RU
RU
TAN (TMP)
RU
ZUBISHI (SHOONK)

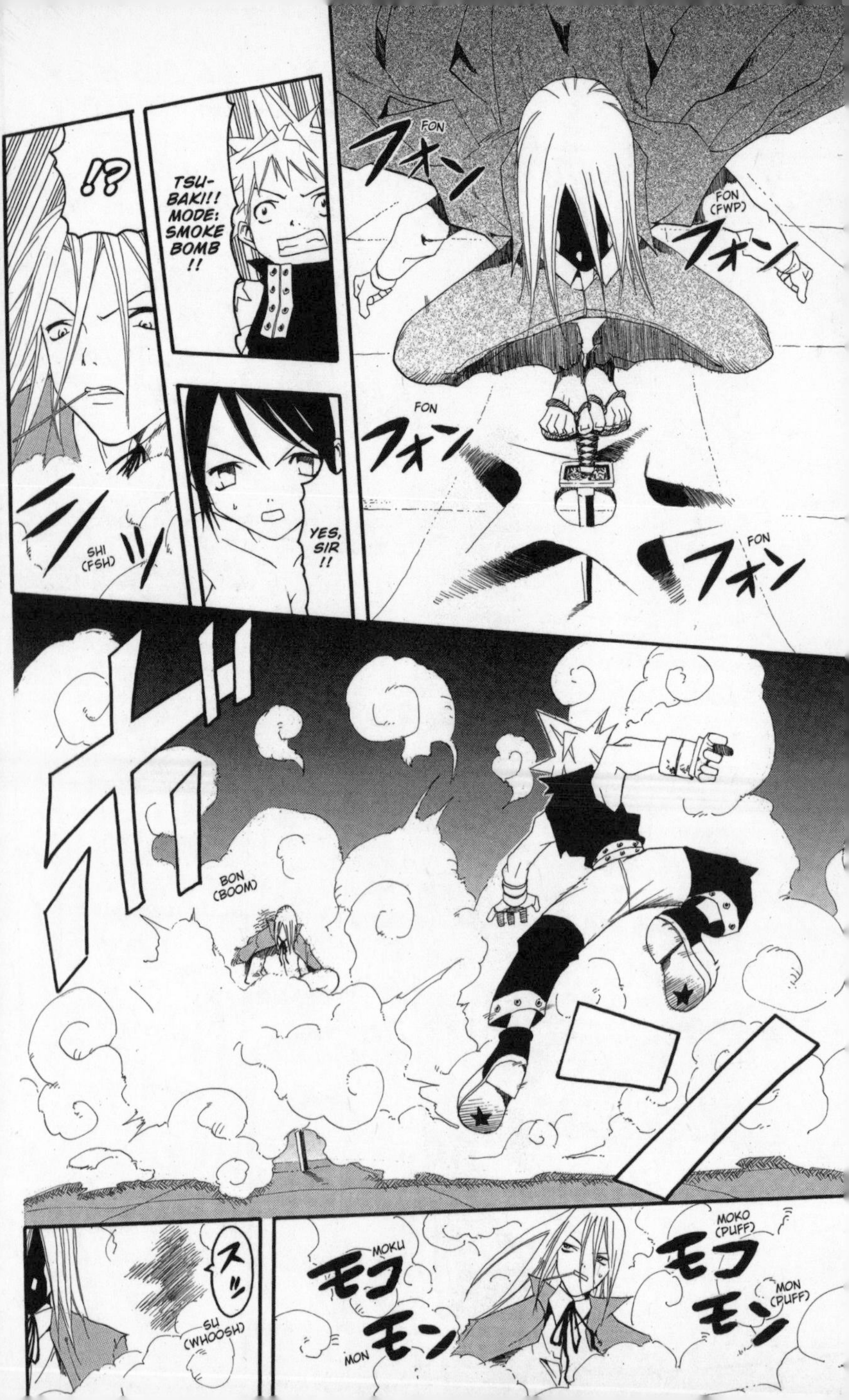
FON
フォン
FON (FWP)
フォン
FON
フォン
FON
フォン
TSU-BAKI!!! MODE: SMOKE BOMB!!
YES, SIR!!
!?
SHI (FSH)
シッ
BON (BOOM)
ボン
MOKO (PUFF)
モコ
MON (PUFF)
モン
MOKU
モコ
MON
モン
スッ
SU (WHOOSH)

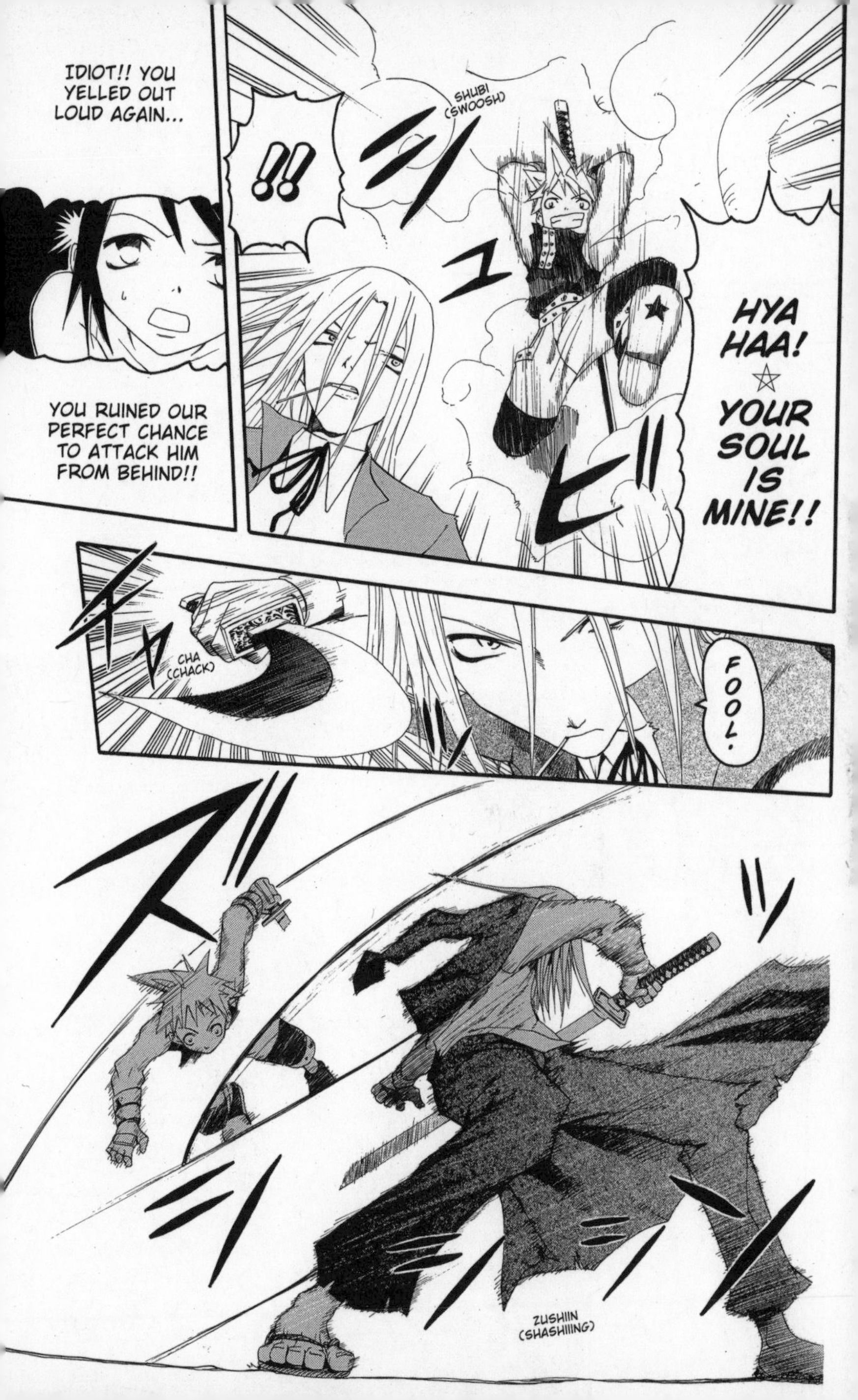
SHUBI (SWOOSH)
!!
HYA HAA! ☆ YOUR SOUL IS MINE!!
IDIOT!! YOU YELLED OUT LOUD AGAIN...
YOU RUINED OUR PERFECT CHANCE TO ATTACK HIM FROM BEHIND!!
FOOL.
CHA (CHACK)
ZUSHIIN (SHASHIIING)

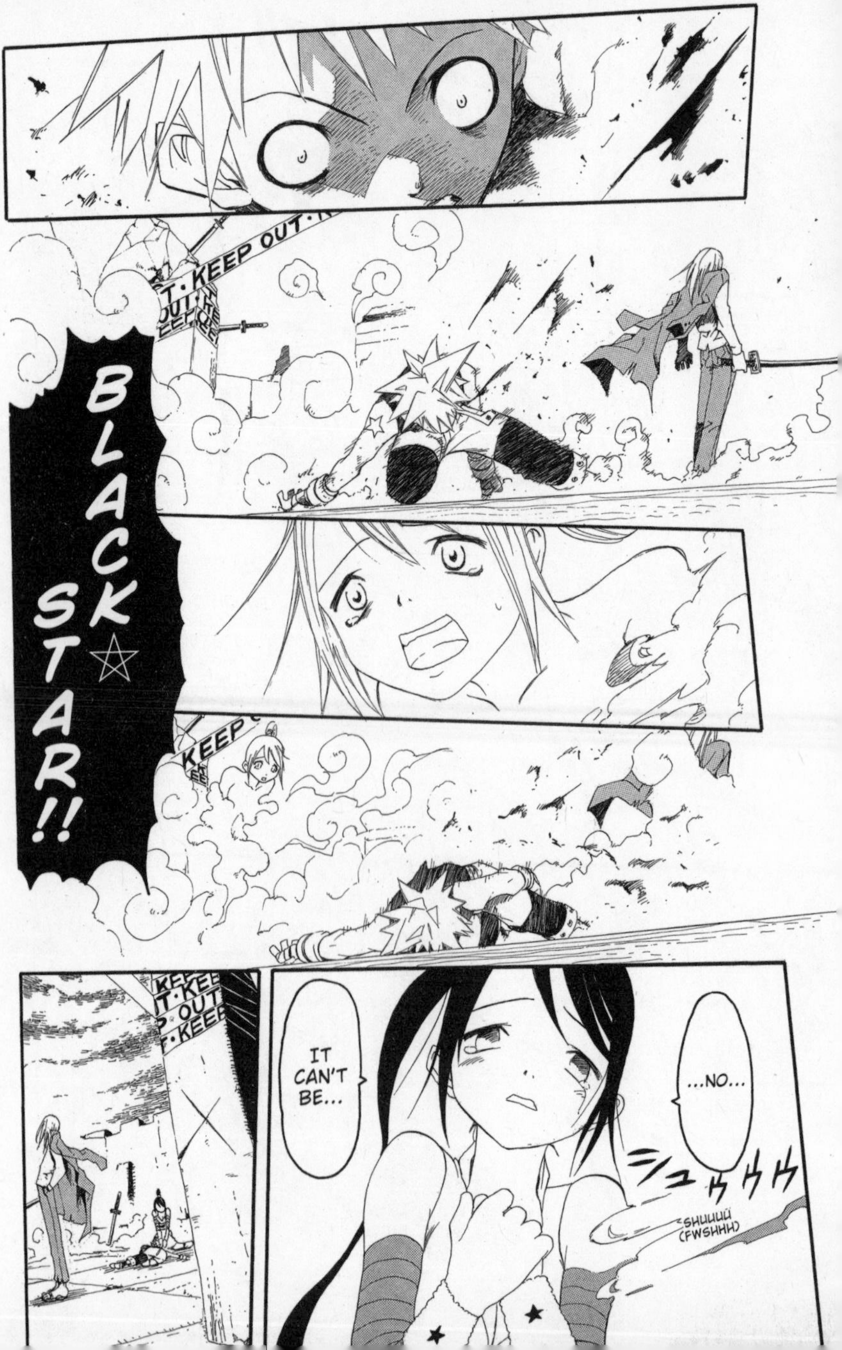
KEEP OUT
BLACK☆STAR!!
...NO...
IT CAN'T BE...
SHUUUU (FWSHHH)

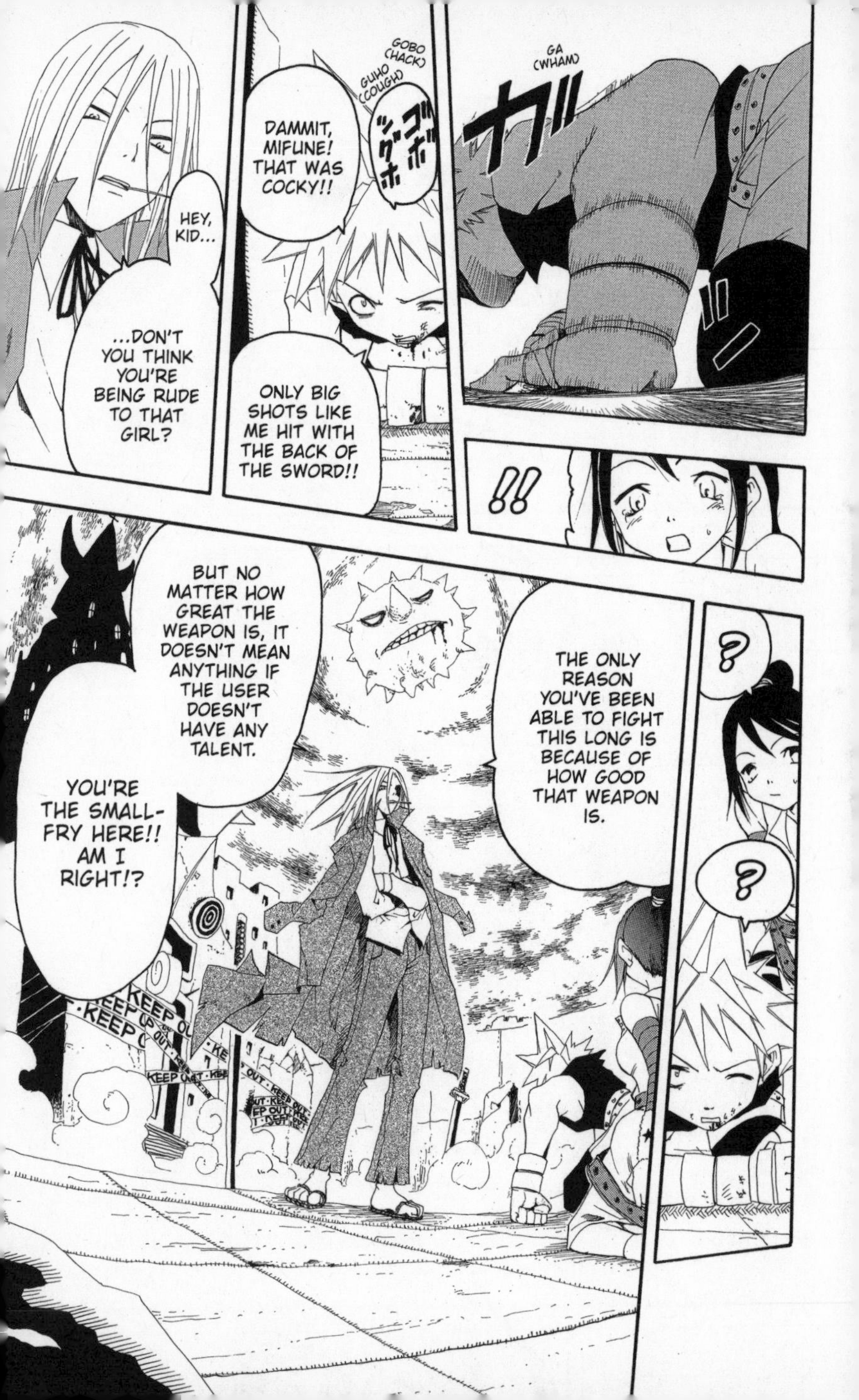
GA (WHAM)
GOBO (HACK)
GUHO (COUGH)
DAMMIT, MIFUNE! THAT WAS COCKY!!
ONLY BIG SHOTS LIKE ME HIT WITH THE BACK OF THE SWORD!!
HEY, KID...
...DON'T YOU THINK YOU'RE BEING RUDE TO THAT GIRL?
!!
?
?
THE ONLY REASON YOU'VE BEEN ABLE TO FIGHT THIS LONG IS BECAUSE OF HOW GOOD THAT WEAPON IS.
BUT NO MATTER HOW GREAT THE WEAPON IS, IT DOESN'T MEAN ANYTHING IF THE USER DOESN'T HAVE ANY TALENT.
YOU'RE THE SMALL-FRY HERE!! AM I RIGHT!?

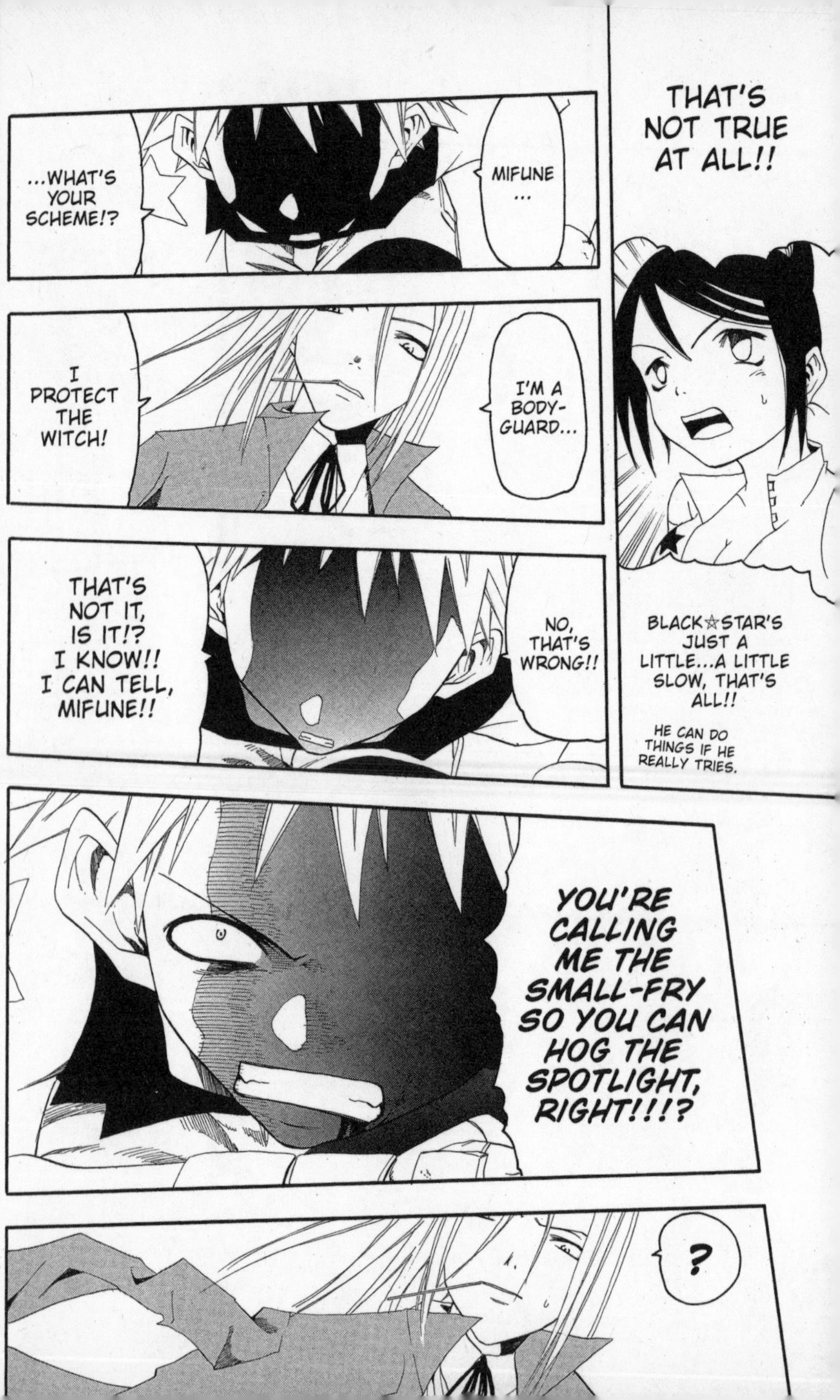
THAT'S NOT TRUE AT ALL!!
BLACK☆STAR'S JUST A LITTLE...A LITTLE SLOW, THAT'S ALL!!
HE CAN DO THINGS IF HE REALLY TRIES.
MIFUNE...
...WHAT'S YOUR SCHEME!?
I'M A BODY-GUARD...
I PROTECT THE WITCH!
NO, THAT'S WRONG!!
THAT'S NOT IT, IS IT!? I KNOW!! I CAN TELL, MIFUNE!!
YOU'RE CALLING ME THE SMALL-FRY SO YOU CAN HOG THE SPOTLIGHT, RIGHT!!!?
?

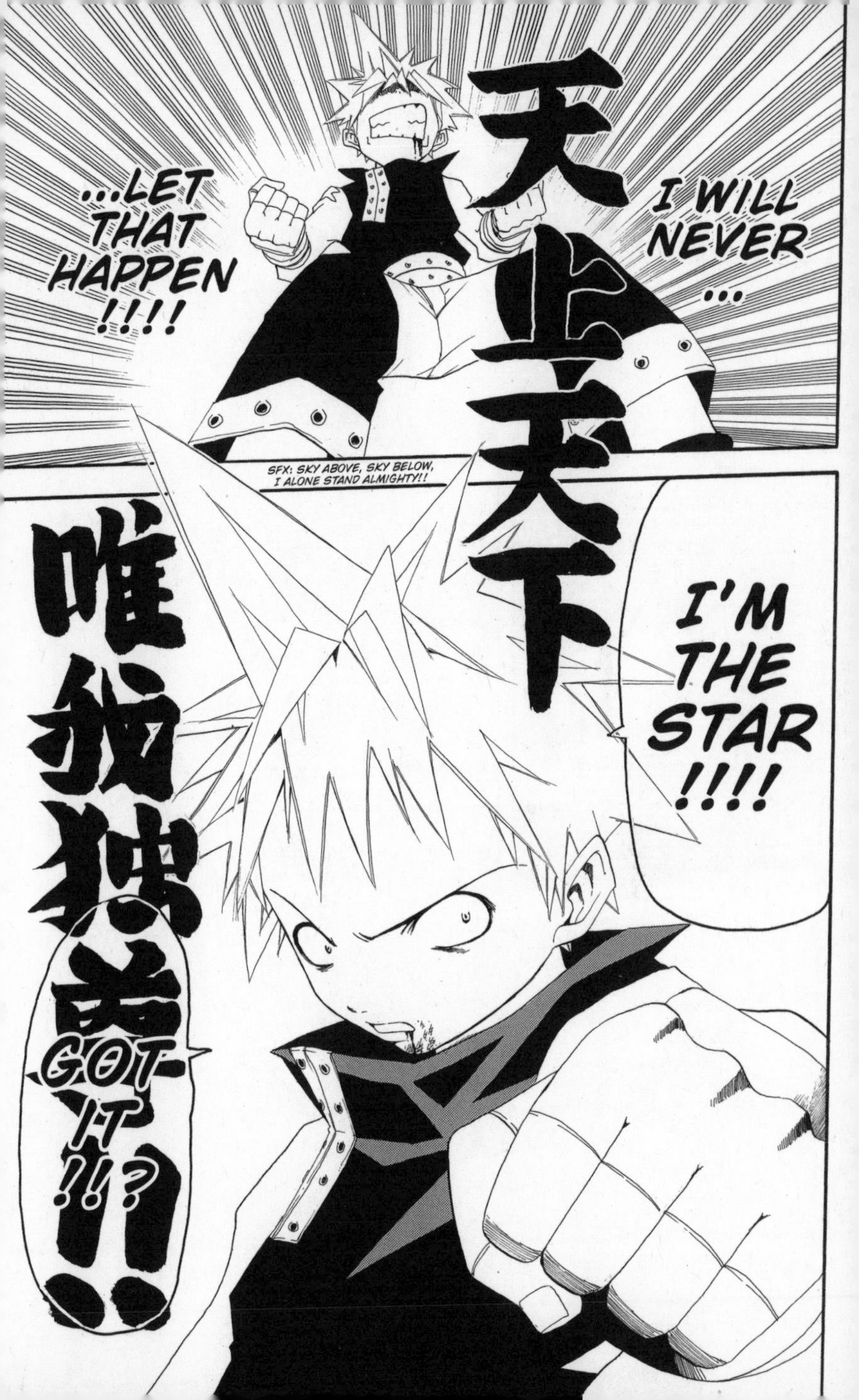
I WILL NEVER...
...LET THAT HAPPEN!!!!
天上天下唯我独尊
SFX: SKY ABOVE, SKY BELOW, I ALONE STAND ALMIGHTY!!
I'M THE STAR!!!!
GOT IT!!?

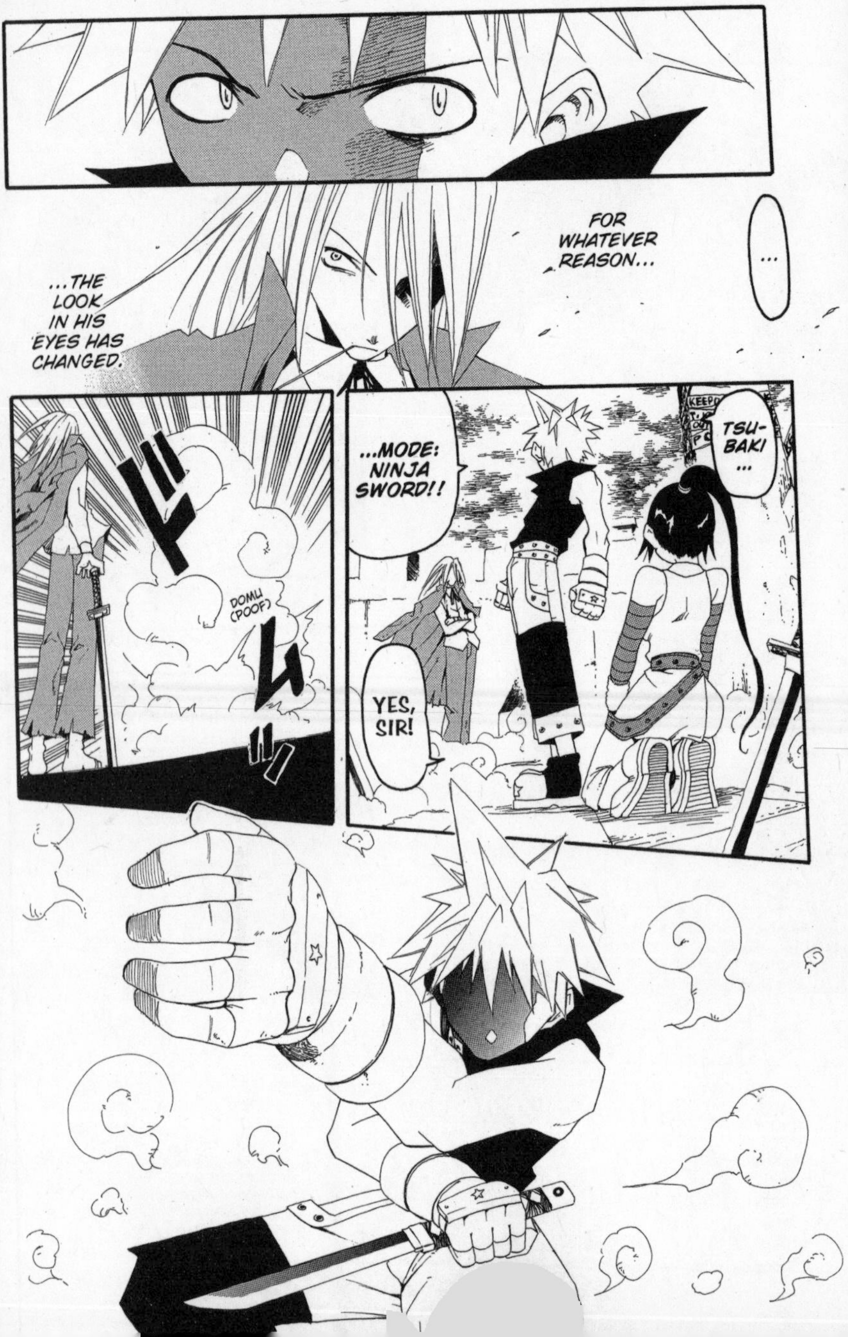

...
FOR WHATEVER REASON...
...THE LOOK IN HIS EYES HAS CHANGED.
TSU-BAKI...
...MODE: NINJA SWORD!!
YES, SIR!
DOMU (POOF)

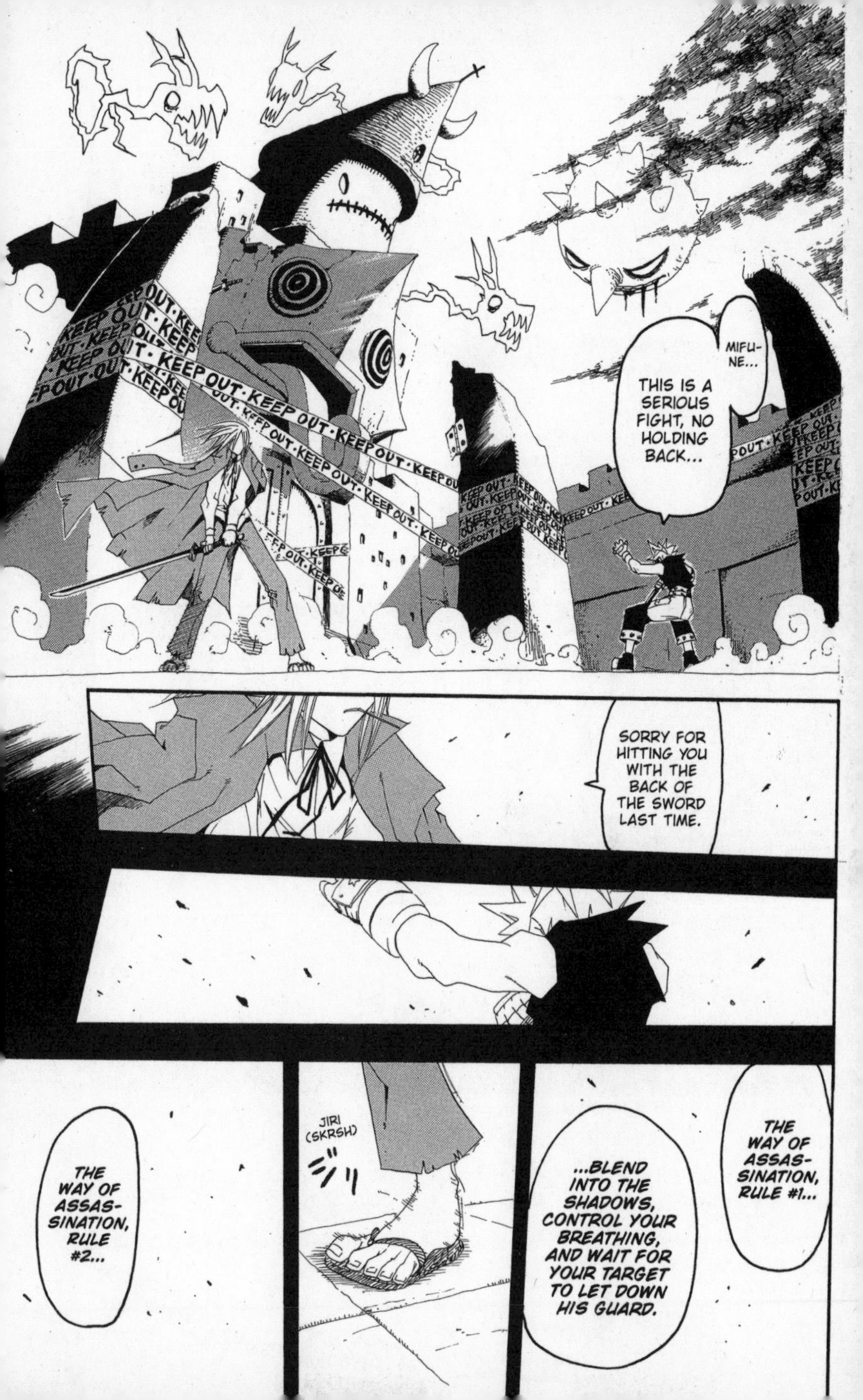

KEEP OUT · KEEP OUT
MIFU-NE...
THIS IS A SERIOUS FIGHT, NO HOLDING BACK...
SORRY FOR HITTING YOU WITH THE BACK OF THE SWORD LAST TIME.
THE WAY OF ASSAS-SINATION, RULE #1...
...BLEND INTO THE SHADOWS, CONTROL YOUR BREATHING, AND WAIT FOR YOUR TARGET TO LET DOWN HIS GUARD.
JIRI (SKRSH)
THE WAY OF ASSAS-SINATION, RULE #2...

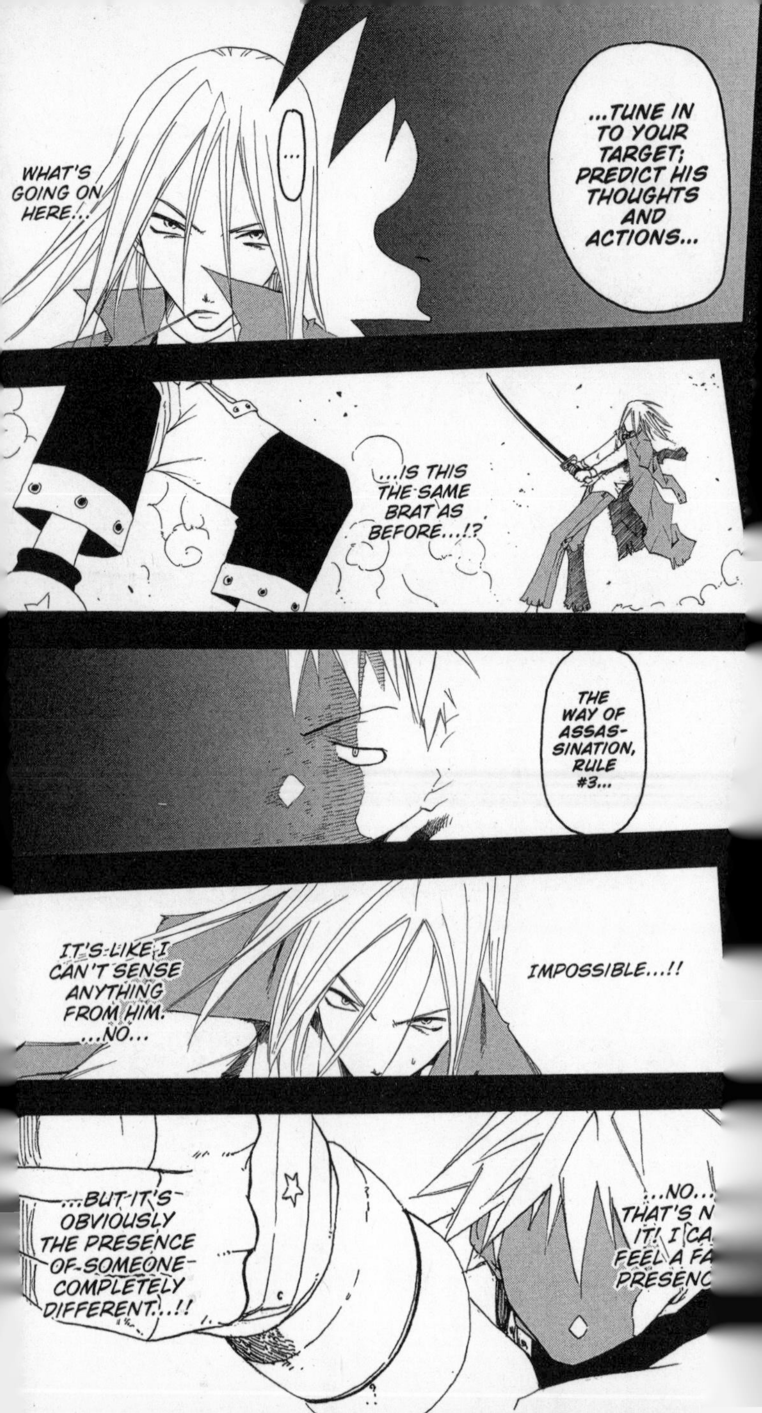
...TUNE IN TO YOUR TARGET; PREDICT HIS THOUGHTS AND ACTIONS...
...
WHAT'S GOING ON HERE...
...IS THIS THE SAME BRAT AS BEFORE...!?
THE WAY OF ASSAS-SINATION, RULE #3...
IMPOSSIBLE...!!
IT'S LIKE I CAN'T SENSE ANYTHING FROM HIM. ...NO...
...NO... THAT'S N IT! I CA FEEL A FA PRESENC
...BUT IT'S OBVIOUSLY THE PRESENCE OF SOMEONE COMPLETELY DIFFERENT...!!

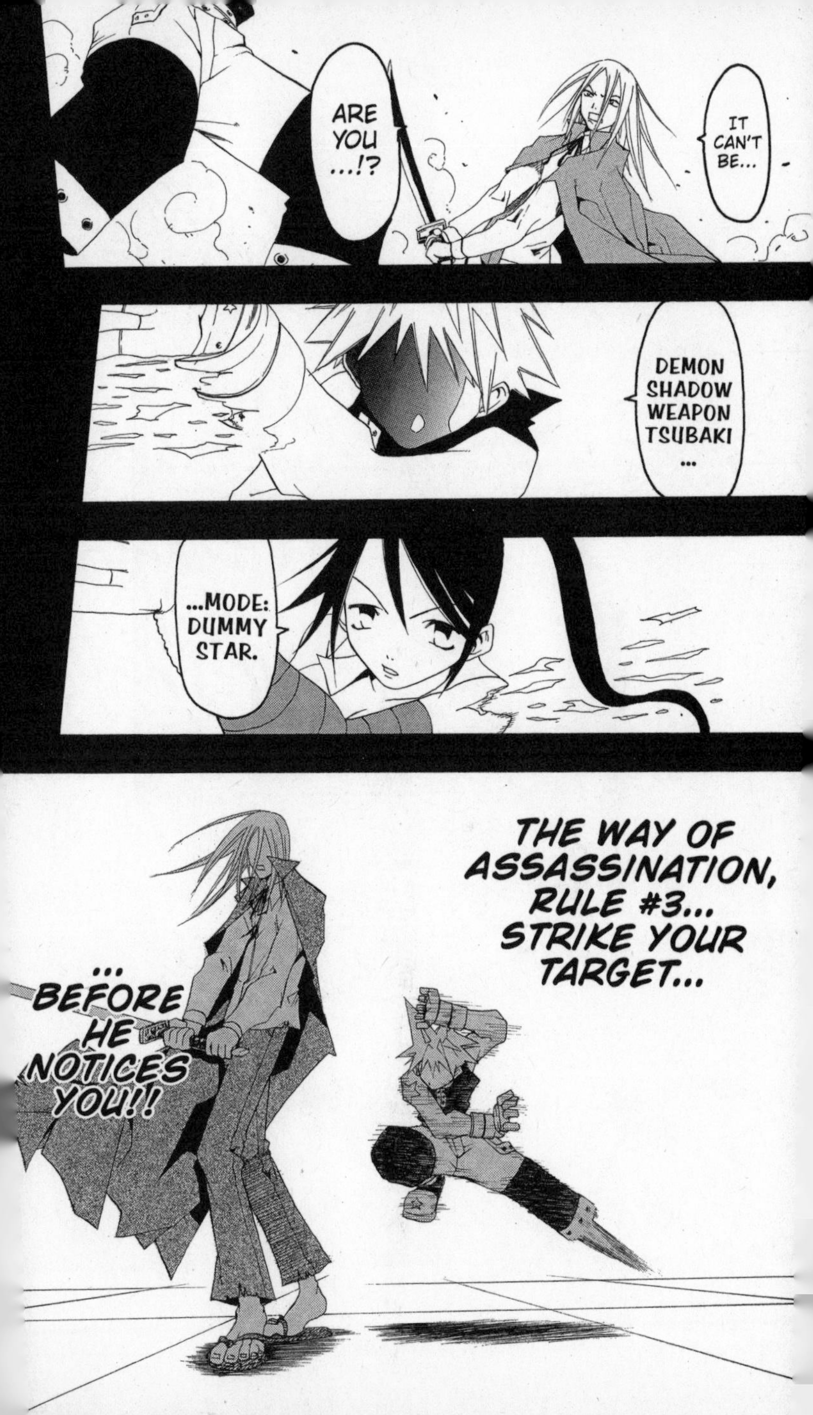
IT CAN'T BE...
ARE YOU ...!?
DEMON SHADOW WEAPON TSUBAKI ...
...MODE: DUMMY STAR.
THE WAY OF ASSASSINATION, RULE #3... STRIKE YOUR TARGET...
... BEFORE HE NOTICES YOU!!

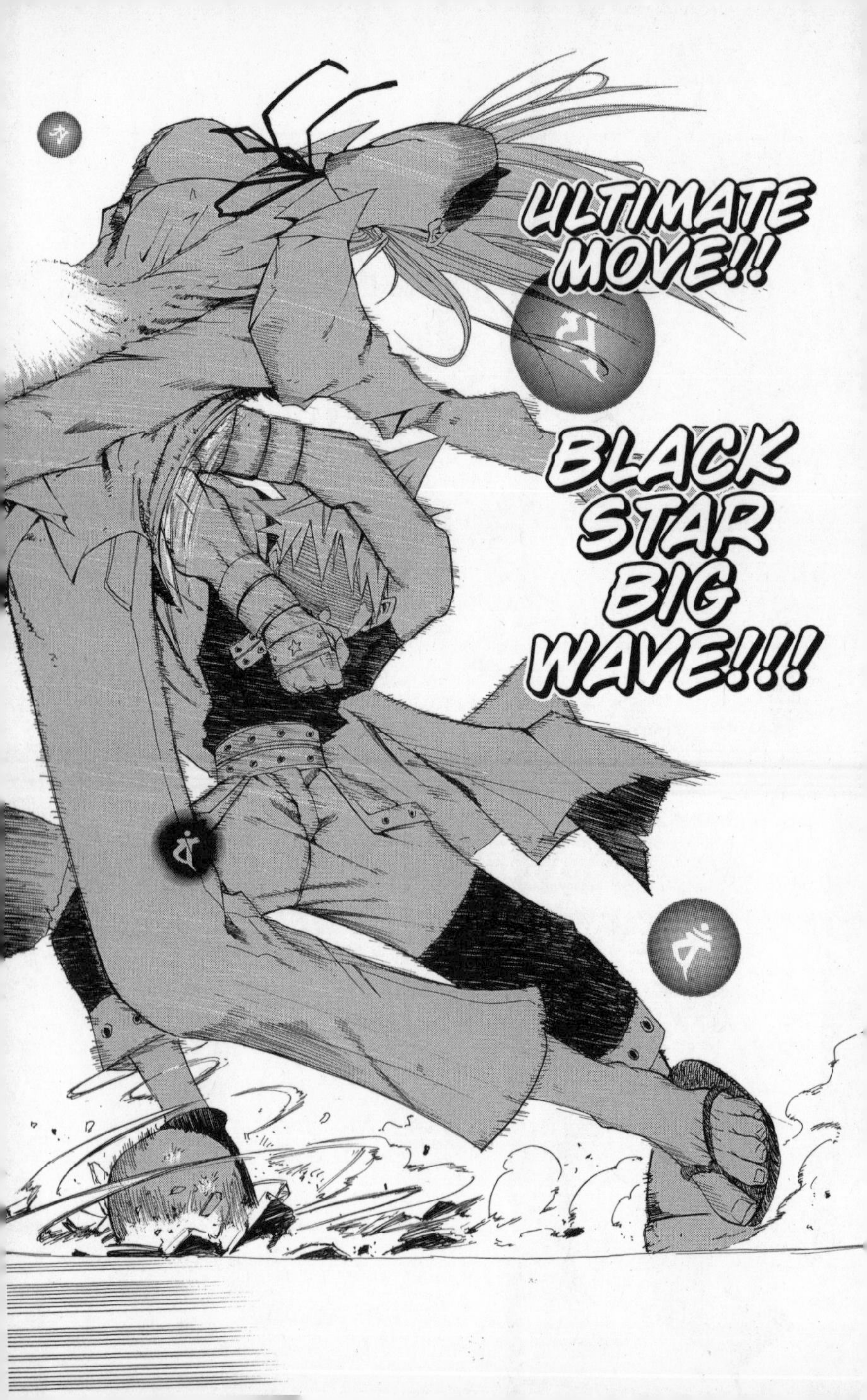
ULTIMATE MOVE!!
BLACK STAR BIG WAVE!!!

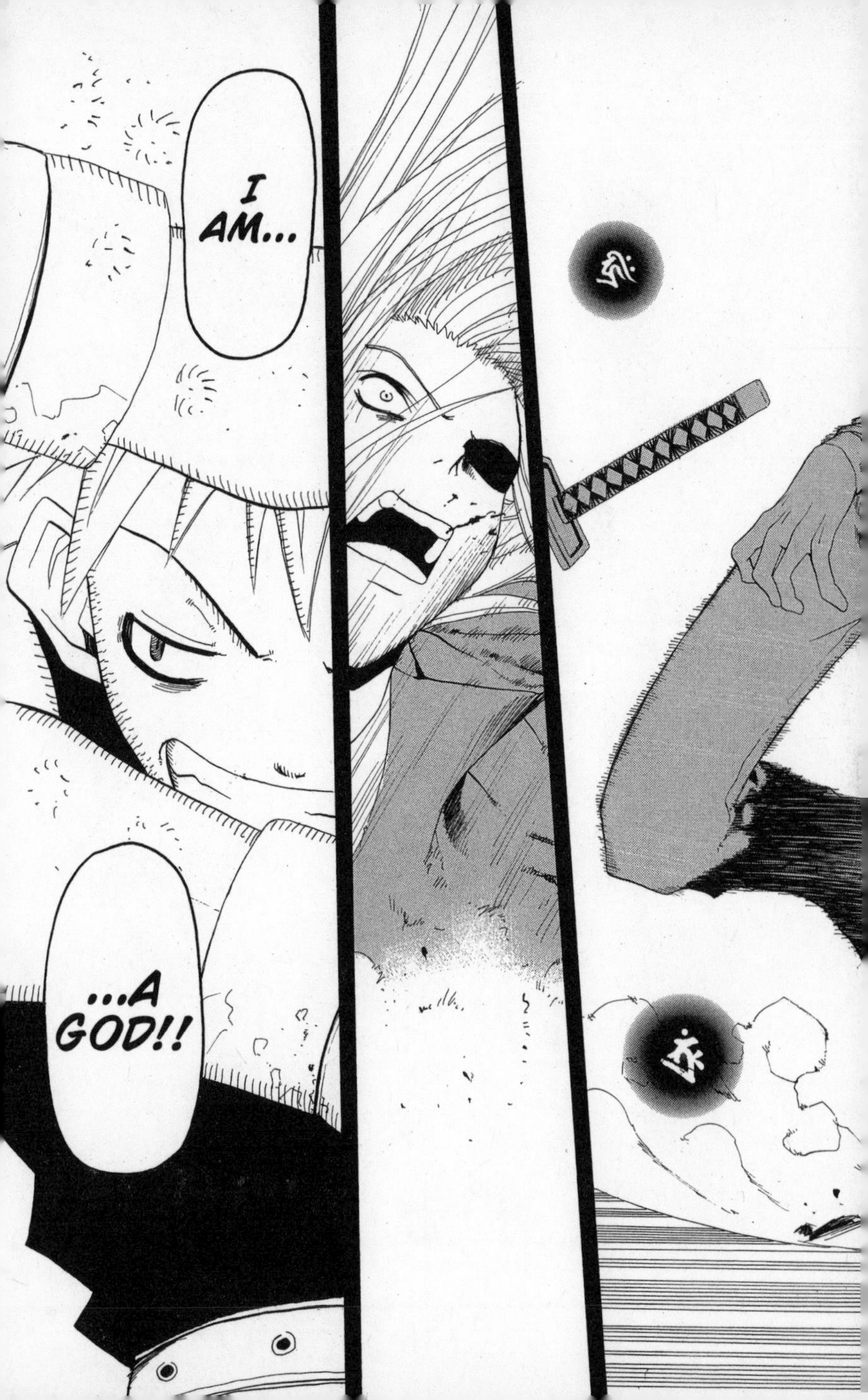
I AM...
...A GOD!!

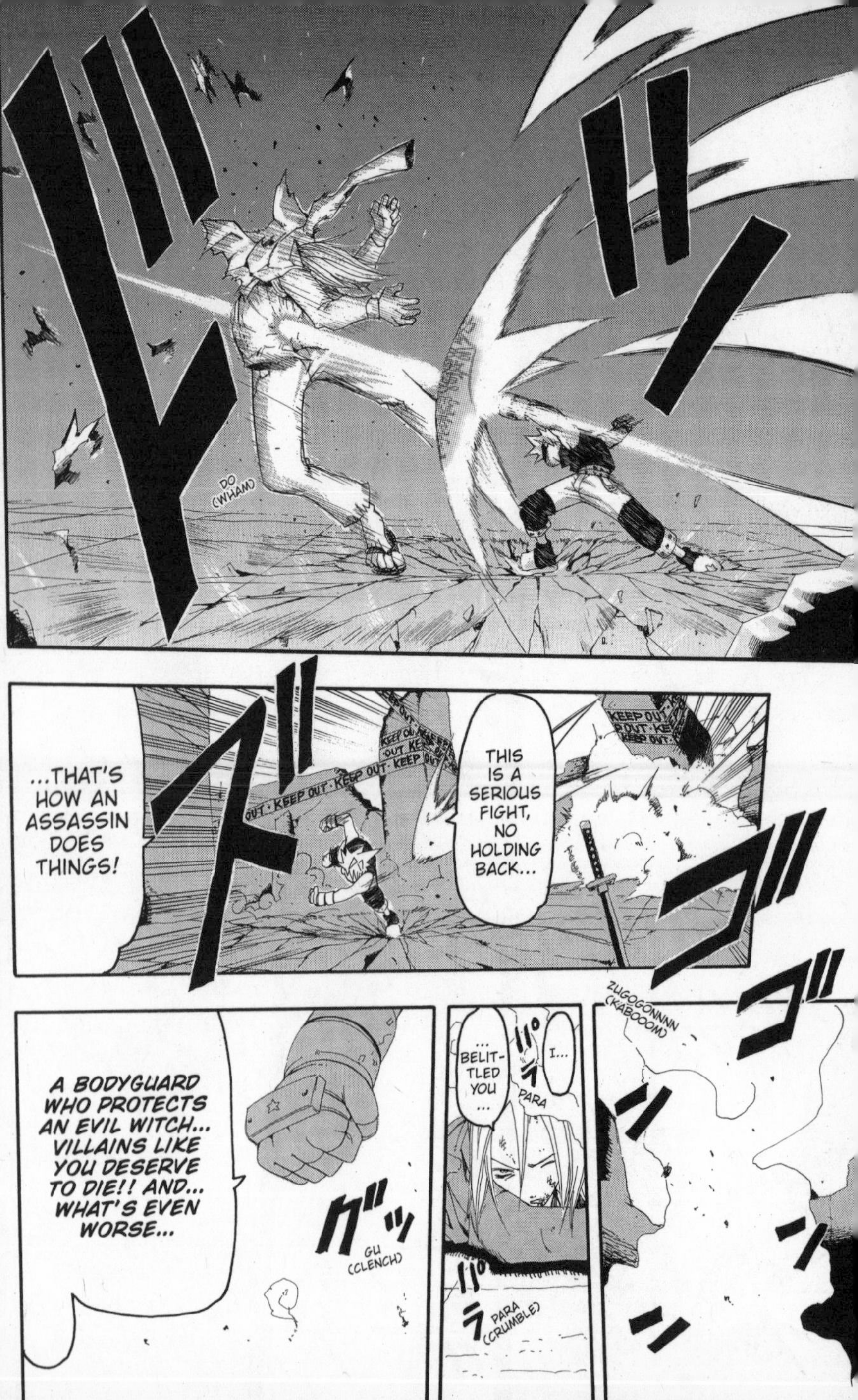
DO (WHAM)
THIS IS A SERIOUS FIGHT, NO HOLDING BACK...
...THAT'S HOW AN ASSASSIN DOES THINGS!
ZUGOGONNNN (KABOOOM)
I...
...BELITTLED YOU...
PARA
PARA (CRUMBLE)
A BODYGUARD WHO PROTECTS AN EVIL WITCH... VILLAINS LIKE YOU DESERVE TO DIE!! AND... WHAT'S EVEN WORSE...
GU (CLENCH)

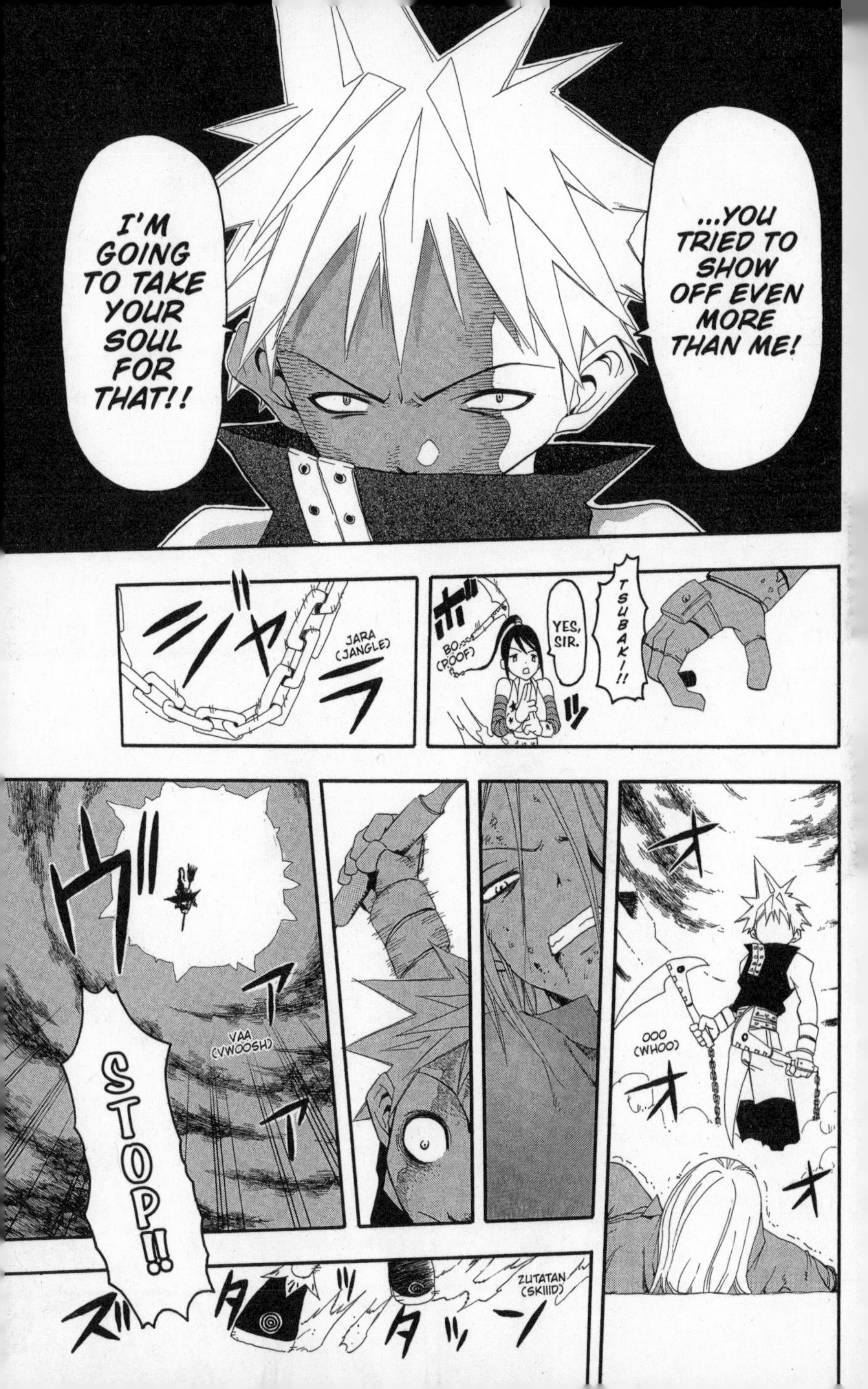
...YOU TRIED TO SHOW OFF EVEN MORE THAN ME!
I'M GOING TO TAKE YOUR SOUL FOR THAT!!
TSUBAKI!!
YES, SIR.
BO (POOF)
JARA (JANGLE)
OOO (WHOO)
VAA (VWOOSH)
STOP!!
ZUTATAN (SKIIID)

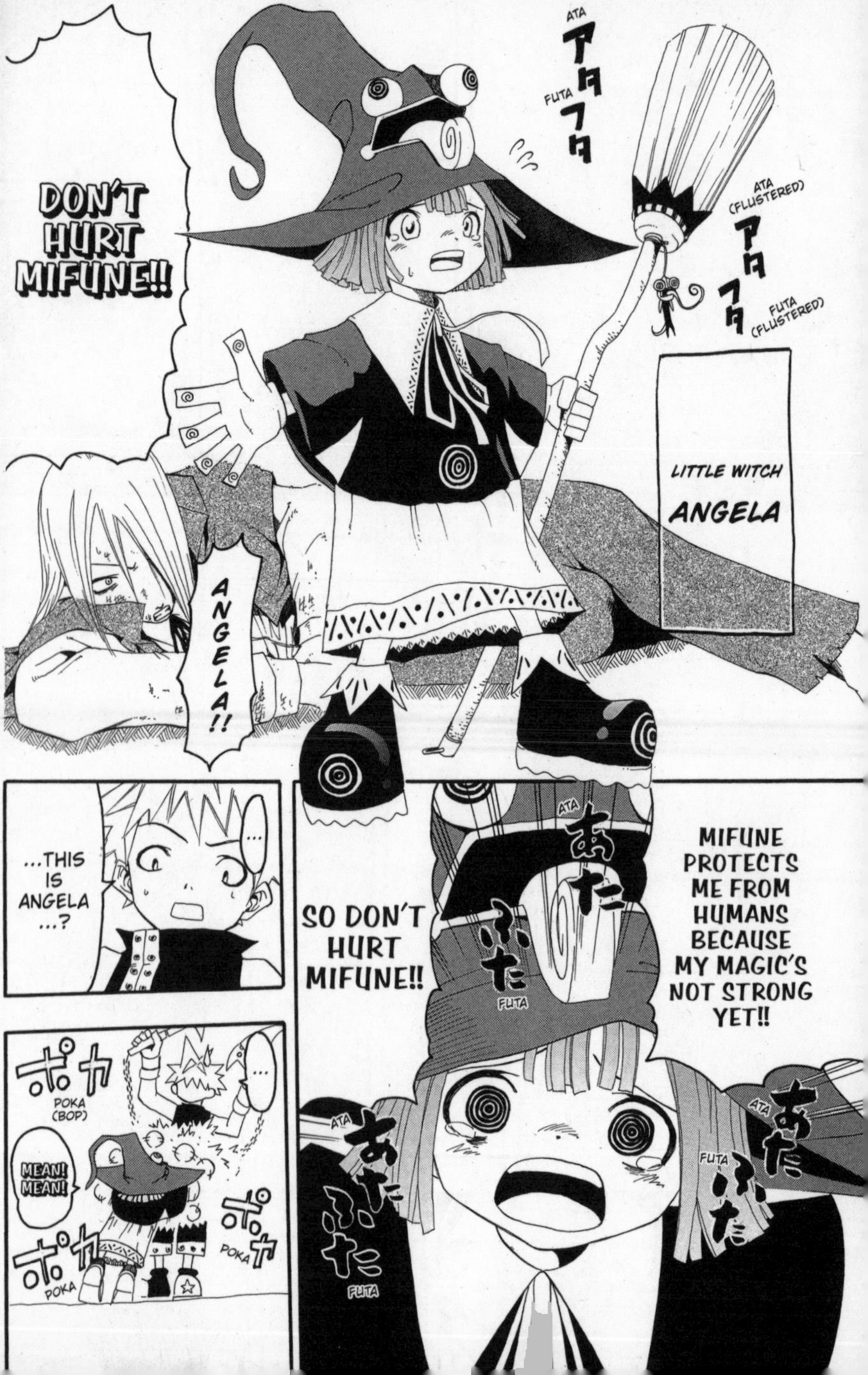
ATA
アタ
FUTA
フタ
ATA (FLUSTERED)
アタフタ
FUTA (FLUSTERED)
LITTLE WITCH
ANGELA
DON'T HURT MIFUNE!!
ANGELA!!
MIFUNE PROTECTS ME FROM HUMANS BECAUSE MY MAGIC'S NOT STRONG YET!!
ATA
あた
ふた
FUTA
SO DON'T HURT MIFUNE!!
ATA
あた
ふた
FUTA
ATA
あた
ふた
FUTA
...
...THIS IS ANGELA ...?
...
ポカ
POKA (BOP)
MEAN! MEAN!
ポカ
POKA
ポカ
POKA

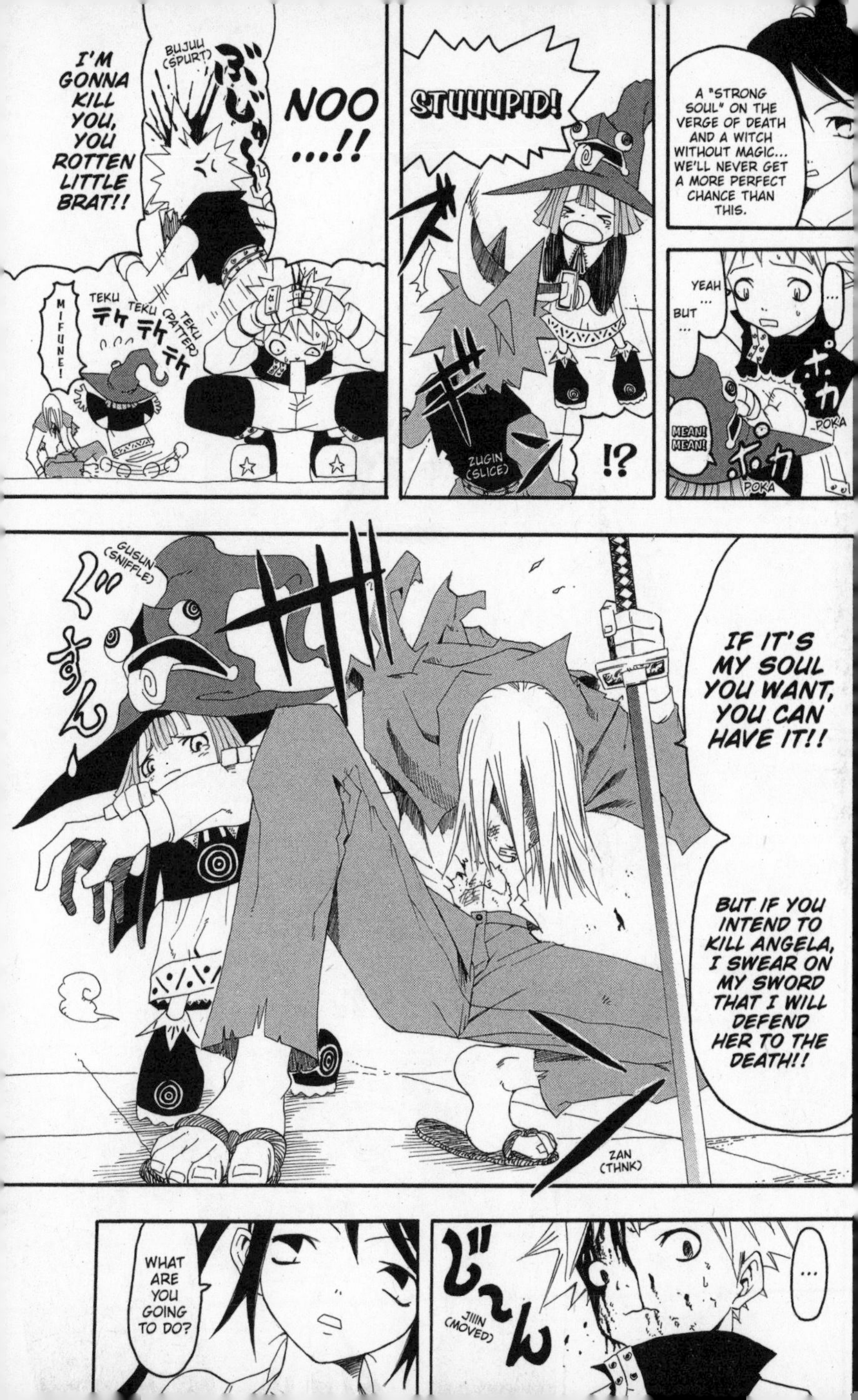
A "STRONG SOUL" ON THE VERGE OF DEATH AND A WITCH WITHOUT MAGIC... WE'LL NEVER GET A MORE PERFECT CHANCE THAN THIS.
YEAH ... BUT ...
...
MEAN! MEAN!
POKA
POKA
STUUUPID!
ZUGIN (SLICE)
!?
I'M GONNA KILL YOU, YOU ROTTEN LITTLE BRAT!!
BUJUU (SPURT)
NOO ...!!
TEKU TEKU TEKU (PATTER)
テケテケテケ
MIFUNE!
IF IT'S MY SOUL YOU WANT, YOU CAN HAVE IT!!
BUT IF YOU INTEND TO KILL ANGELA, I SWEAR ON MY SWORD THAT I WILL DEFEND HER TO THE DEATH!!
ZAN (THNK)
GUSUN (SNIFFLE)
...
JIIIN (MOVED)
WHAT ARE YOU GOING TO DO?

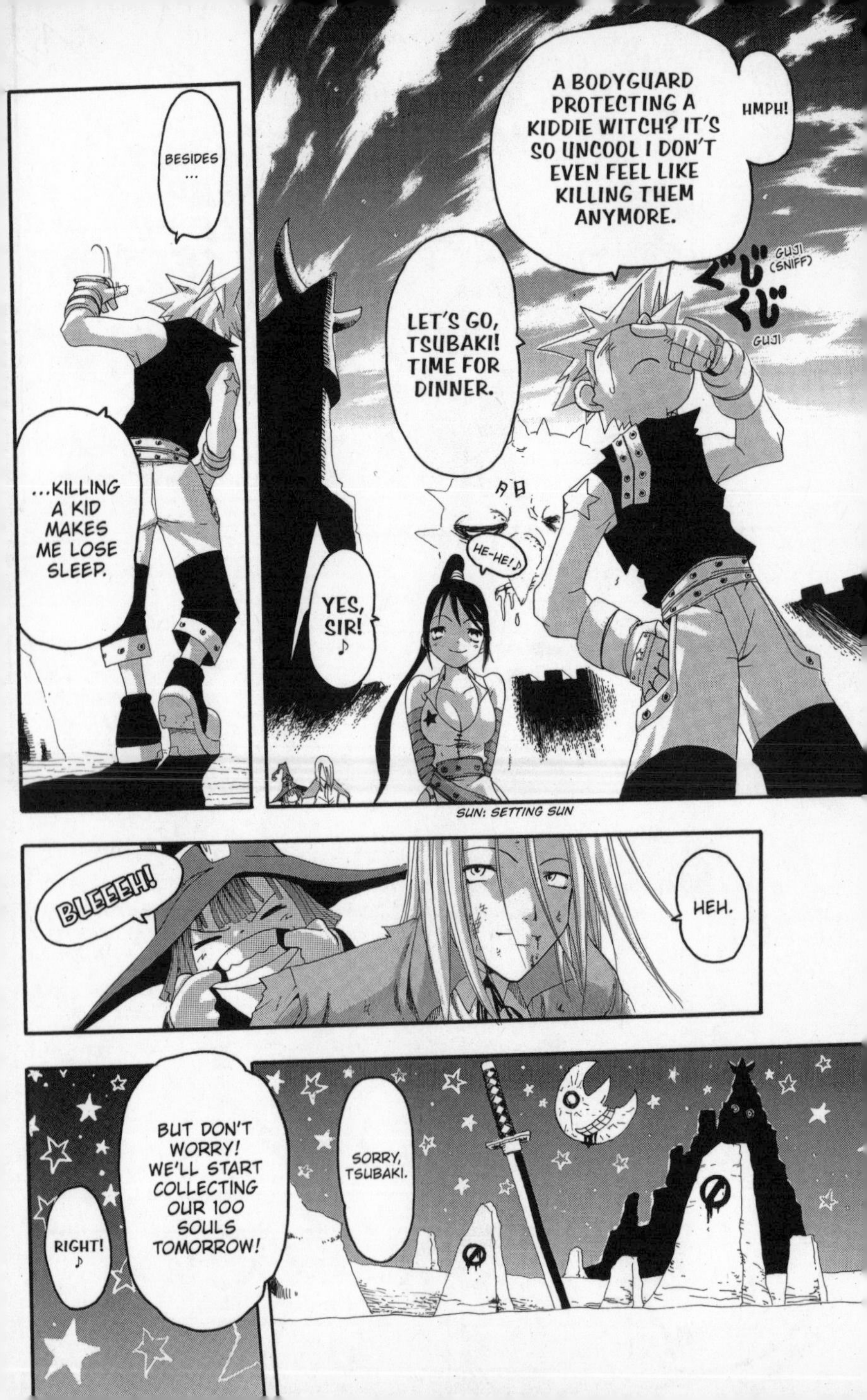
HMPH!
A BODYGUARD PROTECTING A KIDDIE WITCH? IT'S SO UNCOOL I DON'T EVEN FEEL LIKE KILLING THEM ANYMORE.
ぐじ GUJI (SNIFF)
ぐじ GUJI
LET'S GO, TSUBAKI! TIME FOR DINNER.
夕日
HE-HE!♪
YES, SIR! ♪
SUN: SETTING SUN
BESIDES...
...KILLING A KID MAKES ME LOSE SLEEP.
HEH.
BLEEEH!
SORRY, TSUBAKI.
BUT DON'T WORRY! WE'LL START COLLECTING OUR 100 SOULS TOMORROW!
RIGHT! ♪

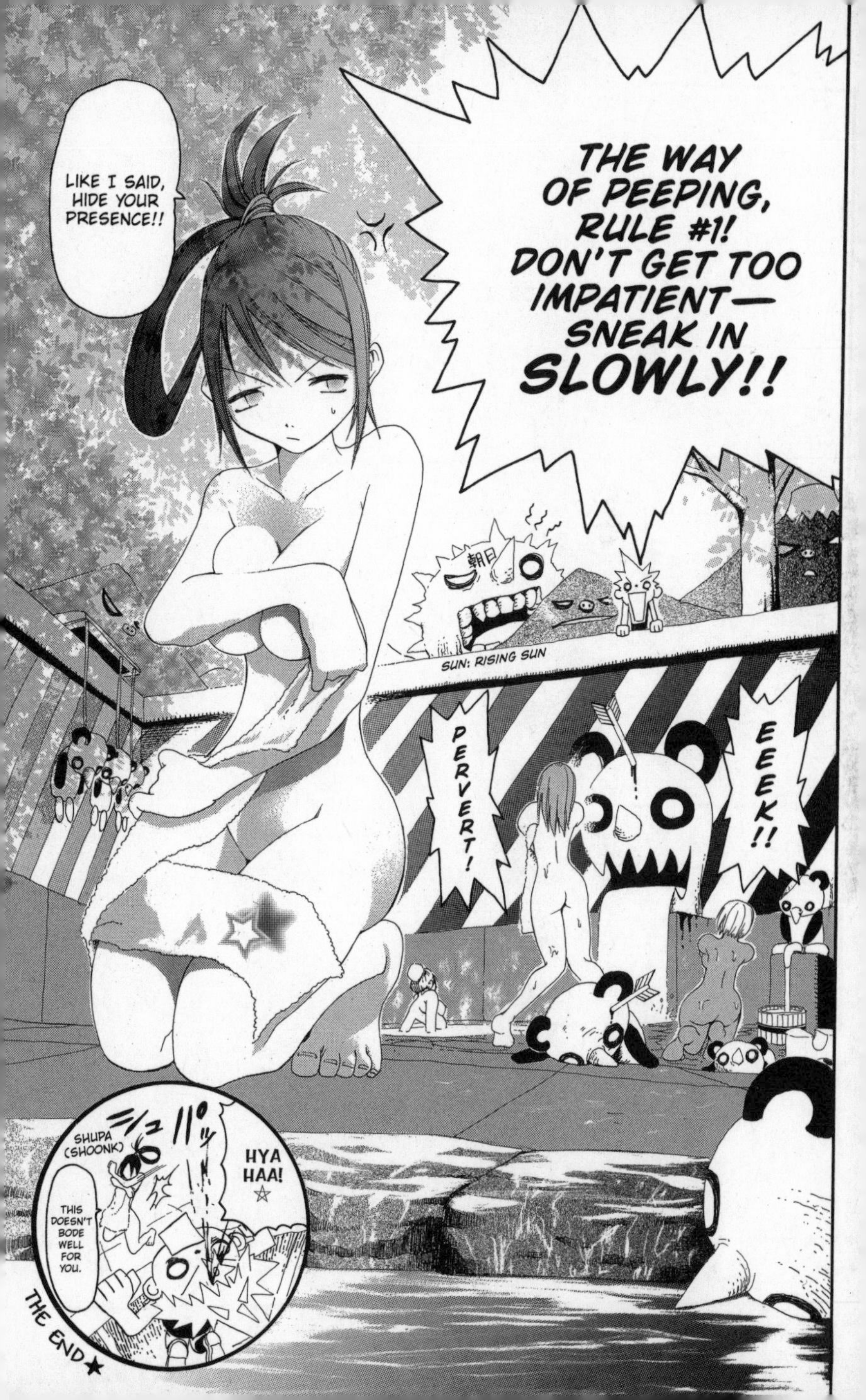
THE WAY OF PEEPING, RULE #1! DON'T GET TOO IMPATIENT— SNEAK IN SLOWLY!!
LIKE I SAID, HIDE YOUR PRESENCE!!
朝日
SUN: RISING SUN
EEEEK!!
PERVERT!
HYA HAA!
SHUPA (SHOONK)
THIS DOESN'T BODE WELL FOR YOU.
THE END★

SOUL EATER

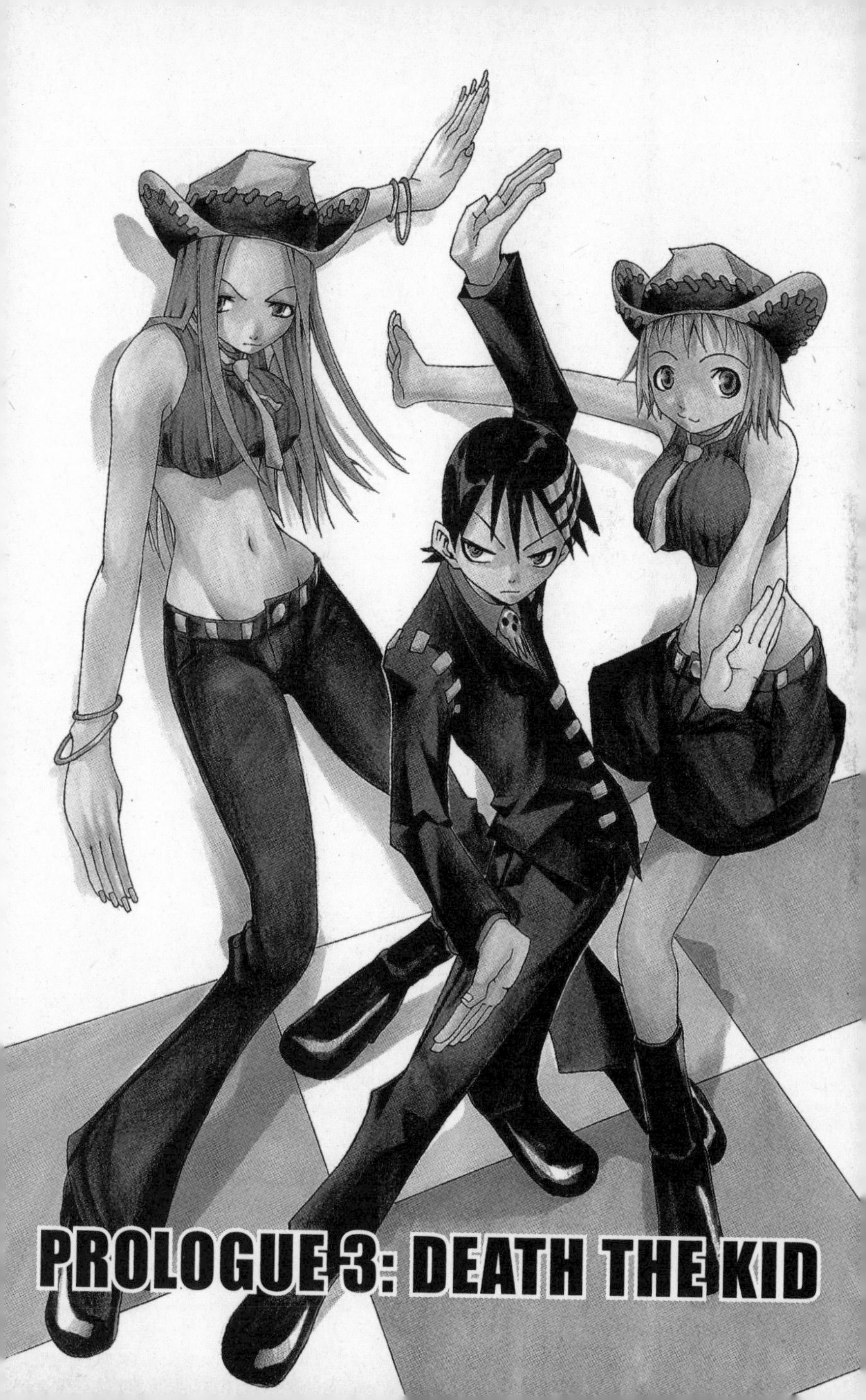
PROLOGUE 3: DEATH THE KID

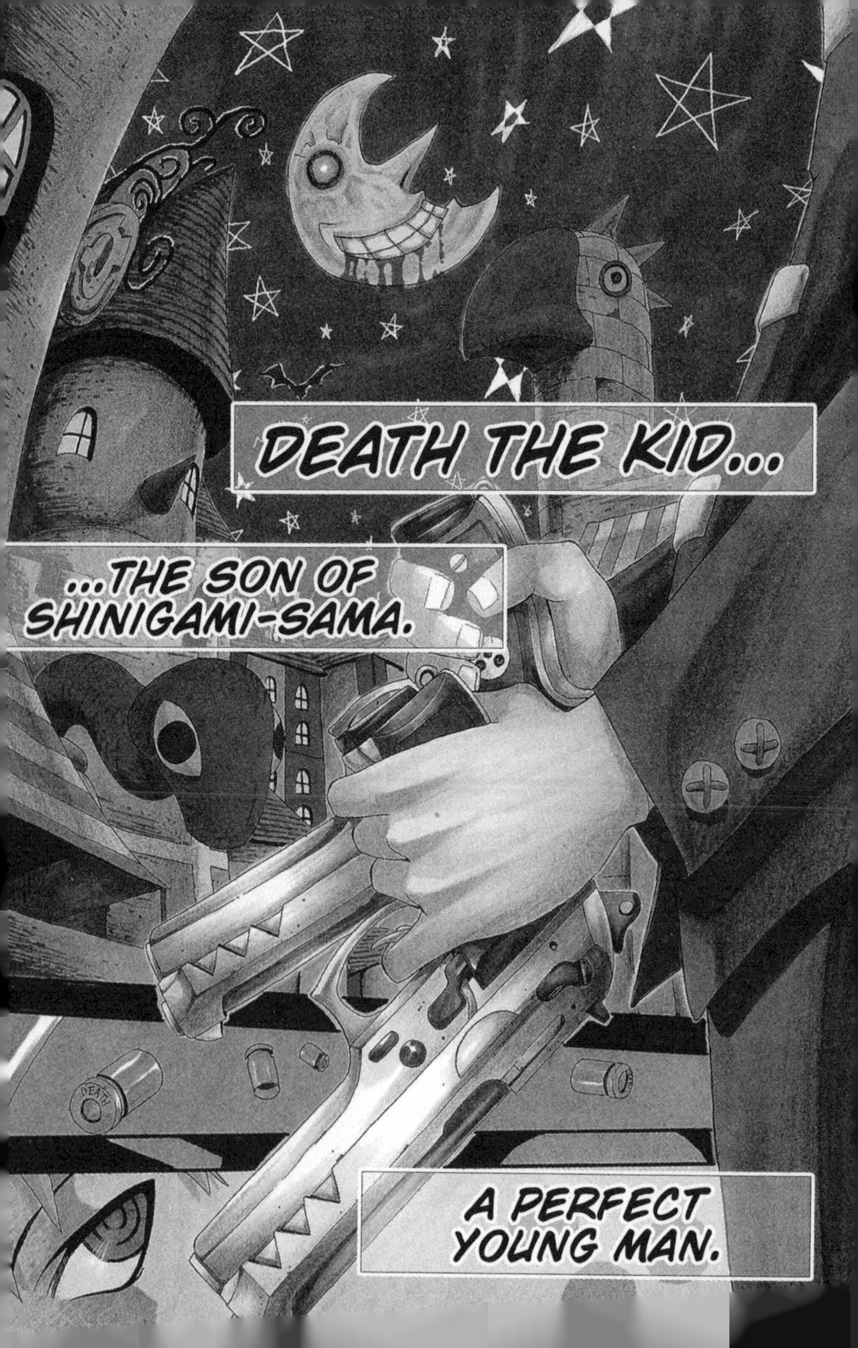
DEATH THE KID...
...THE SON OF SHINIGAMI-SAMA.
A PERFECT YOUNG MAN.
DEATH

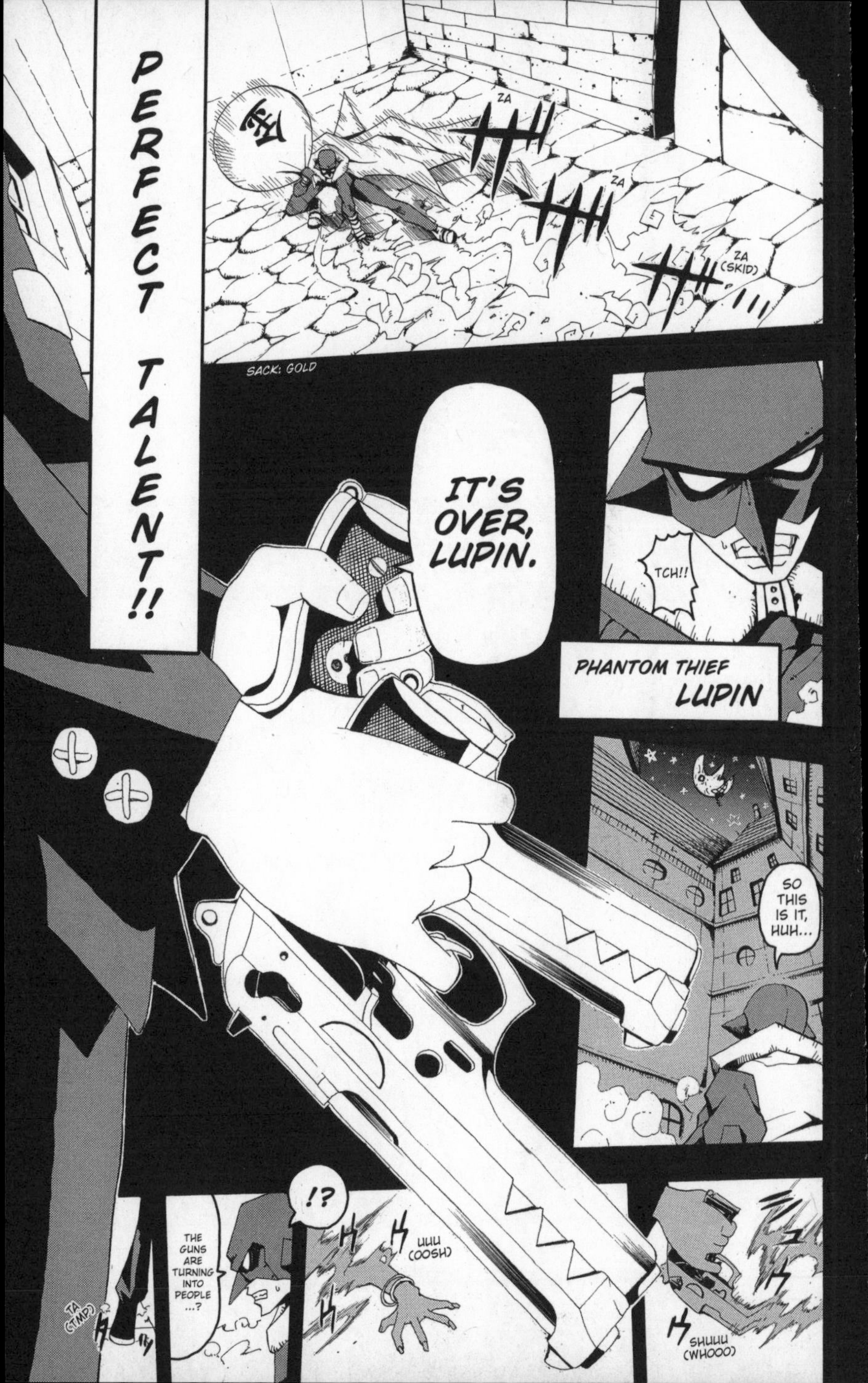
ZA
ZA
ZA (SKID)
SACK: GOLD
TCH!!
PHANTOM THIEF LUPIN
SO THIS IS IT, HUH...
PERFECT TALENT!!
IT'S OVER, LUPIN.
SHUUU (WHOOO)
!?
UUU (OOSH)
THE GUNS ARE TURNING INTO PEOPLE ...?
TA (TMP)

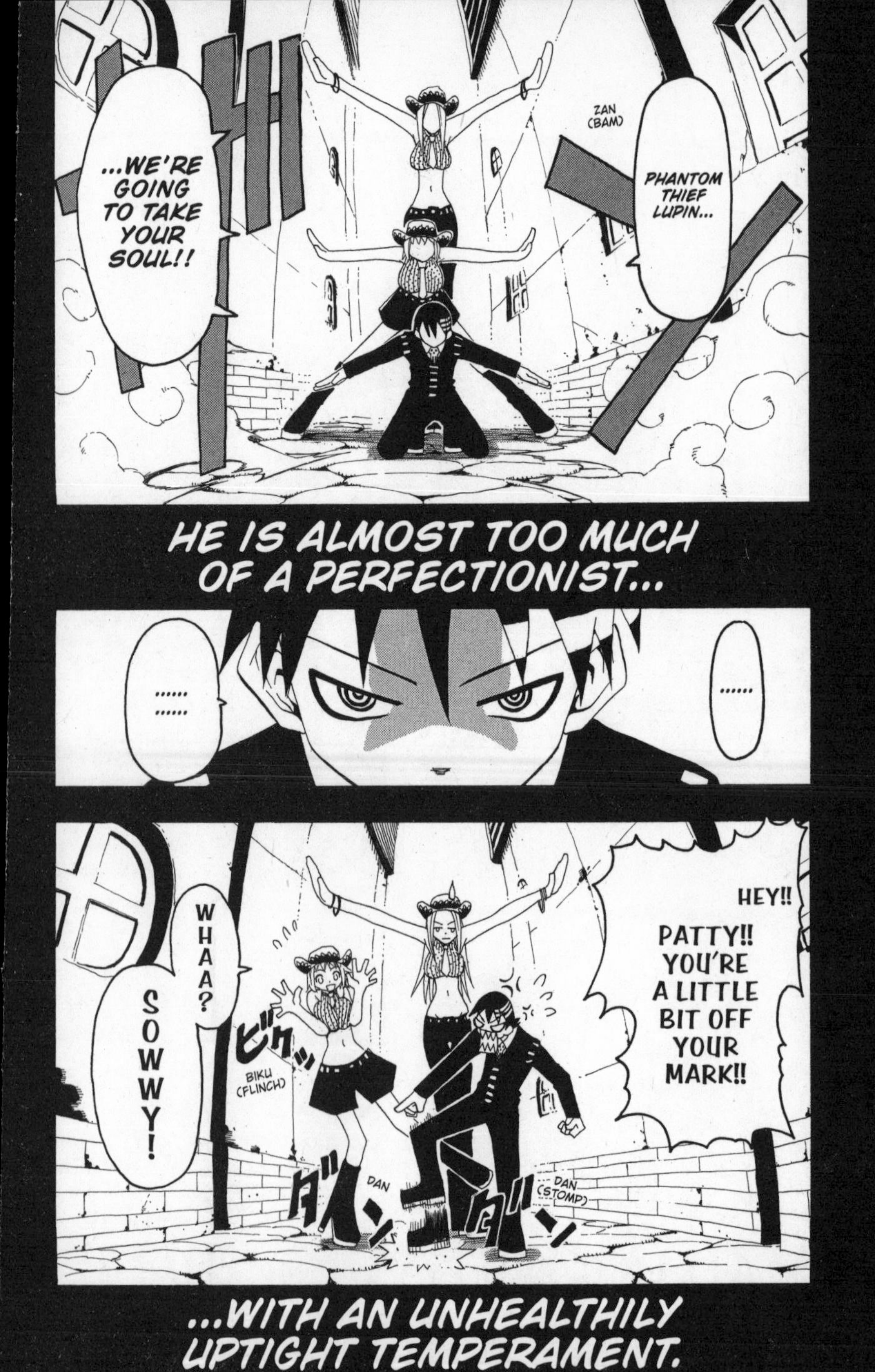
PHANTOM THIEF LUPIN...
ZAN (BAM)
...WE'RE GOING TO TAKE YOUR SOUL!!
HE IS ALMOST TOO MUCH OF A PERFECTIONIST...
......
....
HEY!!
PATTY!! YOU'RE A LITTLE BIT OFF YOUR MARK!!
DAN (STOMP)
DAN
BIKU (FLINCH)
WHAA?
SOWWY!
...WITH AN UNHEALTHILY UPTIGHT TEMPERAMENT.

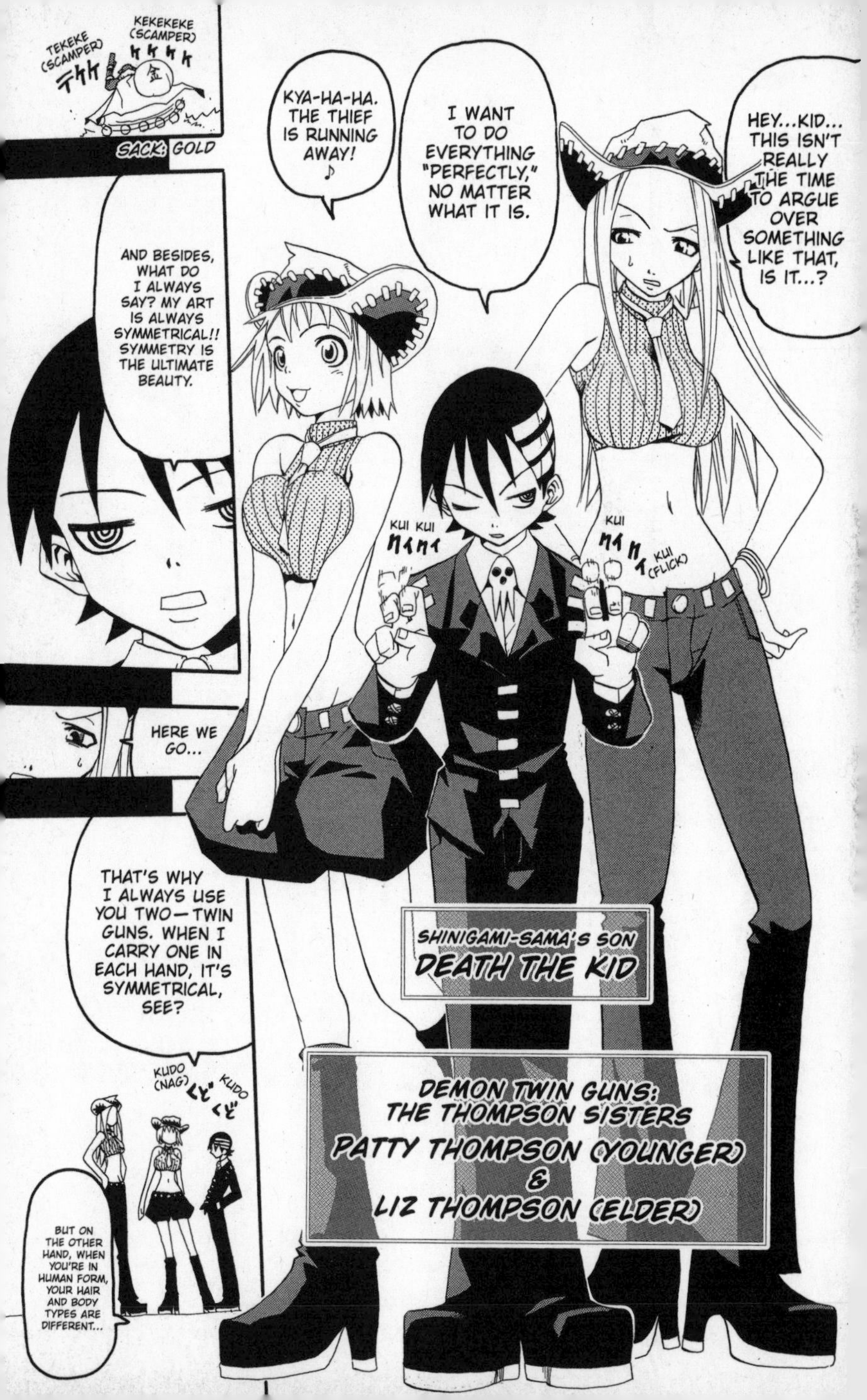
HEY...KID... THIS ISN'T REALLY THE TIME TO ARGUE OVER SOMETHING LIKE THAT, IS IT...?
I WANT TO DO EVERYTHING "PERFECTLY," NO MATTER WHAT IT IS.
KYA-HA-HA. THE THIEF IS RUNNING AWAY! ♪
KUI (FLICK) KUI
KUI KUI
SHINIGAMI-SAMA'S SON
DEATH THE KID
DEMON TWIN GUNS: THE THOMPSON SISTERS
PATTY THOMPSON (YOUNGER) & LIZ THOMPSON (ELDER)
KEKEKEKE (SCAMPER)
TEKEKE (SCAMPER)
SACK: GOLD
AND BESIDES, WHAT DO I ALWAYS SAY? MY ART IS ALWAYS SYMMETRICAL!! SYMMETRY IS THE ULTIMATE BEAUTY.
HERE WE GO...
THAT'S WHY I ALWAYS USE YOU TWO—TWIN GUNS. WHEN I CARRY ONE IN EACH HAND, IT'S SYMMETRICAL, SEE?
KUDO
KUDO (NAG)
BUT ON THE OTHER HAND, WHEN YOU'RE IN HUMAN FORM, YOUR HAIR AND BODY TYPES ARE DIFFERENT...

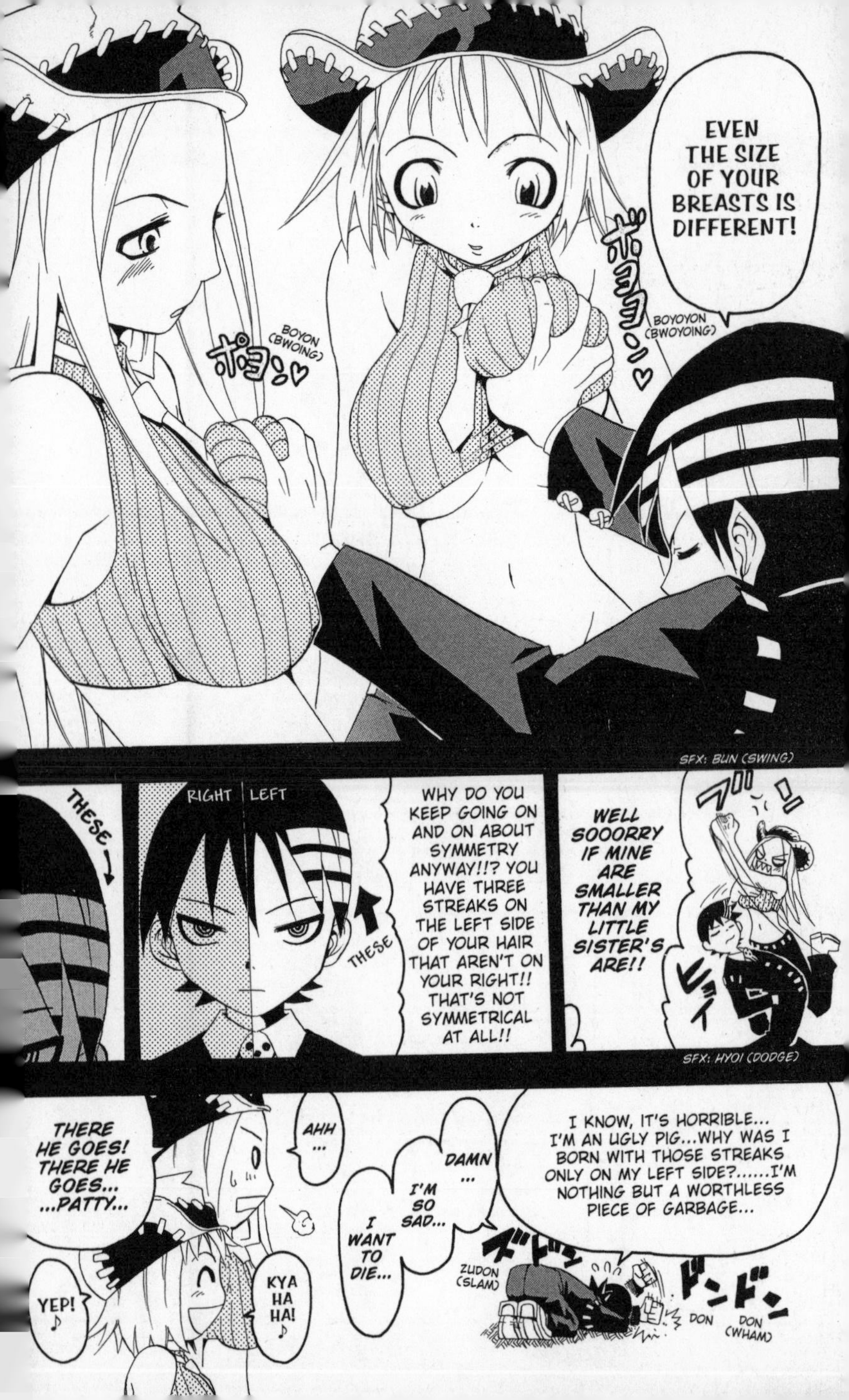

EVEN THE SIZE OF YOUR BREASTS IS DIFFERENT!
BOYOYON (BWOYOING)
BOYON (BWOING)
SFX: BUN (SWING)
WELL SOOORRY IF MINE ARE SMALLER THAN MY LITTLE SISTER'S ARE!!
SFX: HYOI (DODGE)
WHY DO YOU KEEP GOING ON AND ON ABOUT SYMMETRY ANYWAY!!? YOU HAVE THREE STREAKS ON THE LEFT SIDE OF YOUR HAIR THAT AREN'T ON YOUR RIGHT!! THAT'S NOT SYMMETRICAL AT ALL!!
RIGHT | LEFT
THESE
THESE
I KNOW, IT'S HORRIBLE... I'M AN UGLY PIG...WHY WAS I BORN WITH THOSE STREAKS ONLY ON MY LEFT SIDE?......I'M NOTHING BUT A WORTHLESS PIECE OF GARBAGE...
DAMN ...
I'M SO SAD...
I WANT TO DIE...
ZUDON (SLAM)
DON DON (WHAM)
AHH ...
THERE HE GOES! THERE HE GOES... ...PATTY...
KYA HA HA! ♪
YEP! ♪

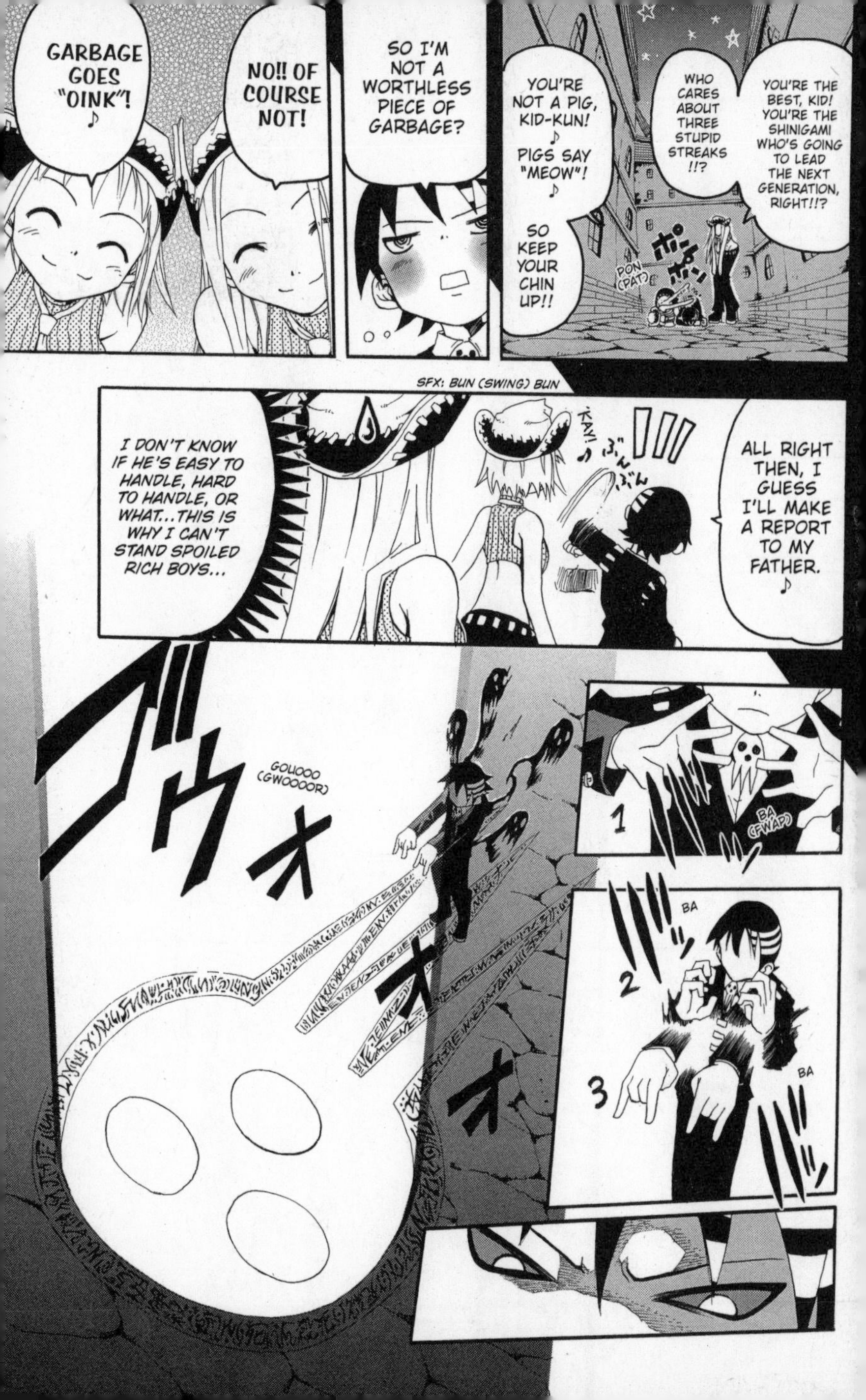
YOU'RE THE BEST, KID! YOU'RE THE SHINIGAMI WHO'S GOING TO LEAD THE NEXT GENERATION, RIGHT!!?
WHO CARES ABOUT THREE STUPID STREAKS !!?
YOU'RE NOT A PIG, KID-KUN! ♪ PIGS SAY "MEOW"! ♪
SO KEEP YOUR CHIN UP!!
PON (PAT)
SO I'M NOT A WORTHLESS PIECE OF GARBAGE?
NO!! OF COURSE NOT!
GARBAGE GOES "OINK"! ♪
SFX: BUN (SWING) BUN
ALL RIGHT THEN, I GUESS I'LL MAKE A REPORT TO MY FATHER. ♪
'KAY! ♪
I DON'T KNOW IF HE'S EASY TO HANDLE, HARD TO HANDLE, OR WHAT...THIS IS WHY I CAN'T STAND SPOILED RICH BOYS...
1
BA (FWAP)
BA
2
3
BA
GOUOOO (GWOOOOR)

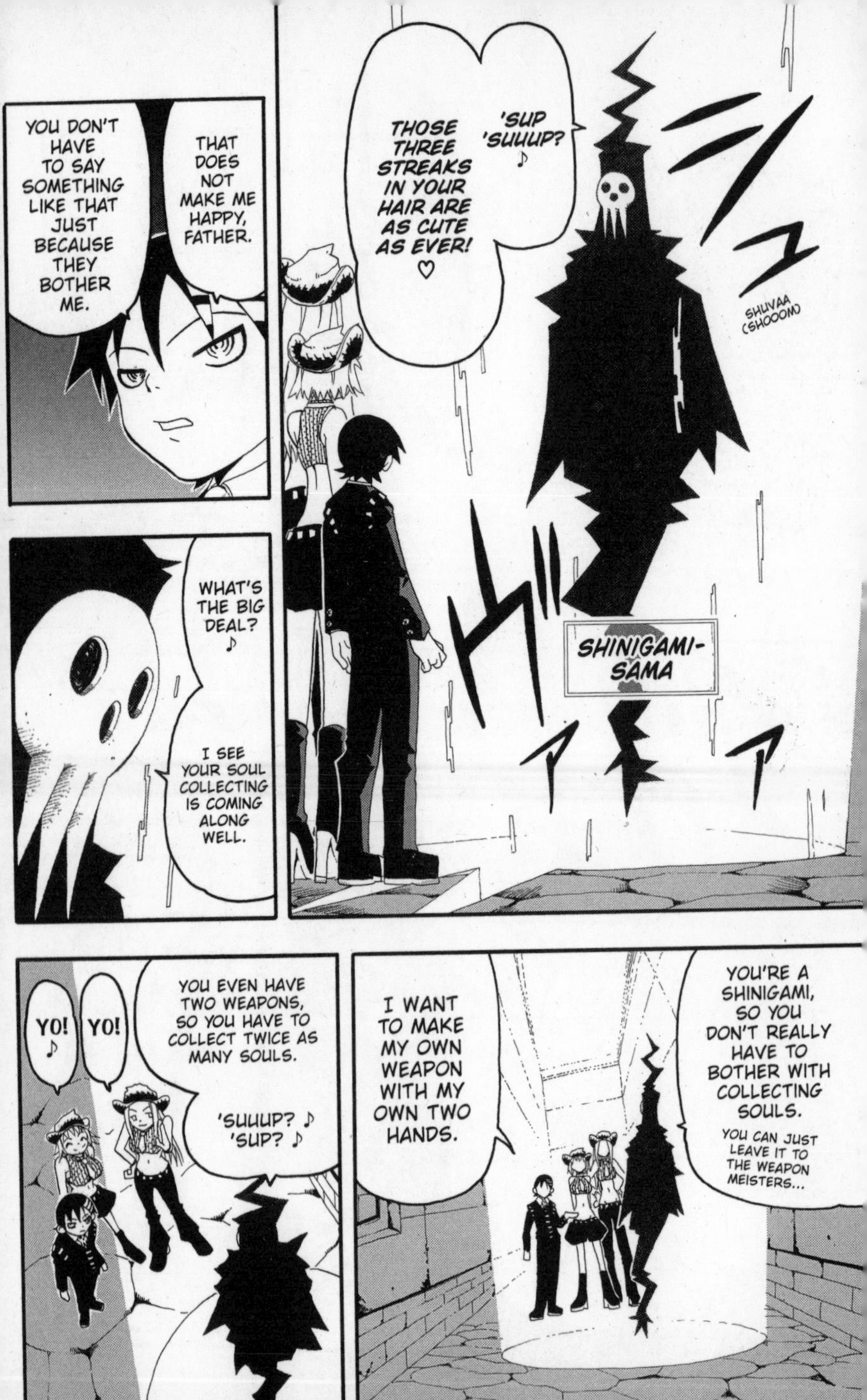
'SUP 'SUUUP? ♪
THOSE THREE STREAKS IN YOUR HAIR ARE AS CUTE AS EVER! ♡
SHUVAA (SHOOOM)
SHINIGAMI-SAMA
THAT DOES NOT MAKE ME HAPPY, FATHER.
YOU DON'T HAVE TO SAY SOMETHING LIKE THAT JUST BECAUSE THEY BOTHER ME.
WHAT'S THE BIG DEAL? ♪
I SEE YOUR SOUL COLLECTING IS COMING ALONG WELL.
YOU'RE A SHINIGAMI, SO YOU DON'T REALLY HAVE TO BOTHER WITH COLLECTING SOULS.
YOU CAN JUST LEAVE IT TO THE WEAPON MEISTERS...
I WANT TO MAKE MY OWN WEAPON WITH MY OWN TWO HANDS.
YOU EVEN HAVE TWO WEAPONS, SO YOU HAVE TO COLLECT TWICE AS MANY SOULS.
'SUUUP? ♪ 'SUP? ♪
YO!
YO! ♪

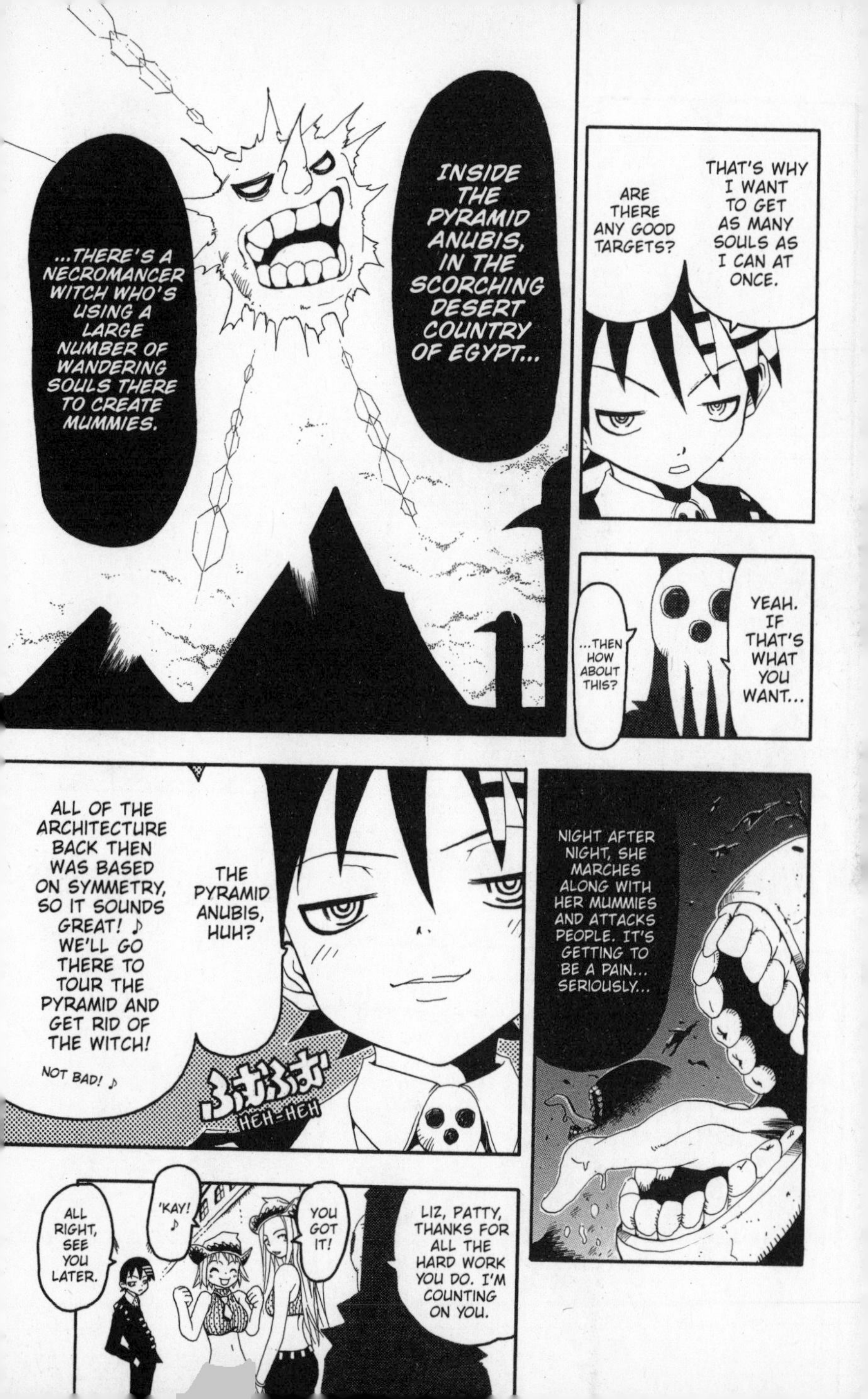
THAT'S WHY I WANT TO GET AS MANY SOULS AS I CAN AT ONCE.
ARE THERE ANY GOOD TARGETS?
YEAH. IF THAT'S WHAT YOU WANT...
...THEN HOW ABOUT THIS?
INSIDE THE PYRAMID ANUBIS, IN THE SCORCHING DESERT COUNTRY OF EGYPT...
...THERE'S A NECROMANCER WITCH WHO'S USING A LARGE NUMBER OF WANDERING SOULS THERE TO CREATE MUMMIES.
NIGHT AFTER NIGHT, SHE MARCHES ALONG WITH HER MUMMIES AND ATTACKS PEOPLE. IT'S GETTING TO BE A PAIN... SERIOUSLY...
THE PYRAMID ANUBIS, HUH?
ALL OF THE ARCHITECTURE BACK THEN WAS BASED ON SYMMETRY, SO IT SOUNDS GREAT! ♪ WE'LL GO THERE TO TOUR THE PYRAMID AND GET RID OF THE WITCH!
NOT BAD! ♪
HEH-HEH
LIZ, PATTY, THANKS FOR ALL THE HARD WORK YOU DO. I'M COUNTING ON YOU.
YOU GOT IT!
'KAY! ♪
ALL RIGHT, SEE YOU LATER.

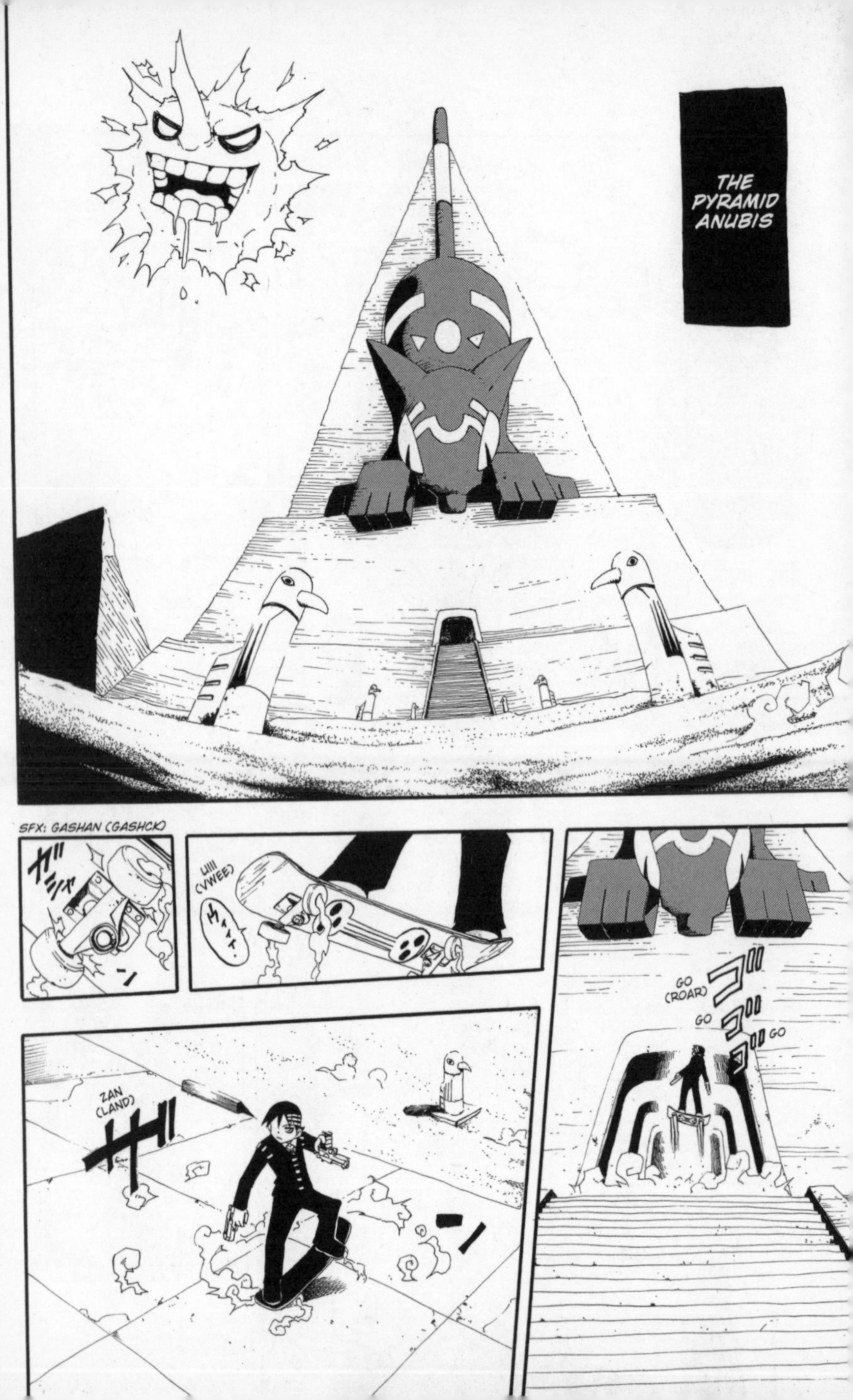
THE PYRAMID ANUBIS
GO (ROAR)
GO
GO
UIII (VWEE)
SFX: GASHAN (GASHCK)
ZAN (LAND)

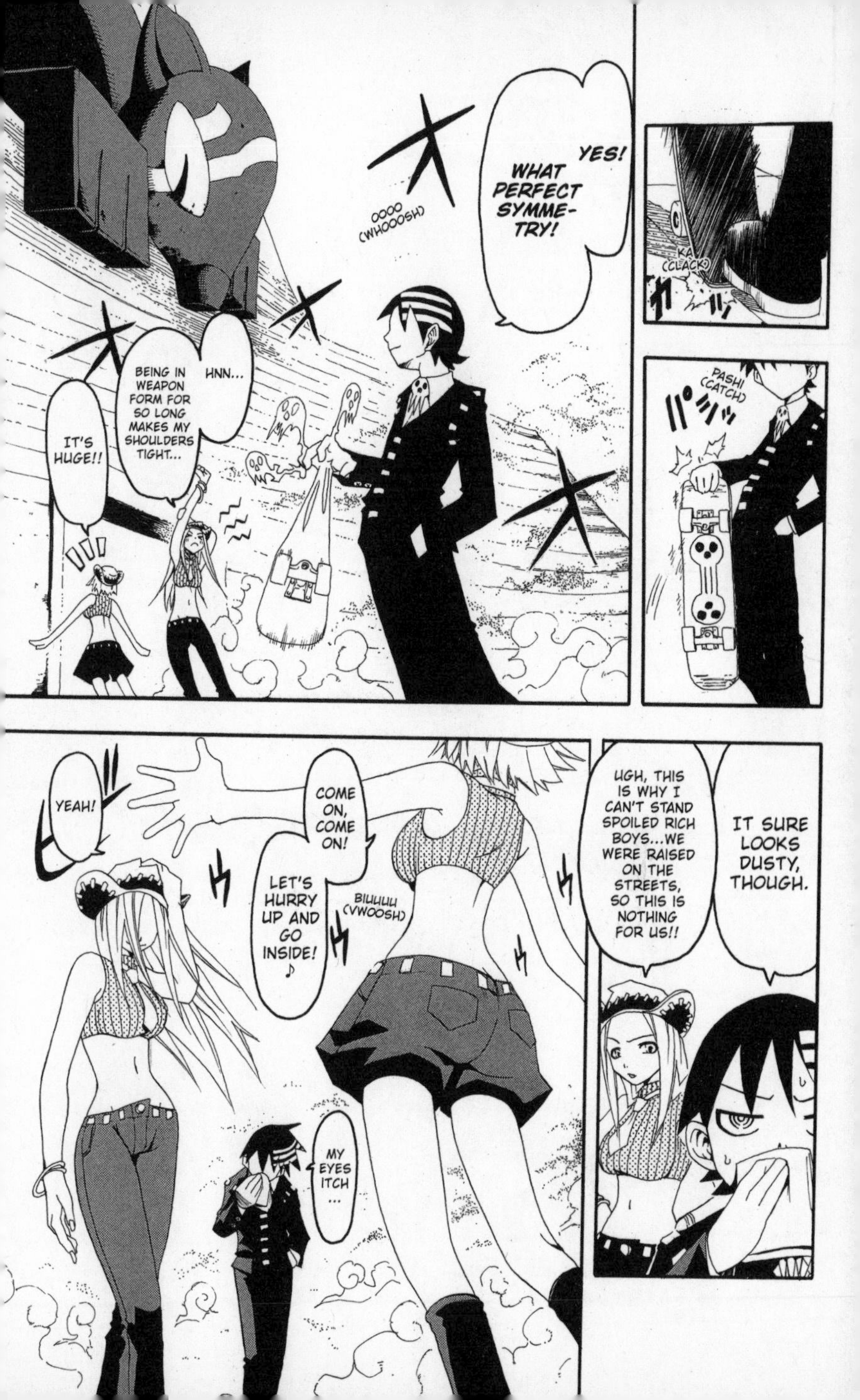
KA (CLACK)
PASHI (CATCH)
YES! WHAT PERFECT SYMMETRY!
OOOO (WHOOOSH)
HNN...
BEING IN WEAPON FORM FOR SO LONG MAKES MY SHOULDERS TIGHT...
IT'S HUGE!!
IT SURE LOOKS DUSTY, THOUGH.
UGH, THIS IS WHY I CAN'T STAND SPOILED RICH BOYS...WE WERE RAISED ON THE STREETS, SO THIS IS NOTHING FOR US!!
COME ON, COME ON!
LET'S HURRY UP AND GO INSIDE! ♪
BIUUUU (VWOOSH)
YEAH!
MY EYES ITCH...

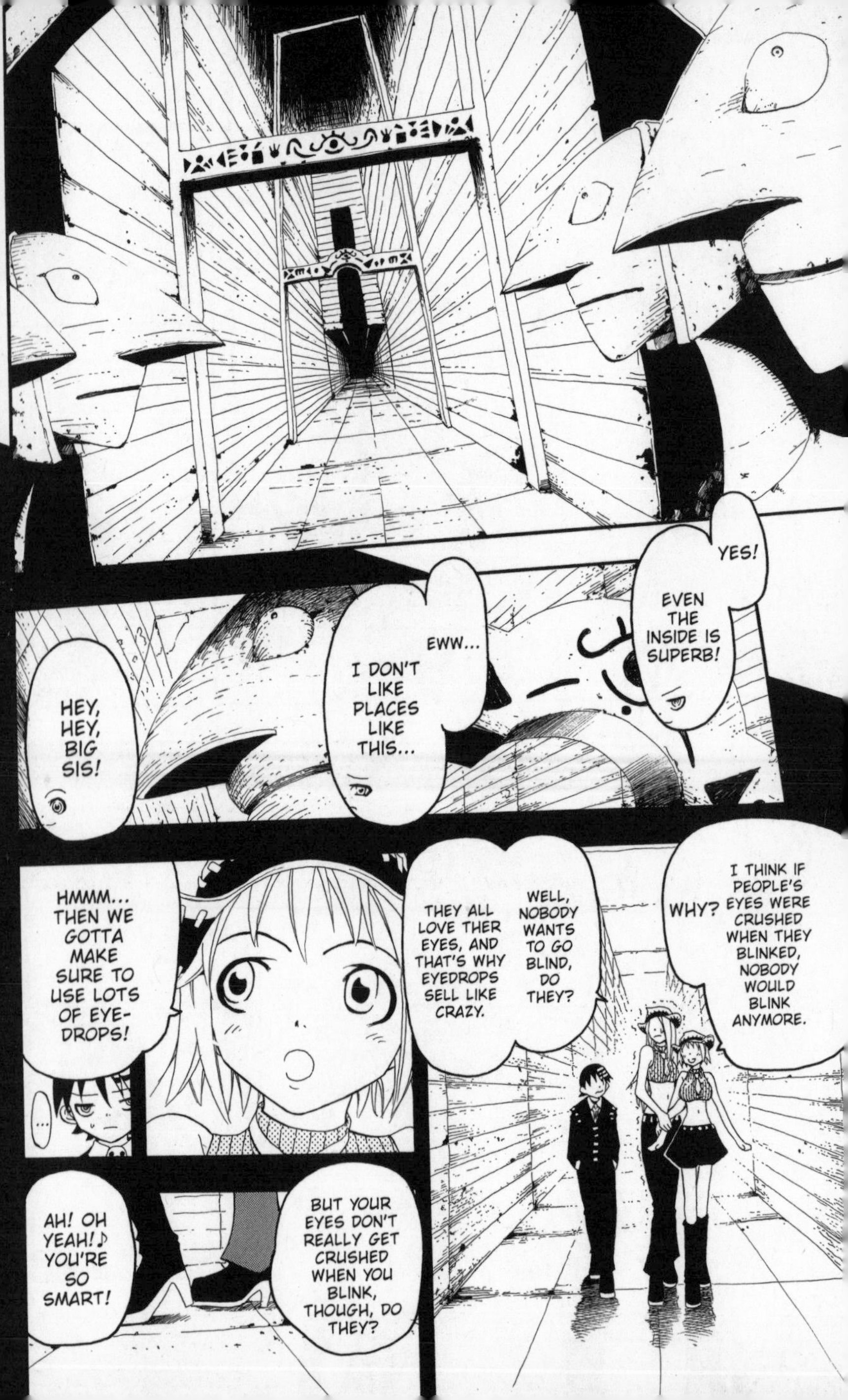
YES!
EVEN THE INSIDE IS SUPERB!
EWW...
I DON'T LIKE PLACES LIKE THIS...
HEY, HEY, BIG SIS!
I THINK IF PEOPLE'S EYES WERE CRUSHED WHEN THEY BLINKED, NOBODY WOULD BLINK ANYMORE.
WHY?
WELL, NOBODY WANTS TO GO BLIND, DO THEY?
THEY ALL LOVE THER EYES, AND THAT'S WHY EYEDROPS SELL LIKE CRAZY.
HMMM... THEN WE GOTTA MAKE SURE TO USE LOTS OF EYE-DROPS!
...
BUT YOUR EYES DON'T REALLY GET CRUSHED WHEN YOU BLINK, THOUGH, DO THEY?
AH! OH YEAH!♪ YOU'RE SO SMART!

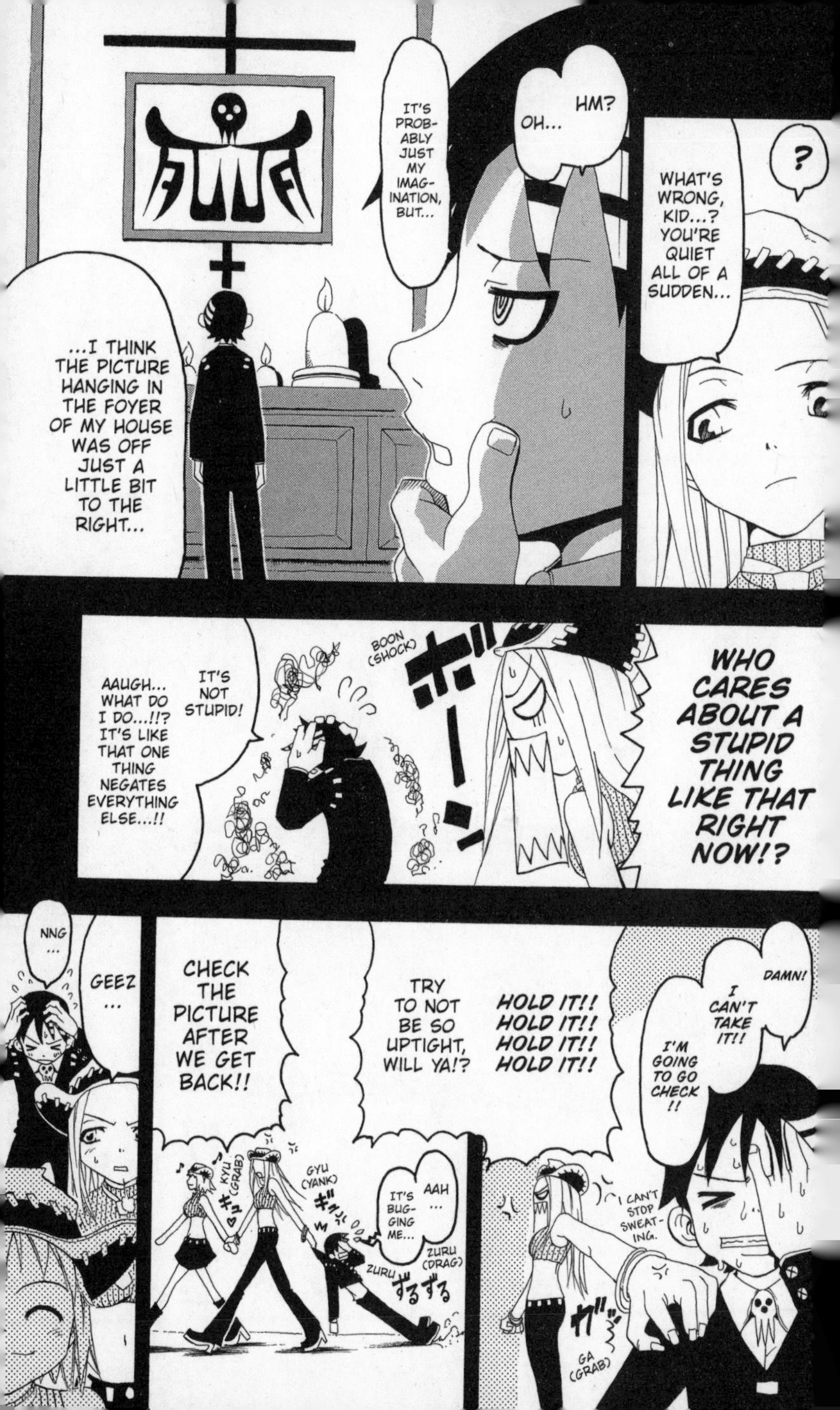
?
WHAT'S WRONG, KID...? YOU'RE QUIET ALL OF A SUDDEN...
HM? OH...
IT'S PROBABLY JUST MY IMAGINATION, BUT...
...I THINK THE PICTURE HANGING IN THE FOYER OF MY HOUSE WAS OFF JUST A LITTLE BIT TO THE RIGHT...
WHO CARES ABOUT A STUPID THING LIKE THAT RIGHT NOW!?
BOON (SHOCK)
IT'S NOT STUPID!
AAUGH... WHAT DO I DO...!!? IT'S LIKE THAT ONE THING NEGATES EVERYTHING ELSE...!!
DAMN!
I CAN'T TAKE IT!!
I'M GOING TO GO CHECK!!
I CAN'T STOP SWEATING.
GA (GRAB)
HOLD IT!! HOLD IT!! HOLD IT!! HOLD IT!!
TRY TO NOT BE SO UPTIGHT, WILL YA!?
CHECK THE PICTURE AFTER WE GET BACK!!
GYU (YANK)
KYU (GRAB)
AAH ...
IT'S BUGGING ME...
ZURU ZURU (DRAG)
GEEZ ...
NNG ...

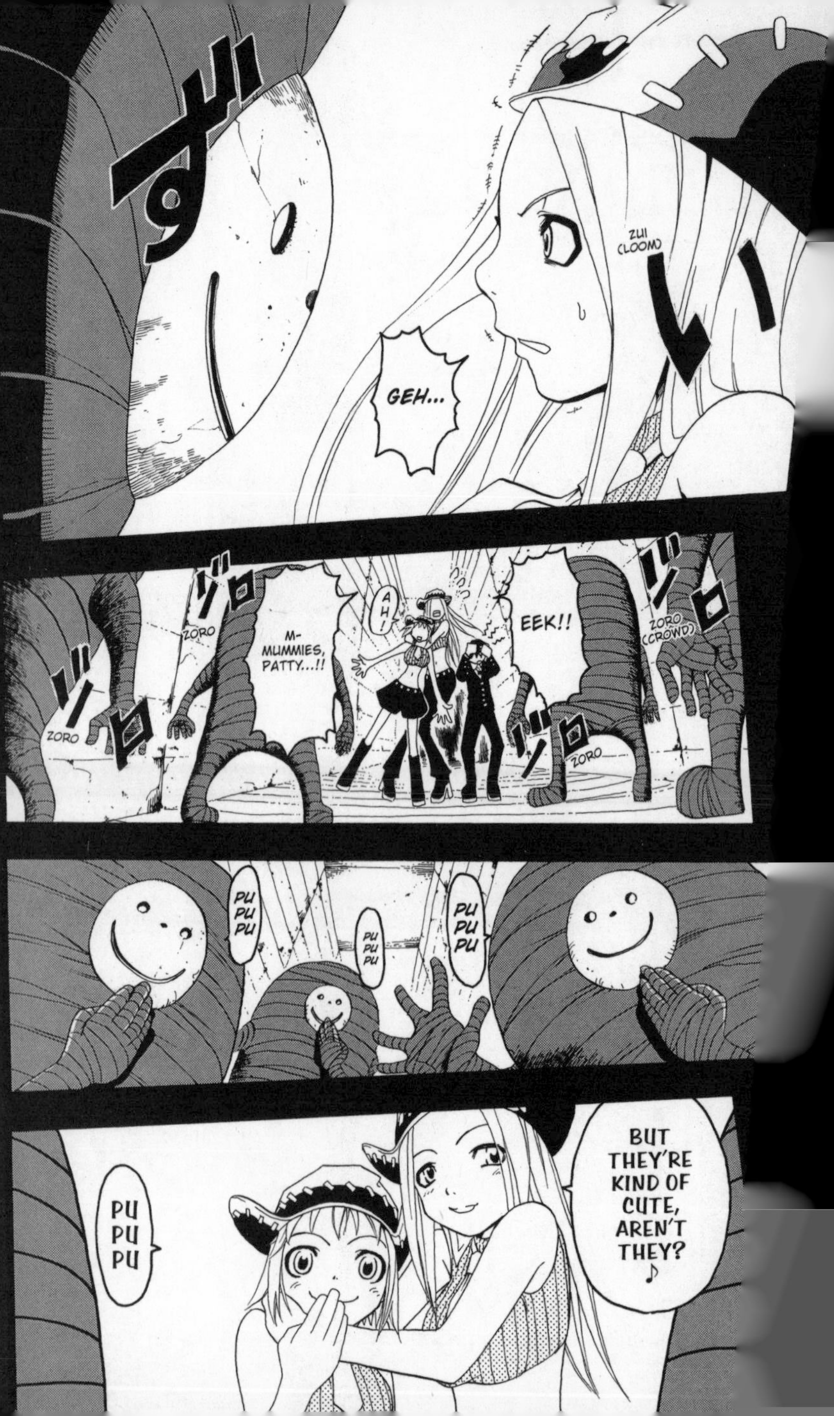
ZUI (LOOM)
GEH...
ZORO (CROWD)
EEK!!
AH!
M-MUMMIES, PATTY...!!
ZORO
ZORO
ZORO
PU PU PU
PU PU PU
PU PU PU
BUT THEY'RE KIND OF CUTE, AREN'T THEY? ♪
PU PU PU

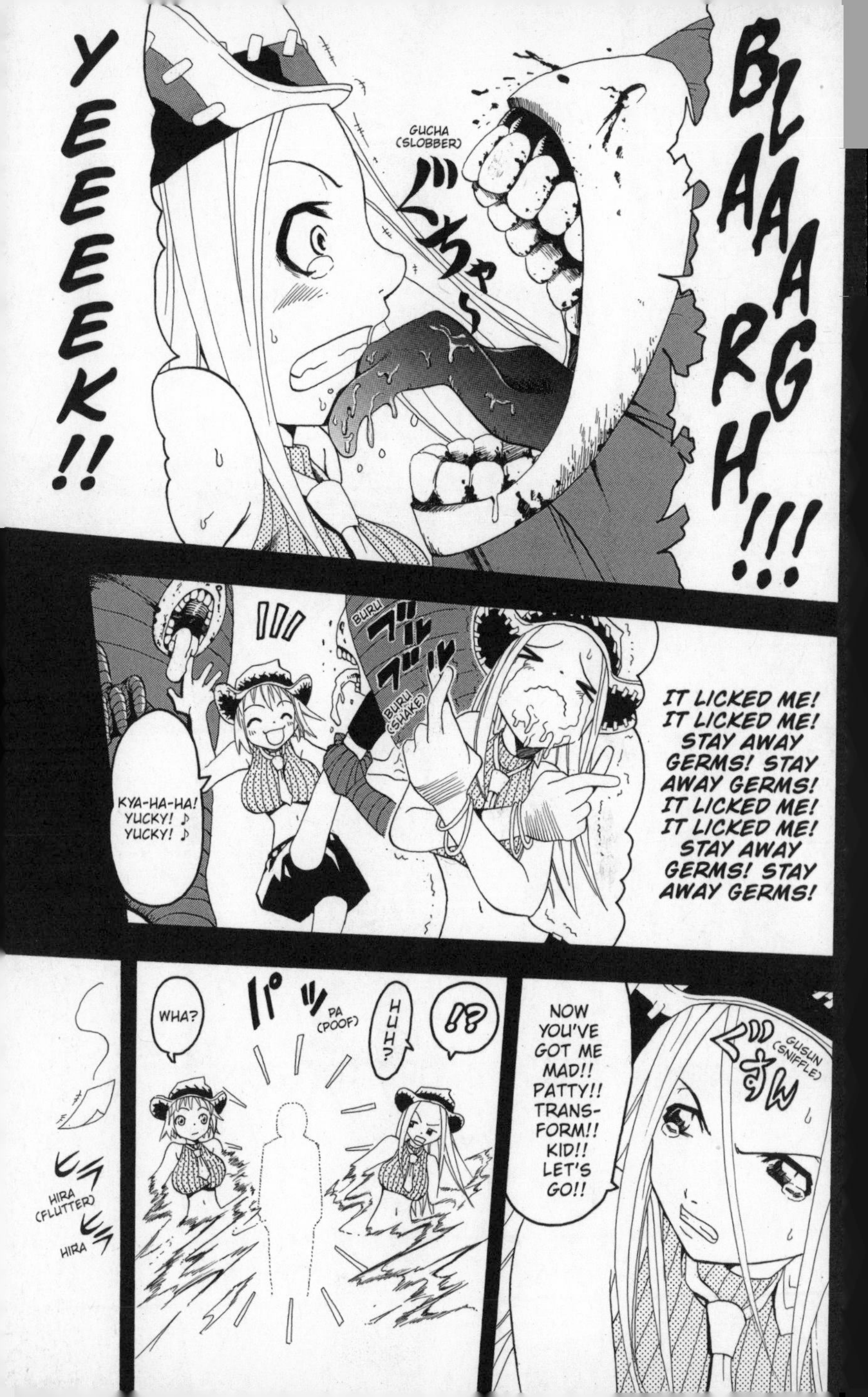
BLAAAARGH!!!
GUCHA (SLOBBER)
ぐちゃ〜
YEEEEEK!!
IT LICKED ME! IT LICKED ME! STAY AWAY GERMS! STAY AWAY GERMS! IT LICKED ME! IT LICKED ME! STAY AWAY GERMS! STAY AWAY GERMS!
ブルブル
BURU BURU (SHAKE)
KYA-HA-HA! YUCKY! ♪ YUCKY! ♪
NOW YOU'VE GOT ME MAD!! PATTY!! TRANS-FORM!! KID!! LET'S GO!!
くすん
GUSUN (SNIFFLE)
!?
HUH?
パッ
PA (POOF)
WHA?
ヒラ
HIRA (FLUTTER)
ヒラ
HIRA

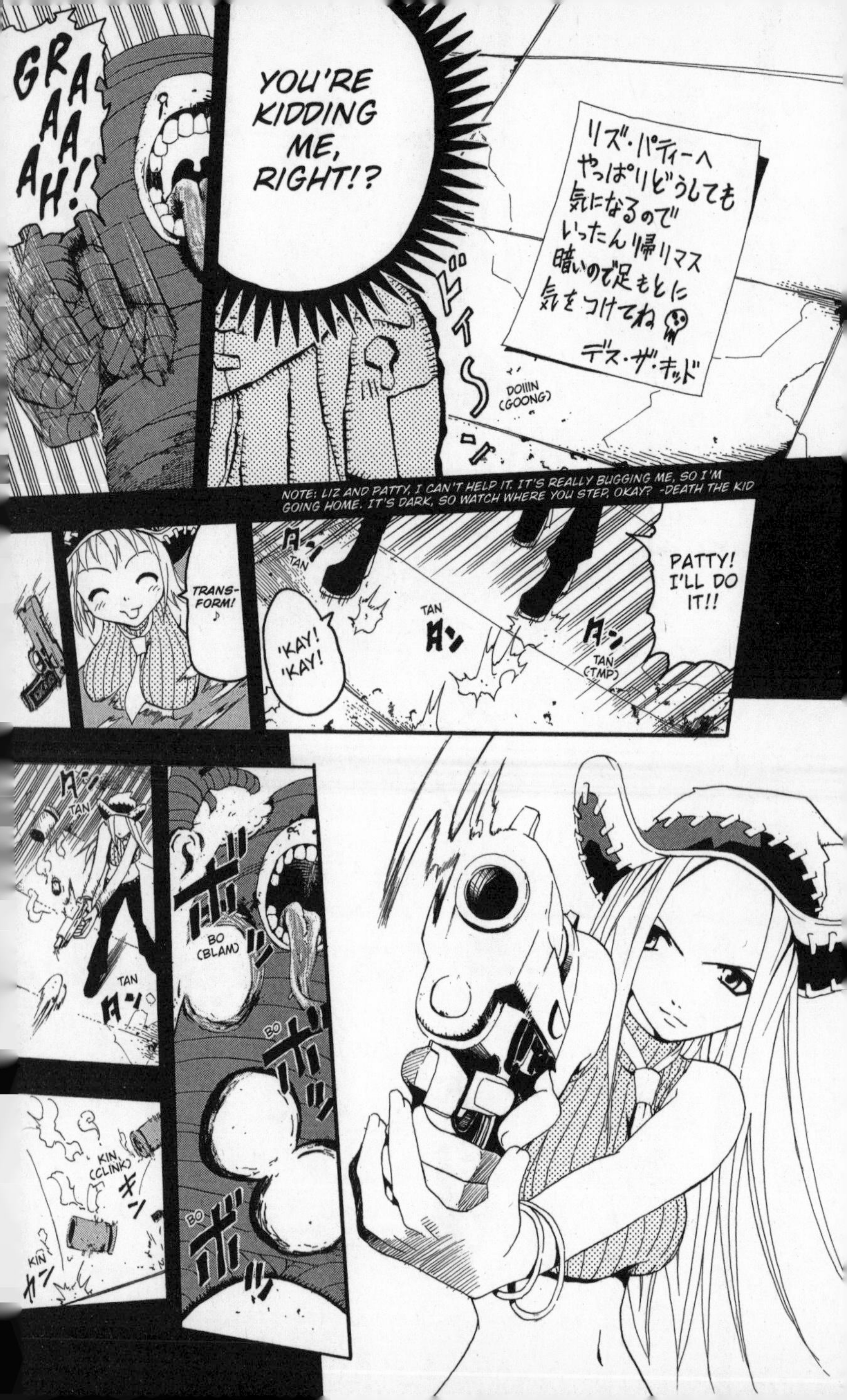
リズ・パティーへ
やっぱりどうしても
気になるので
いったん帰リマス
暗いので足もとに
気をつけてね
デス・ザ・キッド
ドィ～ン
DOIIIN (GOONG)
YOU'RE KIDDING ME, RIGHT!?
GRAAAAH!
NOTE: LIZ AND PATTY, I CAN'T HELP IT. IT'S REALLY BUGGING ME, SO I'M GOING HOME. IT'S DARK, SO WATCH WHERE YOU STEP, OKAY? -DEATH THE KID
PATTY! I'LL DO IT!!
タン
TAN (TMP)
タン
TAN
タン
TAN
'KAY! 'KAY!
TRANS-FORM! ♪
ボッ
BO (BLAM)
ボッ
BO
ボッ
BO
タン
TAN
タン
TAN
KIN (CLINK)
キン
KIN
カン

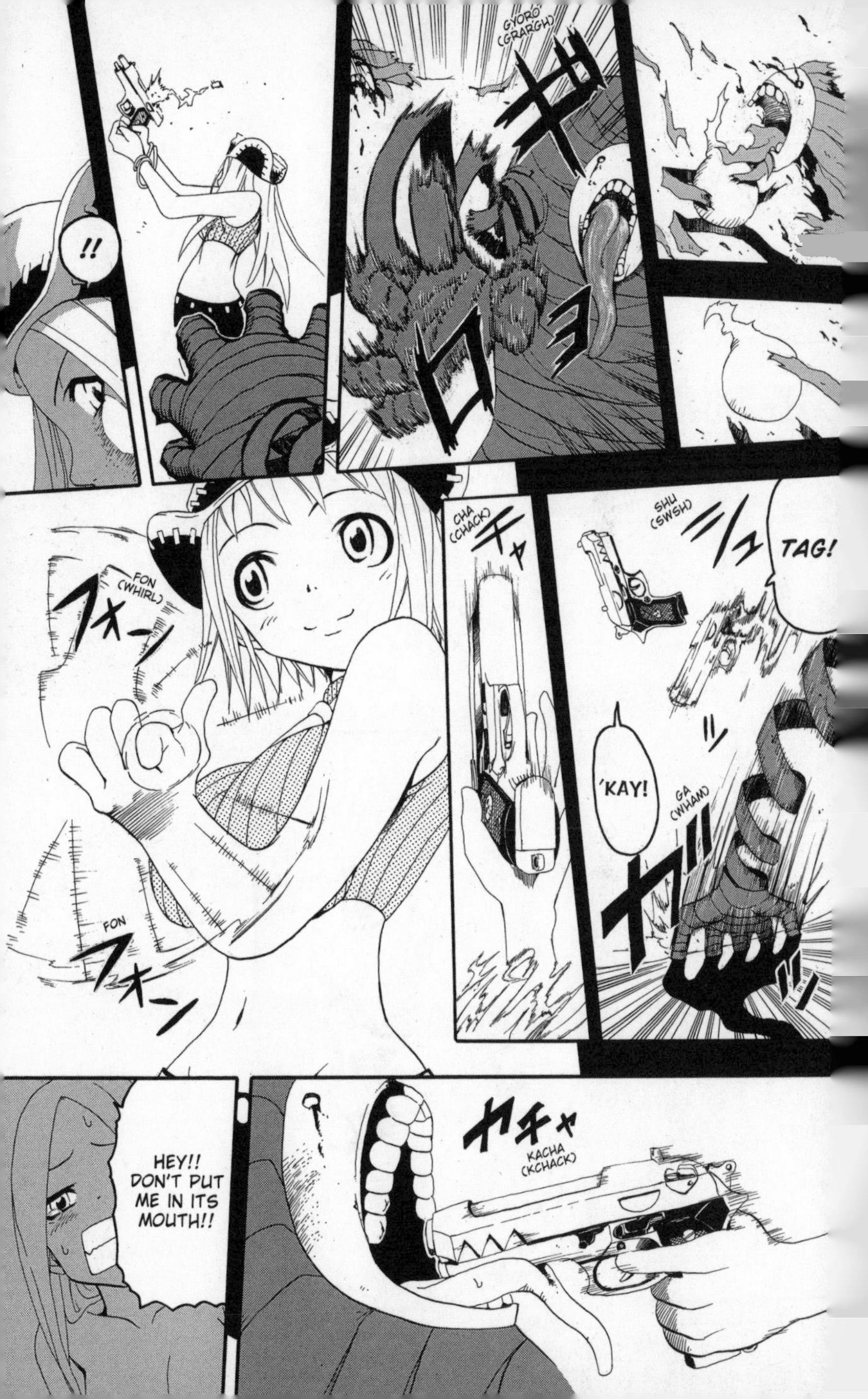
GYORO (GRARGH)
!!
TAG!
SHU (SWSH)
'KAY!
GA (WHAM)
CHA (CHACK)
FON (WHIRL)
FON
KACHA (KCHACK)
HEY!! DON'T PUT ME IN ITS MOUTH!!

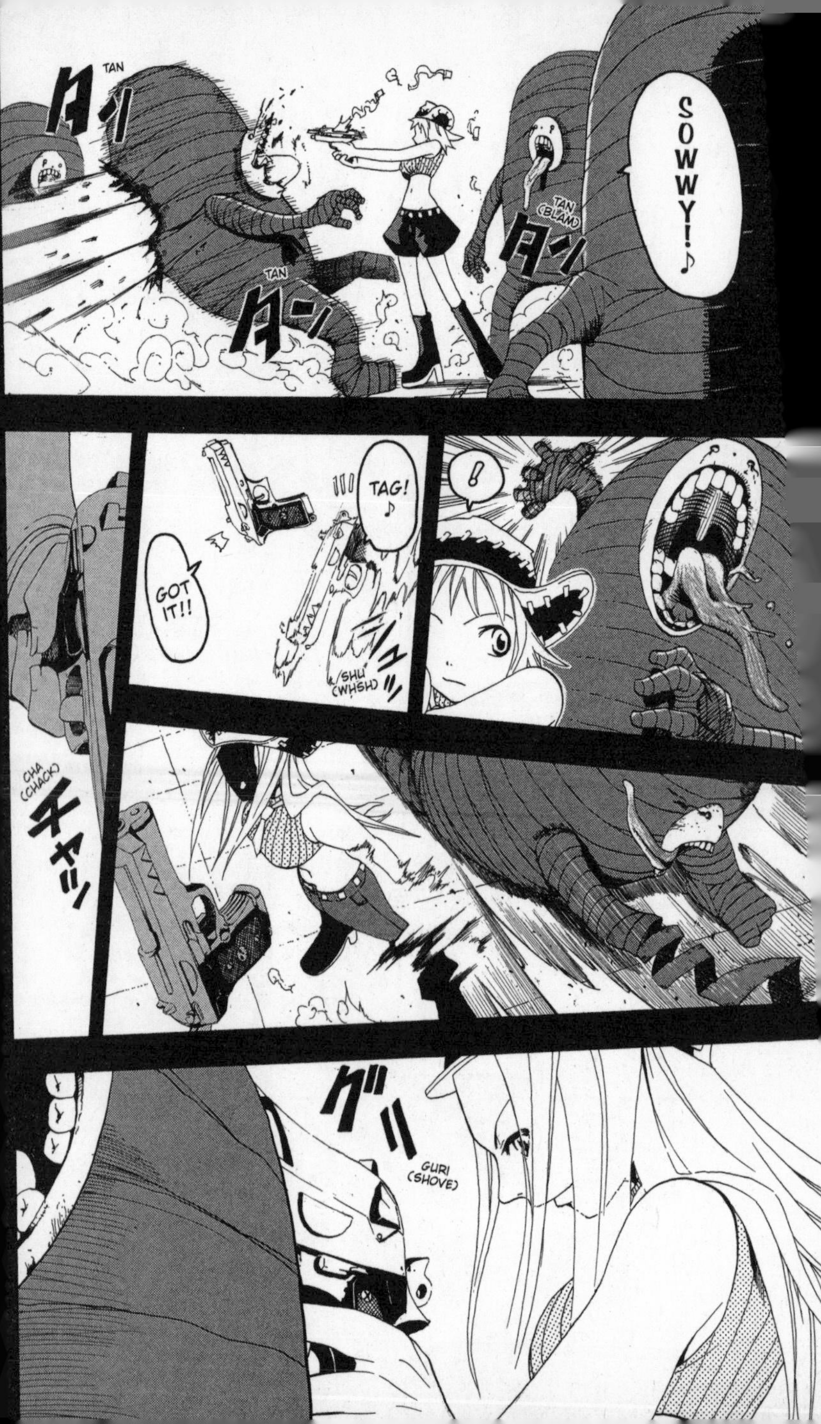
SOWWY!♪
TAN (BLAM)
タン
TAN
タン
TAN
タン
!
TAG! ♪
SHU (WHSH)
GOT IT!!
CHA (CHACK)
チャッ
グリ
GURI (SHOVE)

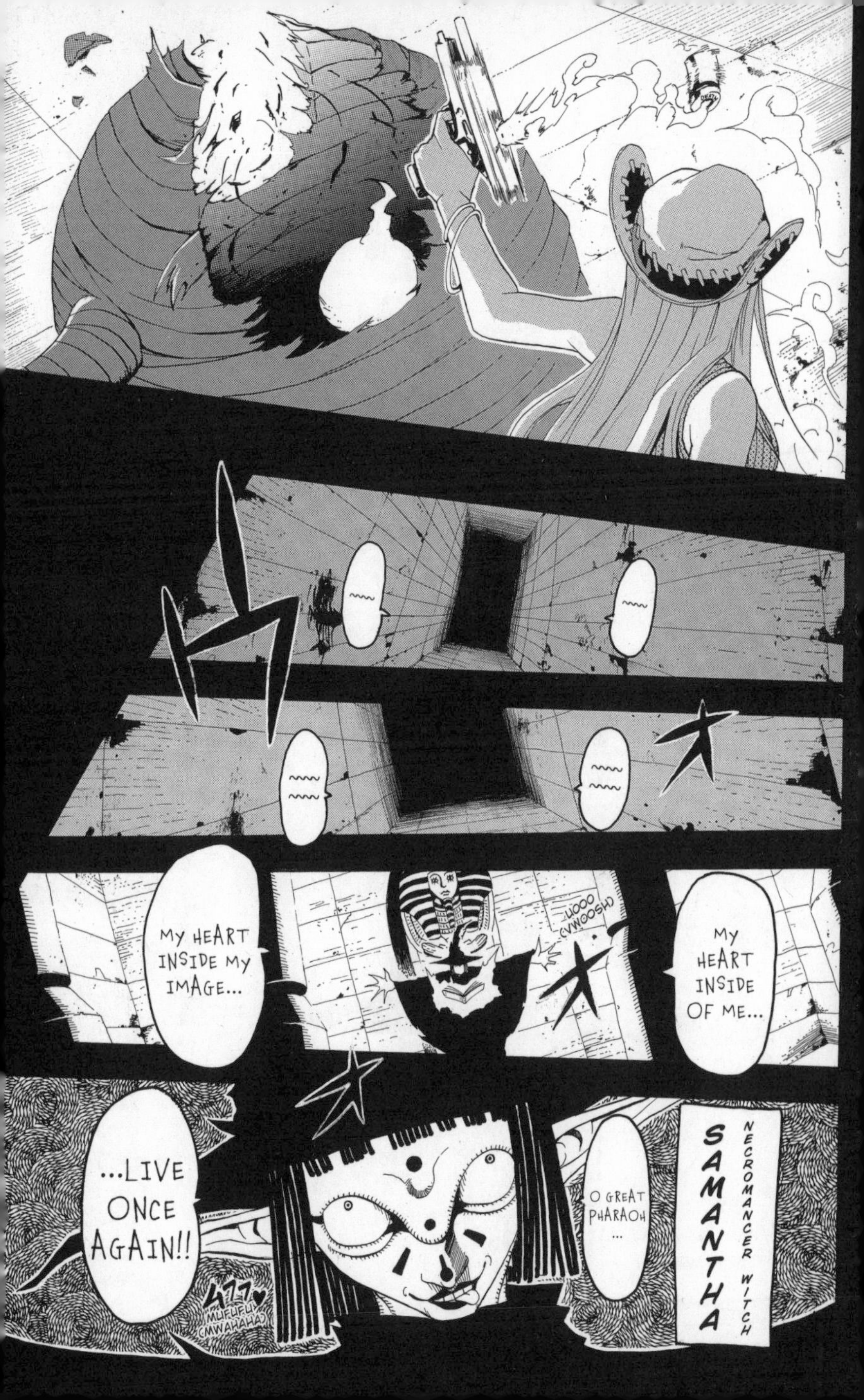

~~~
~~~
~~~ ~~~
~~~ ~~~
MY HEART INSIDE OF ME...
MY HEART INSIDE MY IMAGE...
SAMANTHA
NECROMANCER WITCH
O GREAT PHARAOH ...
...LIVE ONCE AGAIN!!
MUFUFU (MWAHAHA)

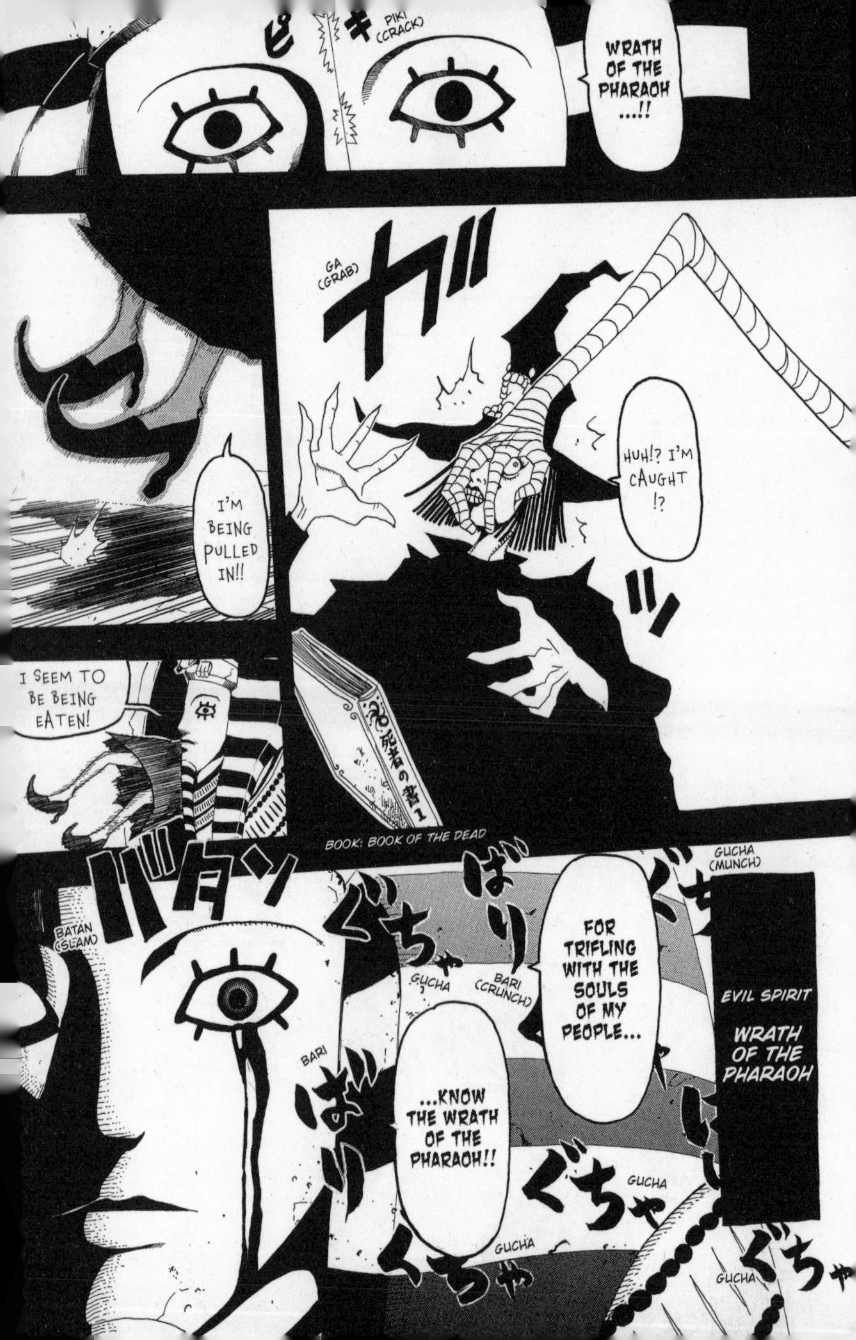
WRATH OF THE PHARAOH ....!!
PIKI (CRACK)
GA (GRAB)
HUH!? I'M CAUGHT !?
死者の書 1
BOOK: BOOK OF THE DEAD
I'M BEING PULLED IN!!
I SEEM TO BE BEING EATEN!
EVIL SPIRIT
WRATH OF THE PHARAOH
GUCHA (MUNCH)
FOR TRIFLING WITH THE SOULS OF MY PEOPLE...
BARI (CRUNCH)
GUCHA
...KNOW THE WRATH OF THE PHARAOH!!
BARI
GUCHA
GUCHA
GUCHA
BATAN (SLAM)

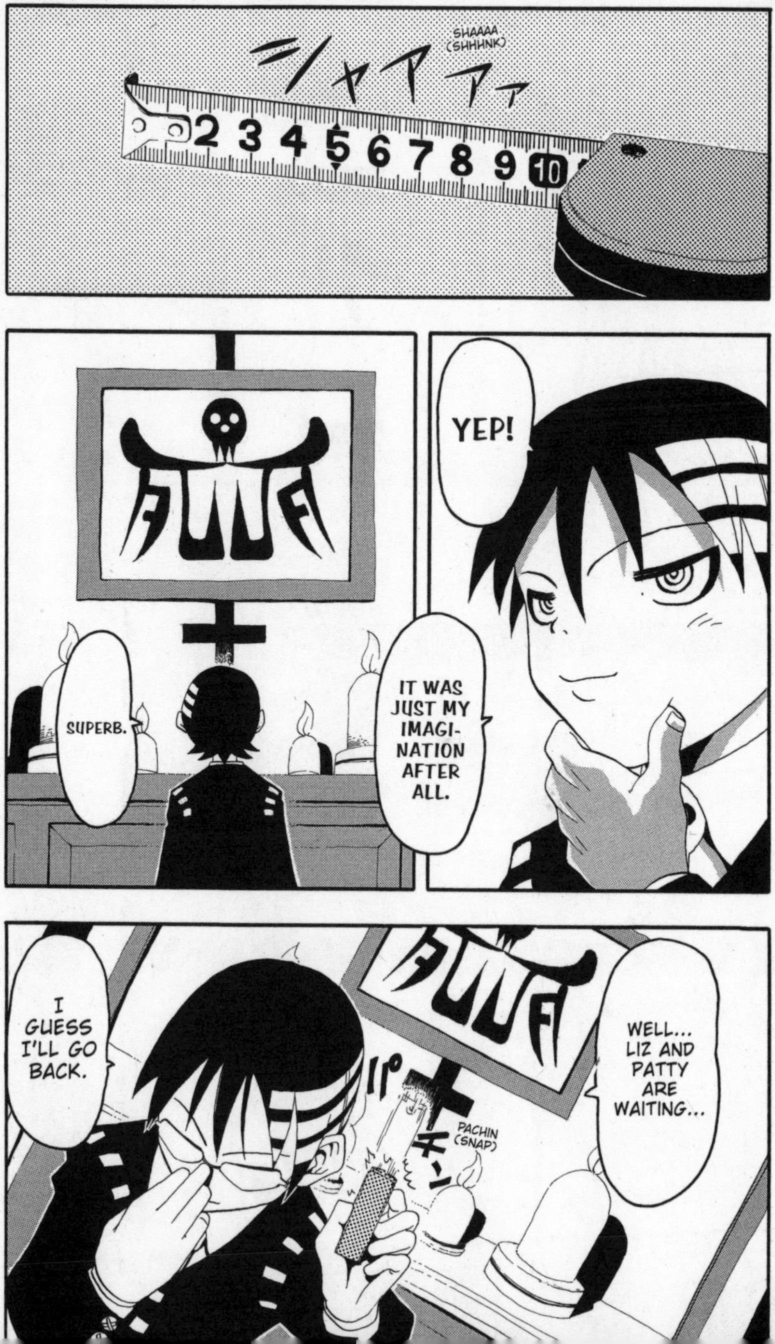
シャアァ
SHAAAA (SHHHNK)
YEP!
IT WAS JUST MY IMAGINATION AFTER ALL.
SUPERB.
WELL... LIZ AND PATTY ARE WAITING...
パチン
PACHIN (SNAP)
I GUESS I'LL GO BACK.

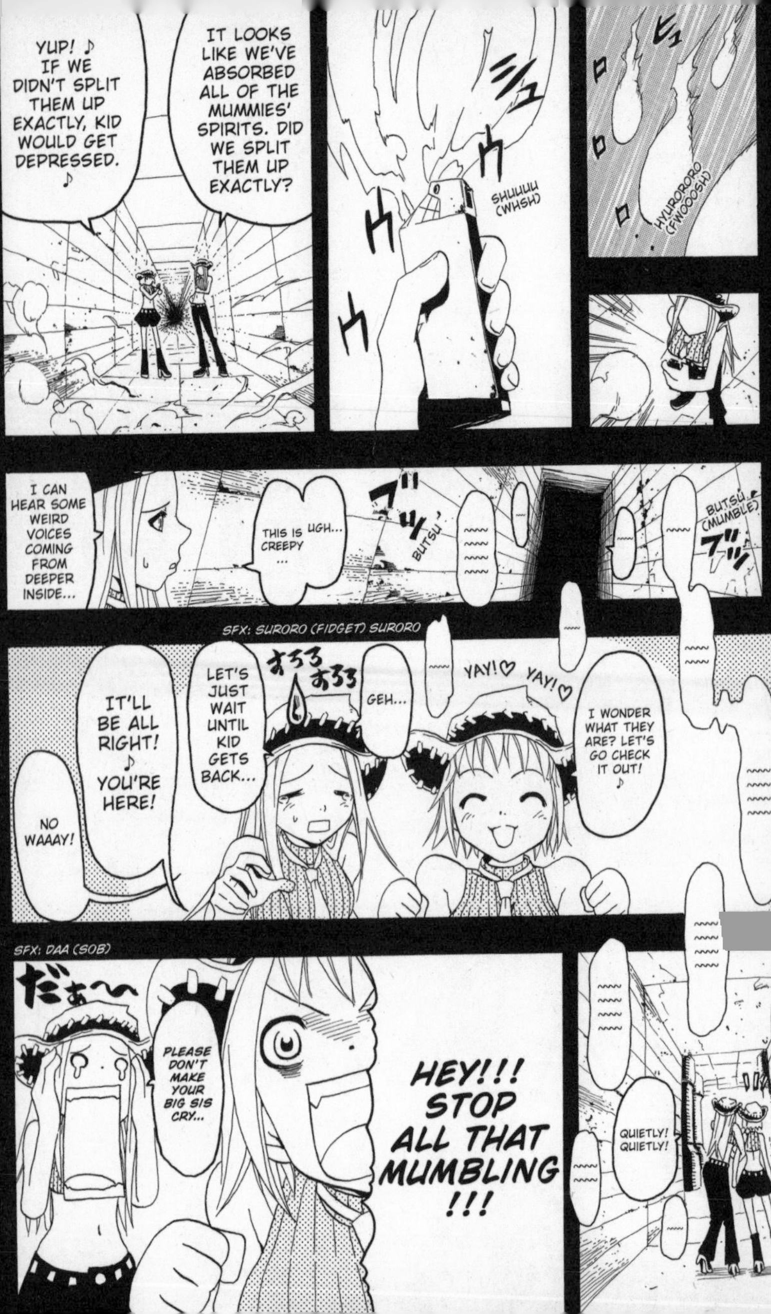
HYURORORO (FWOOOSH)
SHUUUU (WHSH)
IT LOOKS LIKE WE'VE ABSORBED ALL OF THE MUMMIES' SPIRITS. DID WE SPLIT THEM UP EXACTLY?
YUP! ♪ IF WE DIDN'T SPLIT THEM UP EXACTLY, KID WOULD GET DEPRESSED. ♪
BUTSU (MUMBLE)
BUTSU
UGH...
THIS IS CREEPY...
I CAN HEAR SOME WEIRD VOICES COMING FROM DEEPER INSIDE...
SFX: SURORO (FIDGET) SURORO
I WONDER WHAT THEY ARE? LET'S GO CHECK IT OUT! ♪
YAY!♡ YAY!♡
GEH...
LET'S JUST WAIT UNTIL KID GETS BACK...
IT'LL BE ALL RIGHT! ♪ YOU'RE HERE!
NO WAAAY!
IT'S COMING FROM THIS DIREC-TION. ♪
QUIETLY! QUIETLY!
HEY!!! STOP ALL THAT MUMBLING!!!
PLEASE DON'T MAKE YOUR BIG SIS CRY...
SFX: DAA (SOB)

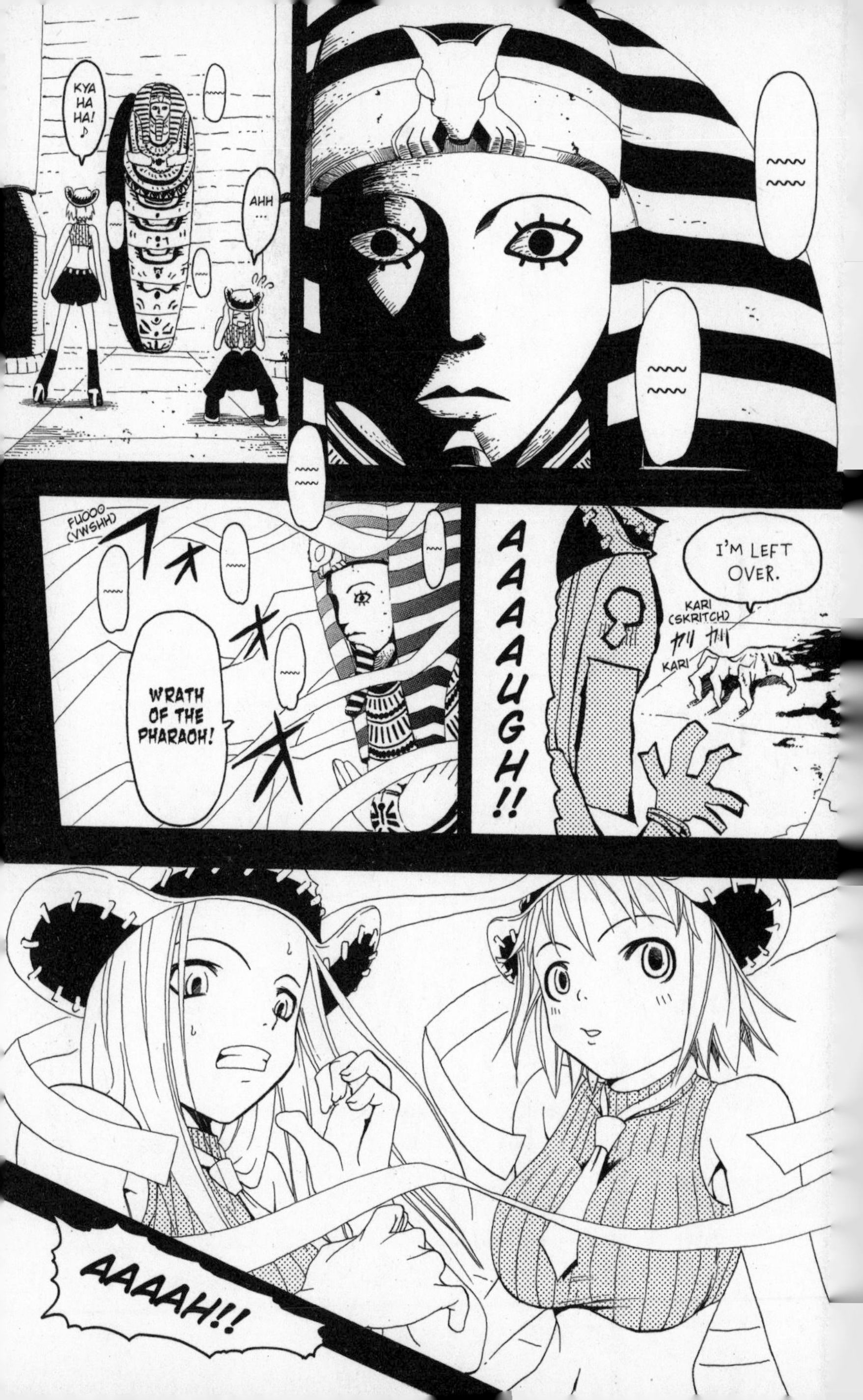
KYA HA HA! ♪
AHH ...
AAAAAUGH!!
I'M LEFT OVER.
KARI (SKRITCH)
カリ カリ
KARI
FUOOO (VWSHH)
WRATH OF THE PHARAOH!
AAAAH!!

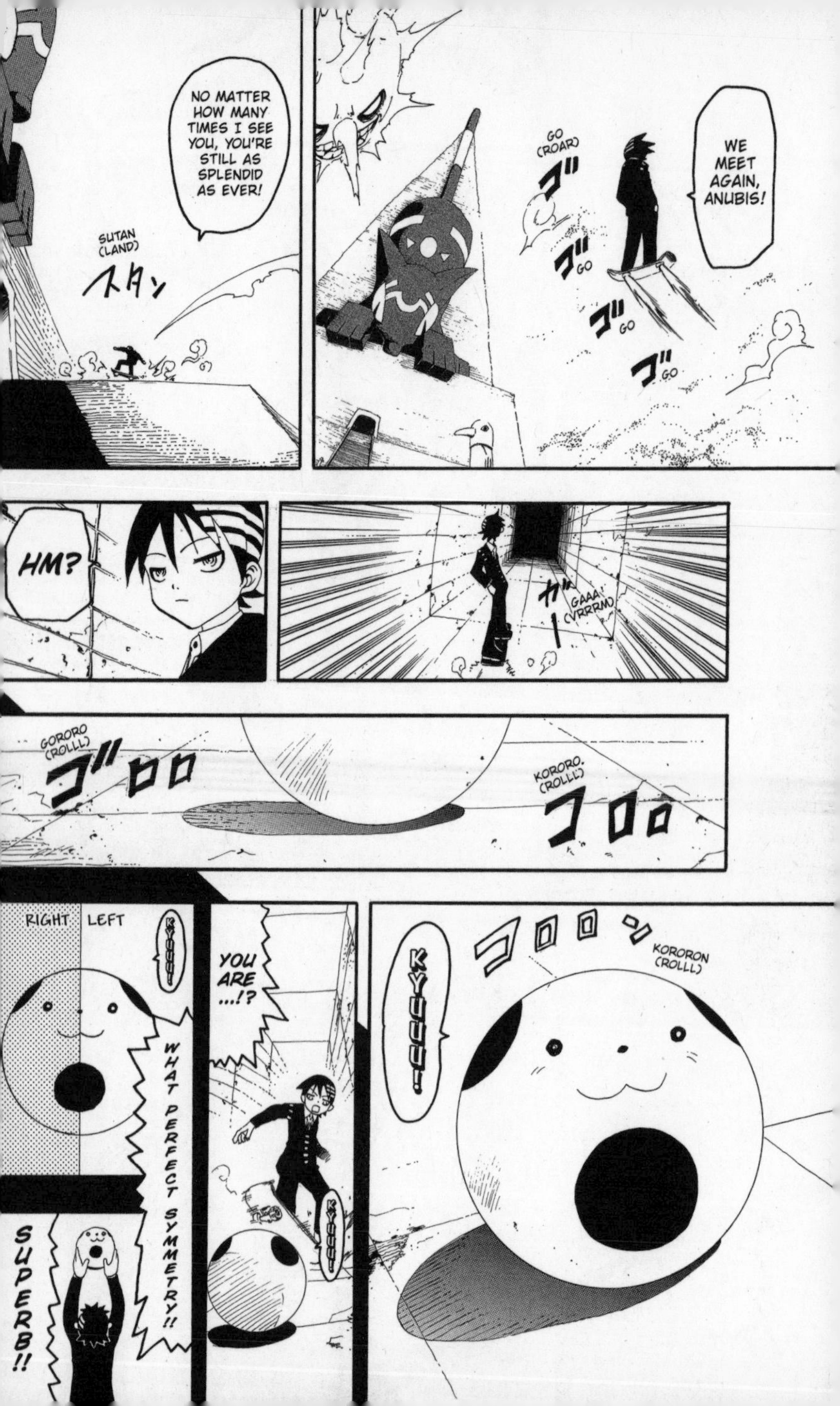

WE MEET AGAIN, ANUBIS!
GO (ROAR)
ゴ
ゴ GO
ゴ GO
ゴ GO
NO MATTER HOW MANY TIMES I SEE YOU, YOU'RE STILL AS SPLENDID AS EVER!
SUTAN (LAND)
スタン
GAAA (VRRRM)
ガー
HM?
KORORO. (ROLLL)
コロロ
GORORO (ROLLL)
ゴロロ
コロロン
KORORON (ROLLL)
KYUUUU!
YOU ARE ...!?
KYUUU!
WHAT PERFECT SYMMETRY!!
RIGHT
LEFT
KYUUU!
SUPERB!!

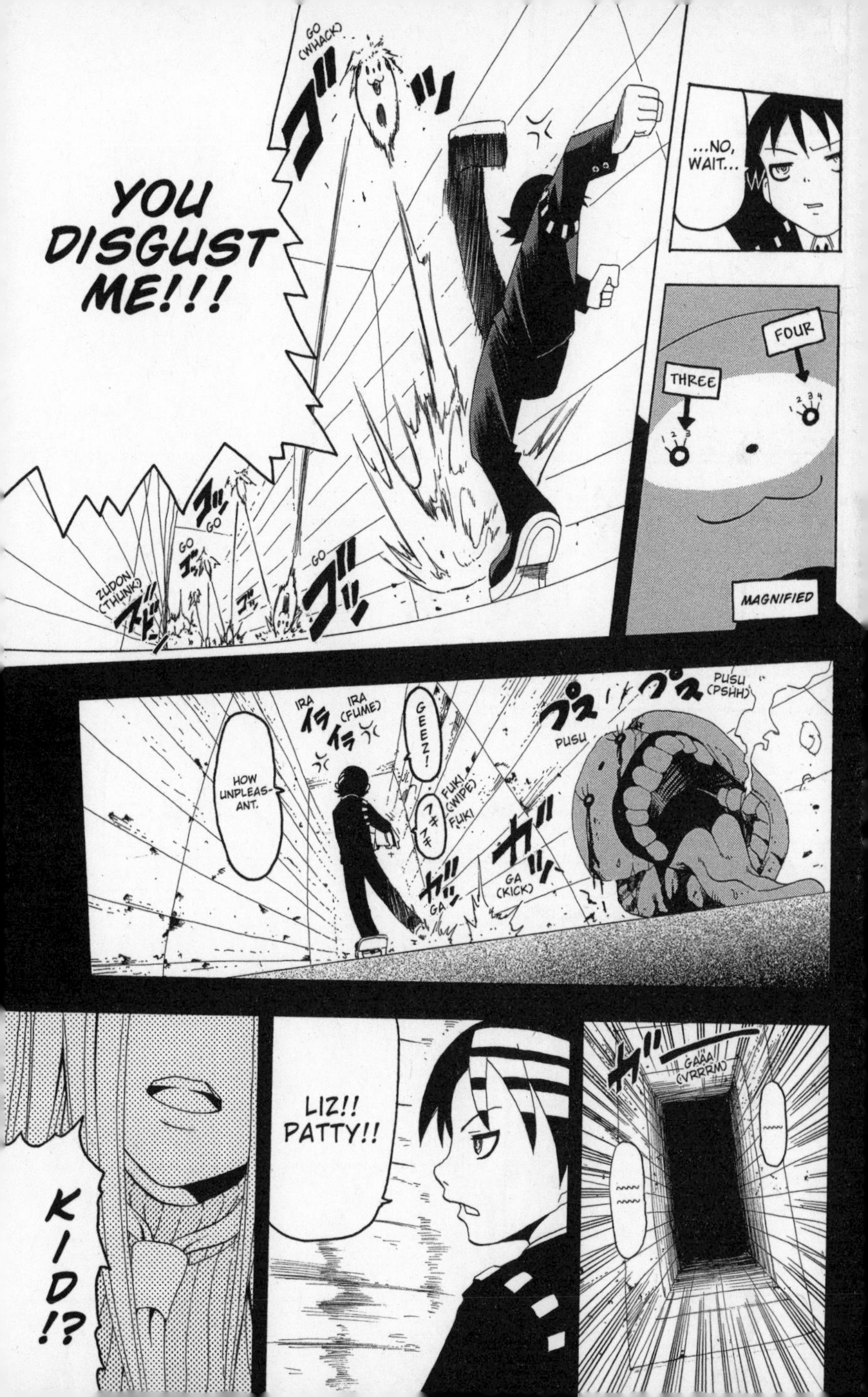
...NO, WAIT...
FOUR
THREE
MAGNIFIED
GO (WHACK)
YOU DISGUST ME!!!
GO
GO
GO
ZUDON (THUNK)
PUSU (PSHH)
PUSU
GA (KICK)
GA
FUKI (WIPE) FUKI
GEEZ!
IRA IRA (FUME)
HOW UNPLEASANT.
GAAA (VRRRM)
LIZ!! PATTY!!
KID!?

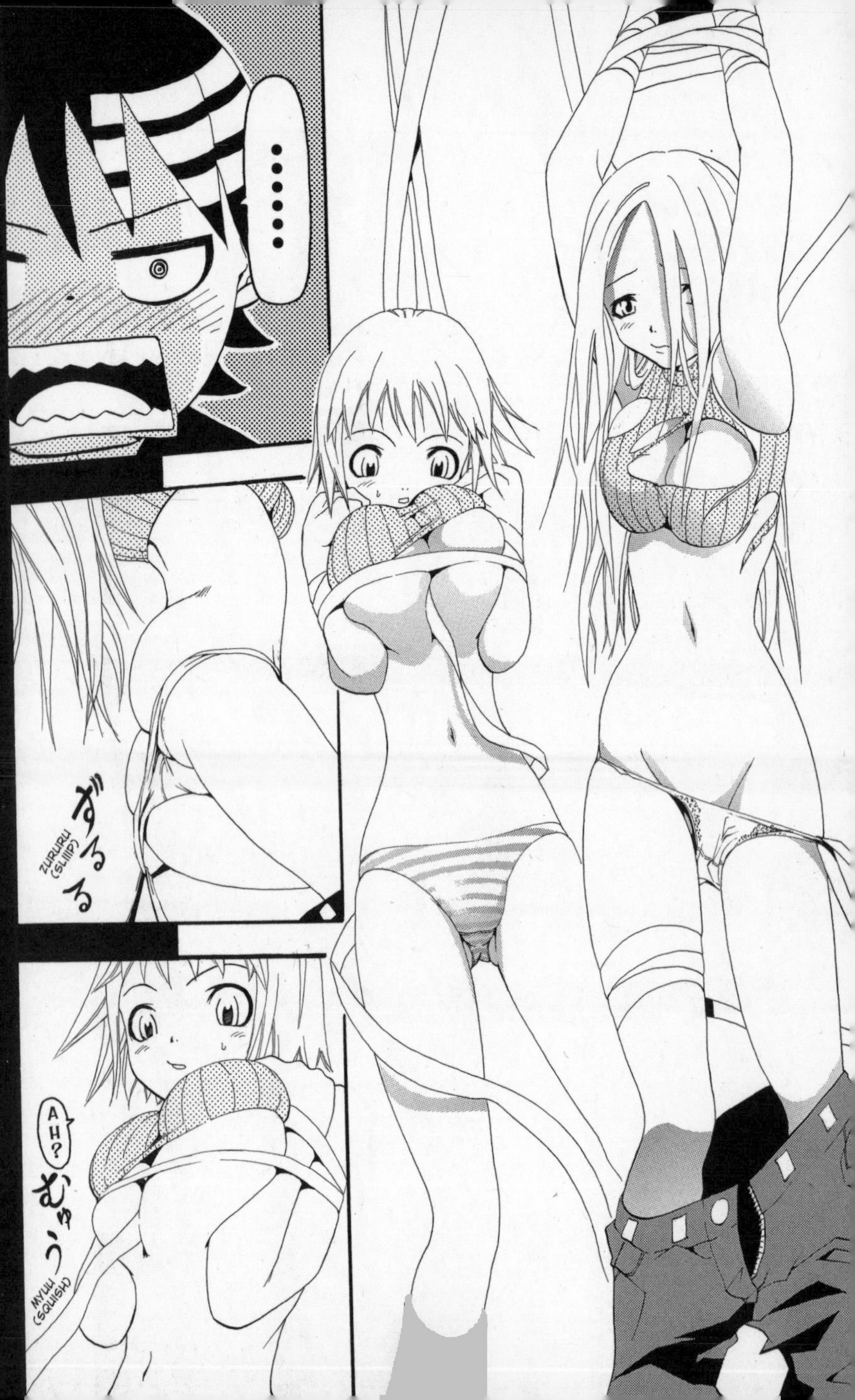
......
ずるる
ZURURU (SLIIIP)
AH?
むゅう
MYUU (SQUISH)

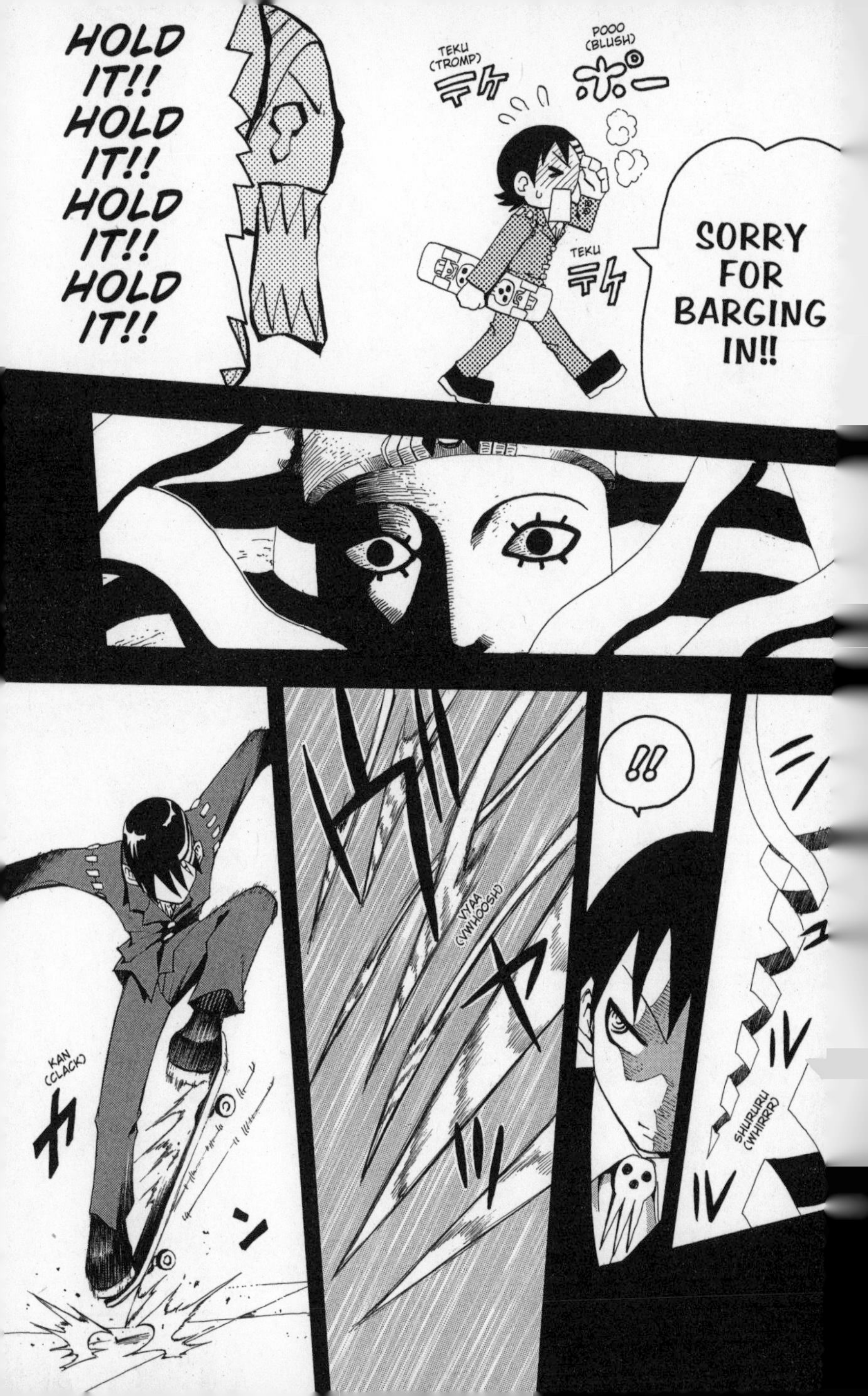
SORRY FOR BARGING IN!!
POOO (BLUSH)
TEKU (TROMP)
TEKU
HOLD IT!! HOLD IT!! HOLD IT!! HOLD IT!!
SHURURU (WHIRRR)
!!
VYAA (VWHOOSH)
KAN (CLACK)

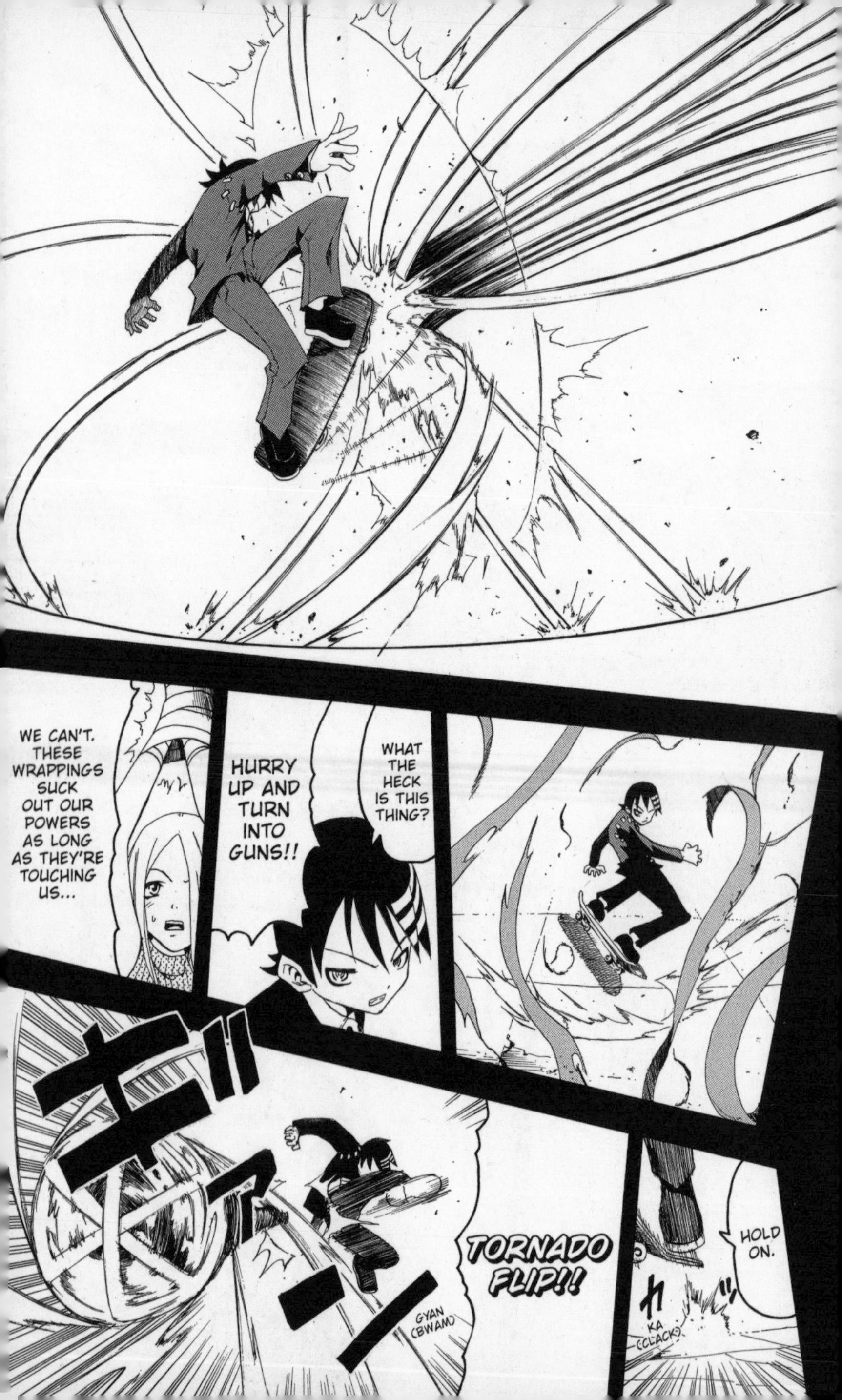
WHAT THE HECK IS THIS THING?
HURRY UP AND TURN INTO GUNS!!
WE CAN'T. THESE WRAPPINGS SUCK OUT OUR POWERS AS LONG AS THEY'RE TOUCHING US...
HOLD ON.
KA (CLACK)
TORNADO FLIP!!
GYAN (BWAM)

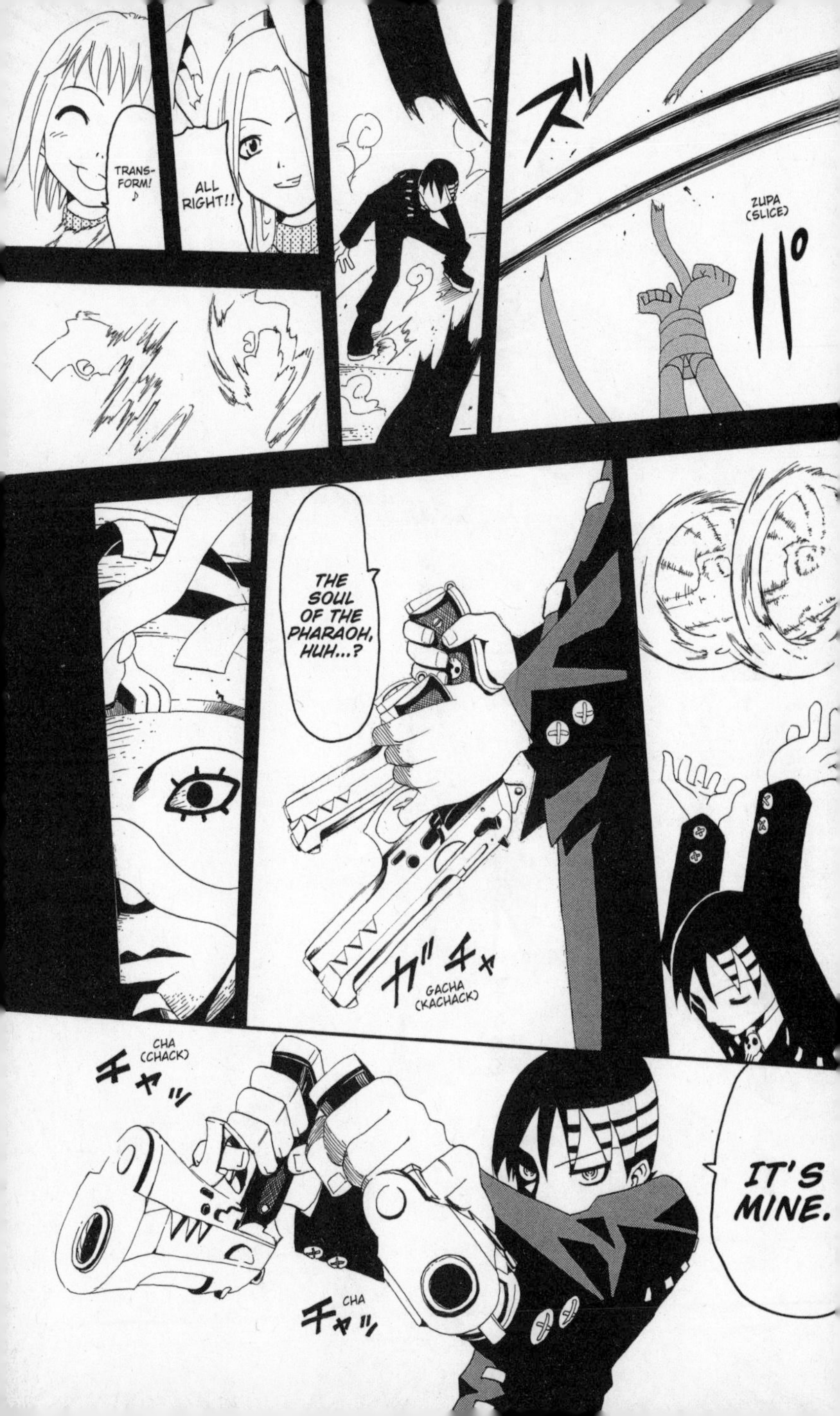
ズ
ZUPA
(SLICE)
パ
ALL
RIGHT!!
TRANS-
FORM!
♪
THE
SOUL
OF THE
PHARAOH,
HUH...?
ガチャ
GACHA
(KACHACK)
IT'S
MINE.
CHA
(CHACK)
チャッ
CHA
チャッ

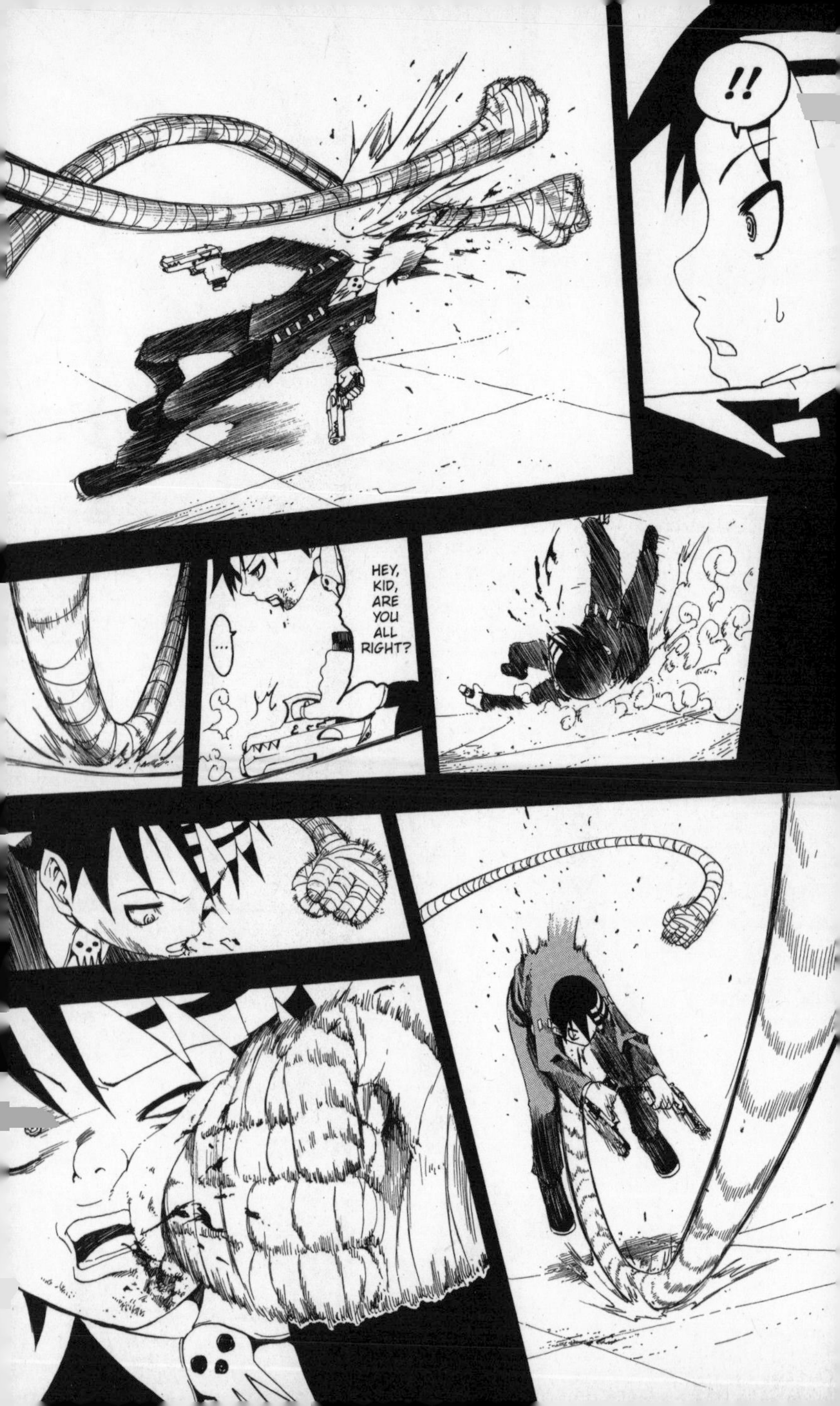
!!
HEY, KID, ARE YOU ALL RIGHT?
...

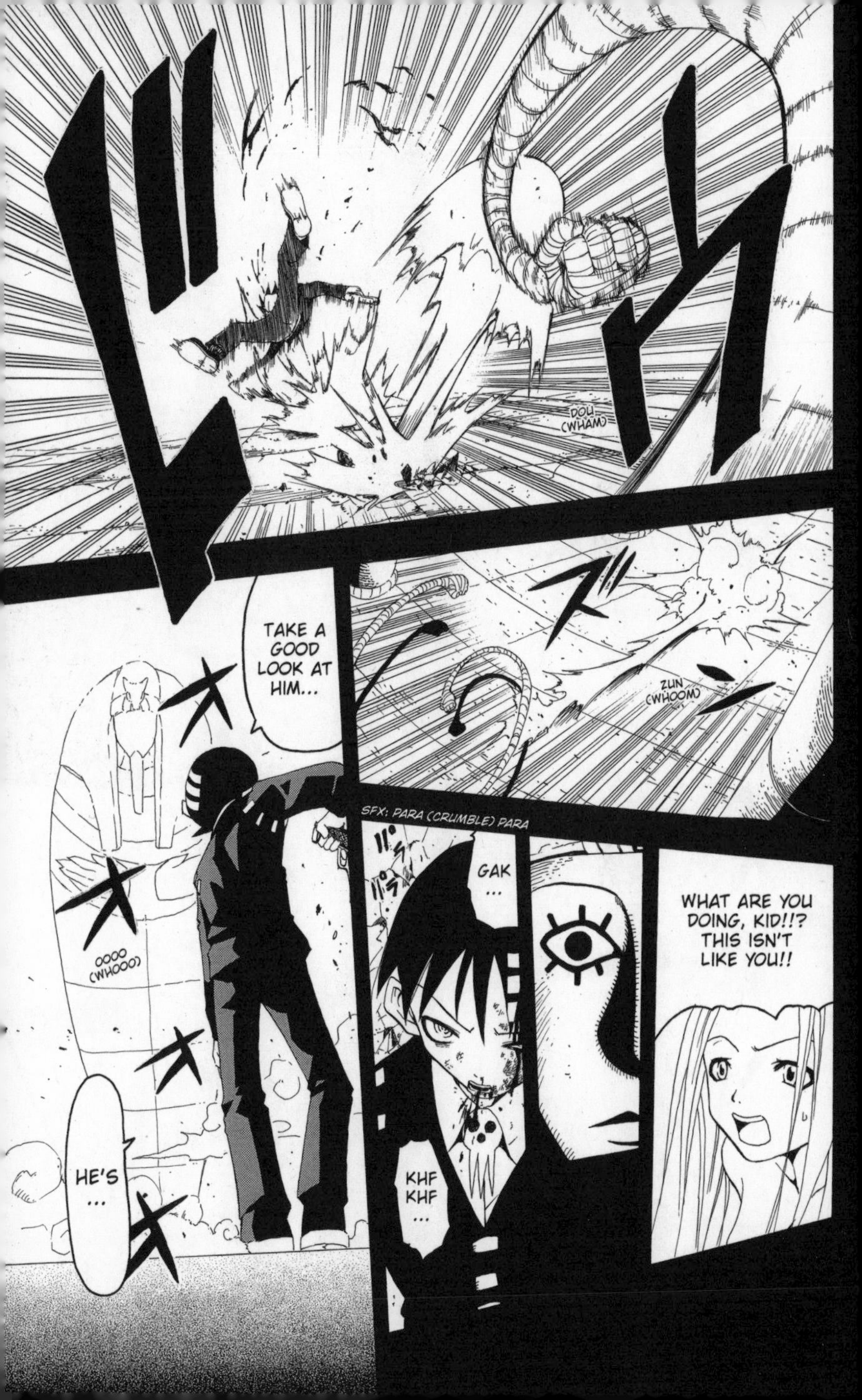
DOU (WHAM)
ZUN (WHOOM)
WHAT ARE YOU DOING, KID!!? THIS ISN'T LIKE YOU!!
SFX: PARA (CRUMBLE) PARA
GAK ...
KHF KHF ...
TAKE A GOOD LOOK AT HIM...
OOOO (WHOOO)
HE'S ...

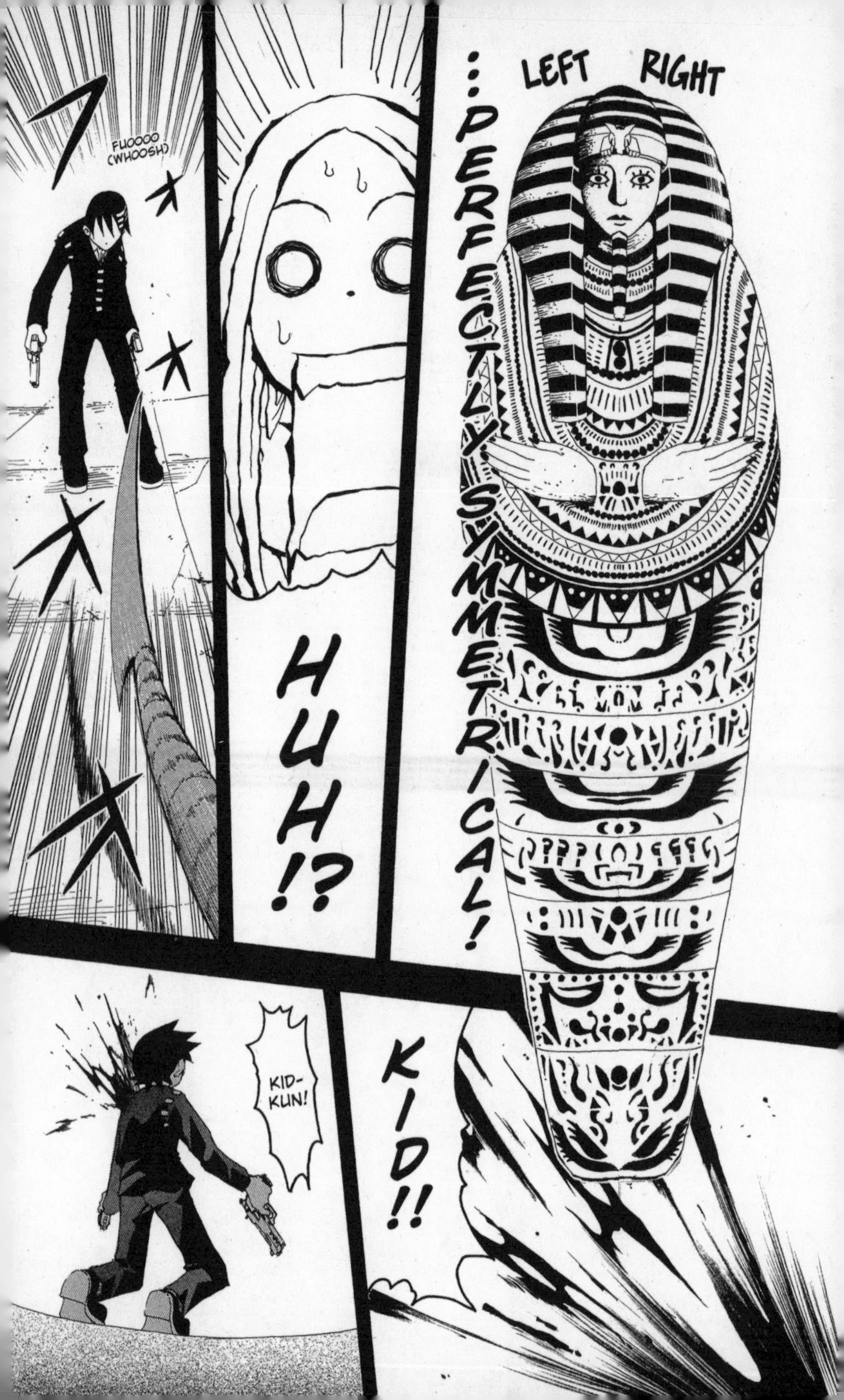
LEFT RIGHT
...PERFECTLY SYMMETRICAL!
HUH!?
FUOOOO (WHOOSH)
KID!!
KID-KUN!

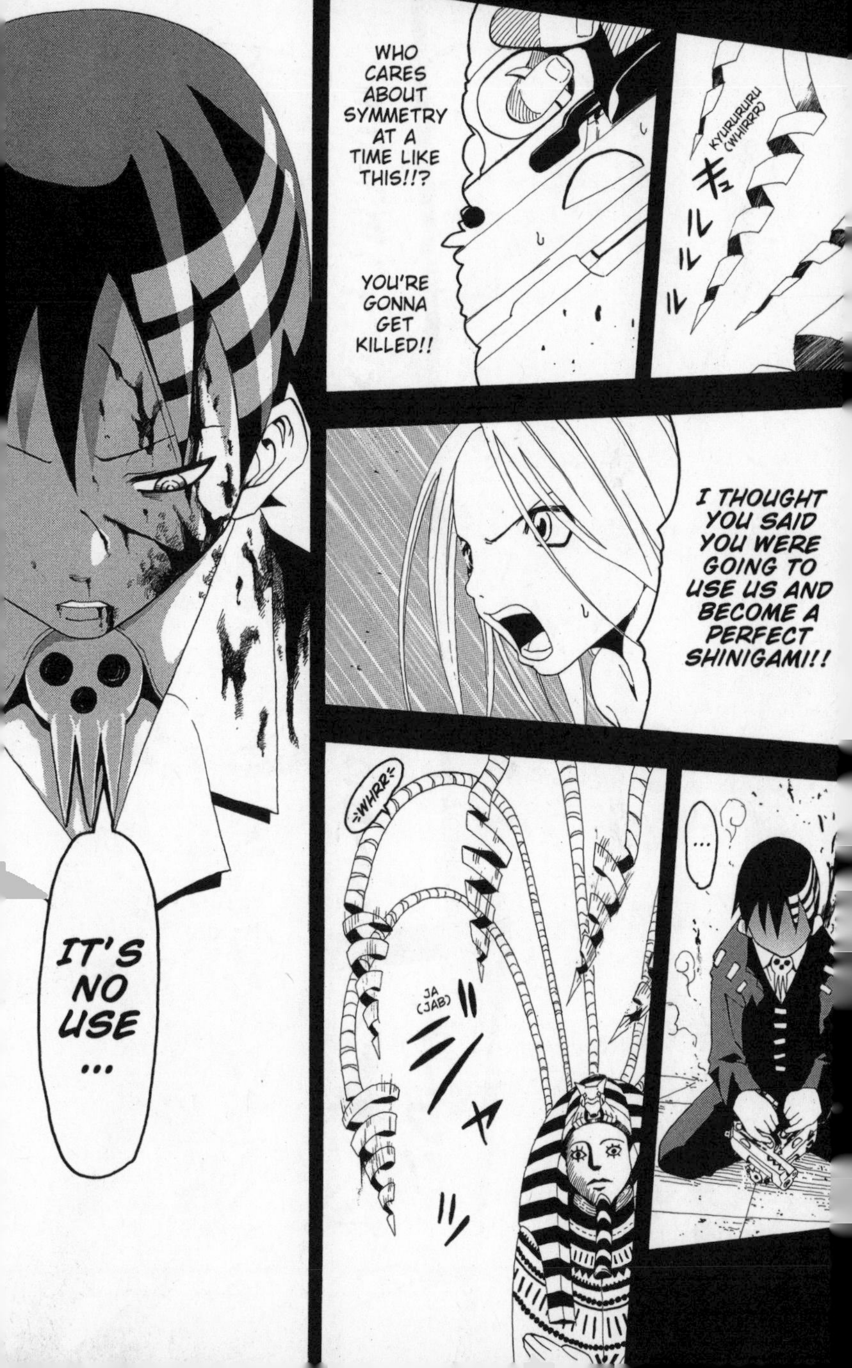
KYURURURU (WHIRRR)
WHO CARES ABOUT SYMMETRY AT A TIME LIKE THIS!!?
YOU'RE GONNA GET KILLED!!
I THOUGHT YOU SAID YOU WERE GOING TO USE US AND BECOME A PERFECT SHINIGAMI!!
...
WHRR
JA (JAB)
IT'S NO USE...

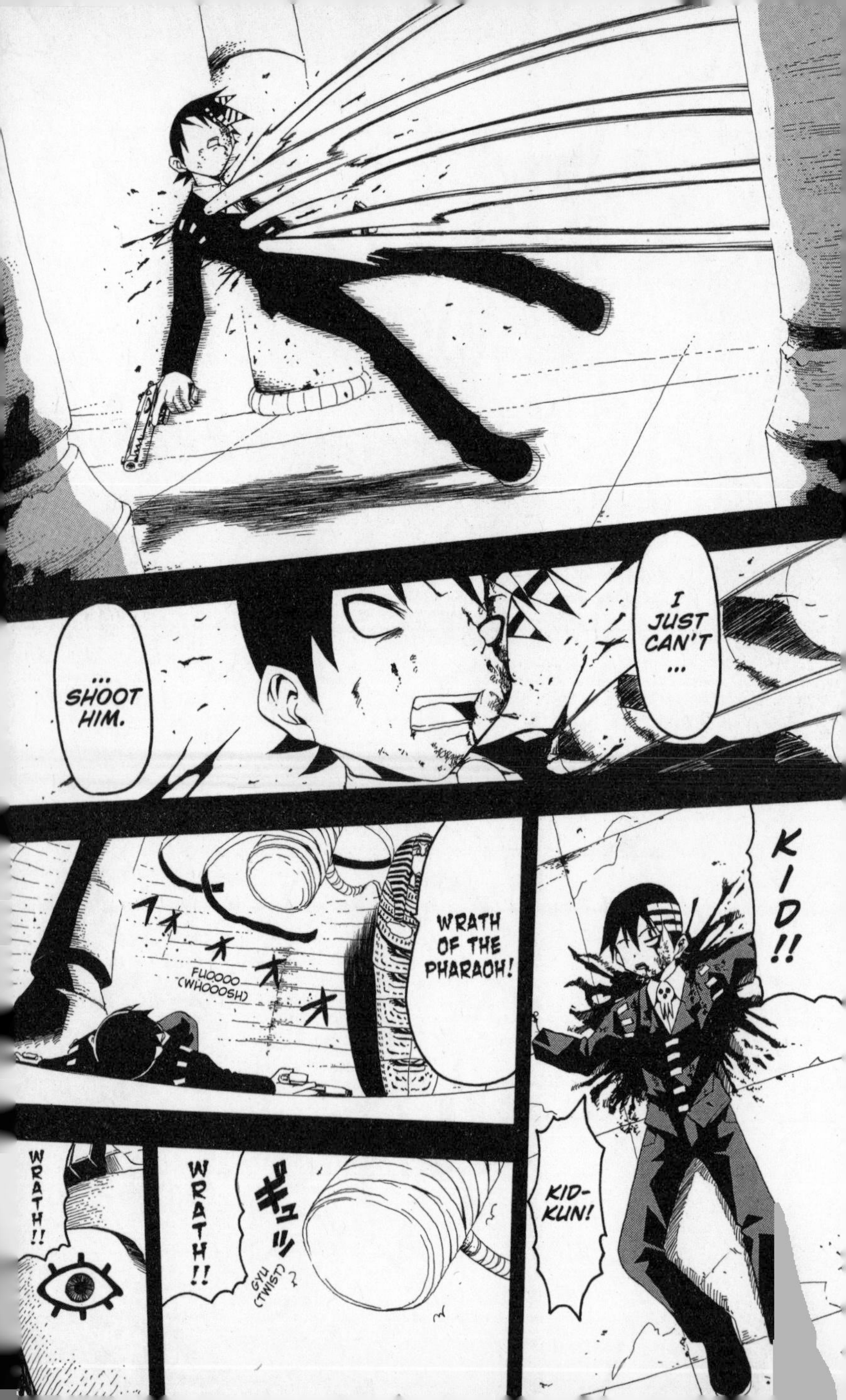
I JUST CAN'T ...
... SHOOT HIM.
KID!!
KID-KUN!
WRATH OF THE PHARAOH!
FUOOOO (WHOOOSH)
ギュッ
GYU (TWIST)
WRATH!!
WRATH!!

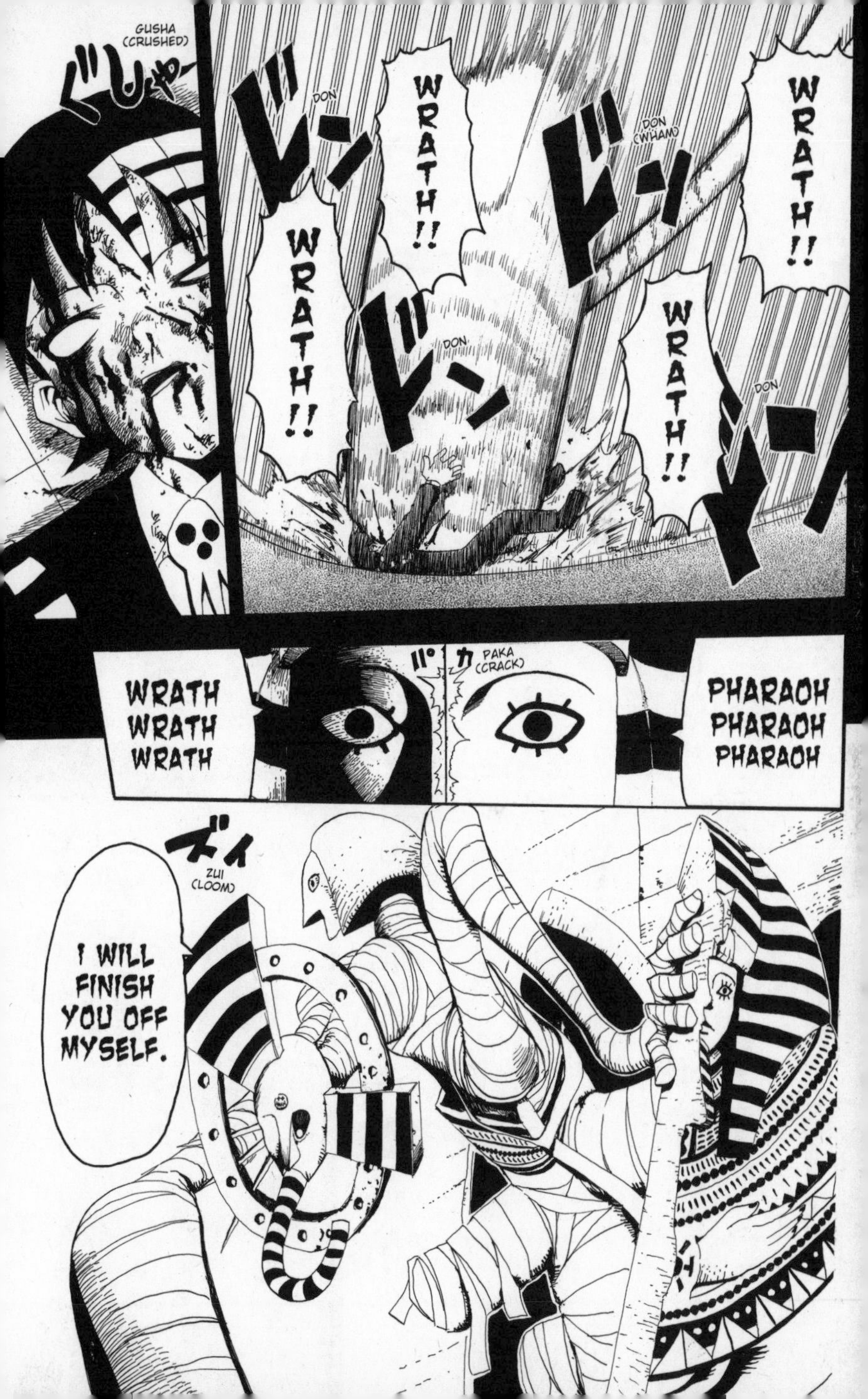
WRATH!!
DON (WHAM)
WRATH!!
DON
WRATH!!
DON
DON
WRATH!!
GUSHA (CRUSHED)
PHARAOH PHARAOH PHARAOH
PAKA (CRACK)
WRATH WRATH WRATH
ZUI (LOOM)
I WILL FINISH YOU OFF MYSELF.

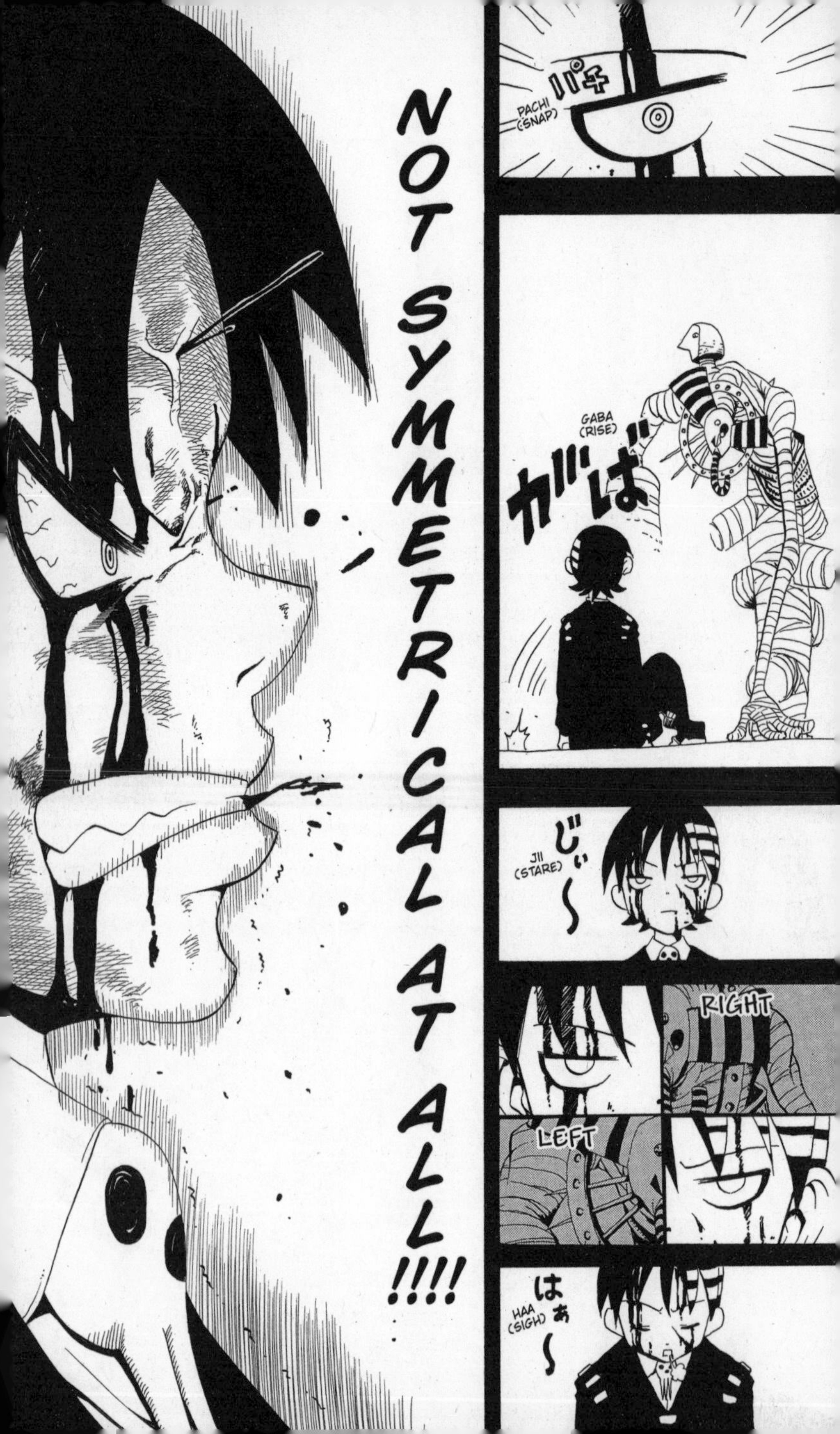
パチ
PACHI (SNAP)
ガば
GABA (RISE)
じぃ～
JII (STARE)
RIGHT
LEFT
はぁ～
HAA (SIGH)
NOT SYMMETRICAL AT ALL!!!!

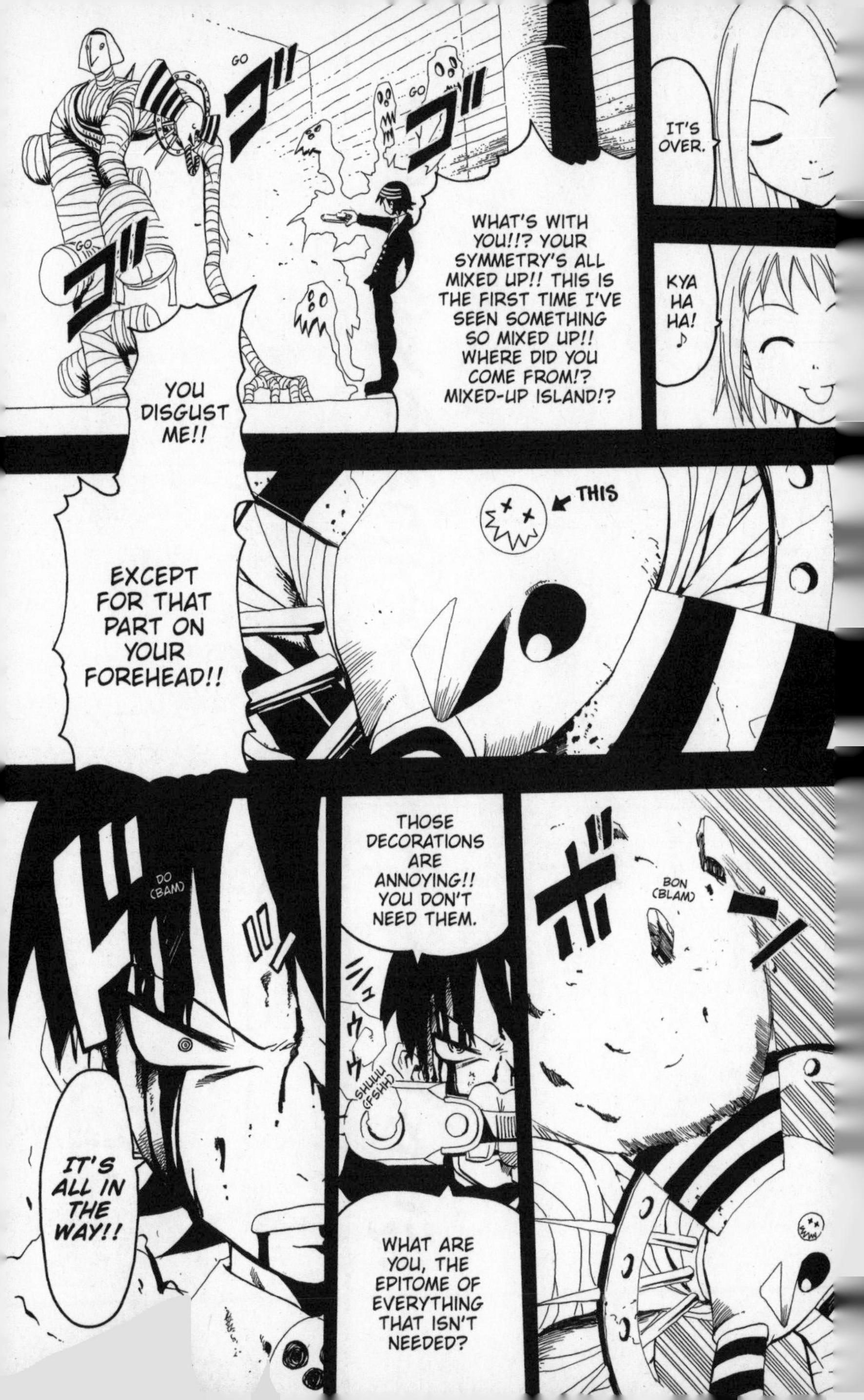
IT'S OVER.
KYA HA HA! ♪
GO
GO
GO
WHAT'S WITH YOU!!? YOUR SYMMETRY'S ALL MIXED UP!! THIS IS THE FIRST TIME I'VE SEEN SOMETHING SO MIXED UP!! WHERE DID YOU COME FROM!? MIXED-UP ISLAND!?
YOU DISGUST ME!!
THIS
EXCEPT FOR THAT PART ON YOUR FOREHEAD!!
BON (BLAM)
THOSE DECORATIONS ARE ANNOYING!! YOU DON'T NEED THEM.
SHUUU (FSHH)
WHAT ARE YOU, THE EPITOME OF EVERYTHING THAT ISN'T NEEDED?
DO (BAM)
IT'S ALL IN THE WAY!!

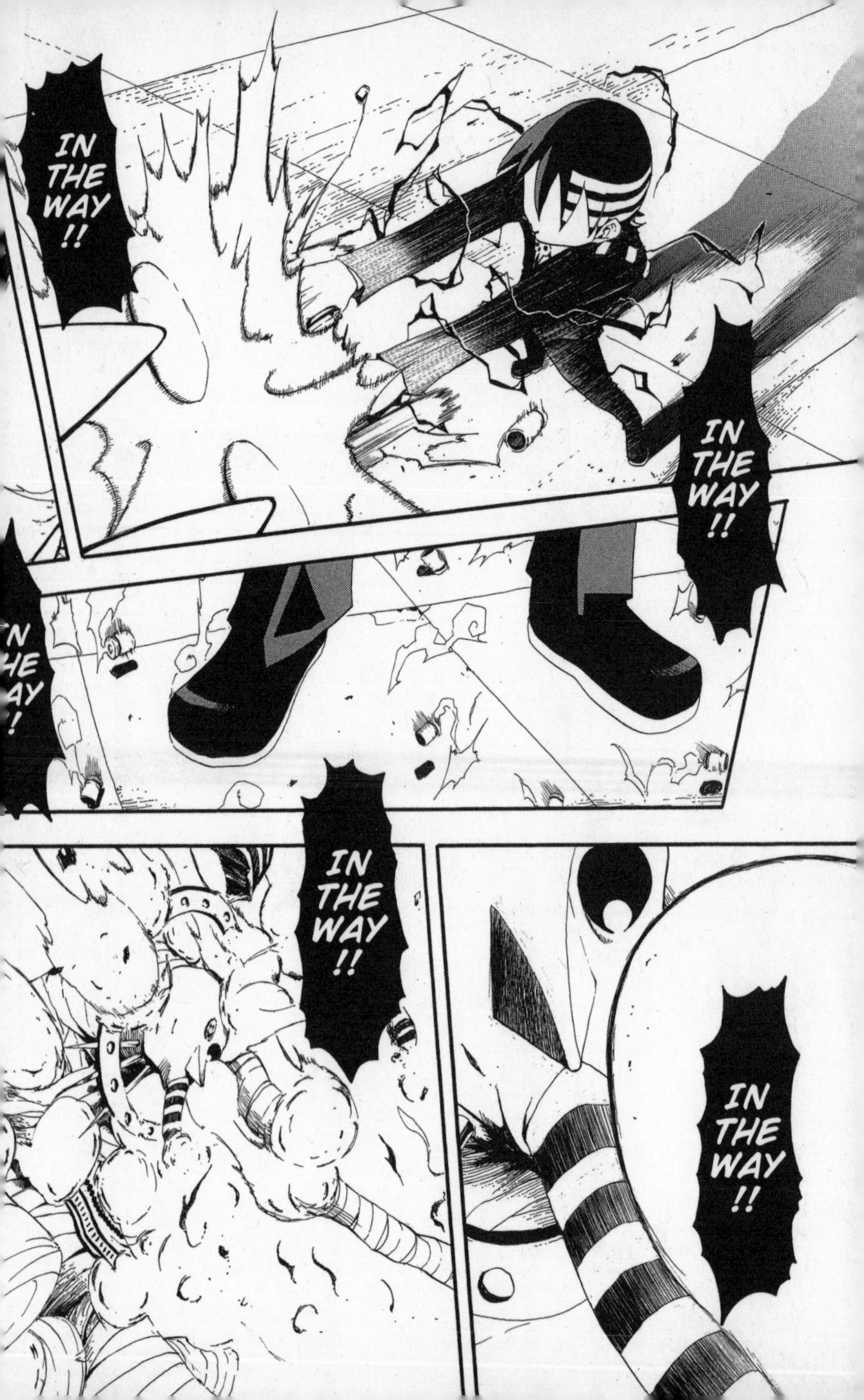
IN THE WAY!!
IN THE WAY!!
IN THE WAY!!
IN THE WAY!!

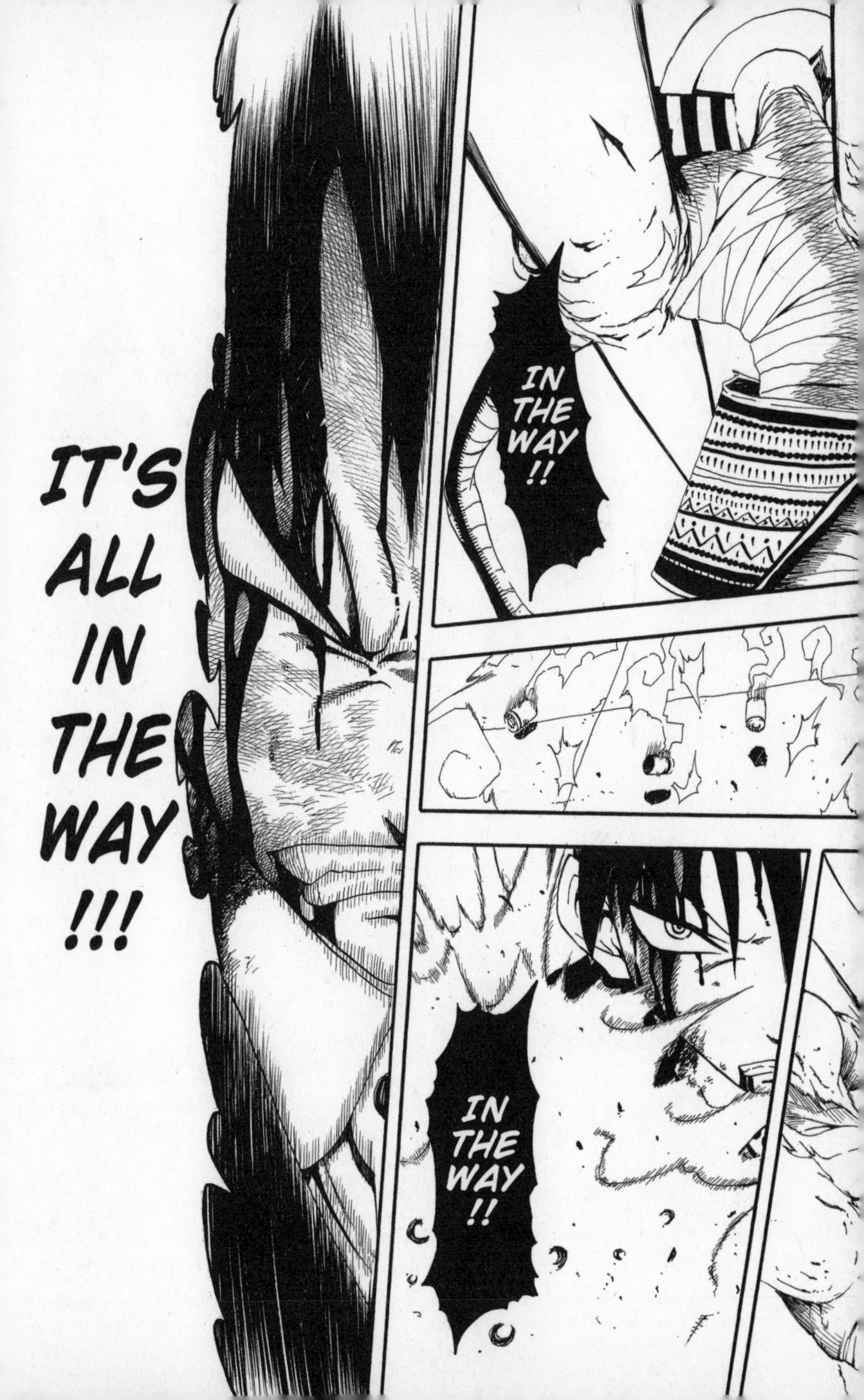
IN THE WAY!!
IN THE WAY!!
IT'S ALL IN THE WAY!!!

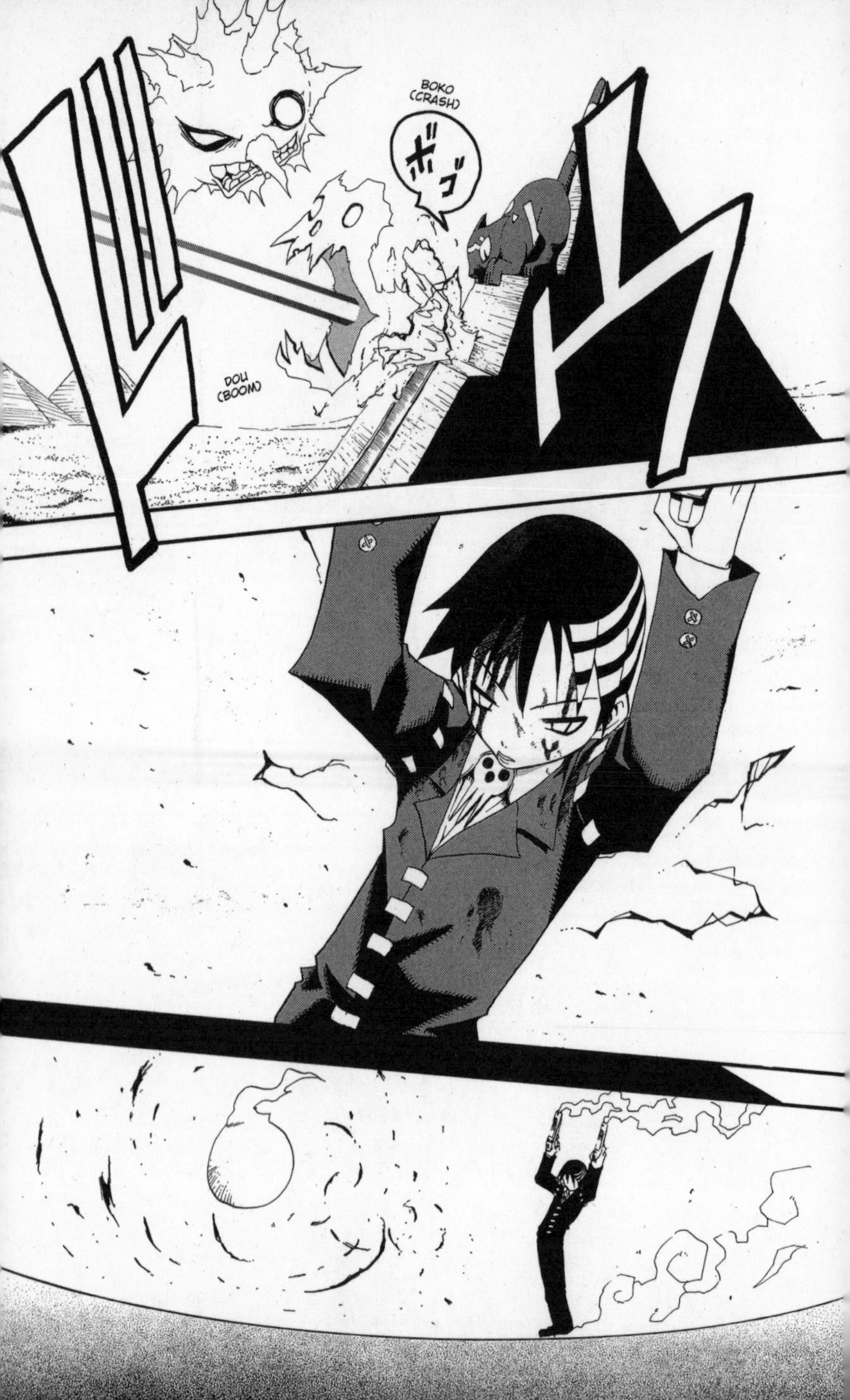

BOKO (CRASH)
ボゴ
DOU (BOOM)

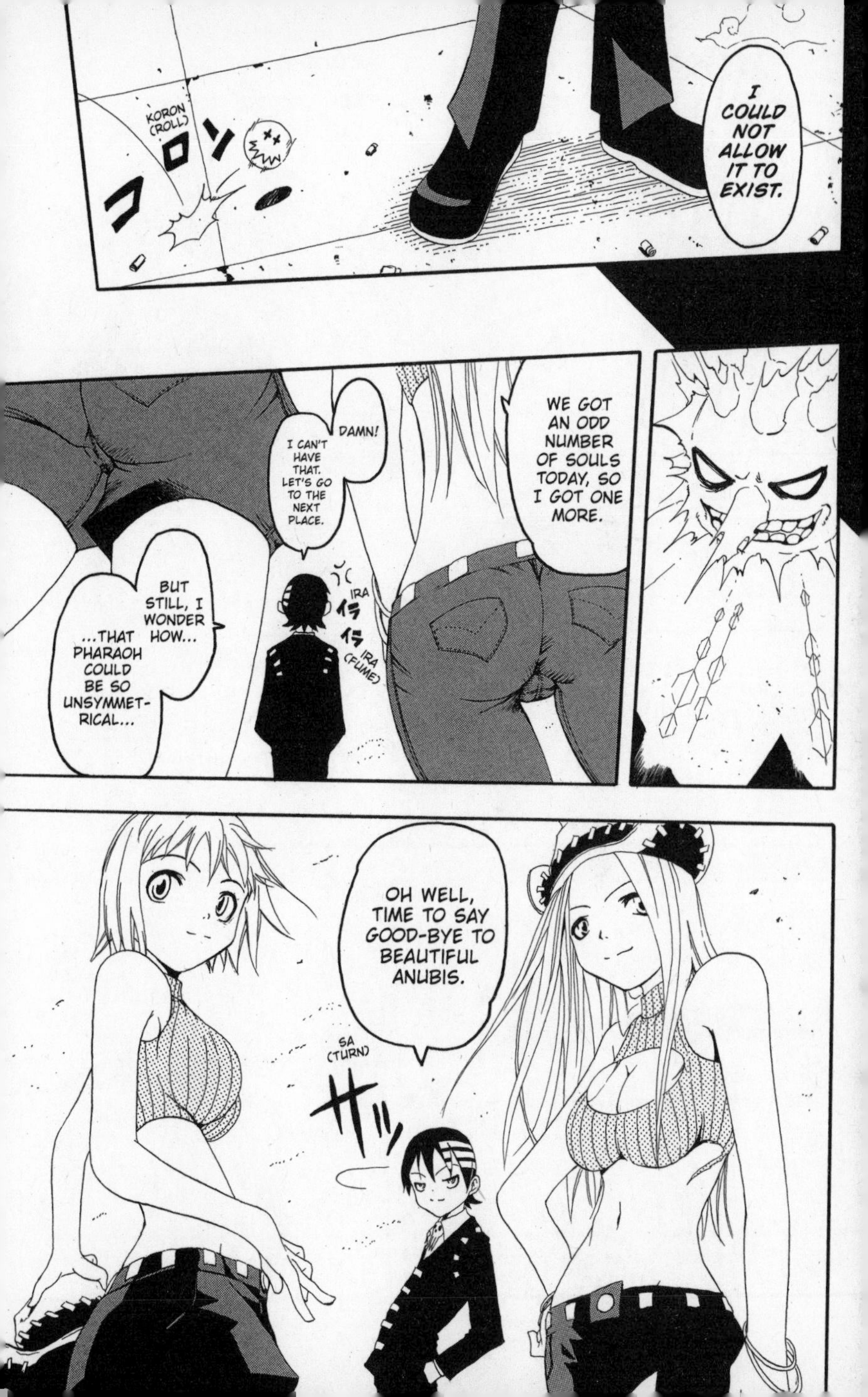
I COULD NOT ALLOW IT TO EXIST.
KORON (ROLL)
WE GOT AN ODD NUMBER OF SOULS TODAY, SO I GOT ONE MORE.
DAMN!
I CAN'T HAVE THAT. LET'S GO TO THE NEXT PLACE.
IRA
IRA (FUME)
BUT STILL, I WONDER HOW...
...THAT PHARAOH COULD BE SO UNSYMMETRICAL...
OH WELL, TIME TO SAY GOOD-BYE TO BEAUTIFUL ANUBIS.
SA (TURN)

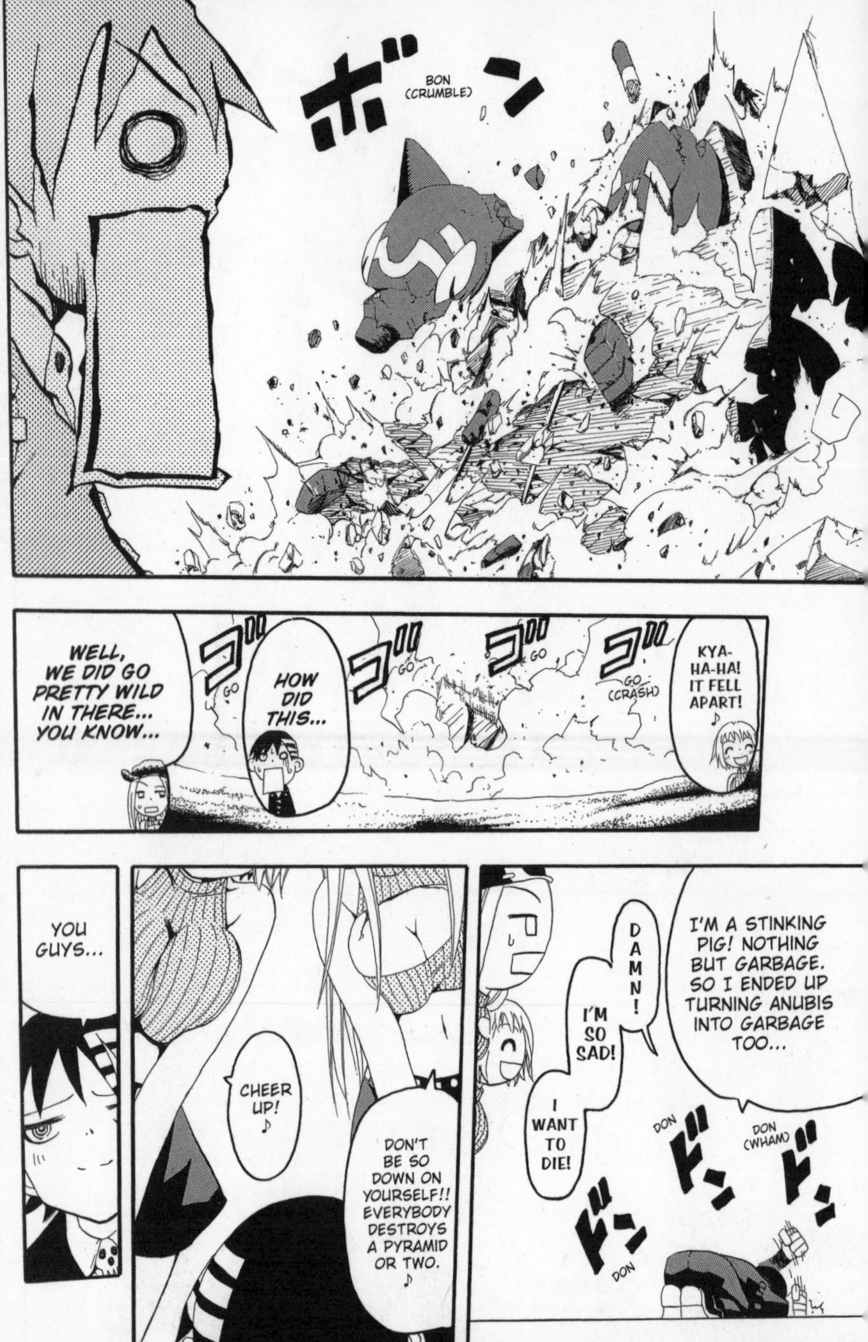
BON (CRUMBLE)
KYA-HA-HA! IT FELL APART! ♪
GO (CRASH)
GO
GO
HOW DID THIS...
GO
WELL, WE DID GO PRETTY WILD IN THERE... YOU KNOW...
I'M A STINKING PIG! NOTHING BUT GARBAGE. SO I ENDED UP TURNING ANUBIS INTO GARBAGE TOO...
DAMN!
I'M SO SAD!
I WANT TO DIE!
DON (WHAM)
DON
DON
CHEER UP! ♪
DON'T BE SO DOWN ON YOURSELF!! EVERYBODY DESTROYS A PYRAMID OR TWO. ♪
YOU GUYS...

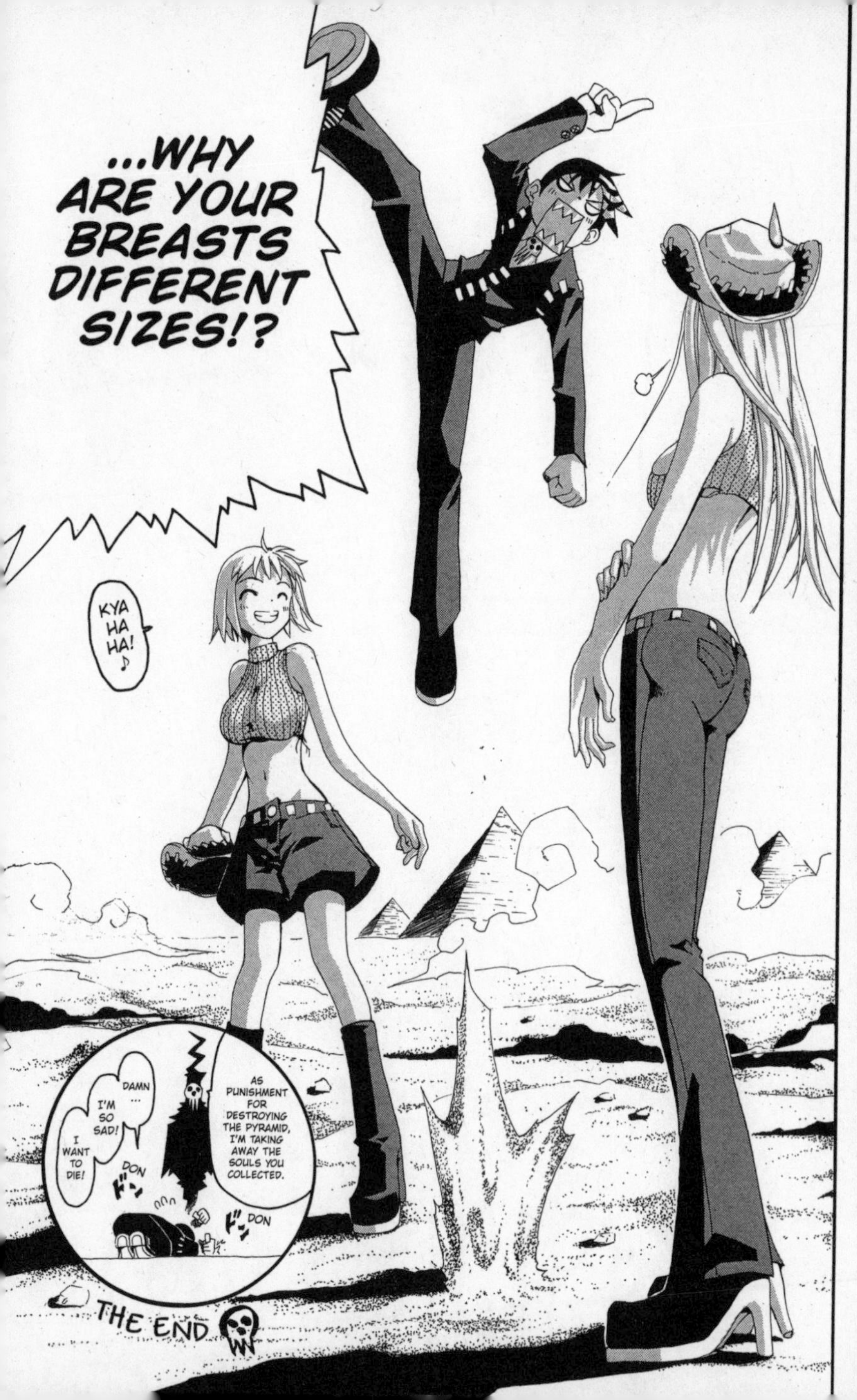
...WHY ARE YOUR BREASTS DIFFERENT SIZES!?
KYA HA HA! ♪
AS PUNISHMENT FOR DESTROYING THE PYRAMID, I'M TAKING AWAY THE SOULS YOU COLLECTED.
DAMN ...
I'M SO SAD!
I WANT TO DIE!
DON
DON
THE END

SOUL EATER

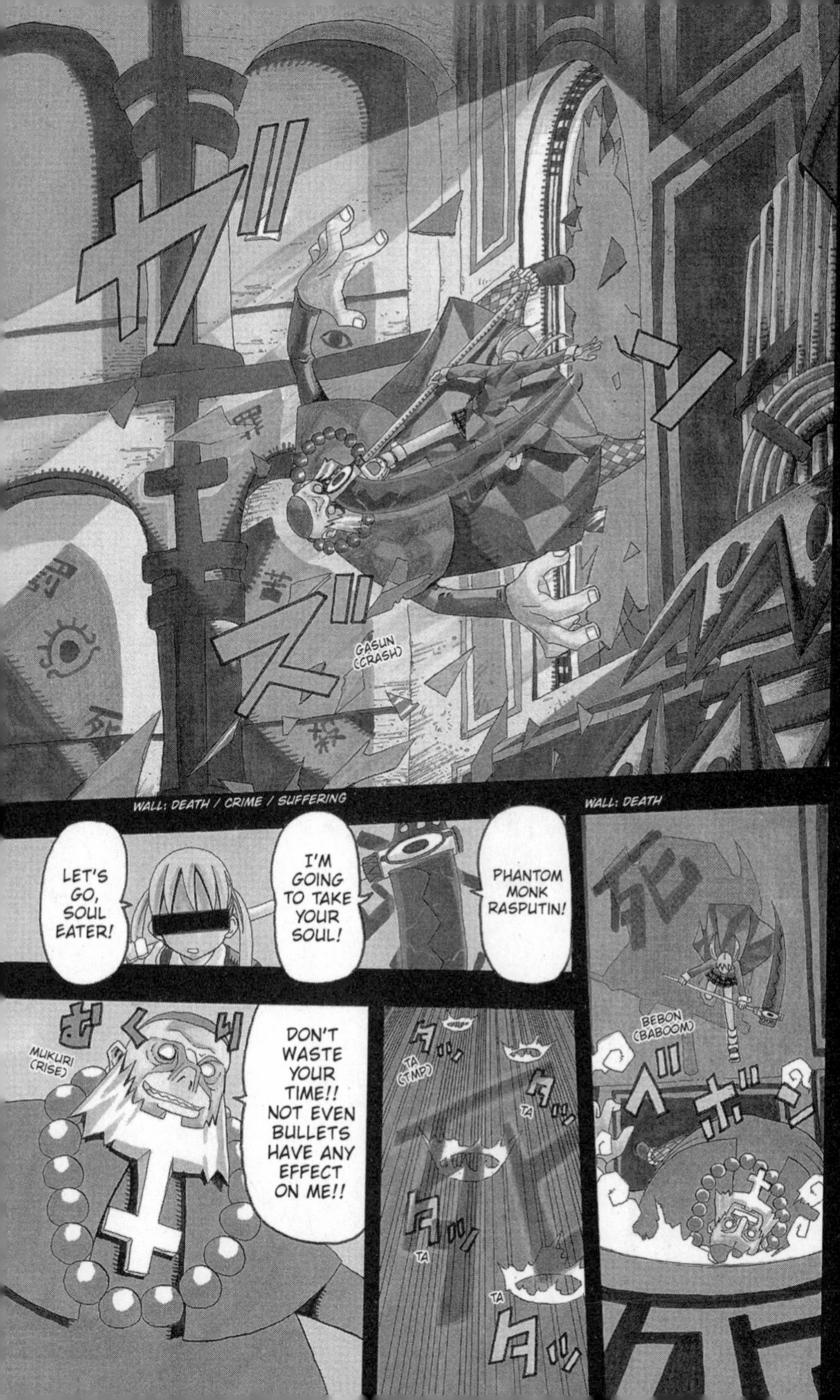
GASUN (CRASH)
WALL: DEATH / CRIME / SUFFERING
WALL: DEATH
BEBON (BABOOM)
PHANTOM MONK RASPUTIN!
I'M GOING TO TAKE YOUR SOUL!
LET'S GO, SOUL EATER!
TA (TMP)
TA
TA
TA
DON'T WASTE YOUR TIME!! NOT EVEN BULLETS HAVE ANY EFFECT ON ME!!
MUKURI (RISE)

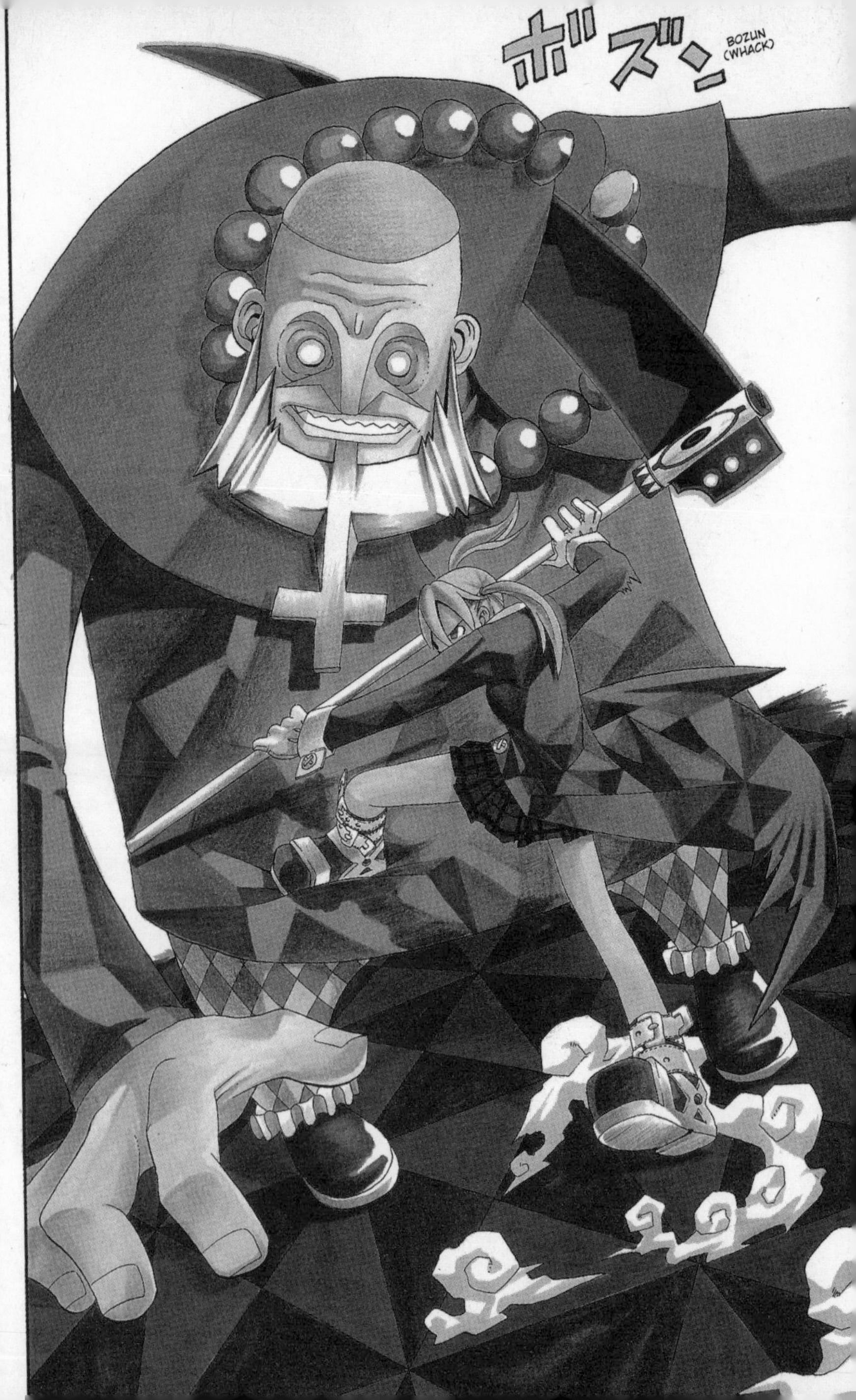
ボズン
BOZUN (WHACK)

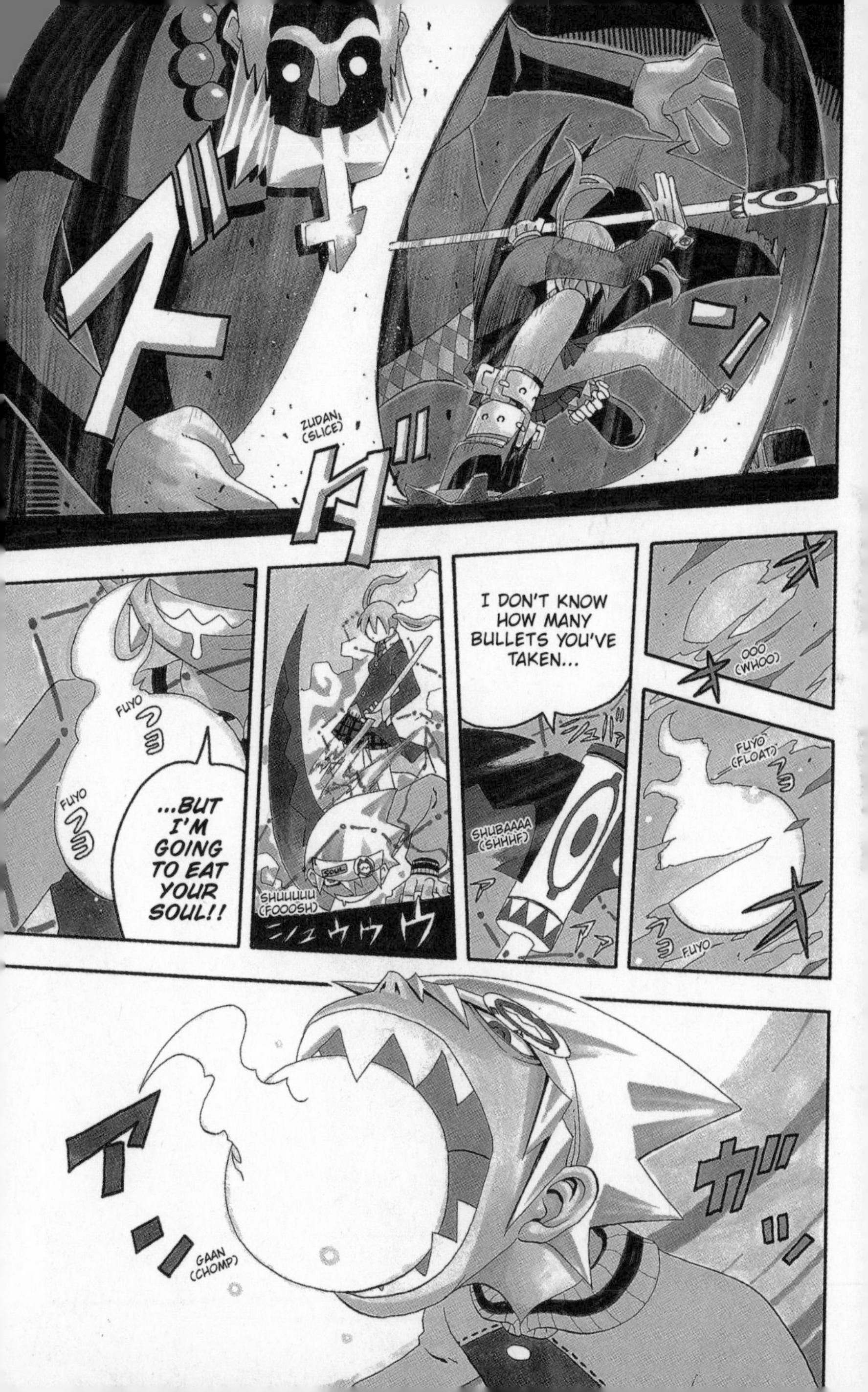
ZUDAN (SLICE)
OOO (WHOO)
FUYO (FLOAT)
FUYO
I DON'T KNOW HOW MANY BULLETS YOU'VE TAKEN...
SHUBAAAA (SHHHF)
SHUUUUU (FOOOSH)
FUYO
FUYO
...BUT I'M GOING TO EAT YOUR SOUL!!
GAAN (CHOMP)

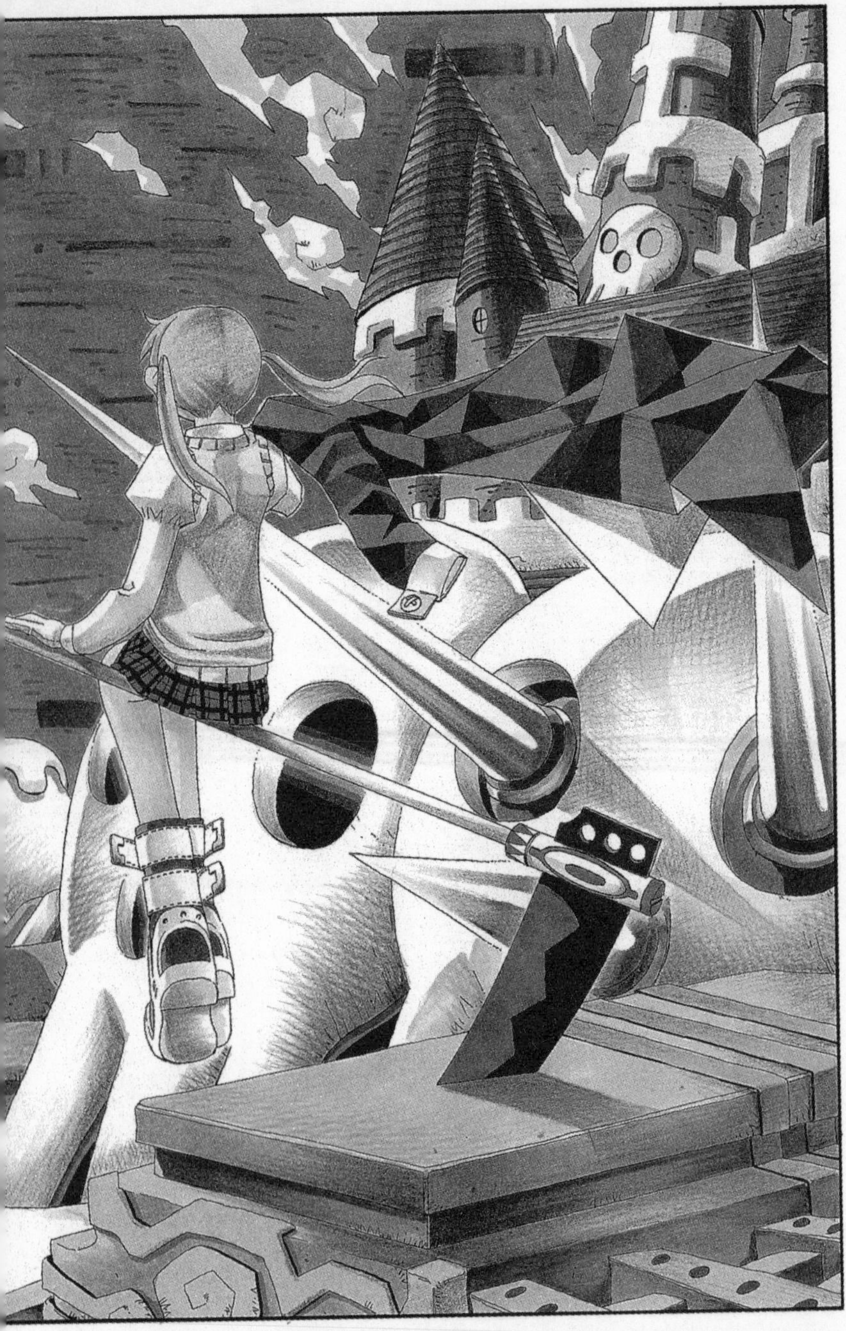

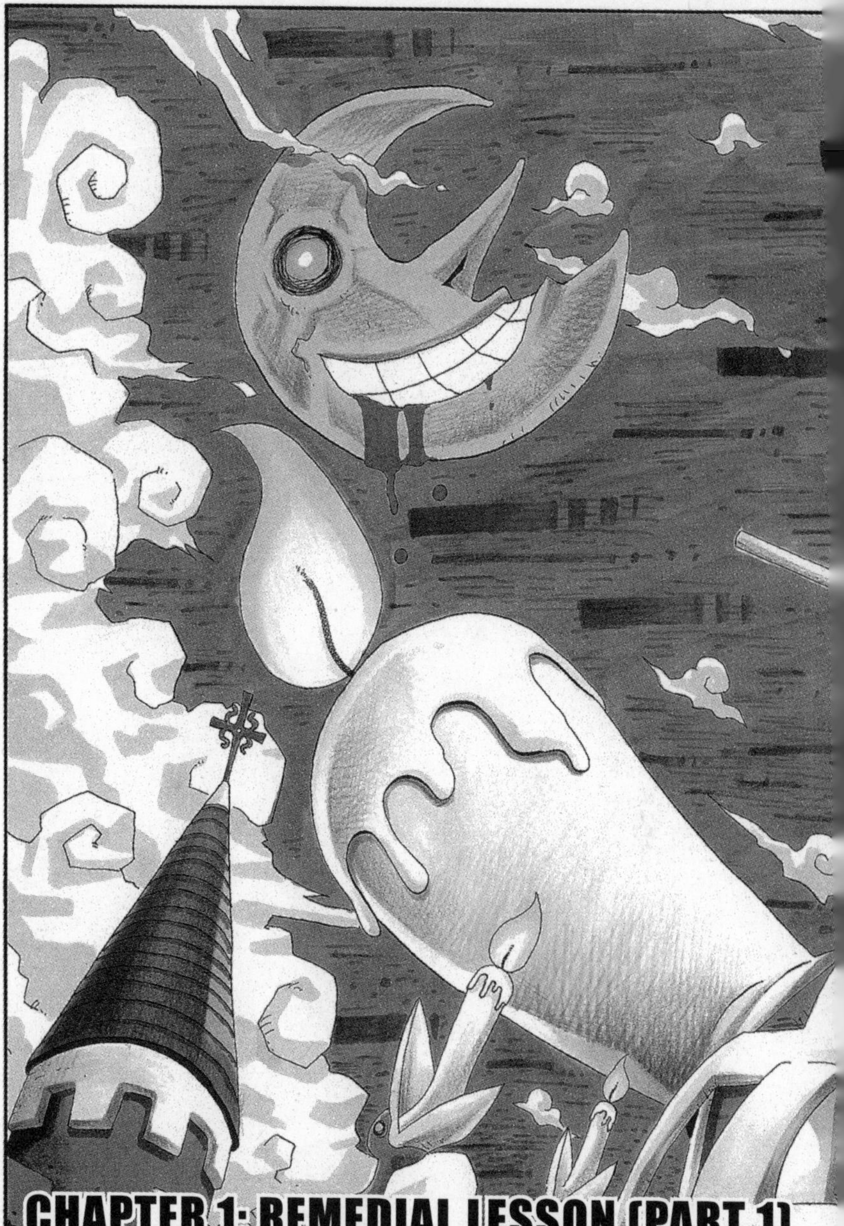
CHAPTER 1: REMEDIAL LESSON (PART 1)

SOUL EATER

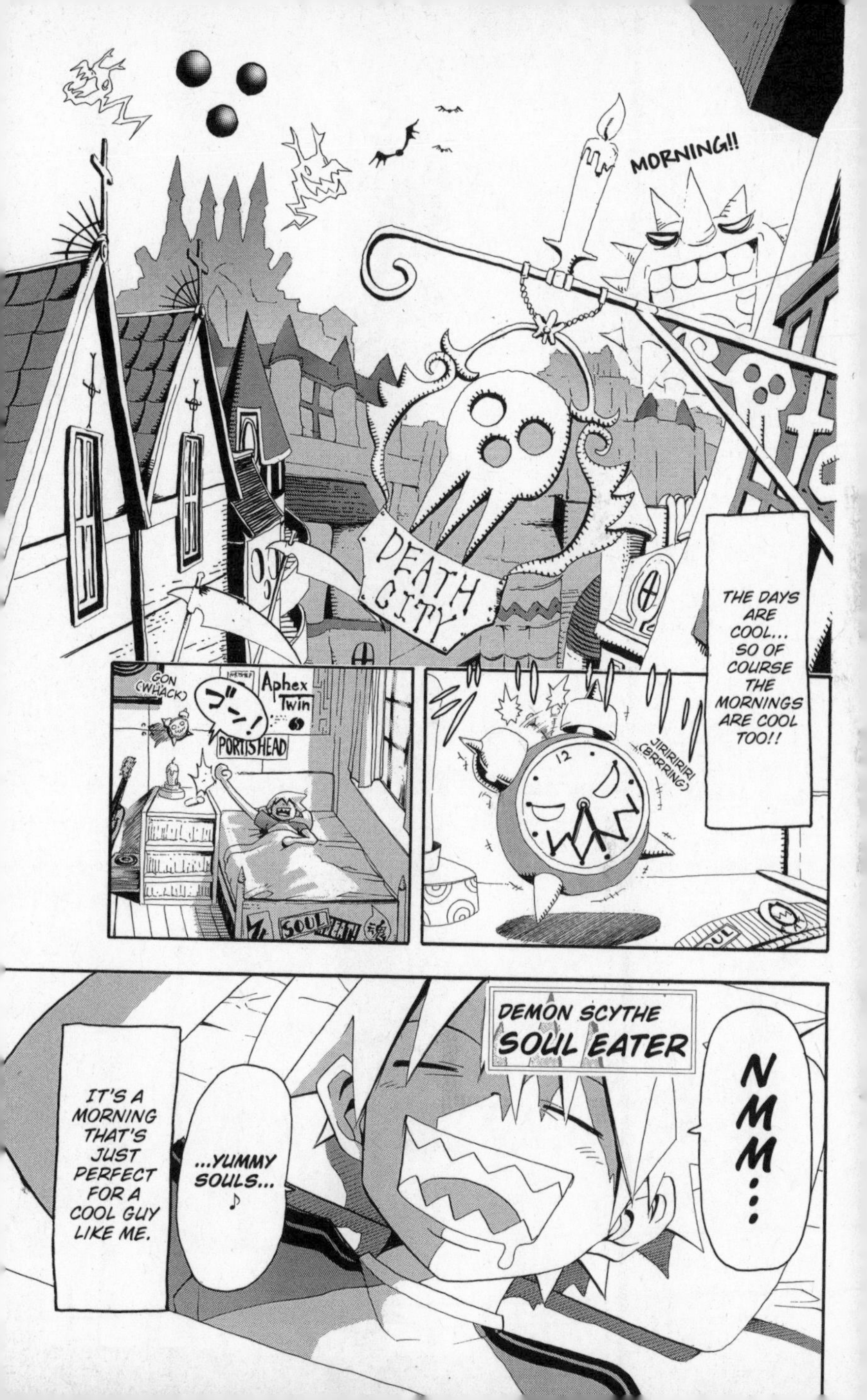

MORNING!!
DEATH CITY
THE DAYS ARE COOL... SO OF COURSE THE MORNINGS ARE COOL TOO!!
JIRIRIRIRI (BRRRING)
SOUL
GON (WHACK)
ゴン!
Aphex Twin
PORTISHEAD
SOUL
NMM...
DEMON SCYTHE SOUL EATER
...YUMMY SOULS... ♪
IT'S A MORNING THAT'S JUST PERFECT FOR A COOL GUY LIKE ME.

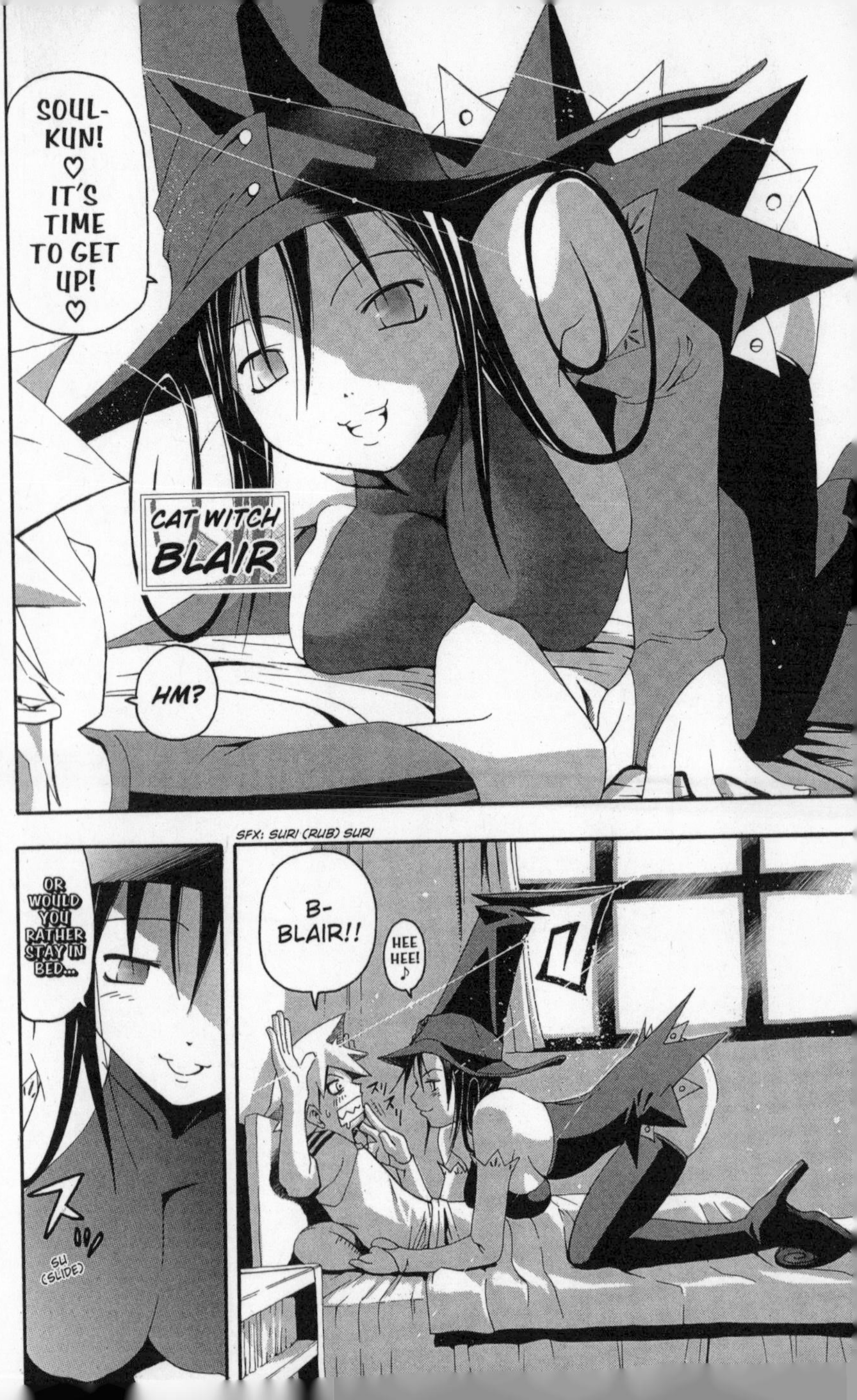
SOUL-KUN! ♡ IT'S TIME TO GET UP! ♡
CAT WITCH BLAIR
HM?
SFX: SURI (RUB) SURI
B-BLAIR!!
HEE HEE! ♪
OR WOULD YOU RATHER STAY IN BED...
SU (SLIDE)

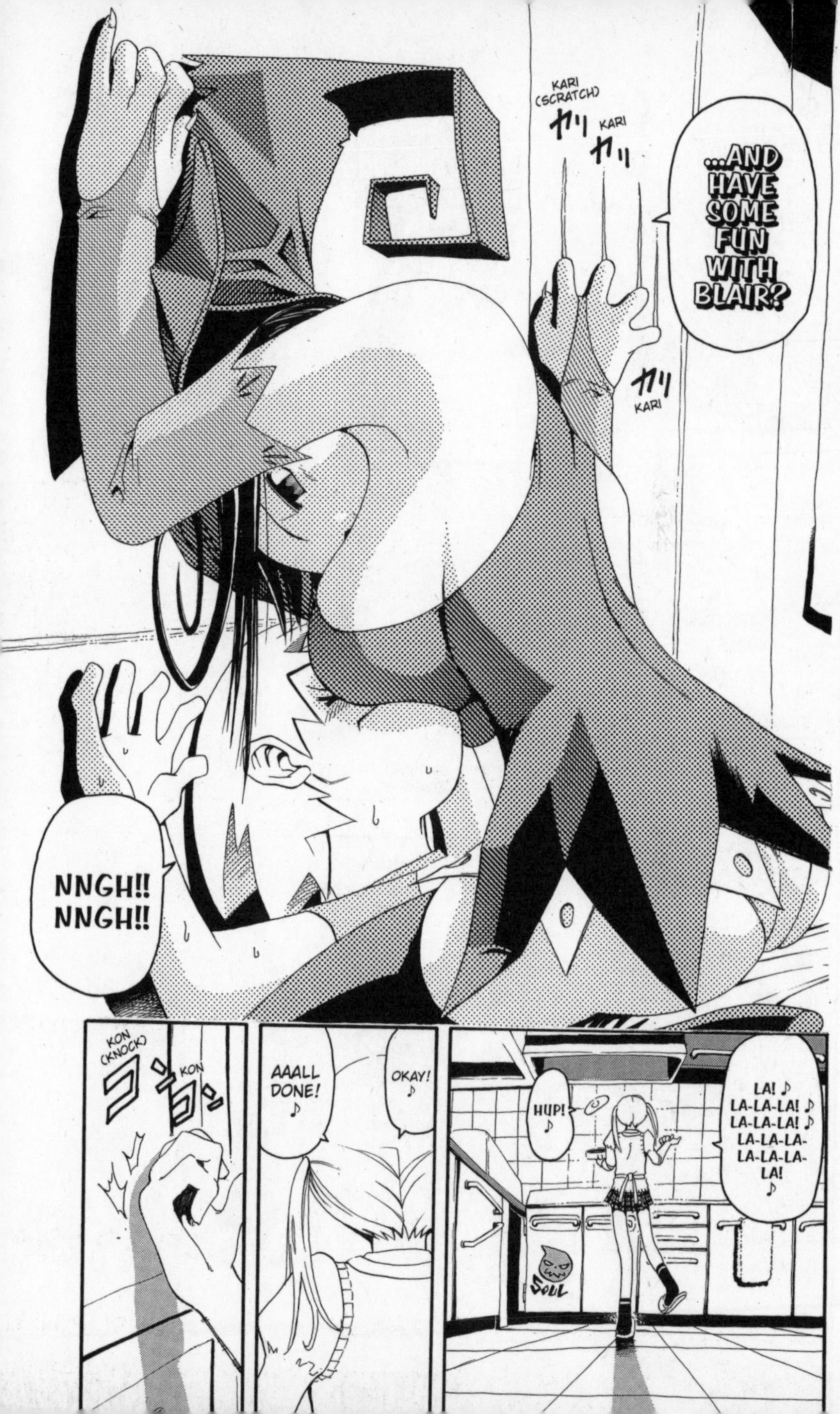
...AND HAVE SOME FUN WITH BLAIR?
ガリ
KARI (SCRATCH)
ガリ
KARI
ガリ
KARI
NNGH!! NNGH!!
LA! ♪ LA-LA-LA! ♪ LA-LA-LA! ♪ LA-LA-LA-LA-LA-LA-LA! ♪
HUP! ♪
SOUL
OKAY! ♪
AAALL DONE! ♪
KON (KNOCK)
KON

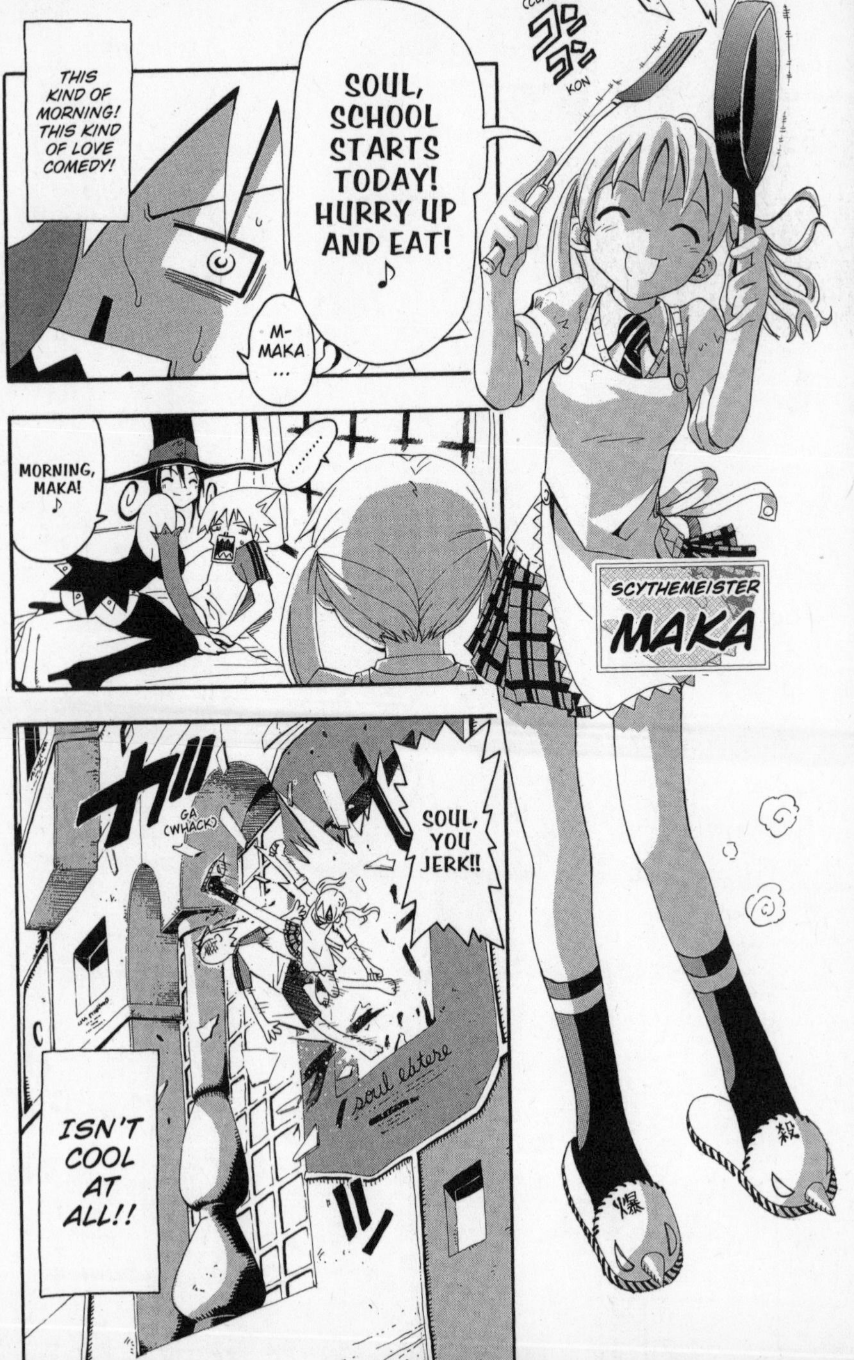

KON (CLANG)
KON
SOUL, SCHOOL STARTS TODAY! HURRY UP AND EAT! ♪
SCYTHEMEISTER
MAKA
THIS KIND OF MORNING! THIS KIND OF LOVE COMEDY!
M-MAKA ...
......
MORNING, MAKA! ♪
SOUL, YOU JERK!!
GA (WHACK)
soul eaters
ISN'T COOL AT ALL!!

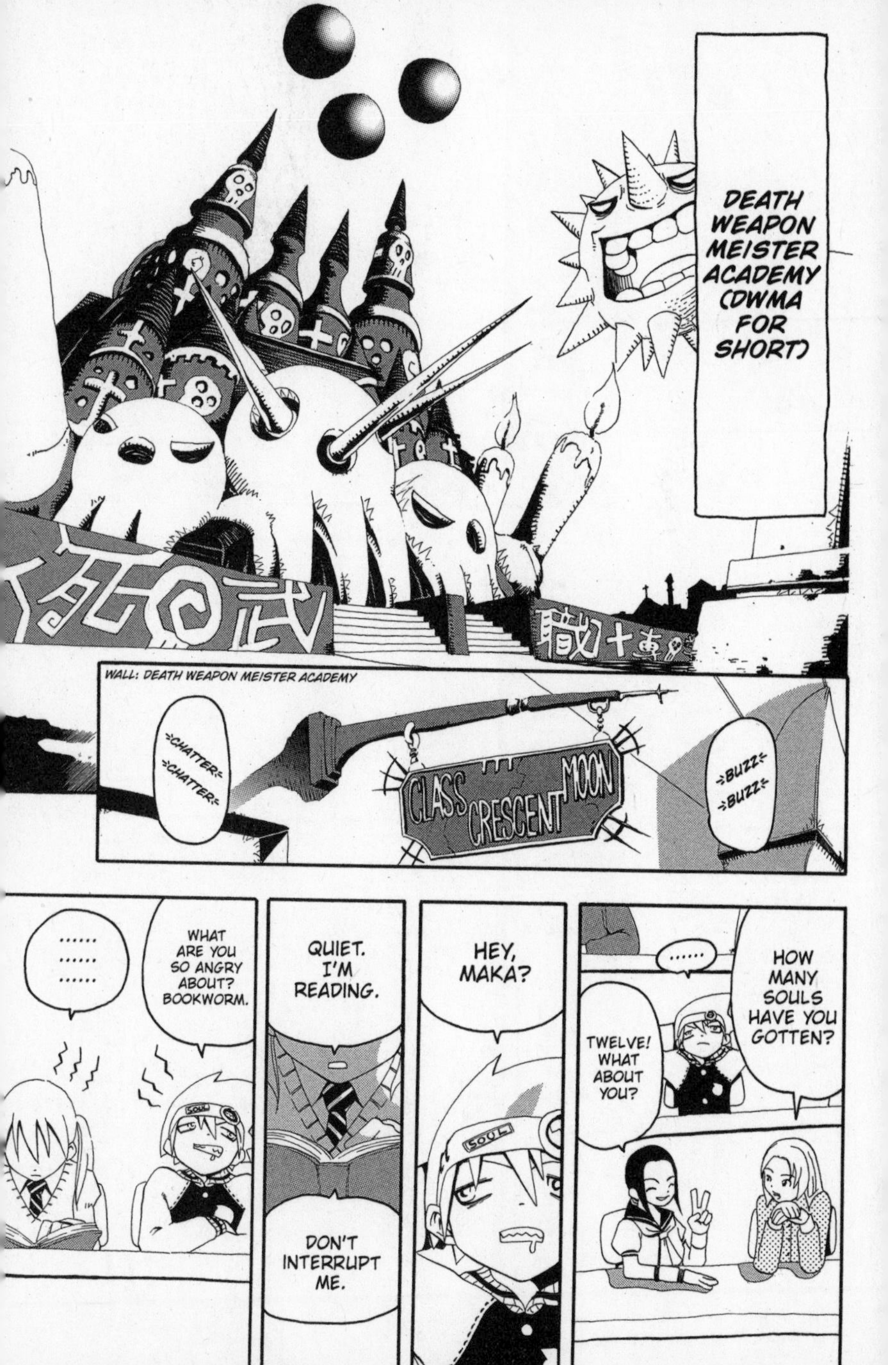
DEATH WEAPON MEISTER ACADEMY (DWMA FOR SHORT)
WALL: DEATH WEAPON MEISTER ACADEMY
BUZZ BUZZ
CLASS CRESCENT MOON
CHATTER CHATTER
HOW MANY SOULS HAVE YOU GOTTEN?
TWELVE! WHAT ABOUT YOU?
......
HEY, MAKA?
QUIET. I'M READING.
DON'T INTERRUPT ME.
WHAT ARE YOU SO ANGRY ABOUT? BOOKWORM.
....

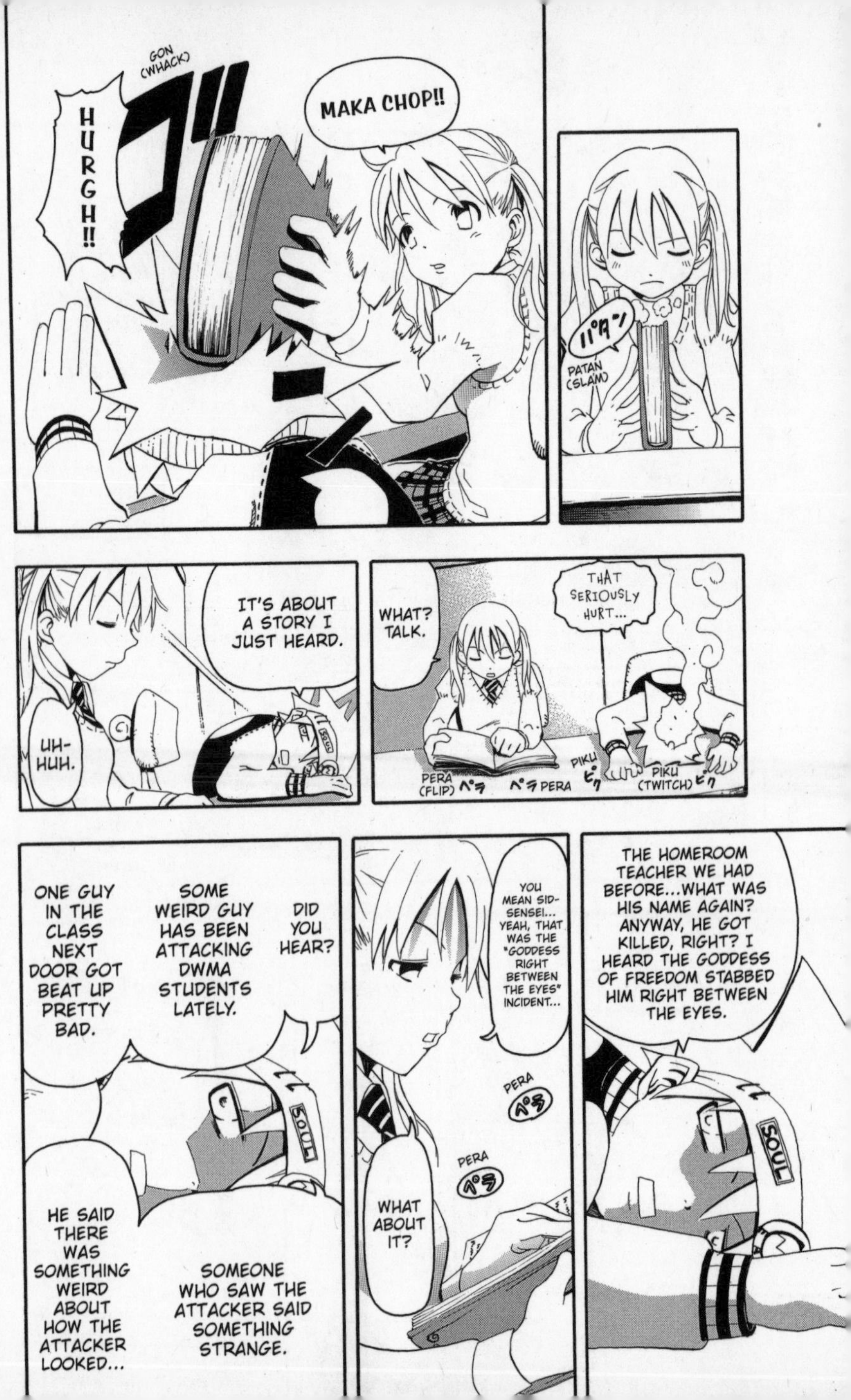

PATAN (SLAM)
MAKA CHOP!!
GON (WHACK)
HURGH!!
THAT SERIOUSLY HURT...
WHAT? TALK.
PIKU (TWITCH)
PIKU
PERA
PERA (FLIP)
IT'S ABOUT A STORY I JUST HEARD.
UH-HUH.
THE HOMEROOM TEACHER WE HAD BEFORE...WHAT WAS HIS NAME AGAIN? ANYWAY, HE GOT KILLED, RIGHT? I HEARD THE GODDESS OF FREEDOM STABBED HIM RIGHT BETWEEN THE EYES.
YOU MEAN SID-SENSEI... YEAH, THAT WAS THE "GODDESS RIGHT BETWEEN THE EYES" INCIDENT...
PERA
PERA
WHAT ABOUT IT?
DID YOU HEAR?
SOME WEIRD GUY HAS BEEN ATTACKING DWMA STUDENTS LATELY.
ONE GUY IN THE CLASS NEXT DOOR GOT BEAT UP PRETTY BAD.
SOMEONE WHO SAW THE ATTACKER SAID SOMETHING STRANGE.
HE SAID THERE WAS SOMETHING WEIRD ABOUT HOW THE ATTACKER LOOKED...

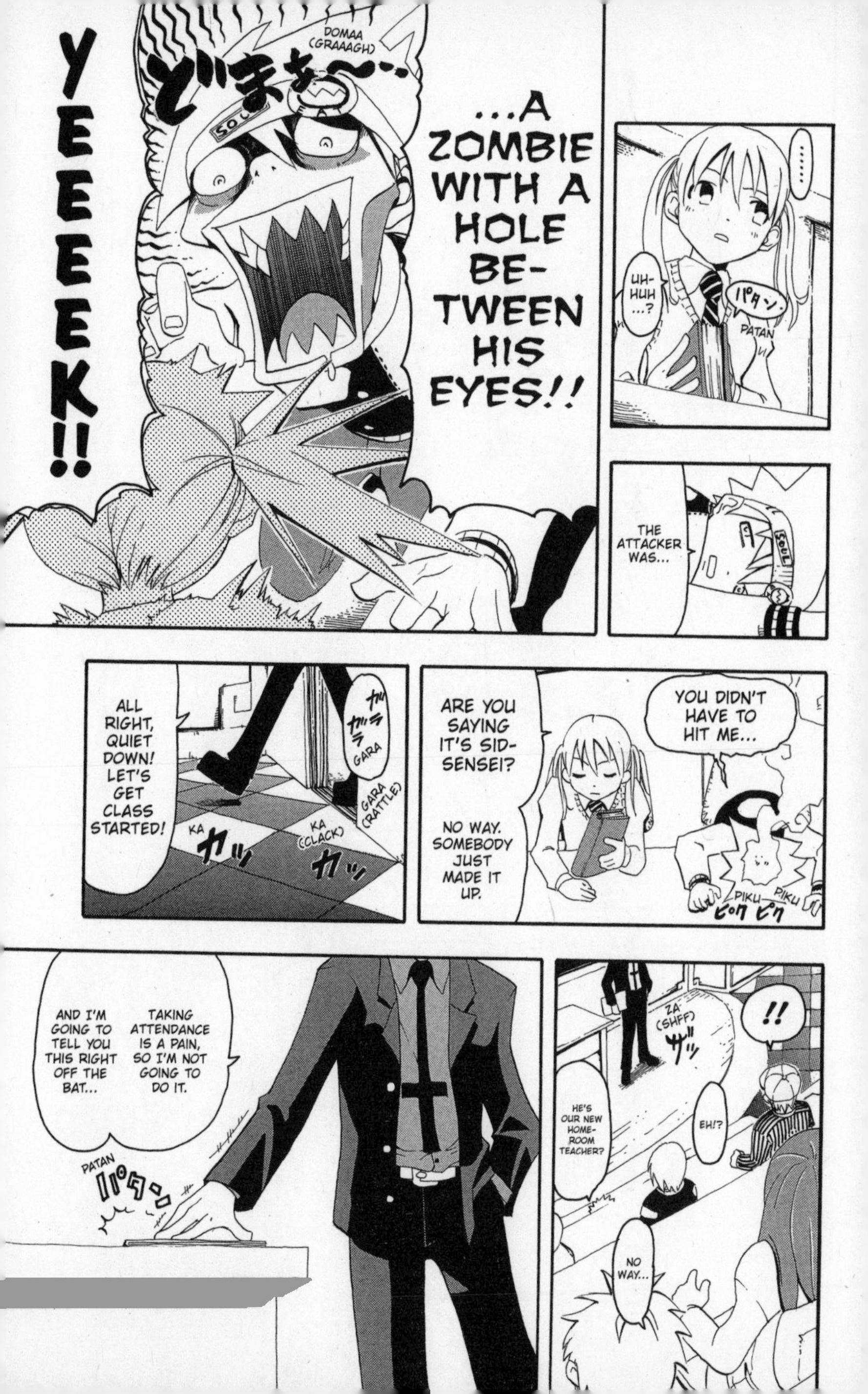
......
UH-HUH...?
パタン
PATAN
THE ATTACKER WAS...
...A ZOMBIE WITH A HOLE BE-TWEEN HIS EYES!!
DOMAA (GRAAAGH)
どまぁ〜...
YEEEEEK!!
YOU DIDN'T HAVE TO HIT ME...
ARE YOU SAYING IT'S SID-SENSEI?
NO WAY. SOMEBODY JUST MADE IT UP.
PIKU PIKU
ピクピク
ガラガラ
GARA
GARA (RATTLE)
ALL RIGHT, QUIET DOWN! LET'S GET CLASS STARTED!
KA (CLACK)
カッ
KA
カッ
!!
ZA (SHFF)
ザッ
EH!?
HE'S OUR NEW HOME-ROOM TEACHER?
NO WAY...
TAKING ATTENDANCE IS A PAIN, SO I'M NOT GOING TO DO IT.
AND I'M GOING TO TELL YOU THIS RIGHT OFF THE BAT...
PATAN
パタッ

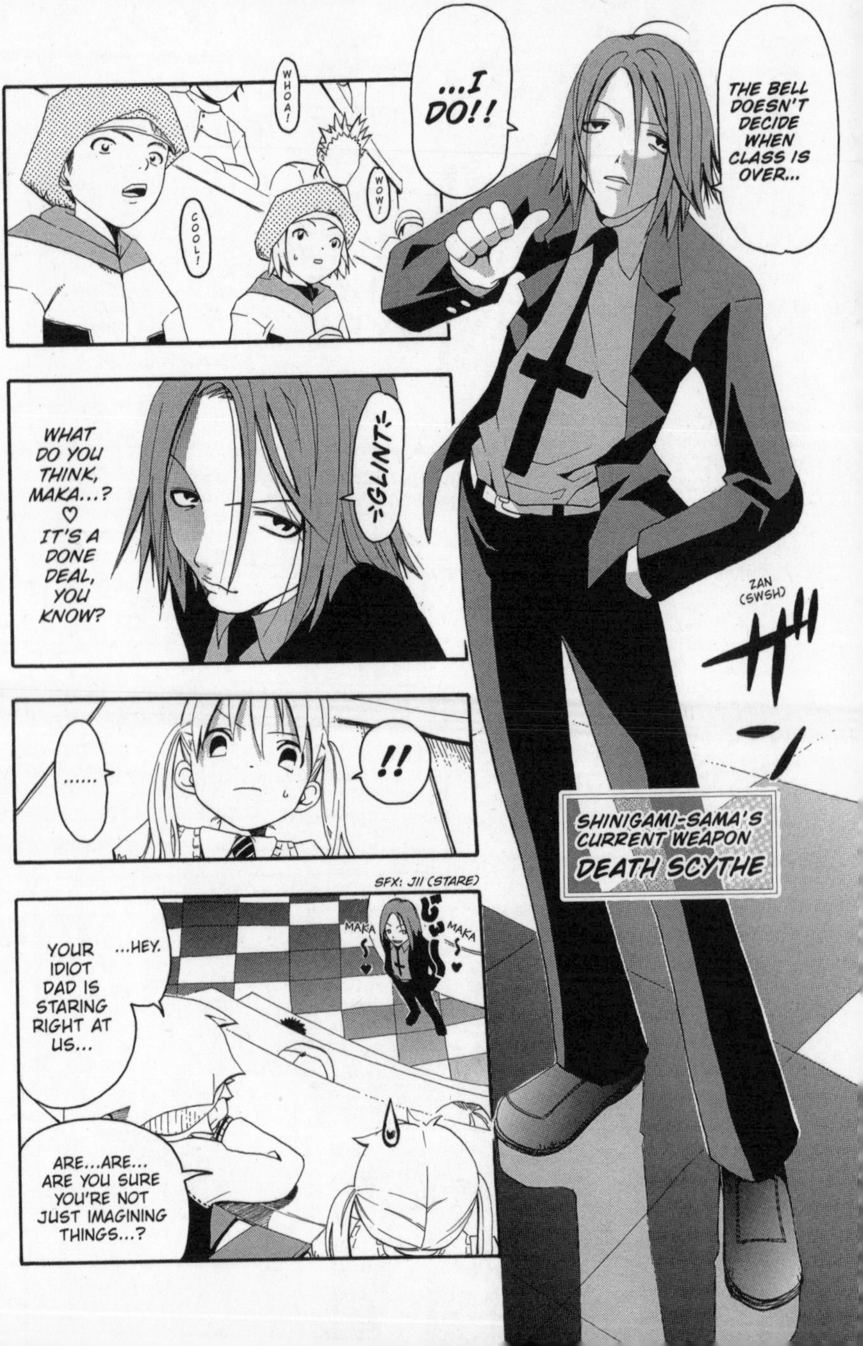

THE BELL DOESN'T DECIDE WHEN CLASS IS OVER...
...I DO!!
ZAN (SWSH)
SHINIGAMI-SAMA'S CURRENT WEAPON
DEATH SCYTHE
WHOA!
WOW!
COOL!
GLINT
WHAT DO YOU THINK, MAKA...? ♡ IT'S A DONE DEAL, YOU KNOW?
!!
......
SFX: JII (STARE)
MAKA ~ ♡
MAKA ~ ♡
...HEY.
YOUR IDIOT DAD IS STARING RIGHT AT US...
ARE...ARE... ARE YOU SURE YOU'RE NOT JUST IMAGINING THINGS...?

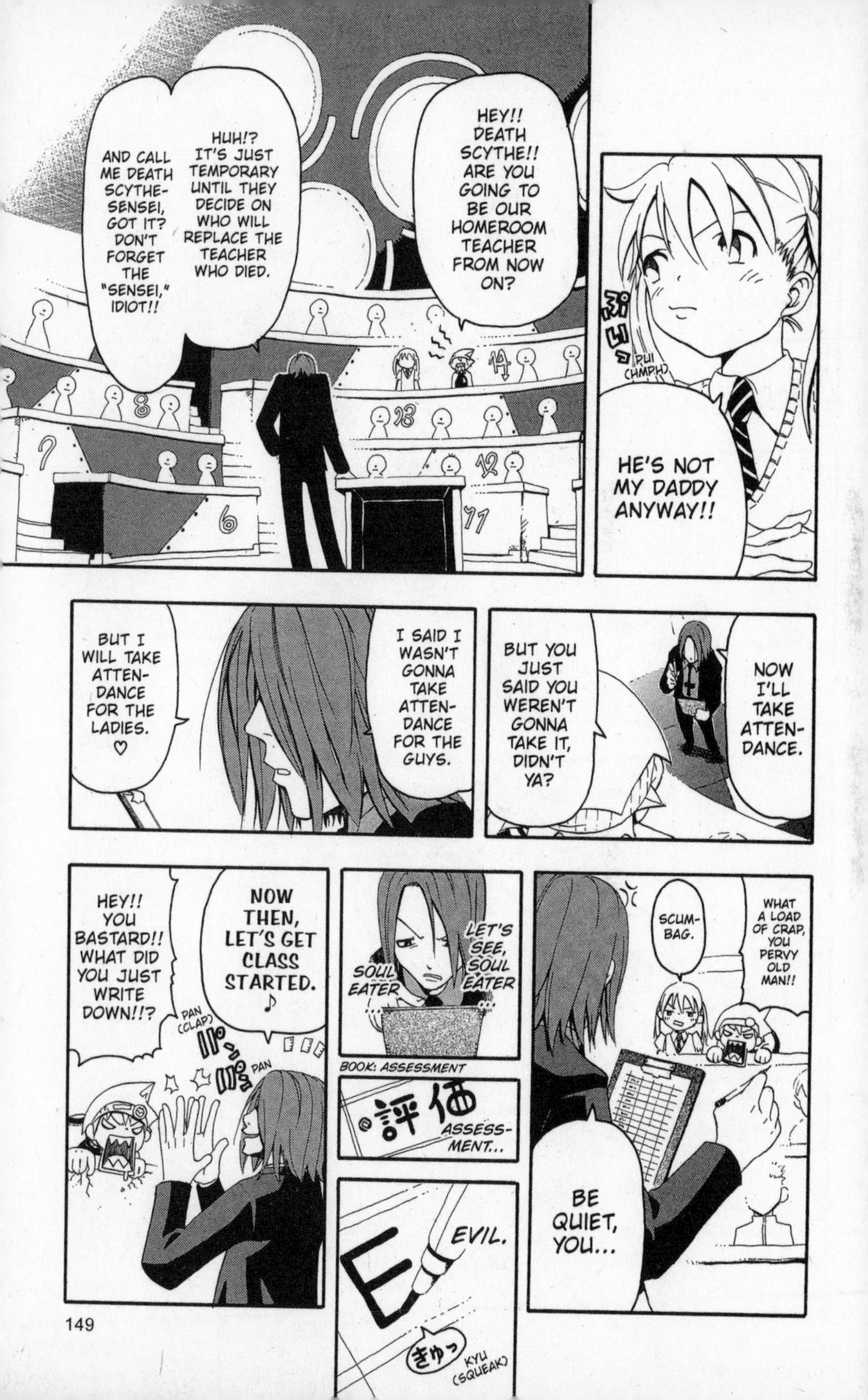
HE'S NOT MY DADDY ANYWAY!!
PUI (HMPH)
HEY!! DEATH SCYTHE!! ARE YOU GOING TO BE OUR HOMEROOM TEACHER FROM NOW ON?
HUH!? IT'S JUST TEMPORARY UNTIL THEY DECIDE ON WHO WILL REPLACE THE TEACHER WHO DIED.
AND CALL ME DEATH SCYTHE-SENSEI, GOT IT? DON'T FORGET THE "SENSEI," IDIOT!!
NOW I'LL TAKE ATTEN-DANCE.
BUT YOU JUST SAID YOU WEREN'T GONNA TAKE IT, DIDN'T YA?
I SAID I WASN'T GONNA TAKE ATTEN-DANCE FOR THE GUYS.
BUT I WILL TAKE ATTEN-DANCE FOR THE LADIES. ♡
WHAT A LOAD OF CRAP, YOU PERVY OLD MAN!!
SCUM-BAG.
BE QUIET, YOU...
LET'S SEE, SOUL EATER
SOUL EATER
BOOK: ASSESSMENT
評価
ASSESS-MENT...
EVIL.
E
きゅっ
KYU (SQUEAK)
NOW THEN, LET'S GET CLASS STARTED. ♪
HEY!! YOU BASTARD!! WHAT DID YOU JUST WRITE DOWN!!?
PAN (CLAP)
パン
PAN

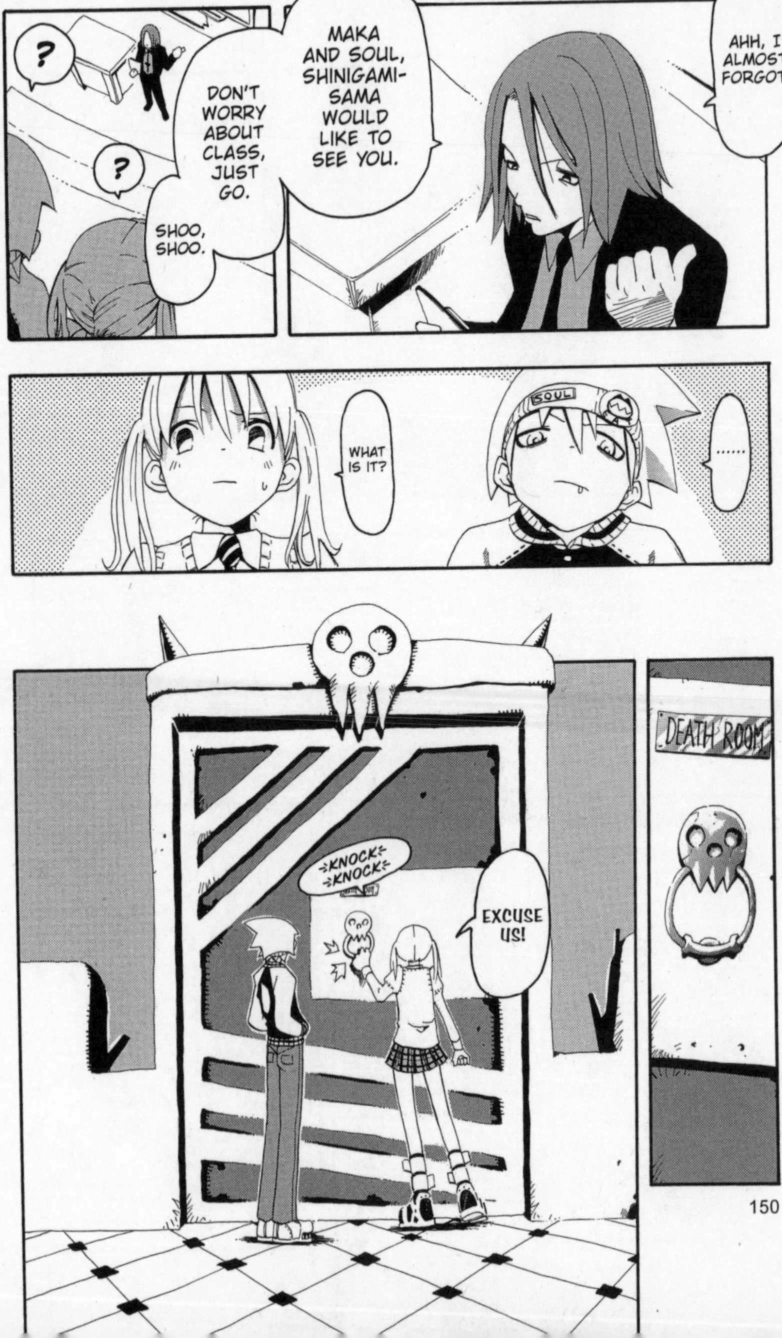
AHH, I ALMOST FORGOT.
MAKA AND SOUL, SHINIGAMI-SAMA WOULD LIKE TO SEE YOU.
?
?
DON'T WORRY ABOUT CLASS, JUST GO.
SHOO, SHOO.
......
WHAT IS IT?
DEATH ROOM
KNOCK KNOCK
EXCUSE US!

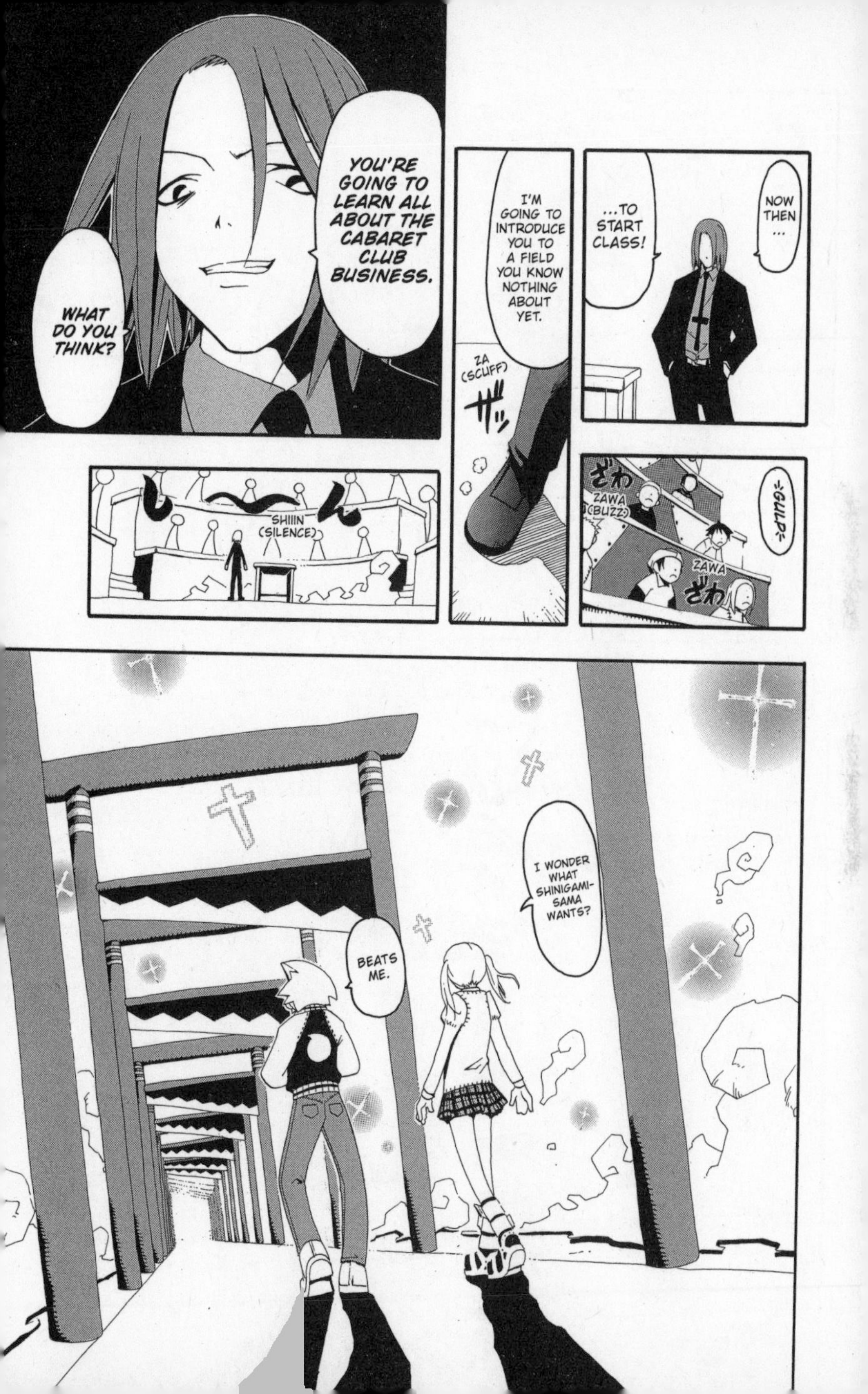
NOW THEN ...
...TO START CLASS!
-GULP-
ZAWA (BUZZ)
ZAWA
I'M GOING TO INTRODUCE YOU TO A FIELD YOU KNOW NOTHING ABOUT YET.
ZA (SCUFF)
YOU'RE GOING TO LEARN ALL ABOUT THE CABARET CLUB BUSINESS.
WHAT DO YOU THINK?
SHIIIN (SILENCE)
I WONDER WHAT SHINIGAMI-SAMA WANTS?
BEATS ME.

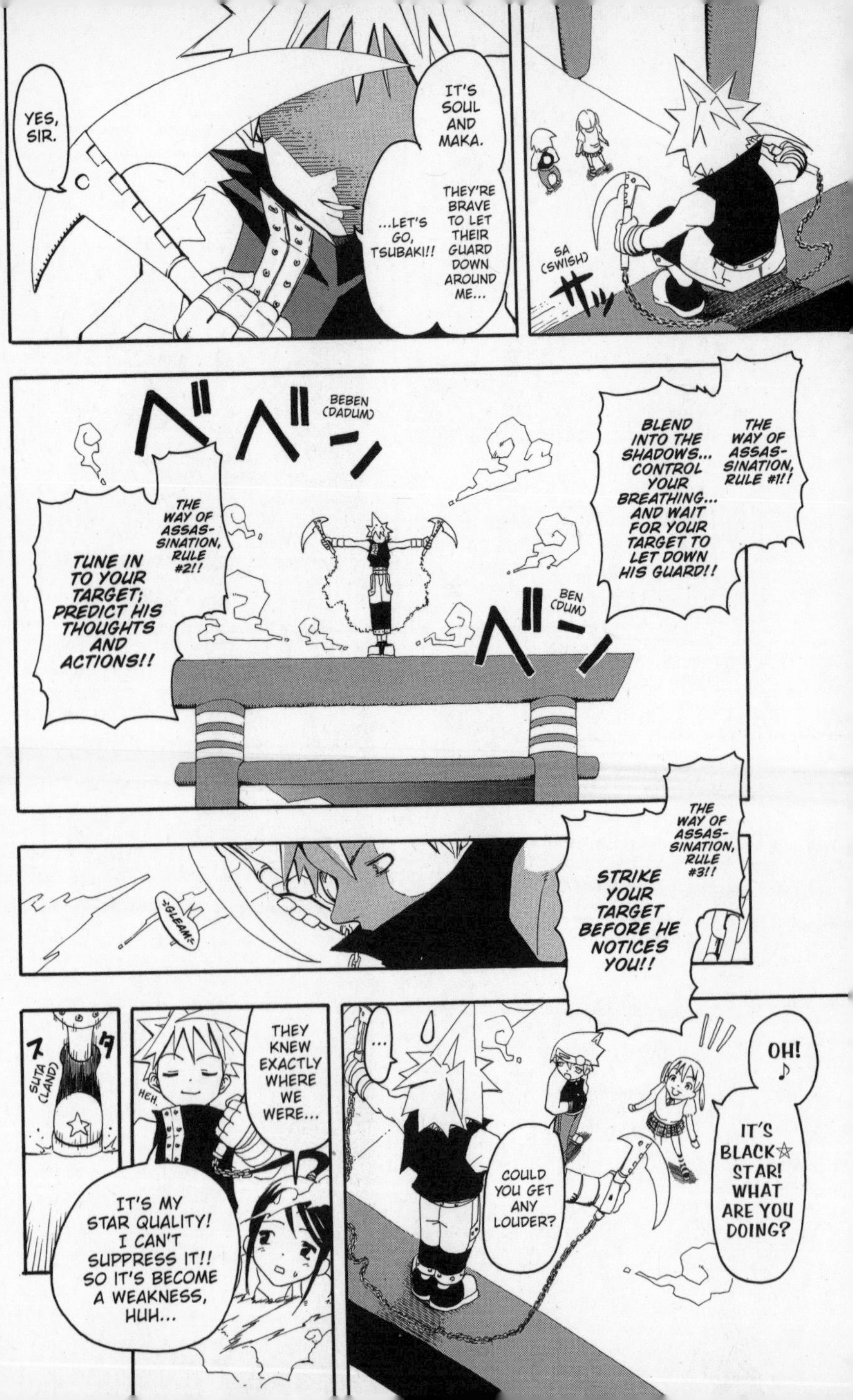
SA (SWISH)
IT'S SOUL AND MAKA.
THEY'RE BRAVE TO LET THEIR GUARD DOWN AROUND ME...
...LET'S GO, TSUBAKI!!
YES, SIR.
THE WAY OF ASSAS-SINATION, RULE #1!!
BLEND INTO THE SHADOWS... CONTROL YOUR BREATHING... AND WAIT FOR YOUR TARGET TO LET DOWN HIS GUARD!!
BEBEN (DADUM)
BEN (DUM)
THE WAY OF ASSAS-SINATION, RULE #2!!
TUNE IN TO YOUR TARGET; PREDICT HIS THOUGHTS AND ACTIONS!!
THE WAY OF ASSAS-SINATION, RULE #3!!
STRIKE YOUR TARGET BEFORE HE NOTICES YOU!!
GLEAM
OH! ♪
IT'S BLACK☆STAR! WHAT ARE YOU DOING?
COULD YOU GET ANY LOUDER?
...
THEY KNEW EXACTLY WHERE WE WERE...
HEH.
IT'S MY STAR QUALITY! I CAN'T SUPPRESS IT!! SO IT'S BECOME A WEAKNESS, HUH...
SUTA (LAND)

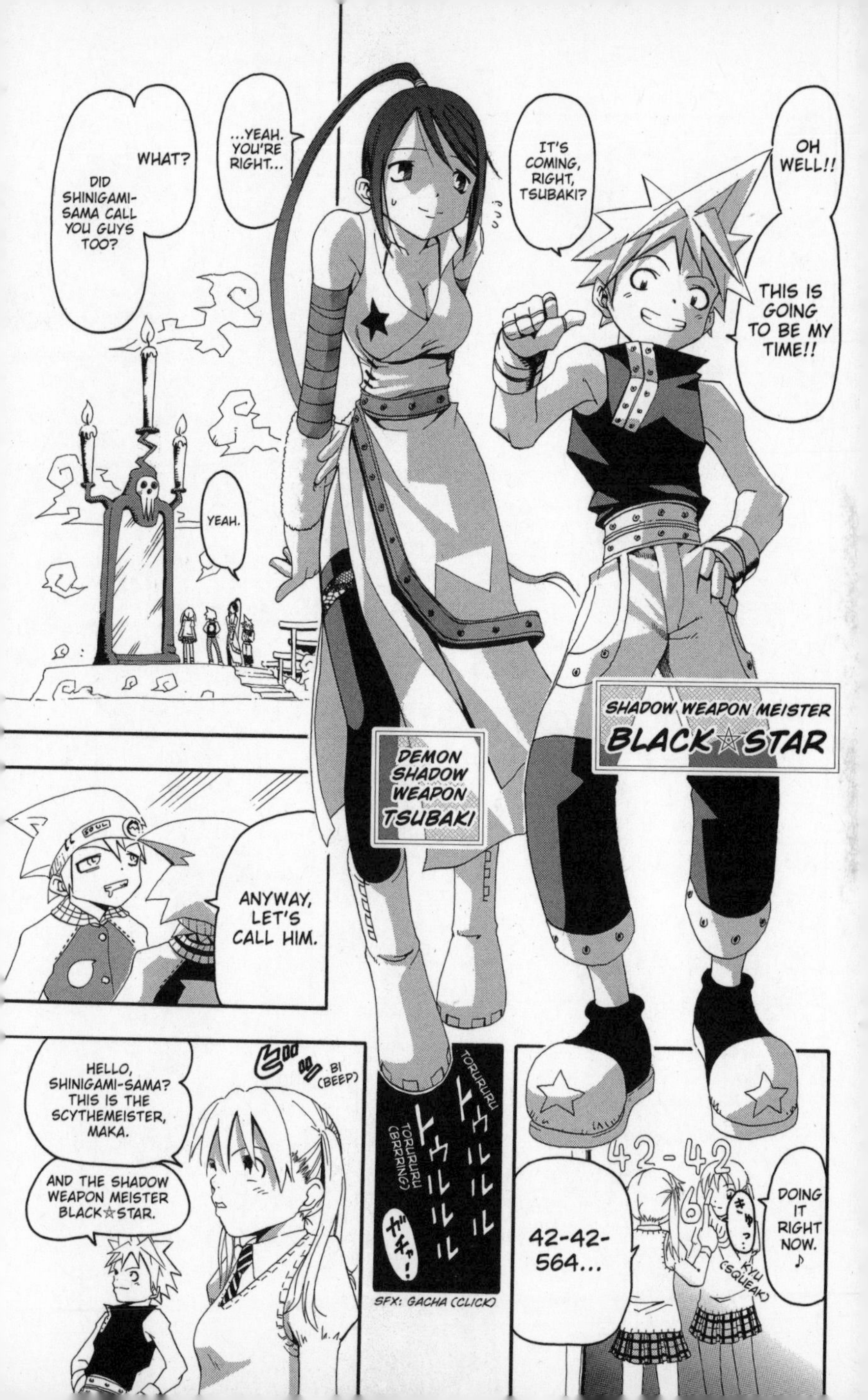
OH WELL!!
THIS IS GOING TO BE MY TIME!!
IT'S COMING, RIGHT, TSUBAKI?
...YEAH. YOU'RE RIGHT...
SHADOW WEAPON MEISTER BLACK☆STAR
DEMON SHADOW WEAPON TSUBAKI
WHAT?
DID SHINIGAMI-SAMA CALL YOU GUYS TOO?
YEAH.
ANYWAY, LET'S CALL HIM.
DOING IT RIGHT NOW. ♪
KYU (SQUEAK)
42-42-564...
TORURURU TORURURU (BRRRING)
SFX: GACHA (CLICK)
HELLO, SHINIGAMI-SAMA? THIS IS THE SCYTHEMEISTER, MAKA.
AND THE SHADOW WEAPON MEISTER BLACK☆STAR.
BI (BEEP)

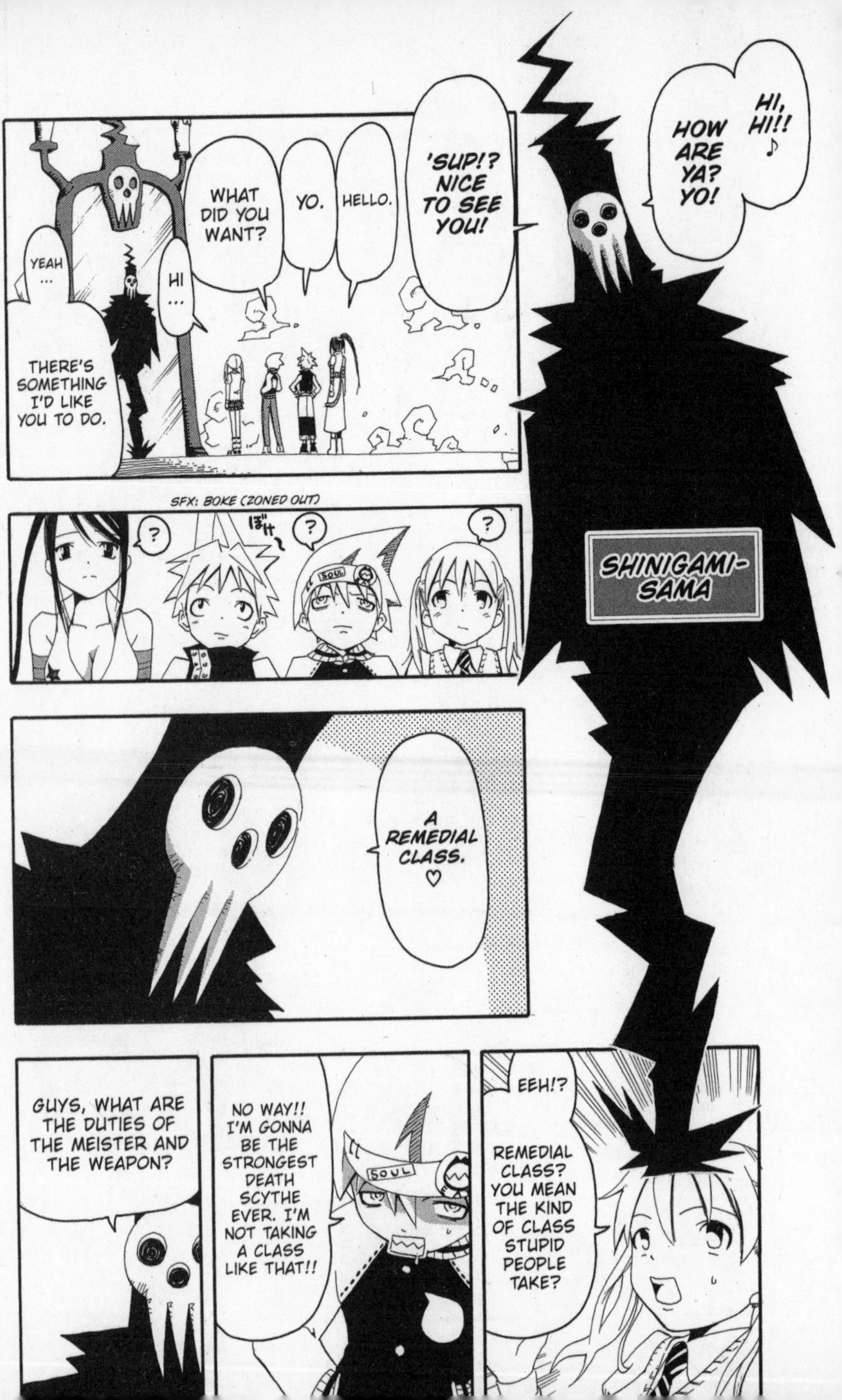
HI, HI!! ♪
HOW ARE YA? YO!
SHINIGAMI-SAMA
'SUP!? NICE TO SEE YOU!
HELLO.
YO.
WHAT DID YOU WANT?
HI ...
YEAH ...
THERE'S SOMETHING I'D LIKE YOU TO DO.
SFX: BOKE (ZONED OUT)
?
?
ぼけ
?
A REMEDIAL CLASS. ♡
EEH!?
REMEDIAL CLASS? YOU MEAN THE KIND OF CLASS STUPID PEOPLE TAKE?
NO WAY!! I'M GONNA BE THE STRONGEST DEATH SCYTHE EVER. I'M NOT TAKING A CLASS LIKE THAT!!
GUYS, WHAT ARE THE DUTIES OF THE MEISTER AND THE WEAPON?

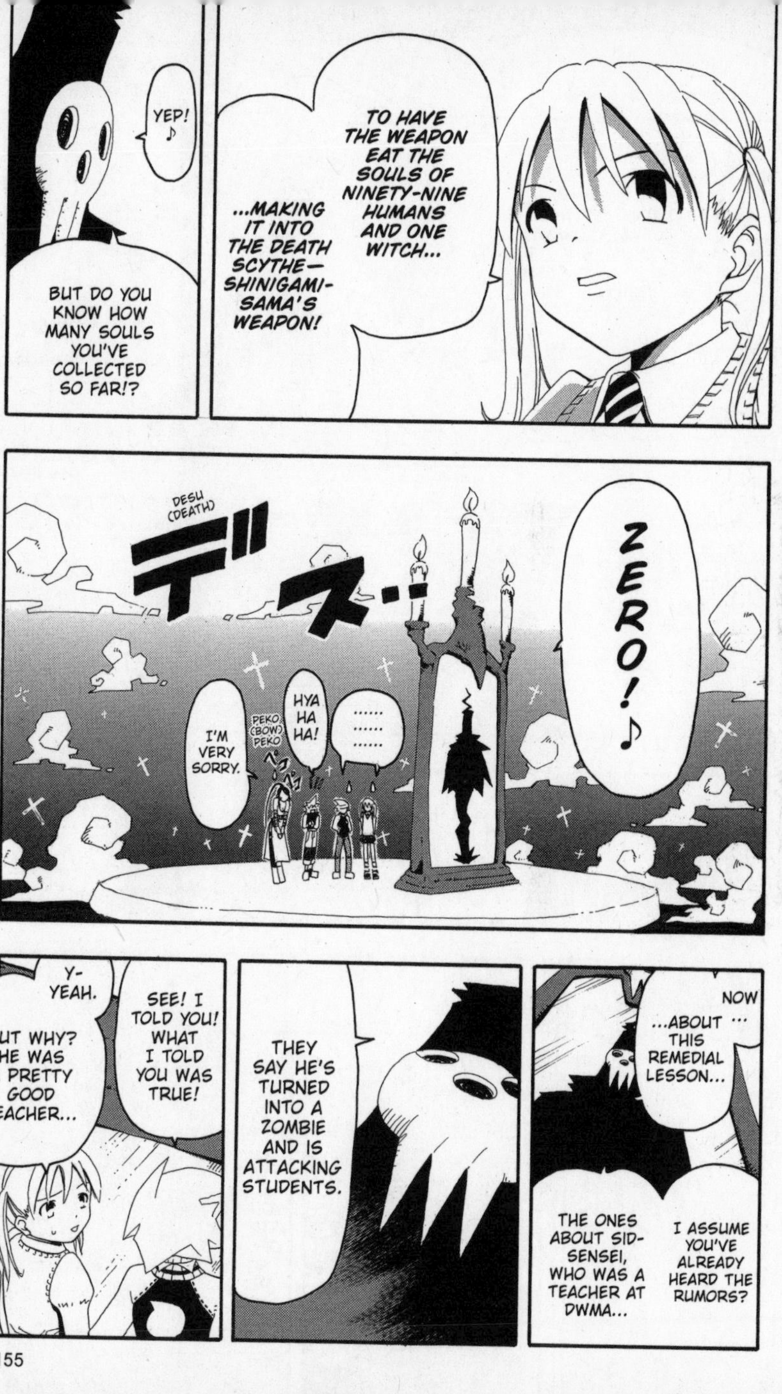
TO HAVE THE WEAPON EAT THE SOULS OF NINETY-NINE HUMANS AND ONE WITCH...
...MAKING IT INTO THE DEATH SCYTHE—SHINIGAMI-SAMA'S WEAPON!
YEP! ♪
BUT DO YOU KNOW HOW MANY SOULS YOU'VE COLLECTED SO FAR!?
ZERO! ♪
DESU (DEATH)
......
HYA HA HA!
PEKO (BOW) PEKO
I'M VERY SORRY.
NOW ...ABOUT THIS REMEDIAL LESSON...
I ASSUME YOU'VE ALREADY HEARD THE RUMORS?
THE ONES ABOUT SID-SENSEI, WHO WAS A TEACHER AT DWMA...
THEY SAY HE'S TURNED INTO A ZOMBIE AND IS ATTACKING STUDENTS.
SEE! I TOLD YOU! WHAT I TOLD YOU WAS TRUE!
Y-YEAH.
BUT WHY? HE WAS A PRETTY GOOD TEACHER...

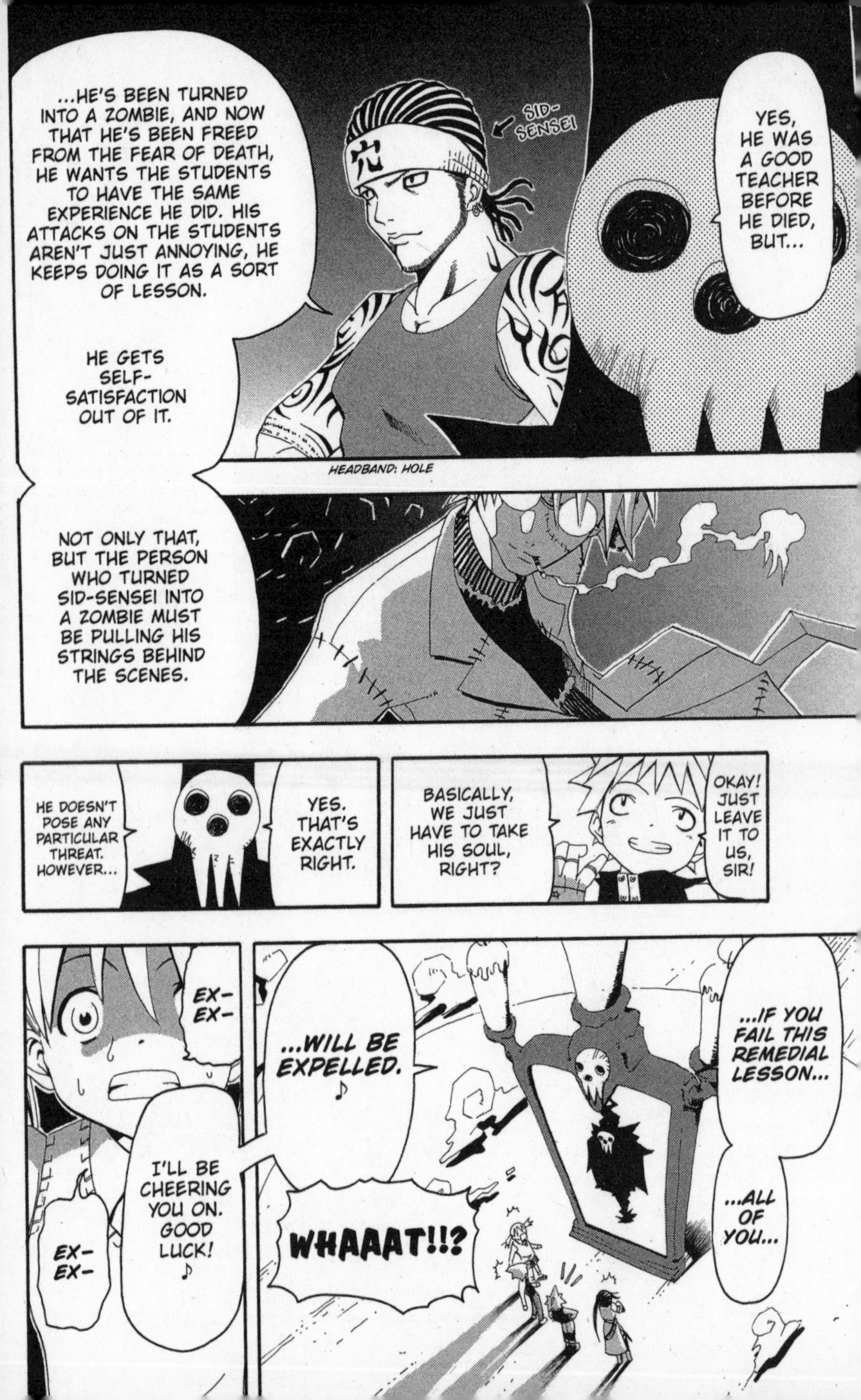
YES, HE WAS A GOOD TEACHER BEFORE HE DIED, BUT...
SID-SENSEI
...HE'S BEEN TURNED INTO A ZOMBIE, AND NOW THAT HE'S BEEN FREED FROM THE FEAR OF DEATH, HE WANTS THE STUDENTS TO HAVE THE SAME EXPERIENCE HE DID. HIS ATTACKS ON THE STUDENTS AREN'T JUST ANNOYING, HE KEEPS DOING IT AS A SORT OF LESSON.
HE GETS SELF-SATISFACTION OUT OF IT.
HEADBAND: HOLE
NOT ONLY THAT, BUT THE PERSON WHO TURNED SID-SENSEI INTO A ZOMBIE MUST BE PULLING HIS STRINGS BEHIND THE SCENES.
OKAY! JUST LEAVE IT TO US, SIR!
BASICALLY, WE JUST HAVE TO TAKE HIS SOUL, RIGHT?
YES. THAT'S EXACTLY RIGHT.
HE DOESN'T POSE ANY PARTICULAR THREAT. HOWEVER...
...IF YOU FAIL THIS REMEDIAL LESSON...
...ALL OF YOU...
...WILL BE EXPELLED. ♪
WHAAAT!!?
EX- EX-
I'LL BE CHEERING YOU ON. GOOD LUCK! ♪
EX- EX-

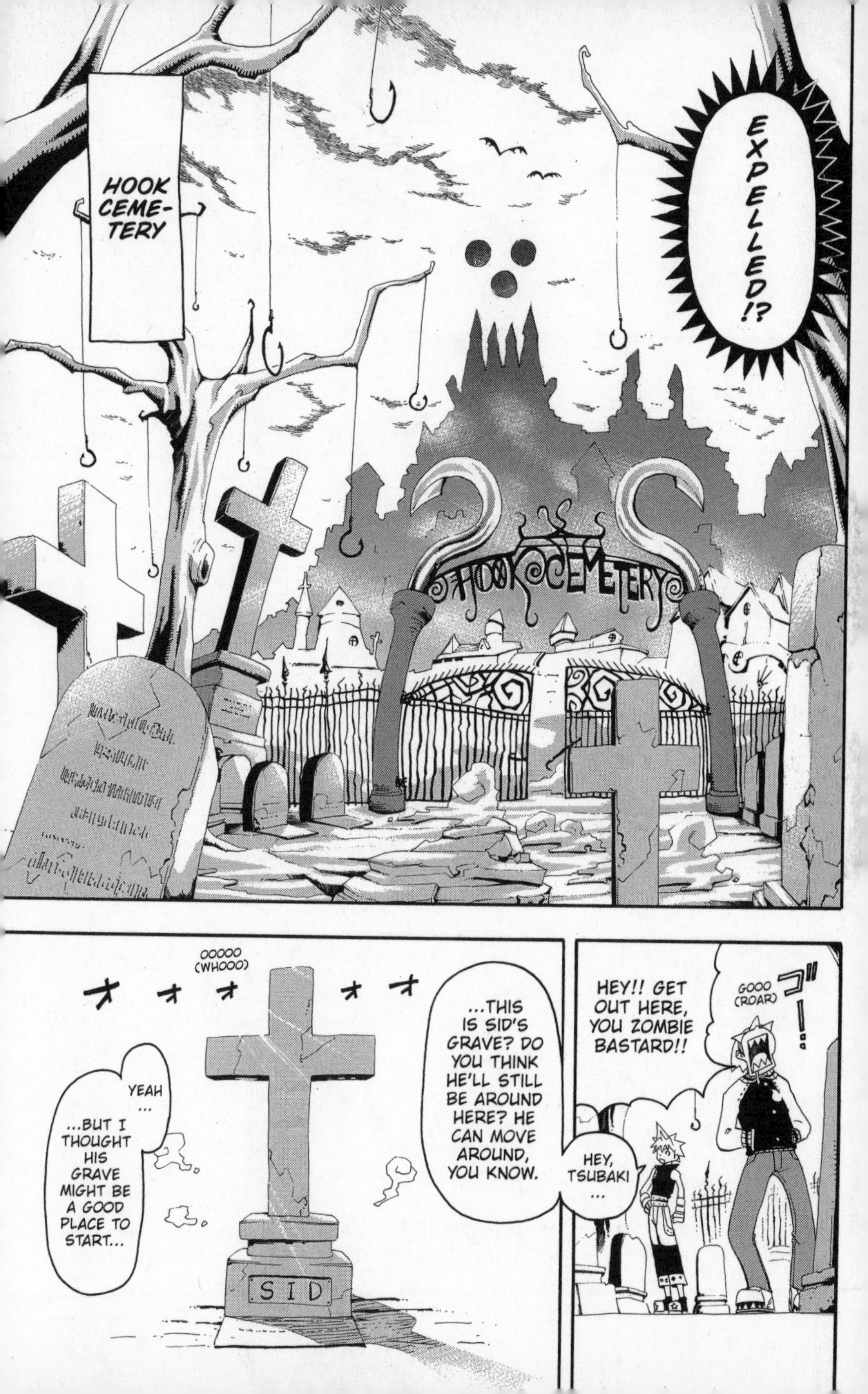
EXPELLED!?
HOOK CEMETERY
HOOK CEMETERY
GOOO (ROAR)
HEY!! GET OUT HERE, YOU ZOMBIE BASTARD!!
HEY, TSUBAKI ...
...THIS IS SID'S GRAVE? DO YOU THINK HE'LL STILL BE AROUND HERE? HE CAN MOVE AROUND, YOU KNOW.
OOOOO (WHOOO)
YEAH ... ...BUT I THOUGHT HIS GRAVE MIGHT BE A GOOD PLACE TO START...
SID

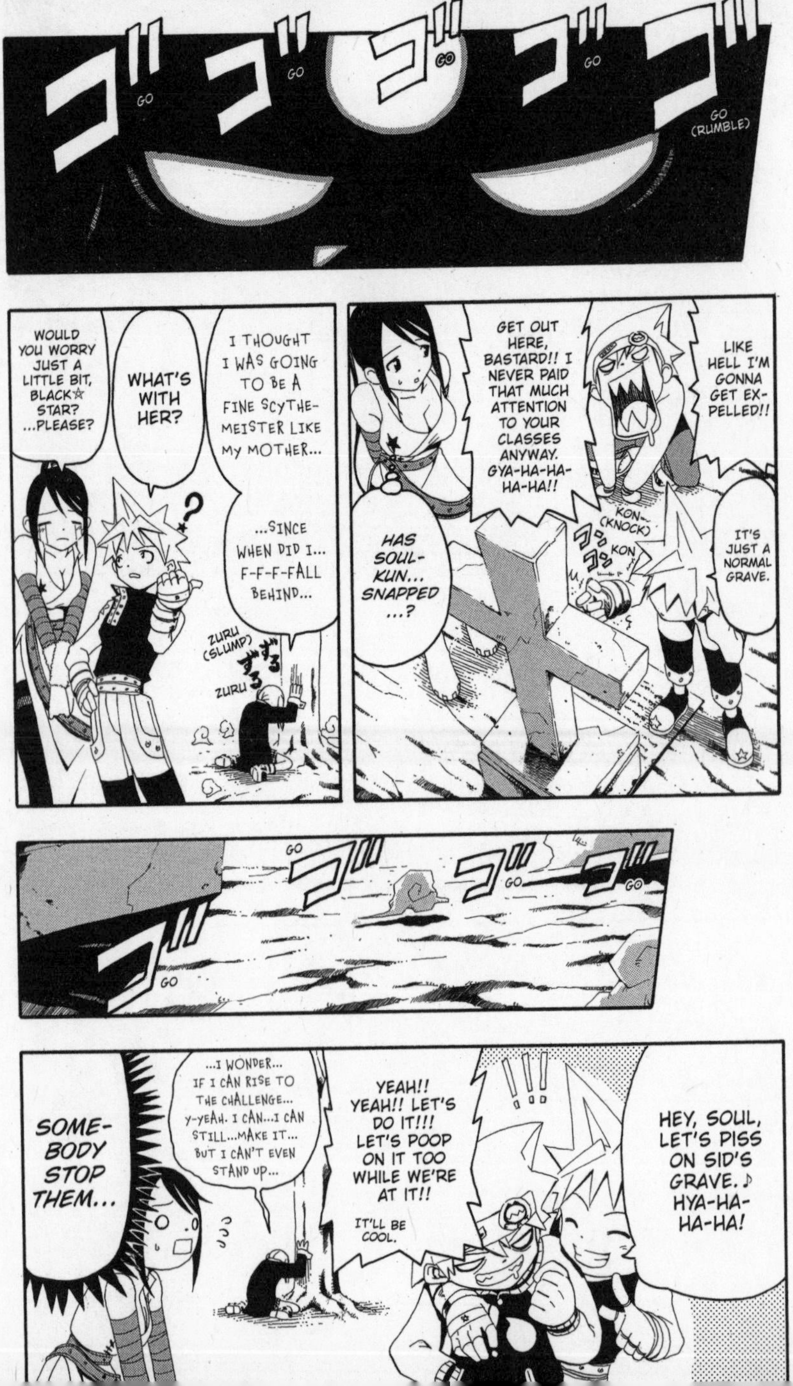
GO GO GO GO GO (RUMBLE)
LIKE HELL I'M GONNA GET EX-PELLED!!
GET OUT HERE, BASTARD!! I NEVER PAID THAT MUCH ATTENTION TO YOUR CLASSES ANYWAY. GYA-HA-HA-HA-HA!!
IT'S JUST A NORMAL GRAVE.
KON (KNOCK) KON
HAS SOUL-KUN... SNAPPED ...?
I THOUGHT I WAS GOING TO BE A FINE SCYTHE-MEISTER LIKE MY MOTHER...
...SINCE WHEN DID I... F-F-F-FALL BEHIND...
WHAT'S WITH HER?
WOULD YOU WORRY JUST A LITTLE BIT, BLACK☆STAR? ...PLEASE?
ZURU (SLUMP) ZURU
GO GO GO GO
HEY, SOUL, LET'S PISS ON SID'S GRAVE.♪ HYA-HA-HA-HA!
YEAH!! YEAH!! LET'S DO IT!!! LET'S POOP ON IT TOO WHILE WE'RE AT IT!!
IT'LL BE COOL.
...I WONDER... IF I CAN RISE TO THE CHALLENGE... Y-YEAH. I CAN...I CAN STILL...MAKE IT... BUT I CAN'T EVEN STAND UP...
SOME-BODY STOP THEM...

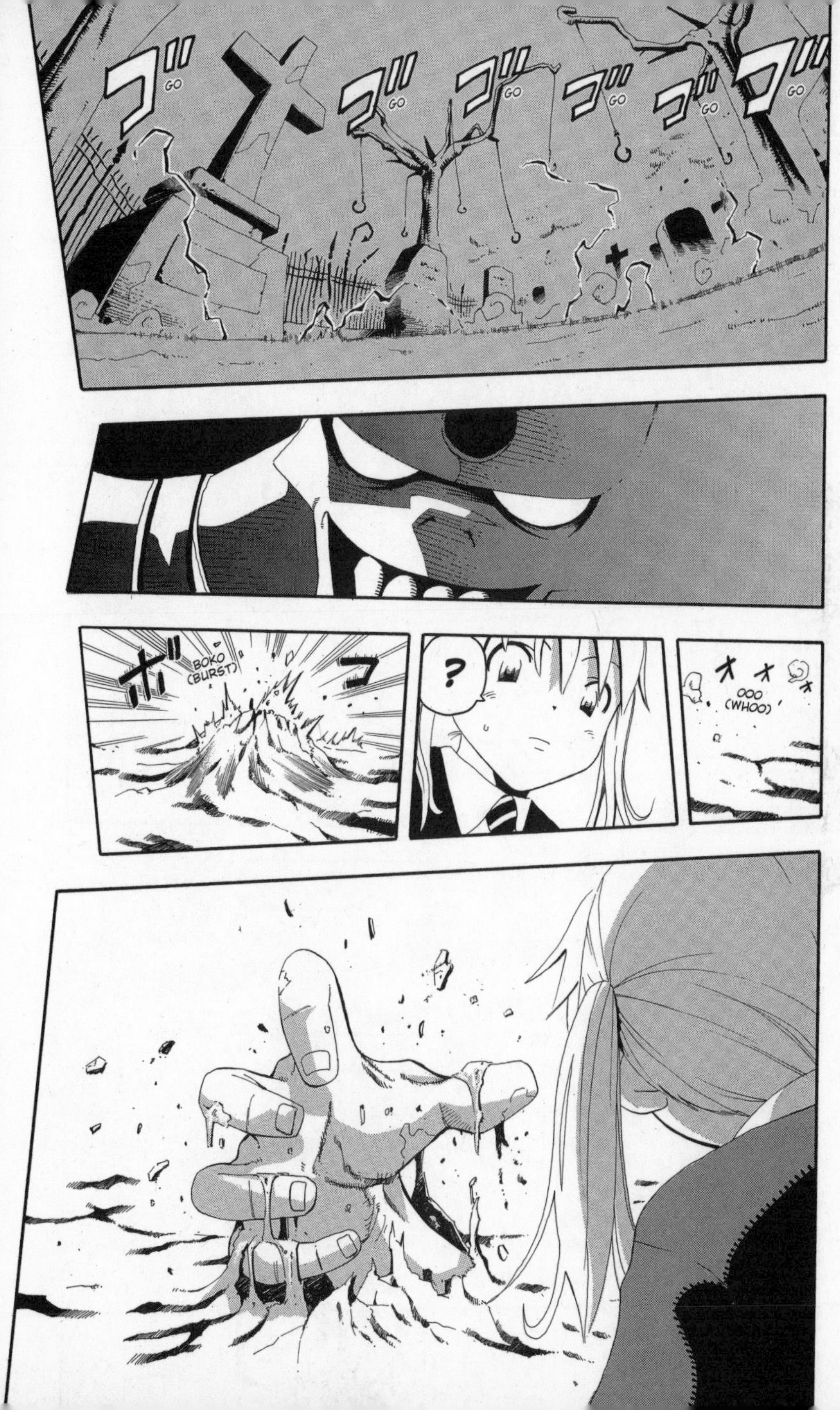
ゴ GO
ゴ GO
ゴ GO
ゴ GO
ゴ GO
ゴ GO
オオ OOO (WHOO)
?
ボコ BOKO (BURST)

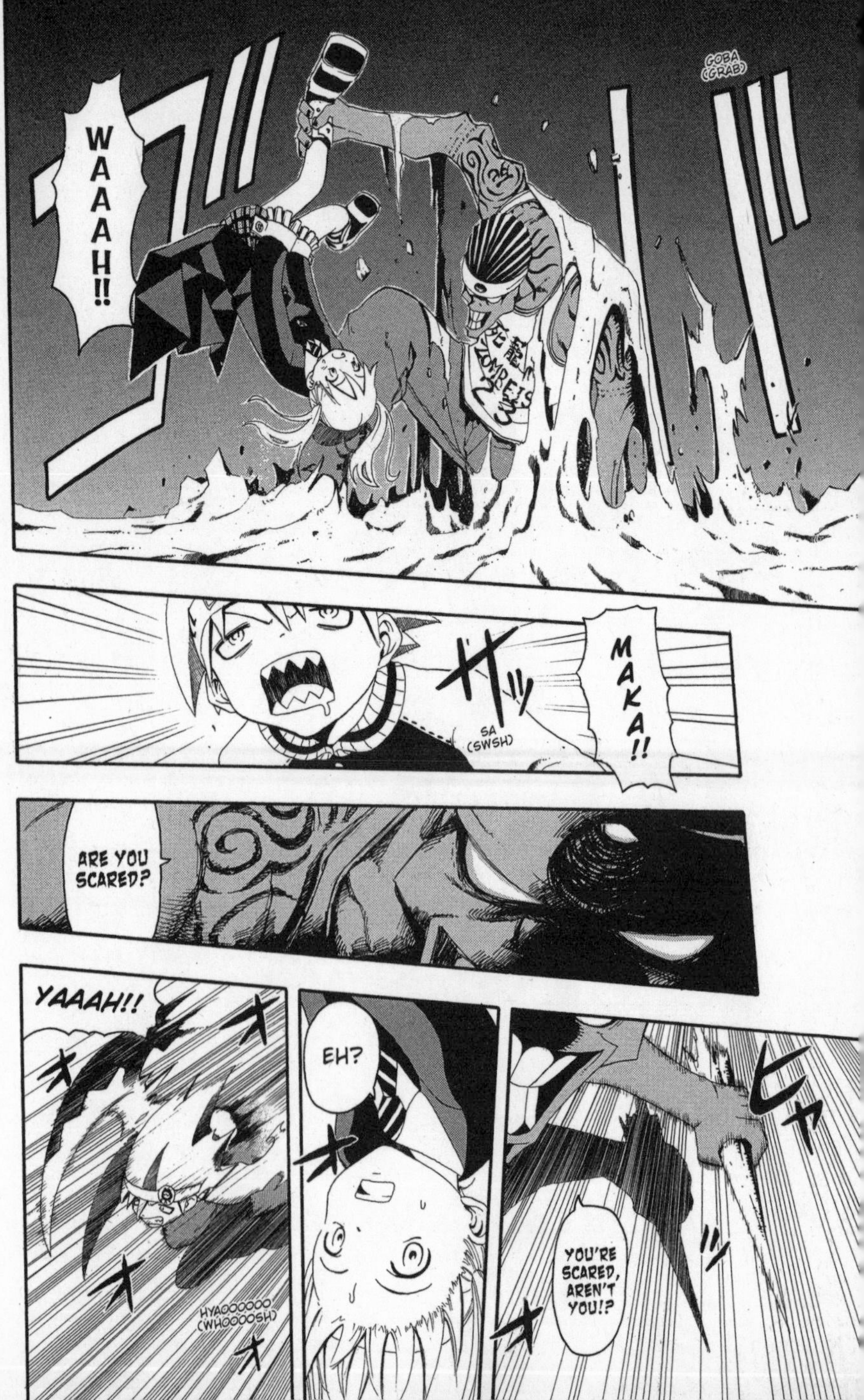
GOBA (GRAB)
WAAAAH!!
MAKA!!
SA (SWSH)
ARE YOU SCARED?
YOU'RE SCARED, AREN'T YOU!?
EH?
YAAAH!!
HYAOOOOOO (WHOOOOSH)

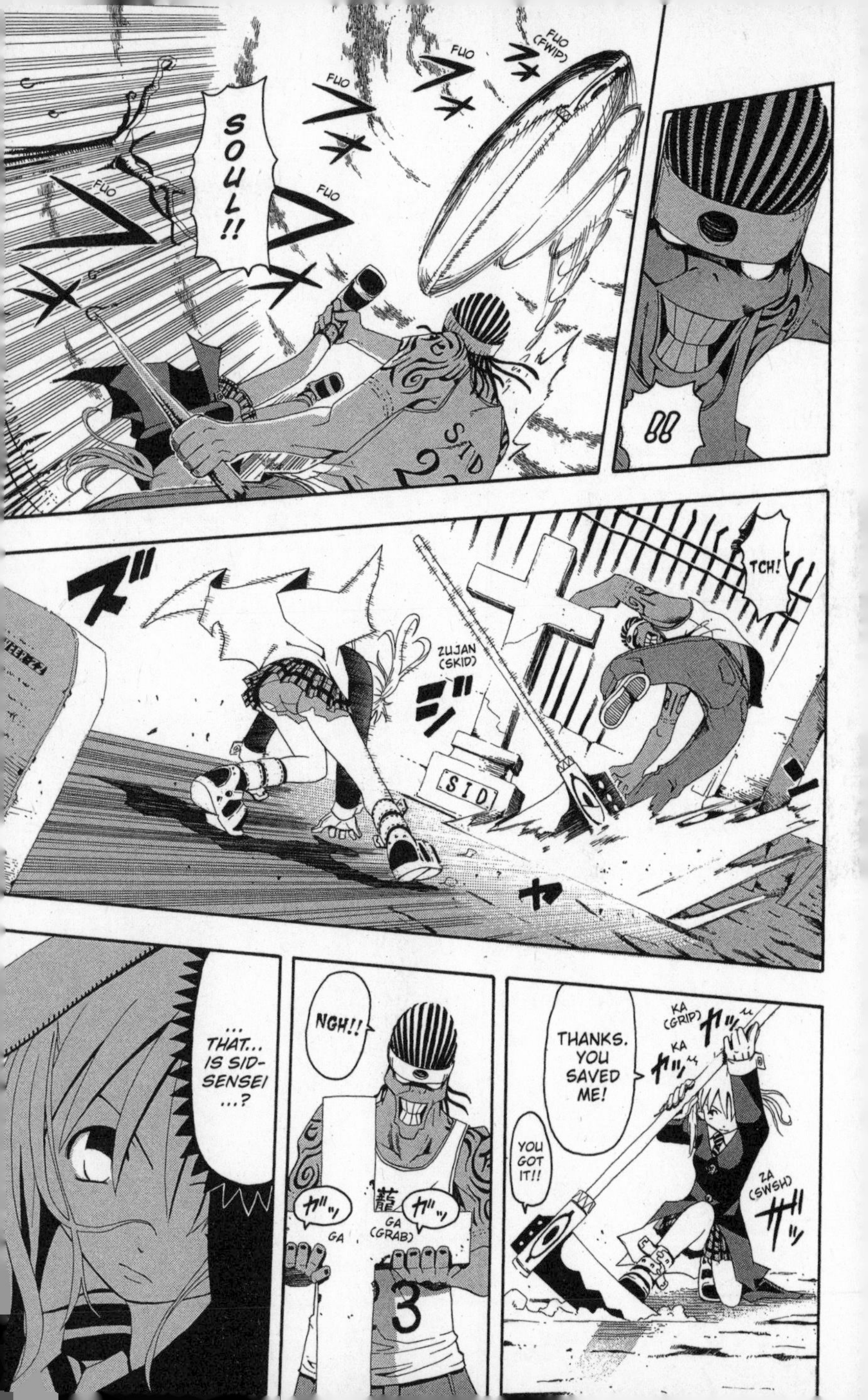
!!
FUO (FWIP)
FUO
FUO
SOUL!!
FUO
FUO
TCH!
ZUJAN (SKID)
KA (GRIP)
KA
THANKS. YOU SAVED ME!
YOU GOT IT!!
ZA (SWSH)
NGH!!
GA (GRAB)
GA
... THAT... IS SID-SENSEI ...?

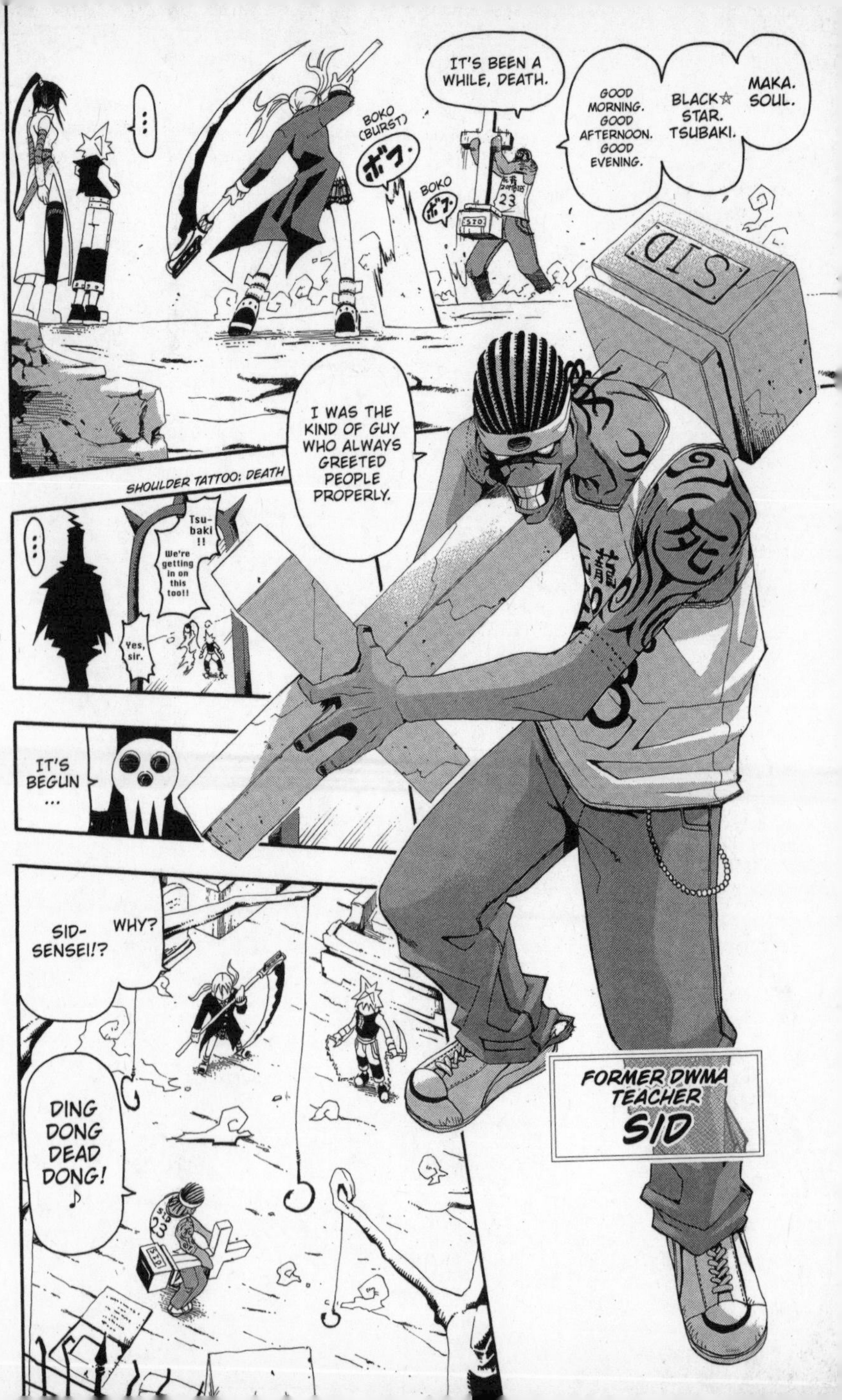

IT'S BEEN A WHILE, DEATH.
MAKA. SOUL.
BLACK☆STAR. TSUBAKI.
GOOD MORNING. GOOD AFTERNOON. GOOD EVENING.
BOKO
ボコ
BOKO (BURST)
ボコ
...
I WAS THE KIND OF GUY WHO ALWAYS GREETED PEOPLE PROPERLY.
SHOULDER TATTOO: DEATH
Tsubaki!!
We're getting in on this too!!
Yes, sir.
...
IT'S BEGUN ...
FORMER DWMA TEACHER SID
WHY?
SID-SENSEI!?
DING DONG DEAD DONG! ♪

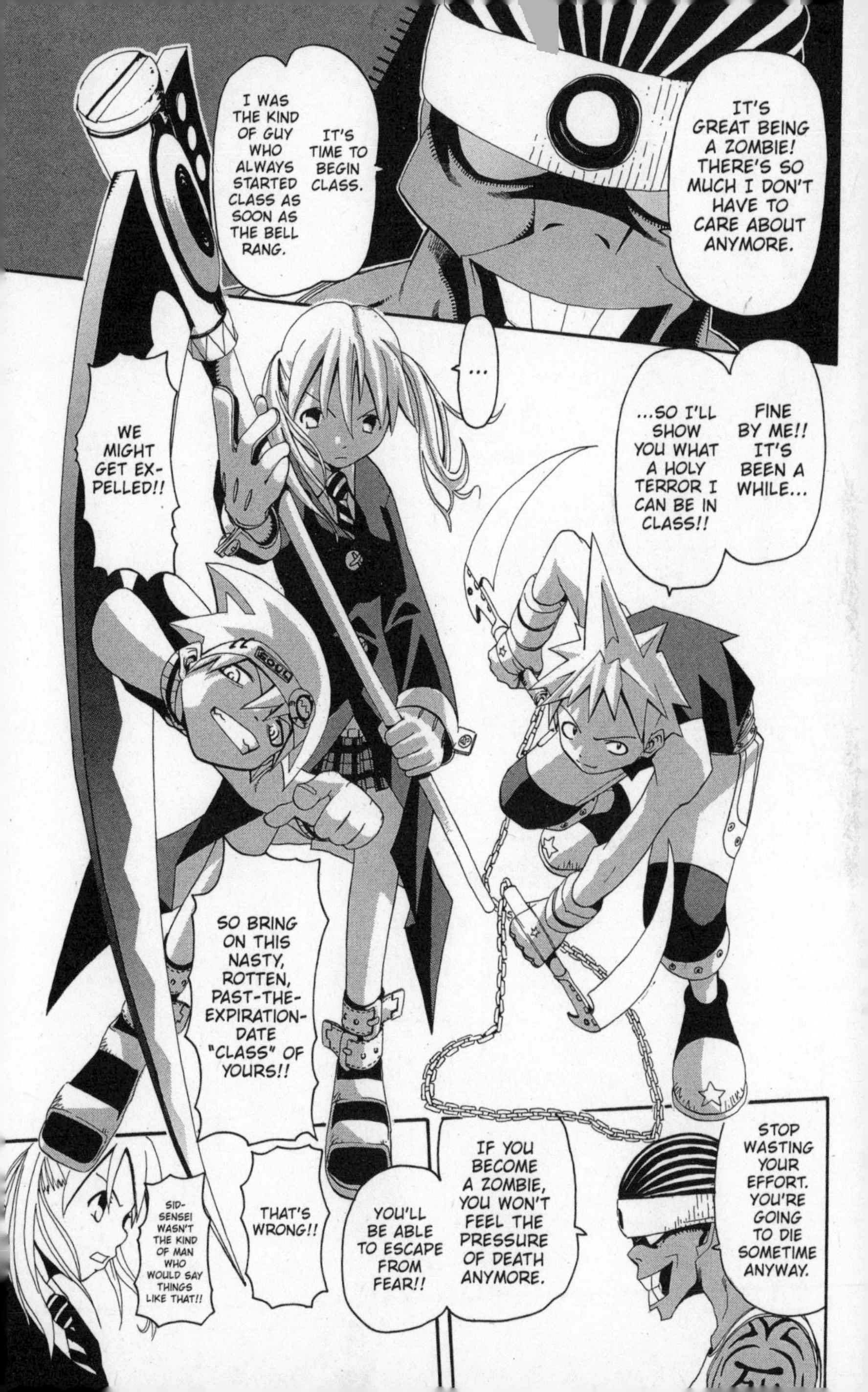

IT'S GREAT BEING A ZOMBIE! THERE'S SO MUCH I DON'T HAVE TO CARE ABOUT ANYMORE.
IT'S TIME TO BEGIN CLASS.
I WAS THE KIND OF GUY WHO ALWAYS STARTED CLASS AS SOON AS THE BELL RANG.
...
FINE BY ME!! IT'S BEEN A WHILE...
...SO I'LL SHOW YOU WHAT A HOLY TERROR I CAN BE IN CLASS!!
WE MIGHT GET EX-PELLED!!
SO BRING ON THIS NASTY, ROTTEN, PAST-THE-EXPIRATION-DATE "CLASS" OF YOURS!!
STOP WASTING YOUR EFFORT. YOU'RE GOING TO DIE SOMETIME ANYWAY.
IF YOU BECOME A ZOMBIE, YOU WON'T FEEL THE PRESSURE OF DEATH ANYMORE.
YOU'LL BE ABLE TO ESCAPE FROM FEAR!!
THAT'S WRONG!!
SID-SENSEI WASN'T THE KIND OF MAN WHO WOULD SAY THINGS LIKE THAT!!

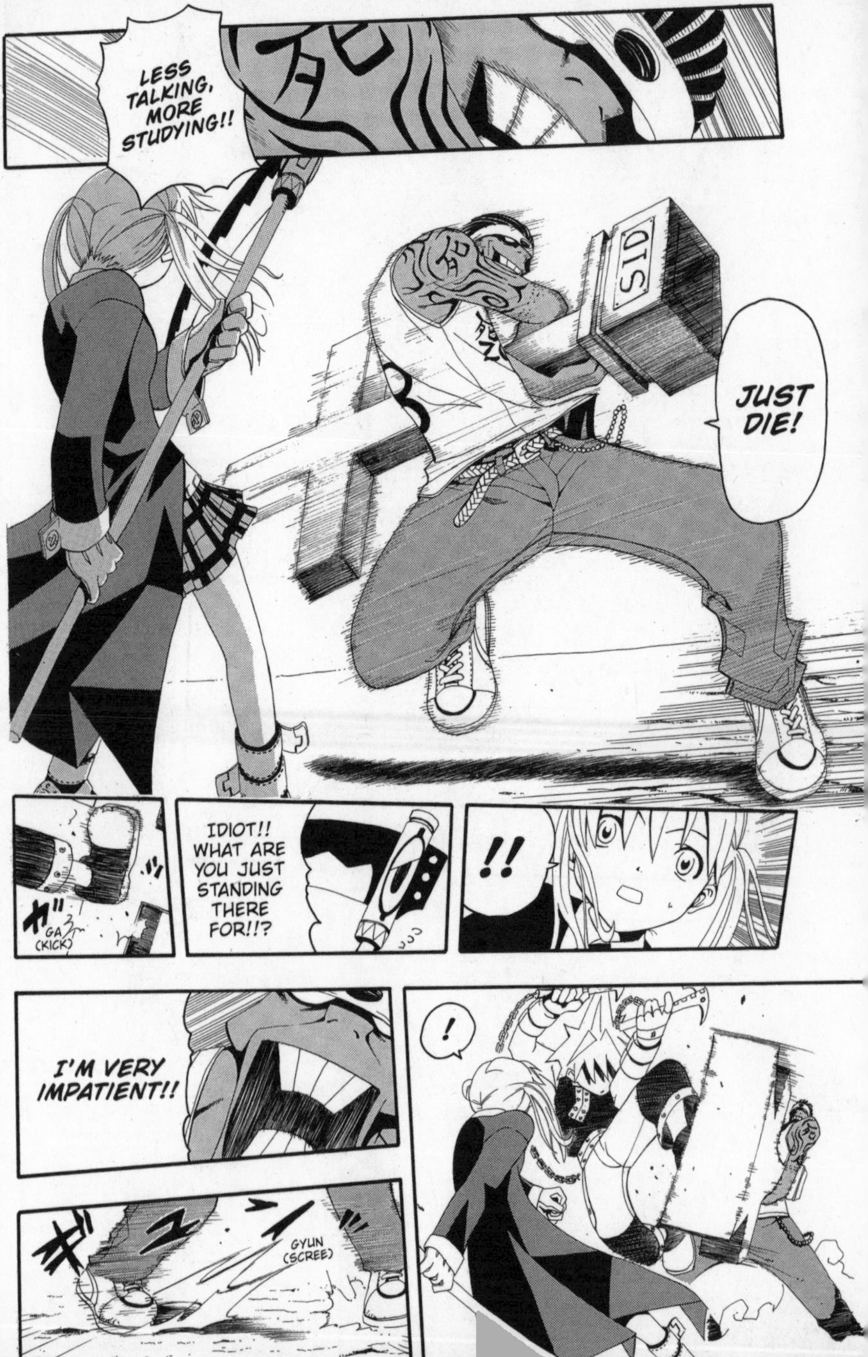
LESS TALKING, MORE STUDYING!!
JUST DIE!
!!
IDIOT!! WHAT ARE YOU JUST STANDING THERE FOR!!?
GA (KICK)
!
I'M VERY IMPATIENT!!
GYUN (SCREE)

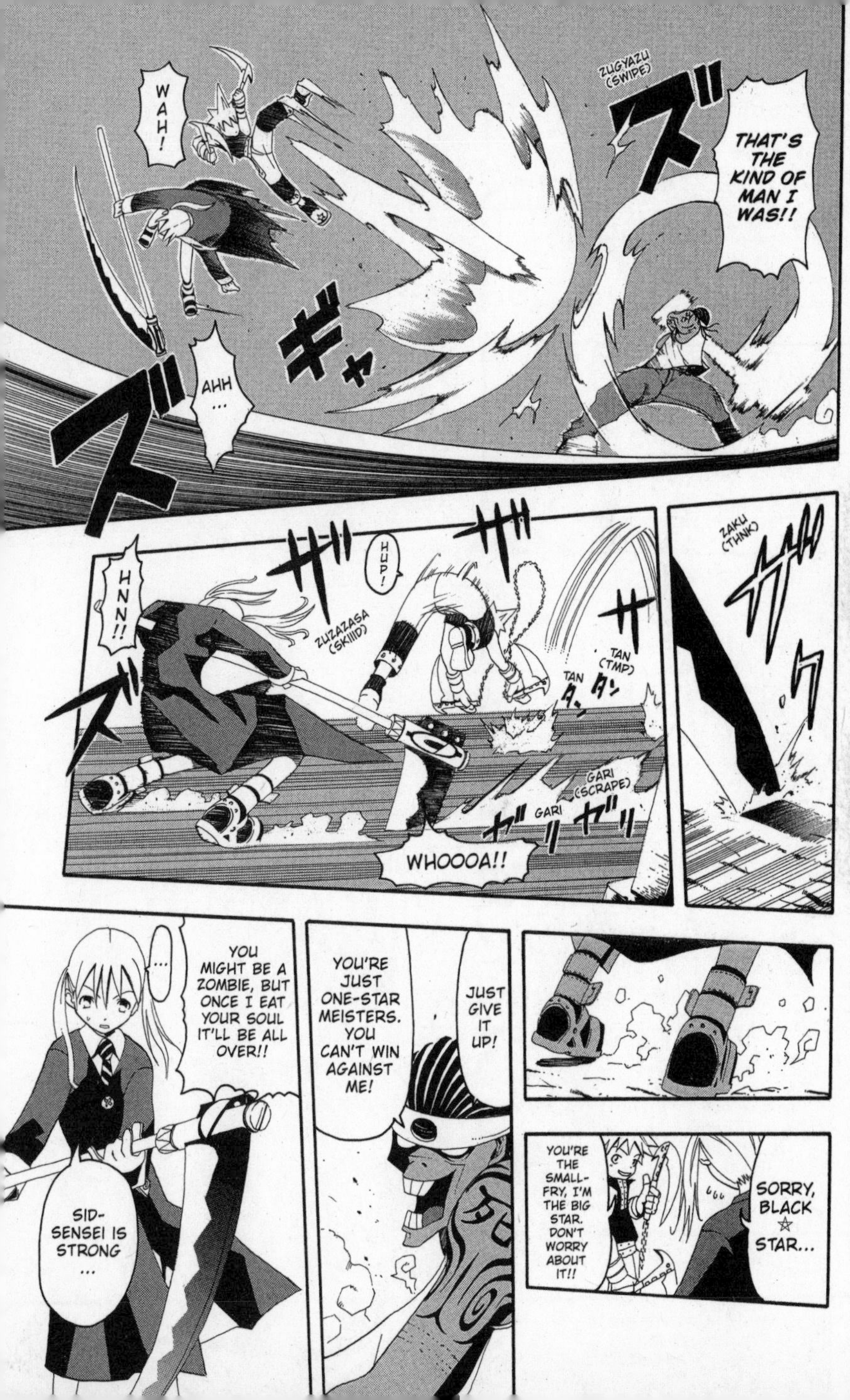
ZUGYAZU (SWIPE)
THAT'S THE KIND OF MAN I WAS!!
WAH!
AHH ...
ZAKU (THNK)
HUP!
HNN!!
ZUZAZASA (SKIIID)
TAN (TMP)
TAN
GARI (SCRAPE)
GARI
WHOOOA!!
SORRY, BLACK☆STAR...
YOU'RE THE SMALL-FRY, I'M THE BIG STAR. DON'T WORRY ABOUT IT!!
JUST GIVE IT UP!
YOU'RE JUST ONE-STAR MEISTERS. YOU CAN'T WIN AGAINST ME!
YOU MIGHT BE A ZOMBIE, BUT ONCE I EAT YOUR SOUL IT'LL BE ALL OVER!!
...
SID-SENSEI IS STRONG ...

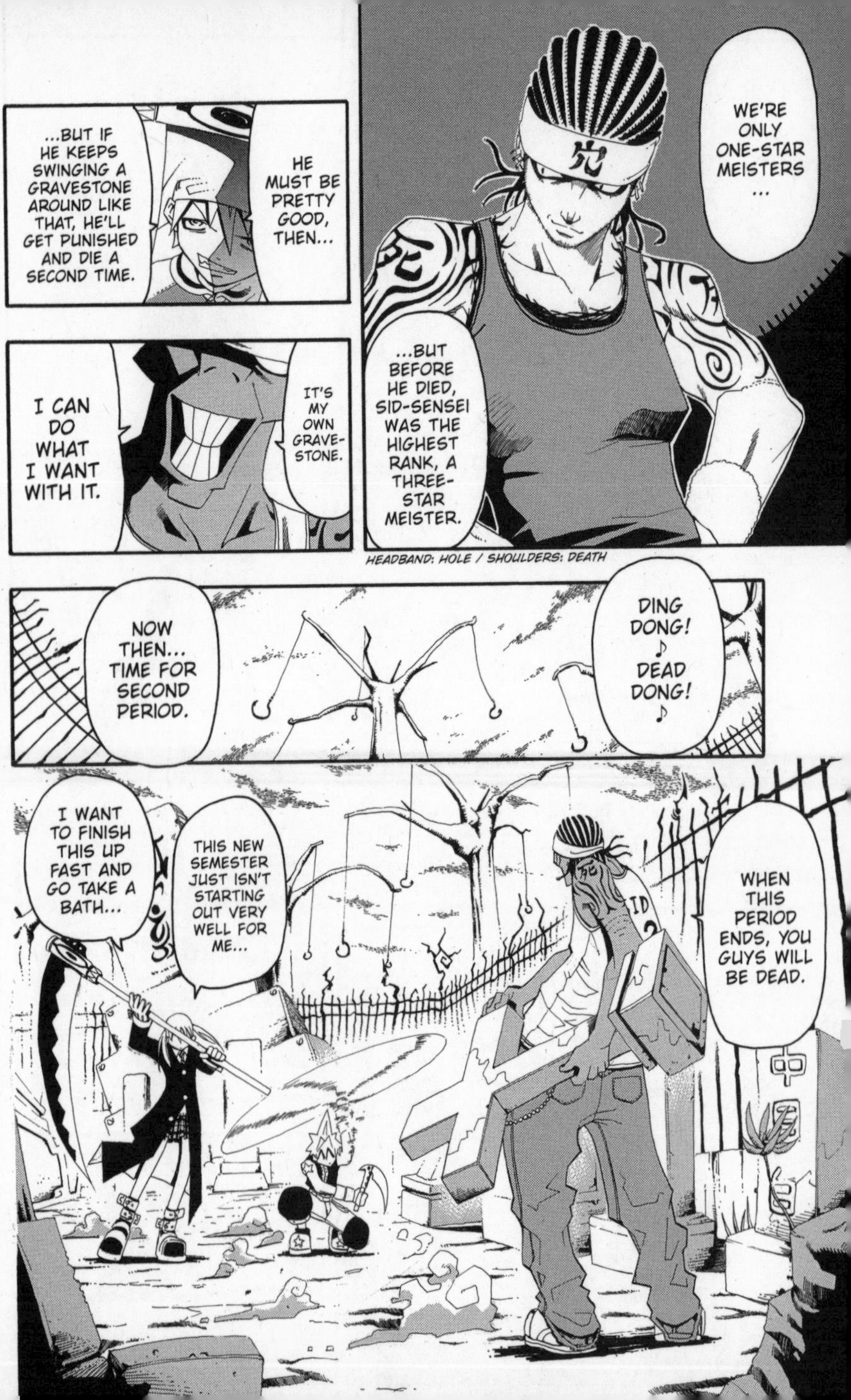
WE'RE ONLY ONE-STAR MEISTERS...
...BUT BEFORE HE DIED, SID-SENSEI WAS THE HIGHEST RANK, A THREE-STAR MEISTER.
HE MUST BE PRETTY GOOD, THEN...
...BUT IF HE KEEPS SWINGING A GRAVESTONE AROUND LIKE THAT, HE'LL GET PUNISHED AND DIE A SECOND TIME.
IT'S MY OWN GRAVESTONE.
I CAN DO WHAT I WANT WITH IT.
HEADBAND: HOLE / SHOULDERS: DEATH
DING DONG! ♪ DEAD DONG! ♪
NOW THEN... TIME FOR SECOND PERIOD.
WHEN THIS PERIOD ENDS, YOU GUYS WILL BE DEAD.
THIS NEW SEMESTER JUST ISN'T STARTING OUT VERY WELL FOR ME...
I WANT TO FINISH THIS UP FAST AND GO TAKE A BATH...

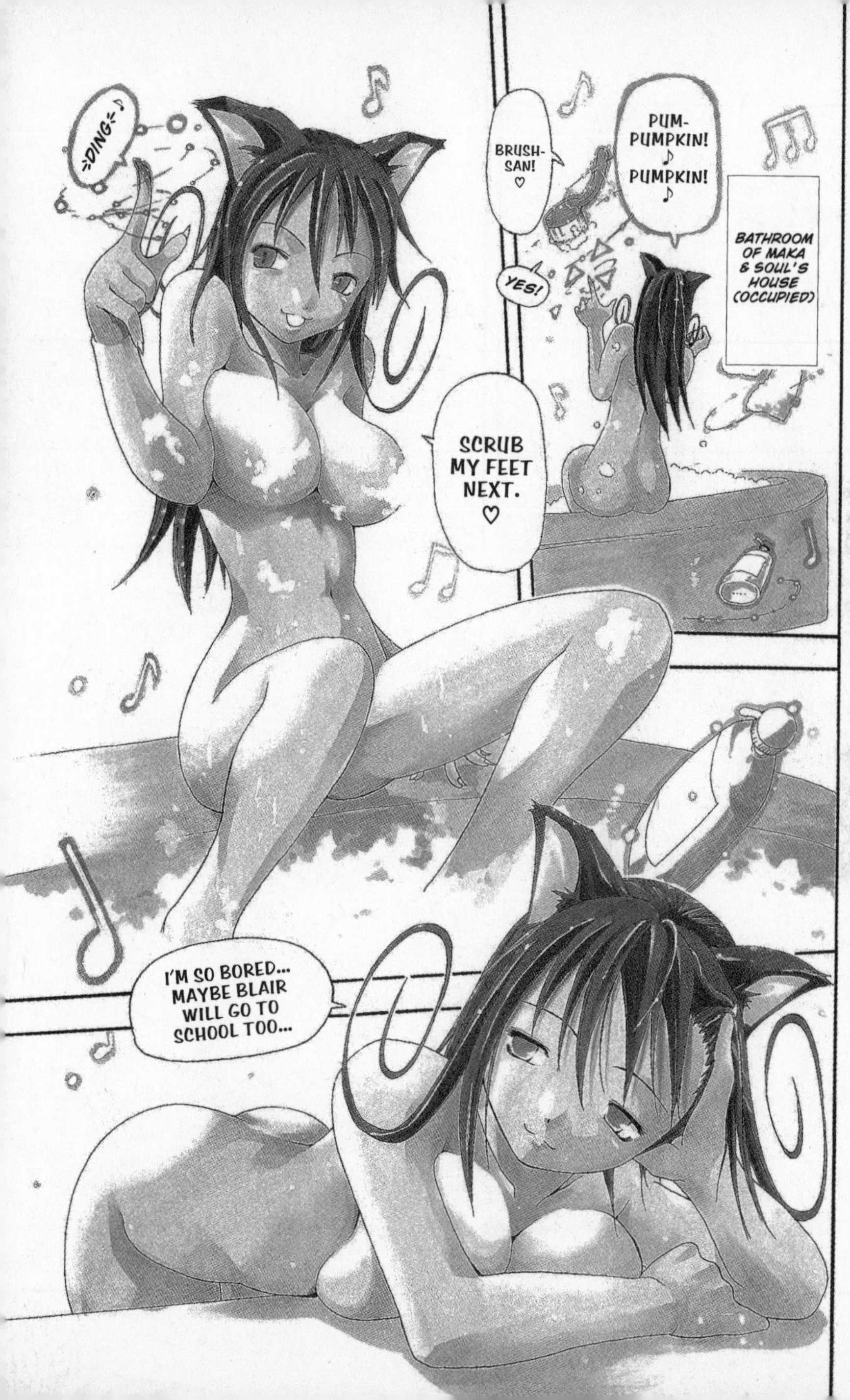
BATHROOM OF MAKA & SOUL'S HOUSE (OCCUPIED)
PUM-PUMPKIN! ♪ PUMPKIN! ♪
BRUSH-SAN! ♡
YES!
SCRUB MY FEET NEXT. ♡
DING ♪
I'M SO BORED... MAYBE BLAIR WILL GO TO SCHOOL TOO...

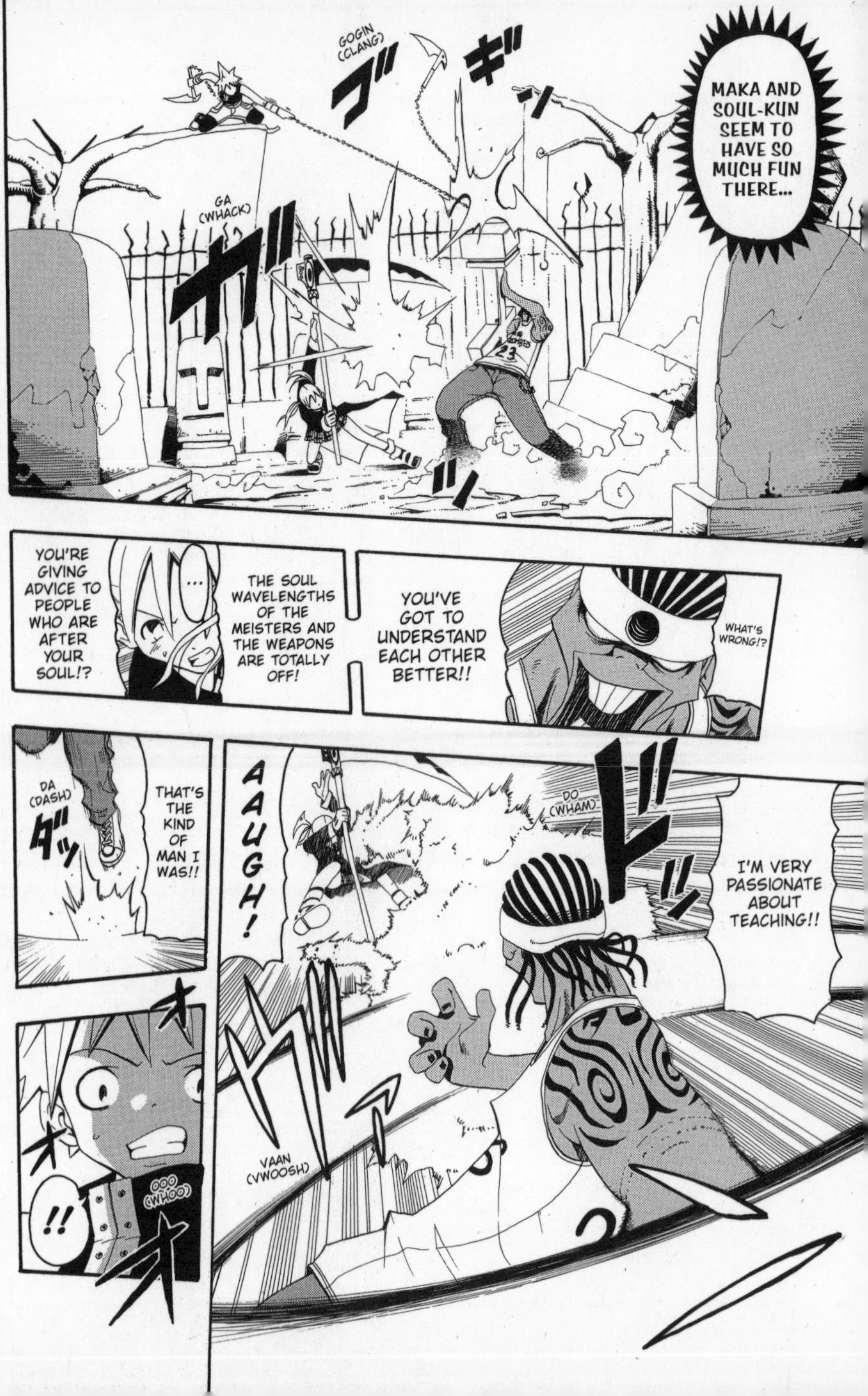
MAKA AND SOUL-KUN SEEM TO HAVE SO MUCH FUN THERE...
GOGIN (CLANG)
GA (WHACK)
WHAT'S WRONG!?
THE SOUL WAVELENGTHS OF THE MEISTERS AND THE WEAPONS ARE TOTALLY OFF!
YOU'VE GOT TO UNDERSTAND EACH OTHER BETTER!!
...
YOU'RE GIVING ADVICE TO PEOPLE WHO ARE AFTER YOUR SOUL!?
I'M VERY PASSIONATE ABOUT TEACHING!!
DO (WHAM)
AAUGH!
THAT'S THE KIND OF MAN I WAS!!
DA (DASH)
VAAN (VWOOSH)
OOO (WHOO)
!!

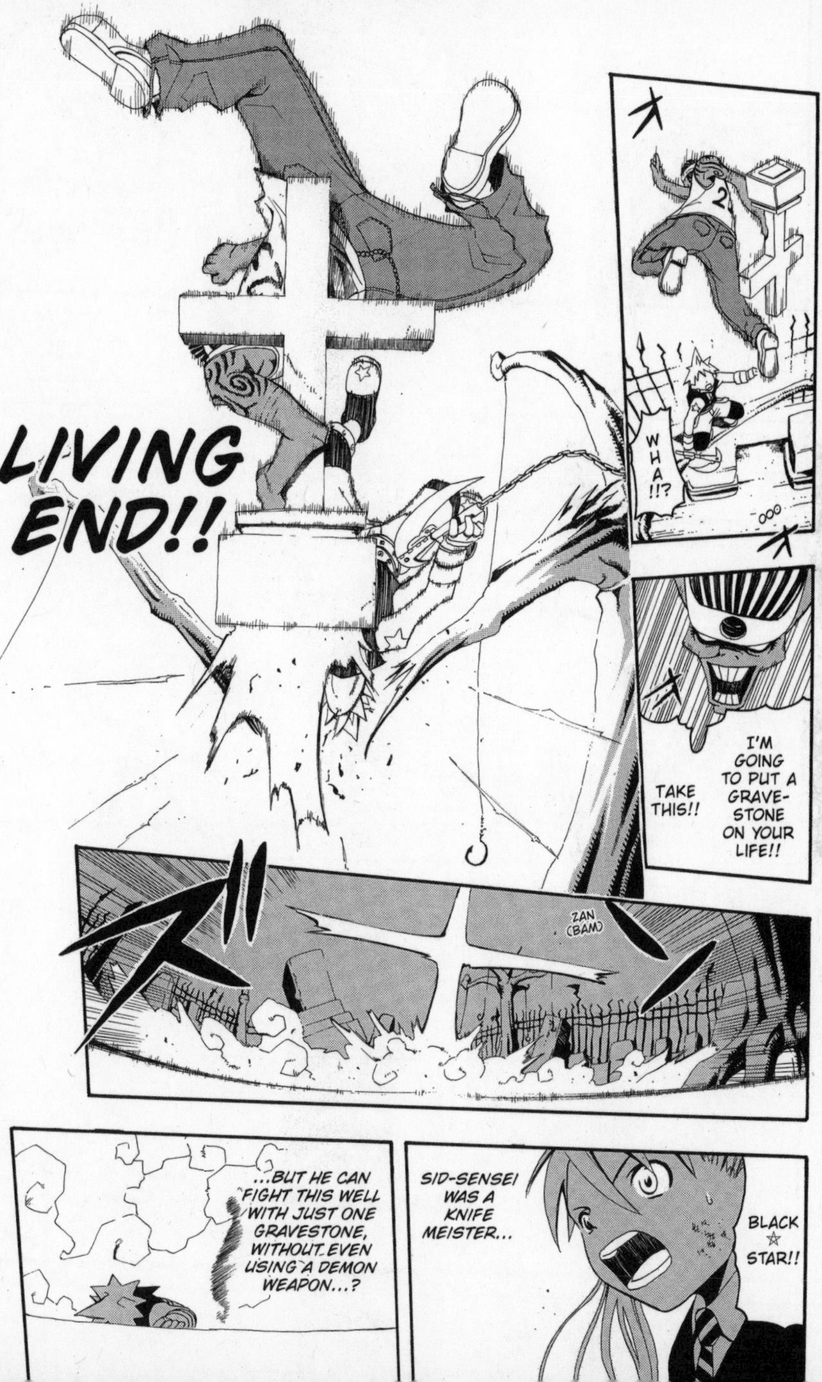
WHA!!?
I'M GOING TO PUT A GRAVESTONE ON YOUR LIFE!!
TAKE THIS!!
LIVING END!!
ZAN (BAM)
BLACK☆STAR!!
SID-SENSEI WAS A KNIFE MEISTER...
...BUT HE CAN FIGHT THIS WELL WITH JUST ONE GRAVESTONE, WITHOUT EVEN USING A DEMON WEAPON...?

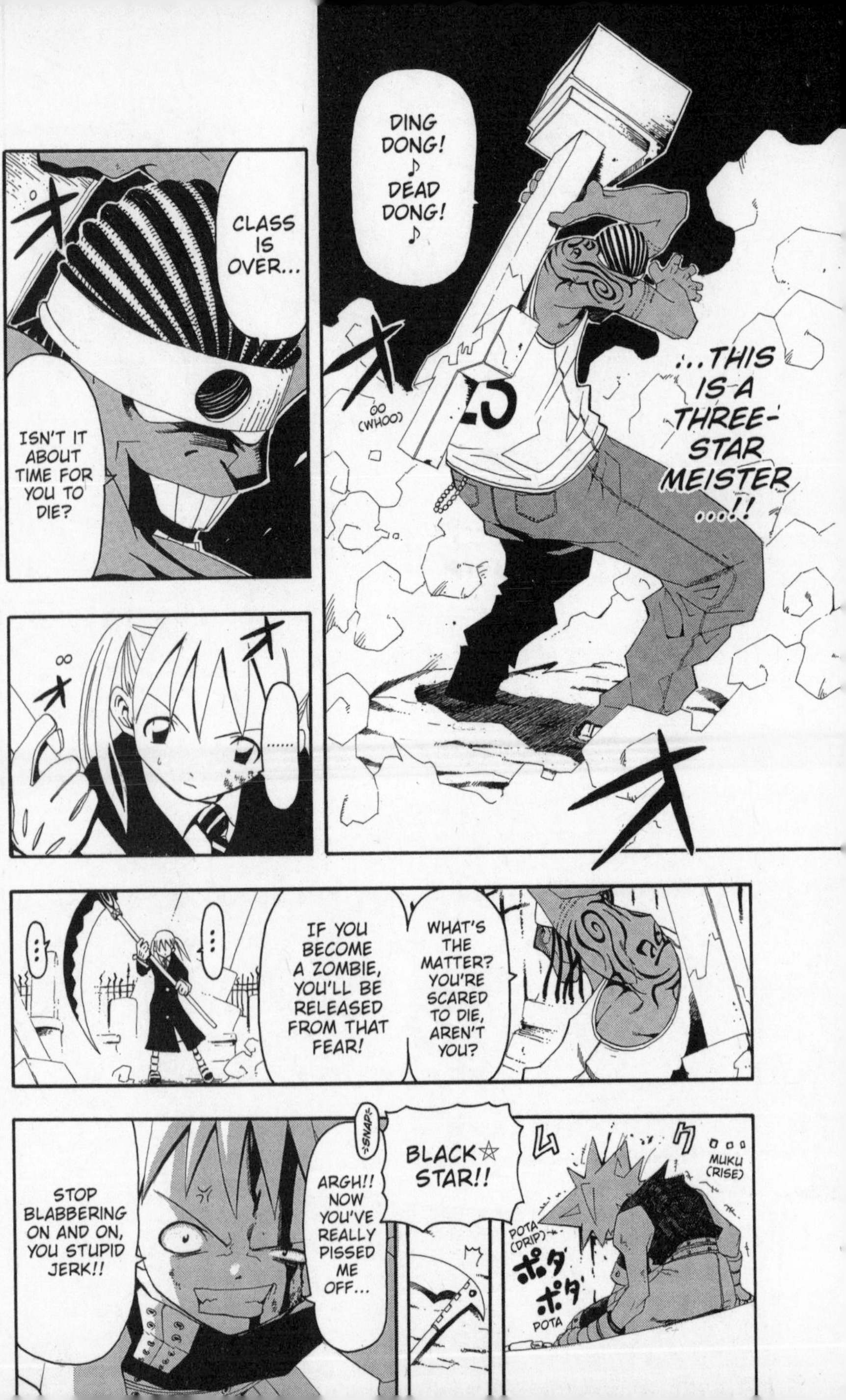
DING DONG! ♪ DEAD DONG! ♪
OO (WHOO)
...THIS IS A THREE-STAR MEISTER ...!!
CLASS IS OVER...
ISN'T IT ABOUT TIME FOR YOU TO DIE?
OO
......
WHAT'S THE MATTER? YOU'RE SCARED TO DIE, AREN'T YOU?
IF YOU BECOME A ZOMBIE, YOU'LL BE RELEASED FROM THAT FEAR!
...
...
MUKU (RISE)
POTA (DRIP)
POTA
BLACK☆ STAR!!
SNAP
ARGH!! NOW YOU'VE REALLY PISSED ME OFF...
STOP BLABBERING ON AND ON, YOU STUPID JERK!!

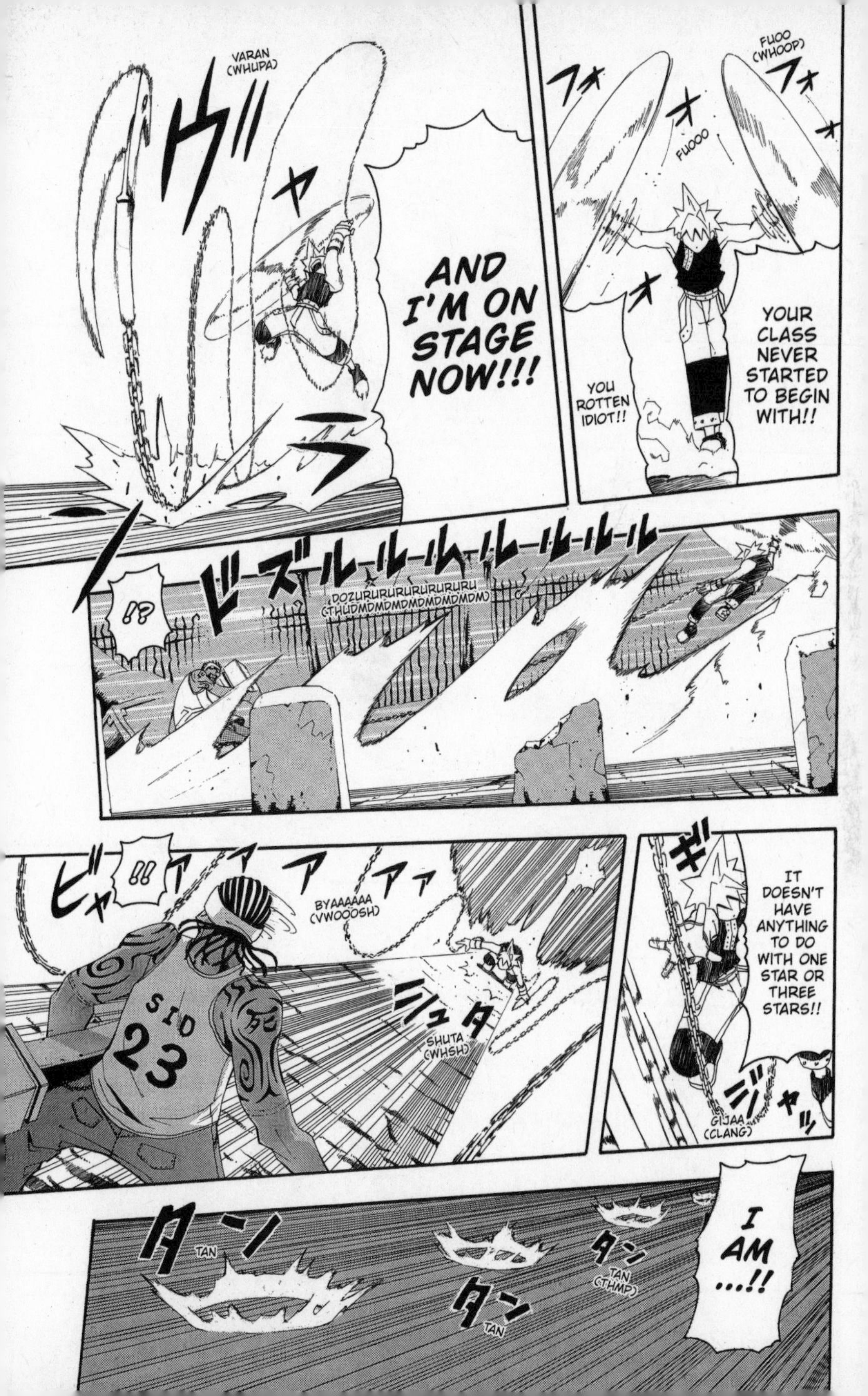
FUOO (WHOOP)
FUOOO
YOUR CLASS NEVER STARTED TO BEGIN WITH!!
YOU ROTTEN IDIOT!!
VARAN (WHUPA)
AND I'M ON STAGE NOW!!!
DOZURURURURURURURU (THUDMDMDMDMDMDMDM)
!?
IT DOESN'T HAVE ANYTHING TO DO WITH ONE STAR OR THREE STARS!!
GIJAA (CLANG)
!!
BYAAAAAA (VWOOOSH)
SID 23
SHUTA (WHSH)
I AM...!!
TAN (THMP)
TAN
TAN

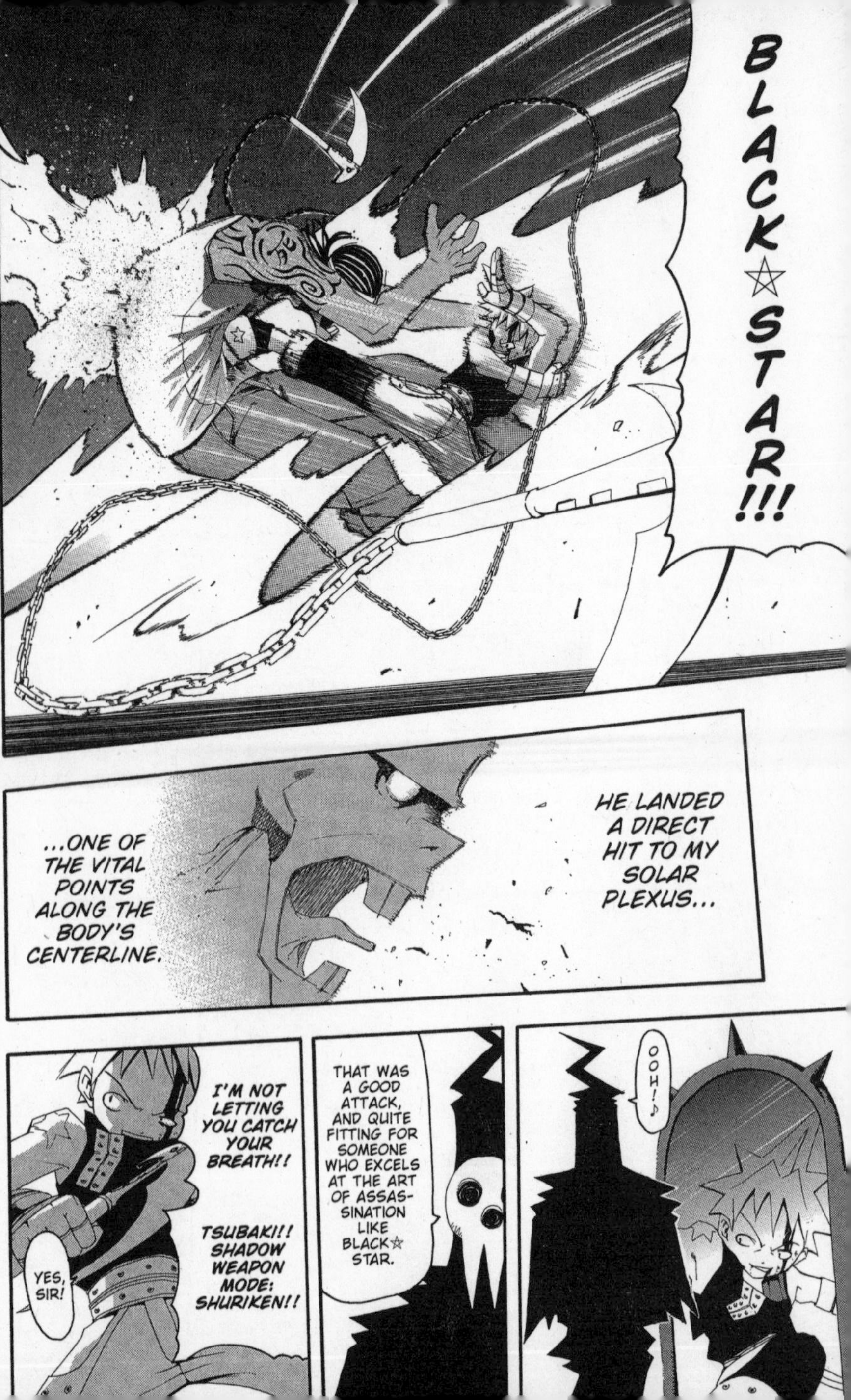
BLACK☆STAR!!!
HE LANDED A DIRECT HIT TO MY SOLAR PLEXUS...
...ONE OF THE VITAL POINTS ALONG THE BODY'S CENTERLINE.
OOH!♪
THAT WAS A GOOD ATTACK, AND QUITE FITTING FOR SOMEONE WHO EXCELS AT THE ART OF ASSAS-SINATION LIKE BLACK☆STAR.
I'M NOT LETTING YOU CATCH YOUR BREATH!!
TSUBAKI!! SHADOW WEAPON MODE: SHURIKEN!!
YES, SIR!

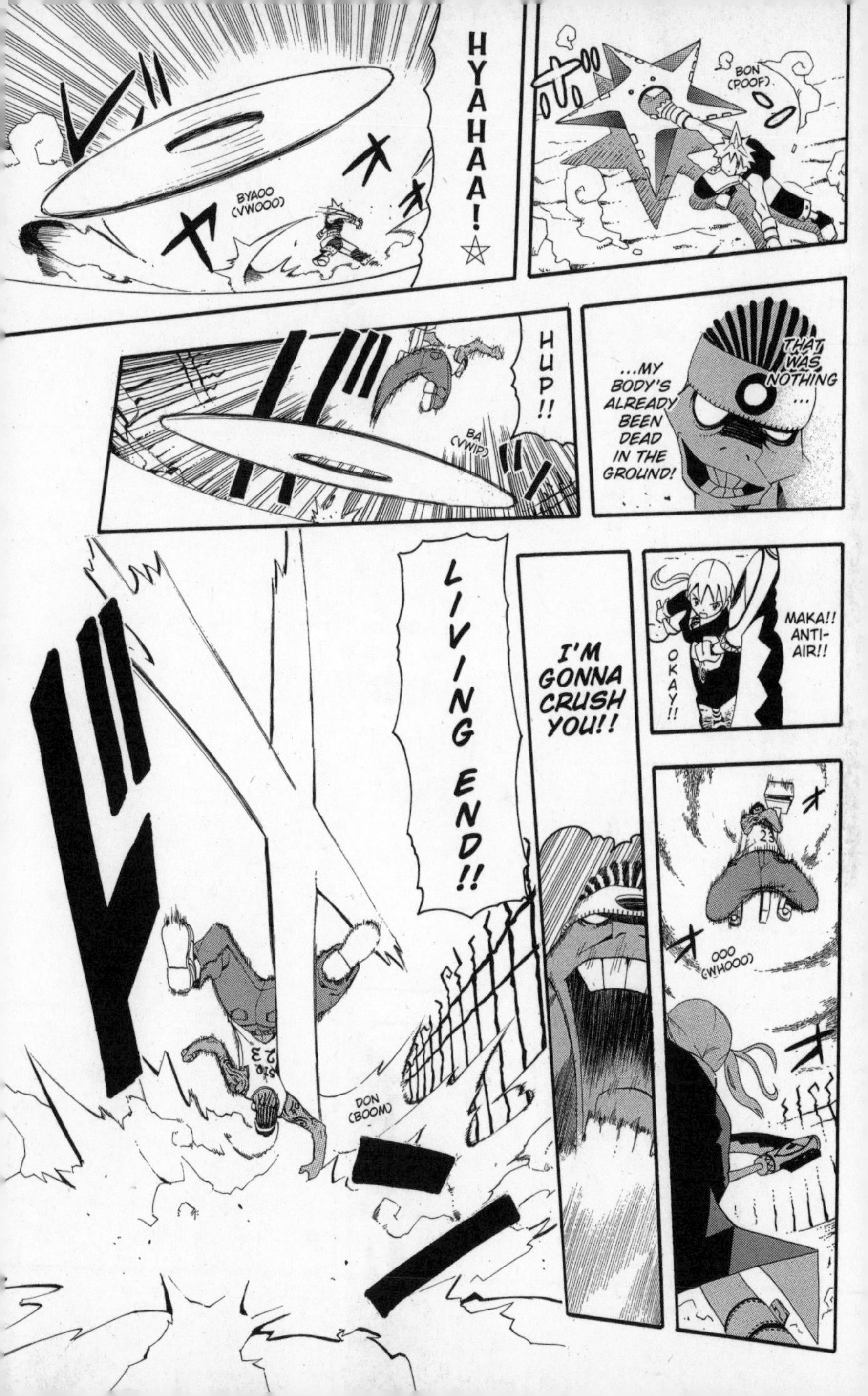
BON (POOF)
BYAOO (VWOOO)
HYAHAA!☆
THAT WAS NOTHING...
...MY BODY'S ALREADY BEEN DEAD IN THE GROUND!
HUP!!
BA (VWIP)
MAKA!! ANTI-AIR!!
OKAY!!
OOO (WHOOO)
I'M GONNA CRUSH YOU!!
LIVING END!!
DON (BOOM)

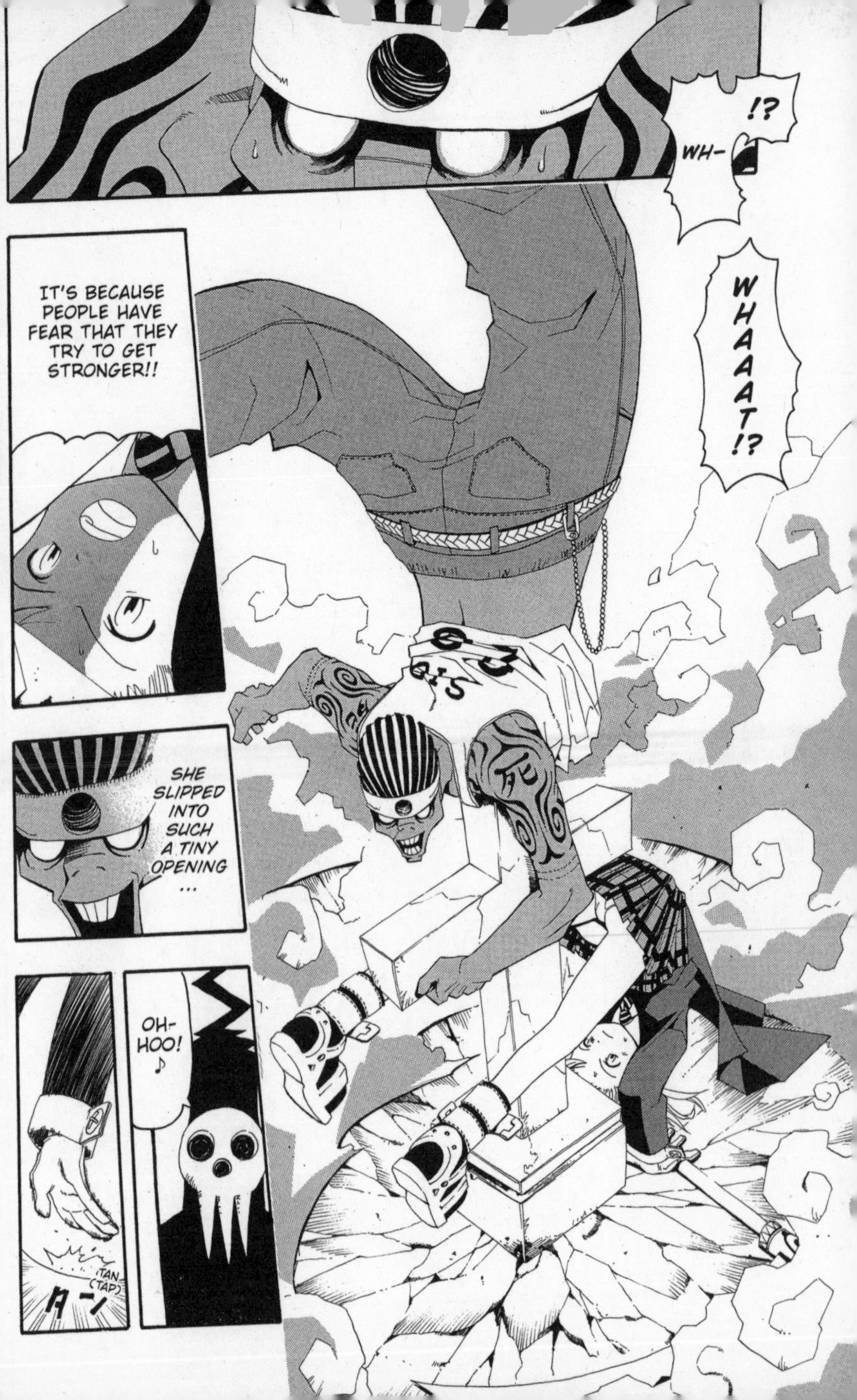
!?
WH-
WHAAAAT!?
IT'S BECAUSE PEOPLE HAVE FEAR THAT THEY TRY TO GET STRONGER!!
SHE SLIPPED INTO SUCH A TINY OPENING ...
OH-HOO! ♪
TAN (TAP)

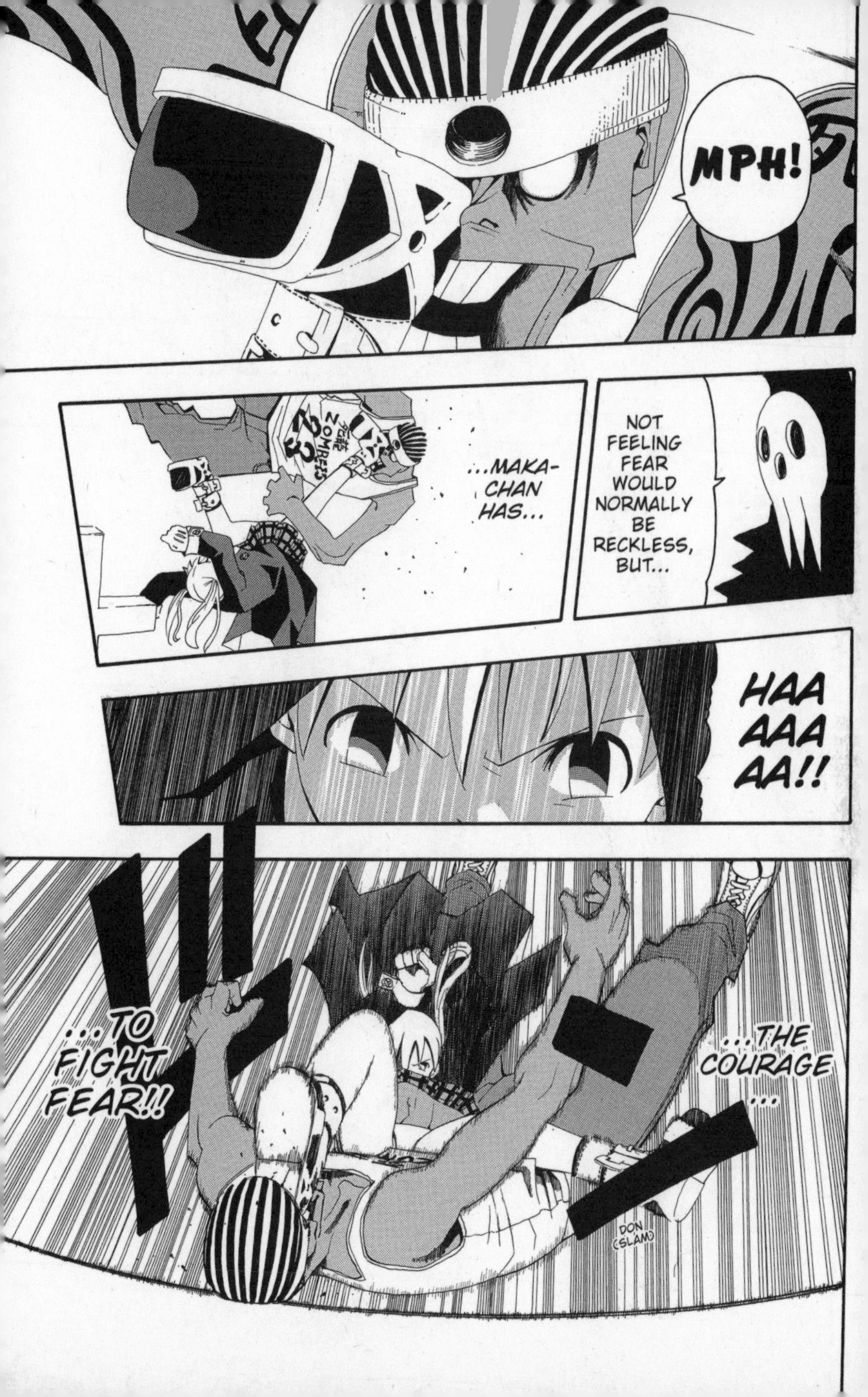
MPH!
NOT FEELING FEAR WOULD NORMALLY BE RECKLESS, BUT...
...MAKA-CHAN HAS...
HAAAAAAA!!
...THE COURAGE...
...TO FIGHT FEAR!!
DON (SLAM)

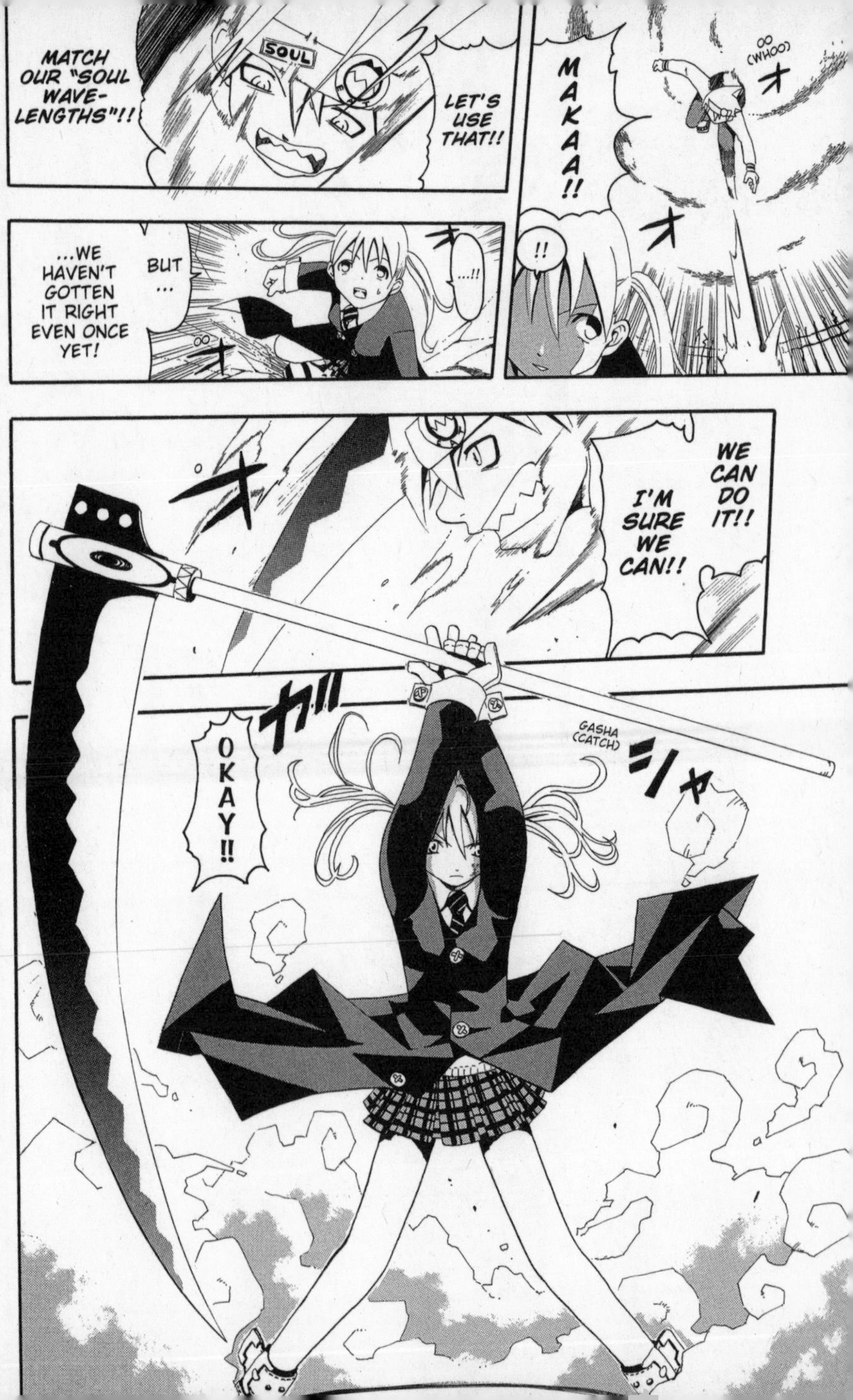

OO (WHOO)
MAKAAA!!
!!
LET'S USE THAT!!
SOUL
MATCH OUR "SOUL WAVE-LENGTHS"!!
...!!
BUT ...
...WE HAVEN'T GOTTEN IT RIGHT EVEN ONCE YET!
OO
WE CAN DO IT!!
I'M SURE WE CAN!!
GASHA (CATCH)
OKAY!!

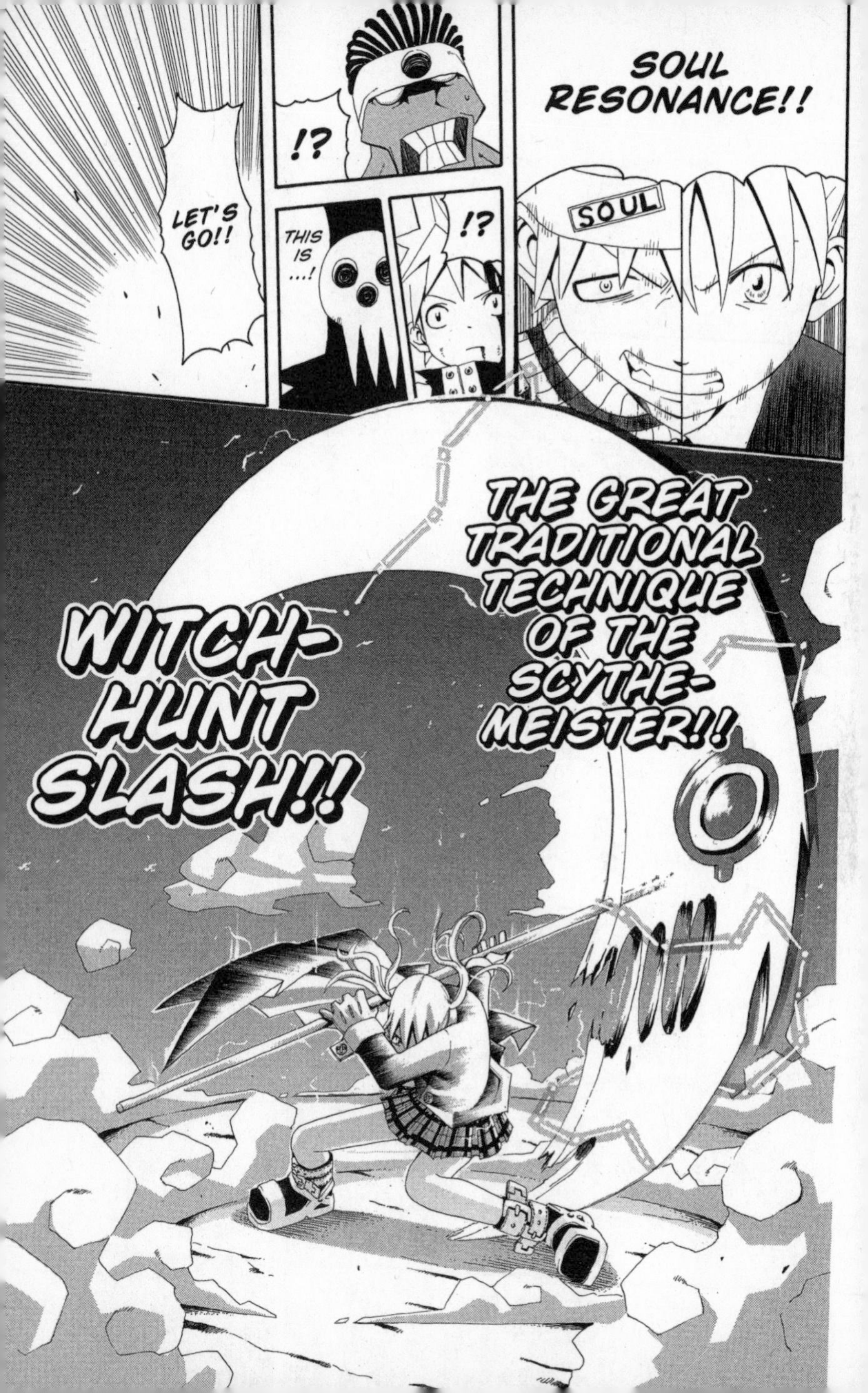
SOUL RESONANCE!!
!?
!?
THIS IS ...!
LET'S GO!!
THE GREAT TRADITIONAL TECHNIQUE OF THE SCYTHE-MEISTER!!
WITCH-HUNT SLASH!!

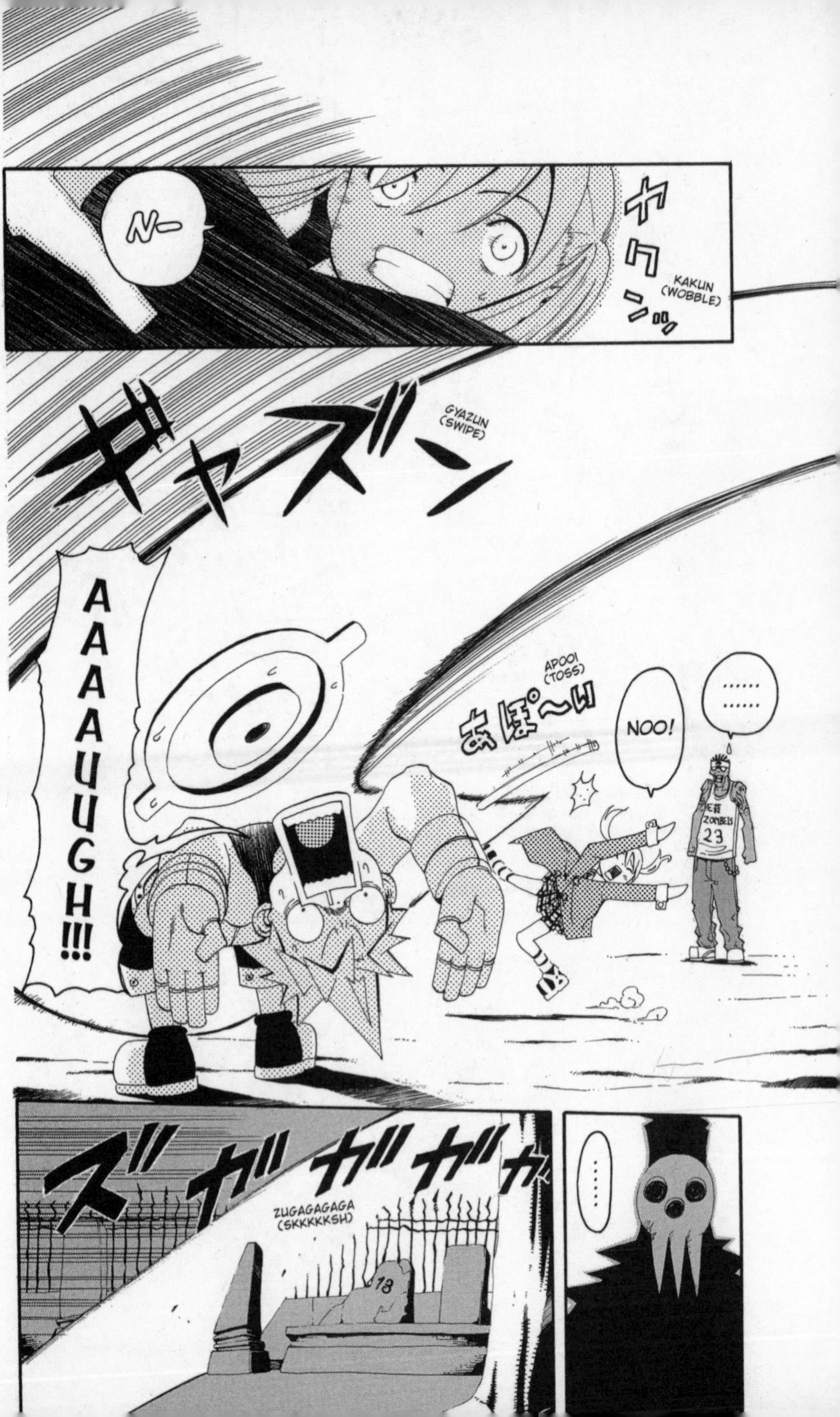
カクン
KAKUN (WOBBLE)
N–
ギャズン
GYAZUN (SWIPE)
……
……
NOO!
あぽ〜い
APOOI (TOSS)
AAAAAUUGH!!!
……
ズガガガガ
ZUGAGAGAGA (SKKKKKSH)

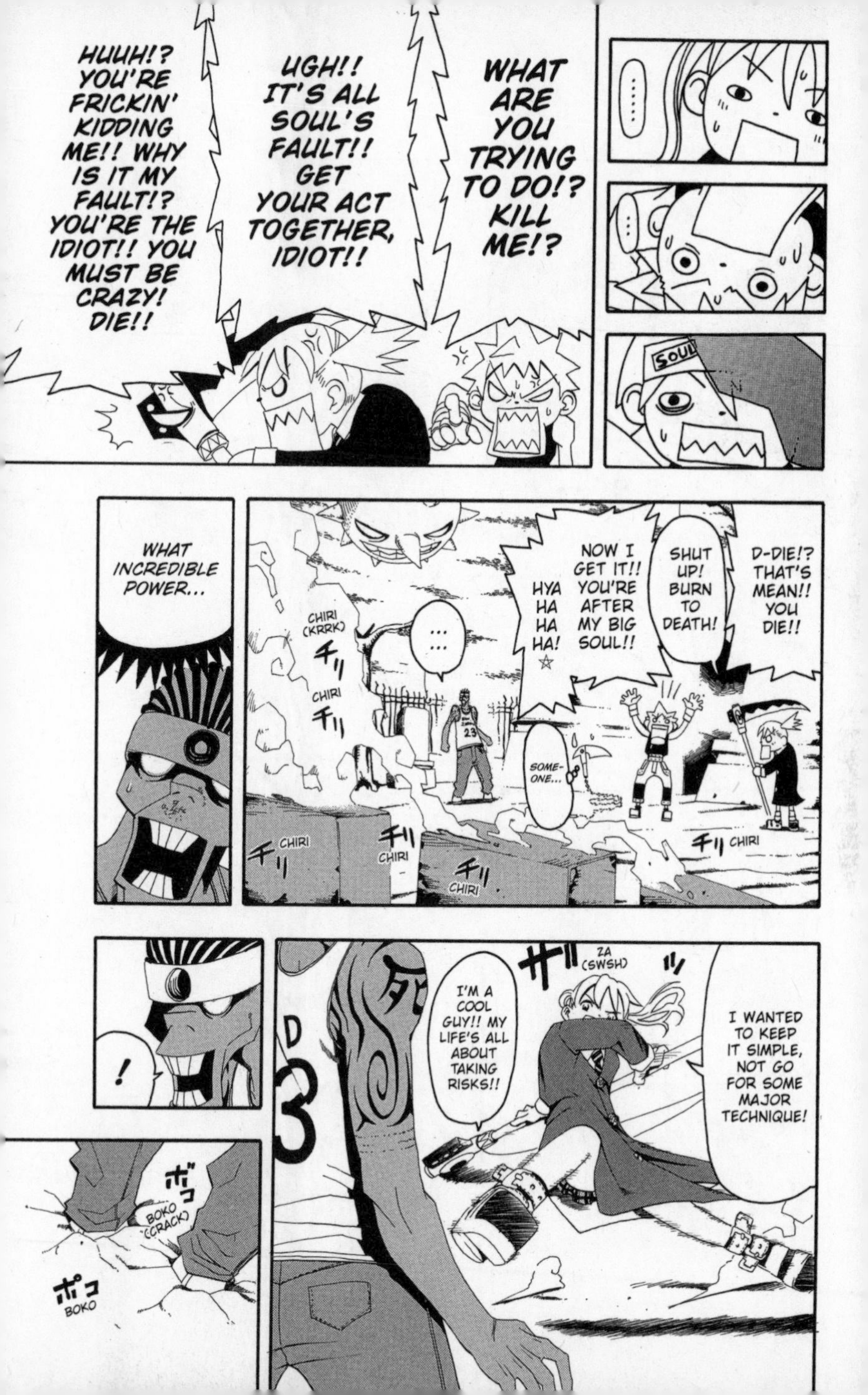

......
...
SOUL
WHAT ARE YOU TRYING TO DO!? KILL ME!?
UGH!! IT'S ALL SOUL'S FAULT!! GET YOUR ACT TOGETHER, IDIOT!!
HUUH!? YOU'RE FRICKIN' KIDDING ME!! WHY IS IT MY FAULT!? YOU'RE THE IDIOT!! YOU MUST BE CRAZY! DIE!!
D-DIE!? THAT'S MEAN!! YOU DIE!!
SHUT UP! BURN TO DEATH!
NOW I GET IT!! YOU'RE AFTER MY BIG SOUL!!
HYA HA HA HA! ☆
......
チリ CHIRI (KRRK)
チリ CHIRI
SOME-ONE...
チリ CHIRI
チリ CHIRI
チリ CHIRI
チリ CHIRI
WHAT INCREDIBLE POWER...
I WANTED TO KEEP IT SIMPLE, NOT GO FOR SOME MAJOR TECHNIQUE!
ザ ZA (SWSH)
I'M A COOL GUY!! MY LIFE'S ALL ABOUT TAKING RISKS!!
!
ボコ BOKO (CRACK)
ボコ BOKO

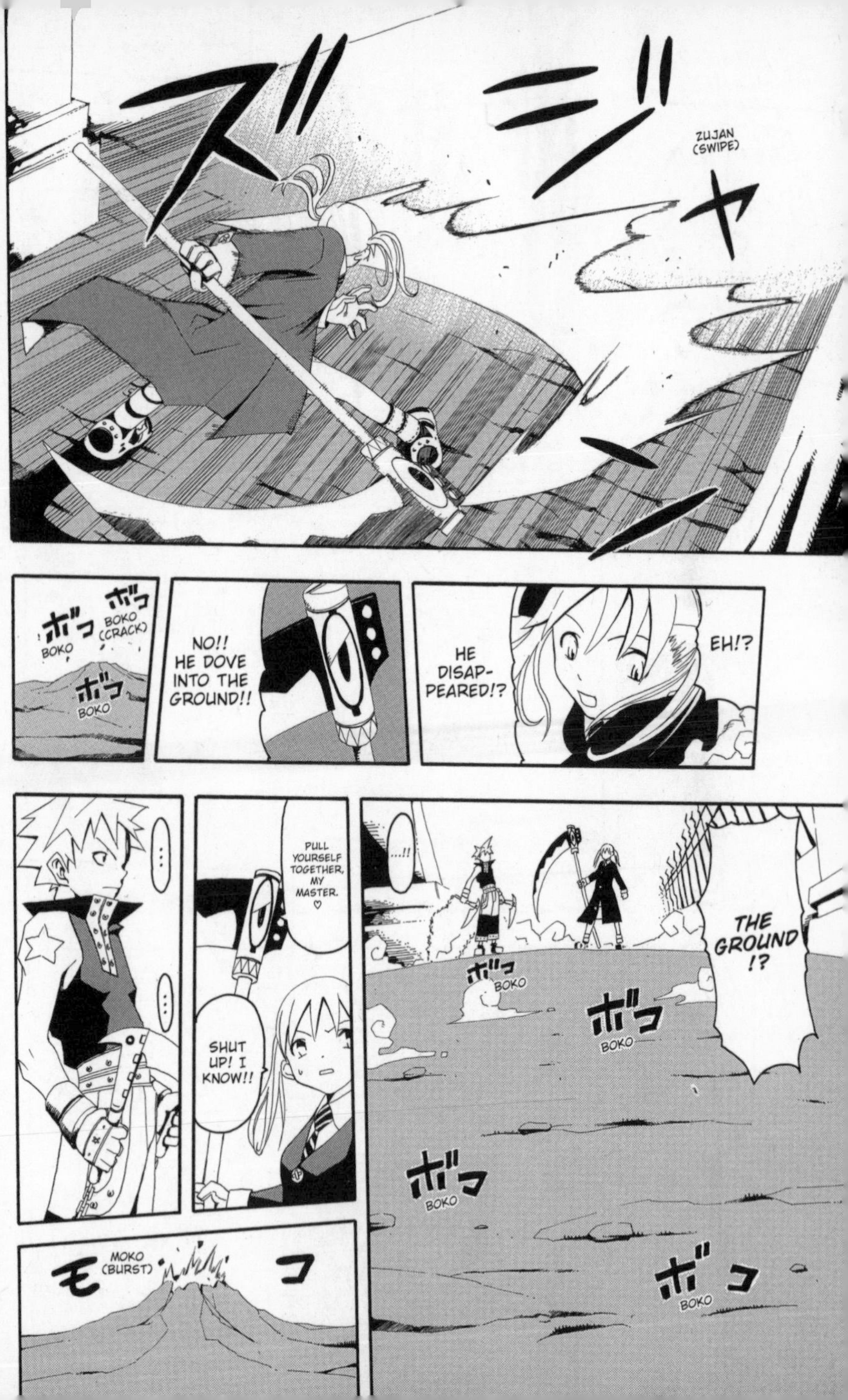
ズジャ
ZUJAN (SWIPE)
EH!?
HE DISAP-PEARED!?
NO!! HE DOVE INTO THE GROUND!!
ボコ
BOKO (CRACK)
ボコ
BOKO
ボコ
BOKO
...!!
THE GROUND!?
ボコ
BOKO
ボコ
BOKO
ボコ
BOKO
ボコ
BOKO
PULL YOURSELF TOGETHER, MY MASTER. ♡
SHUT UP! I KNOW!!
...
...
モコ
MOKO (BURST)

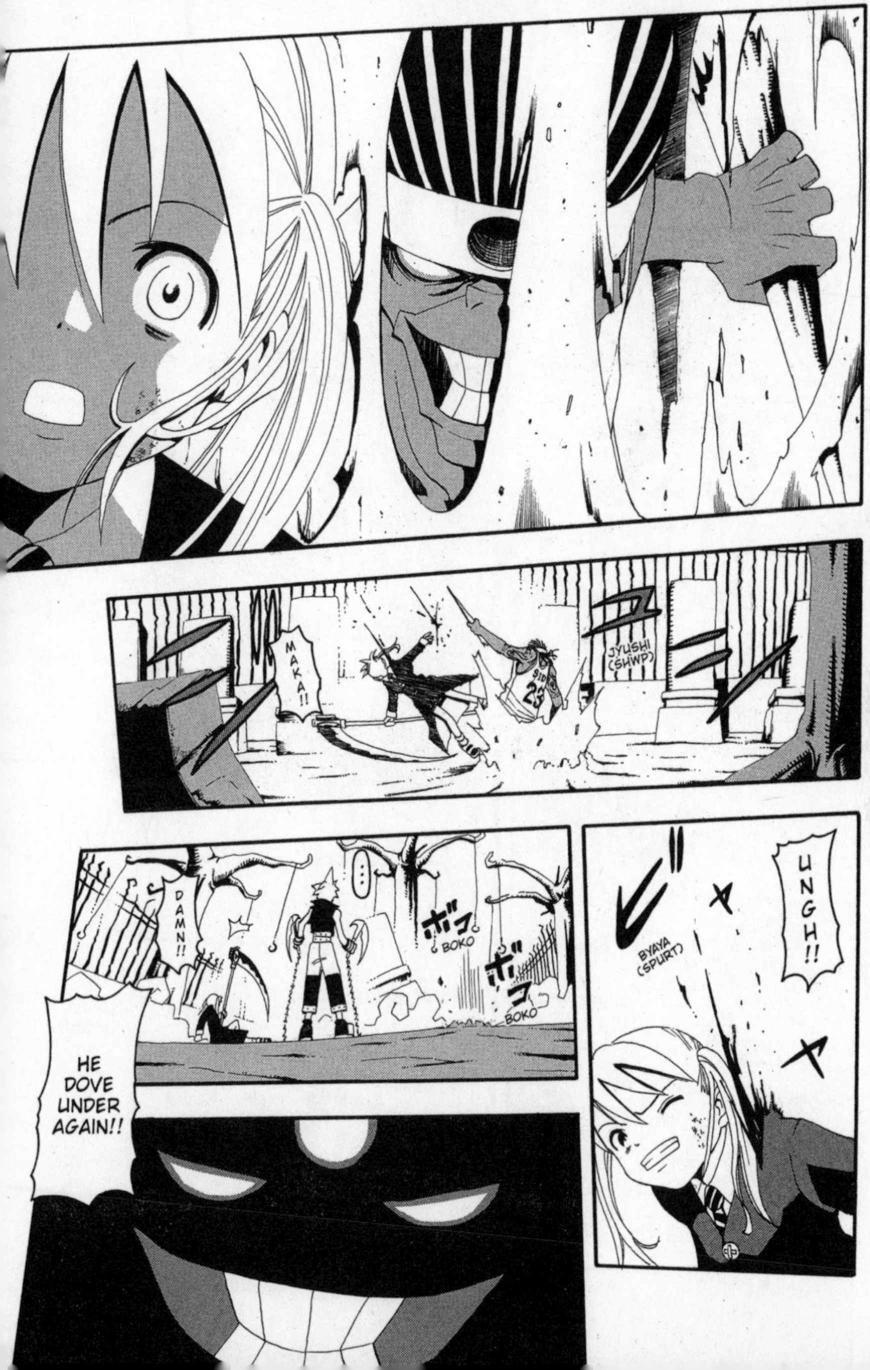
JYUSHI (SHWP)
MAKA!!
UNGH!!
BYAYA (SPURT)
...
ボコ BOKO
ボコ BOKO
DAMN!!
HE DOVE UNDER AGAIN!!

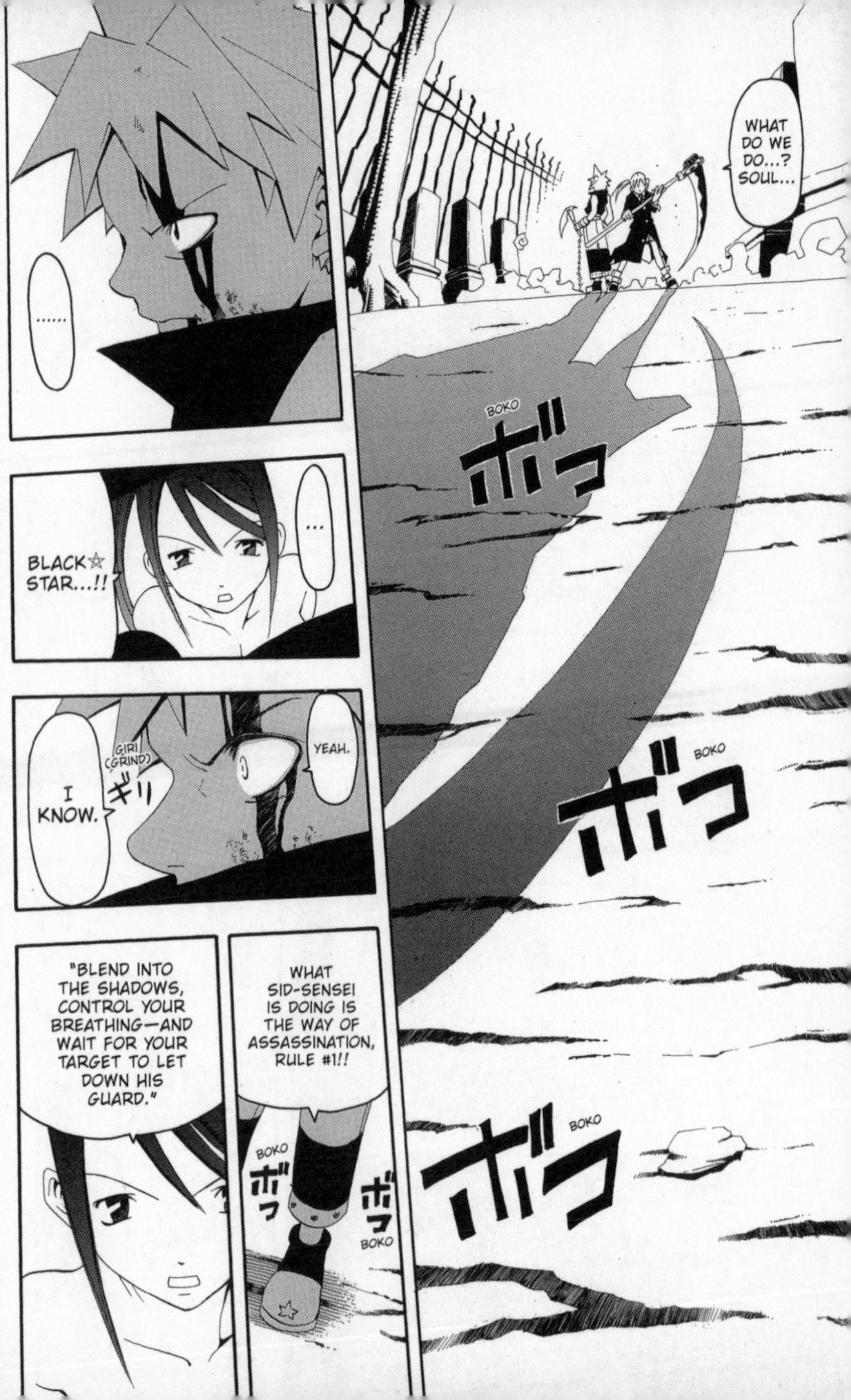
WHAT DO WE DO...? SOUL...
BOKO
ボッ
BOKO
ボッ
BOKO
ボッ
......
...
BLACK☆ STAR...!!
YEAH.
GIRI (GRIND)
ギリ
I KNOW.
WHAT SID-SENSEI IS DOING IS THE WAY OF ASSASSINATION, RULE #1!!
BOKO
ボッ
BOKO
ボッ
"BLEND INTO THE SHADOWS, CONTROL YOUR BREATHING—AND WAIT FOR YOUR TARGET TO LET DOWN HIS GUARD."

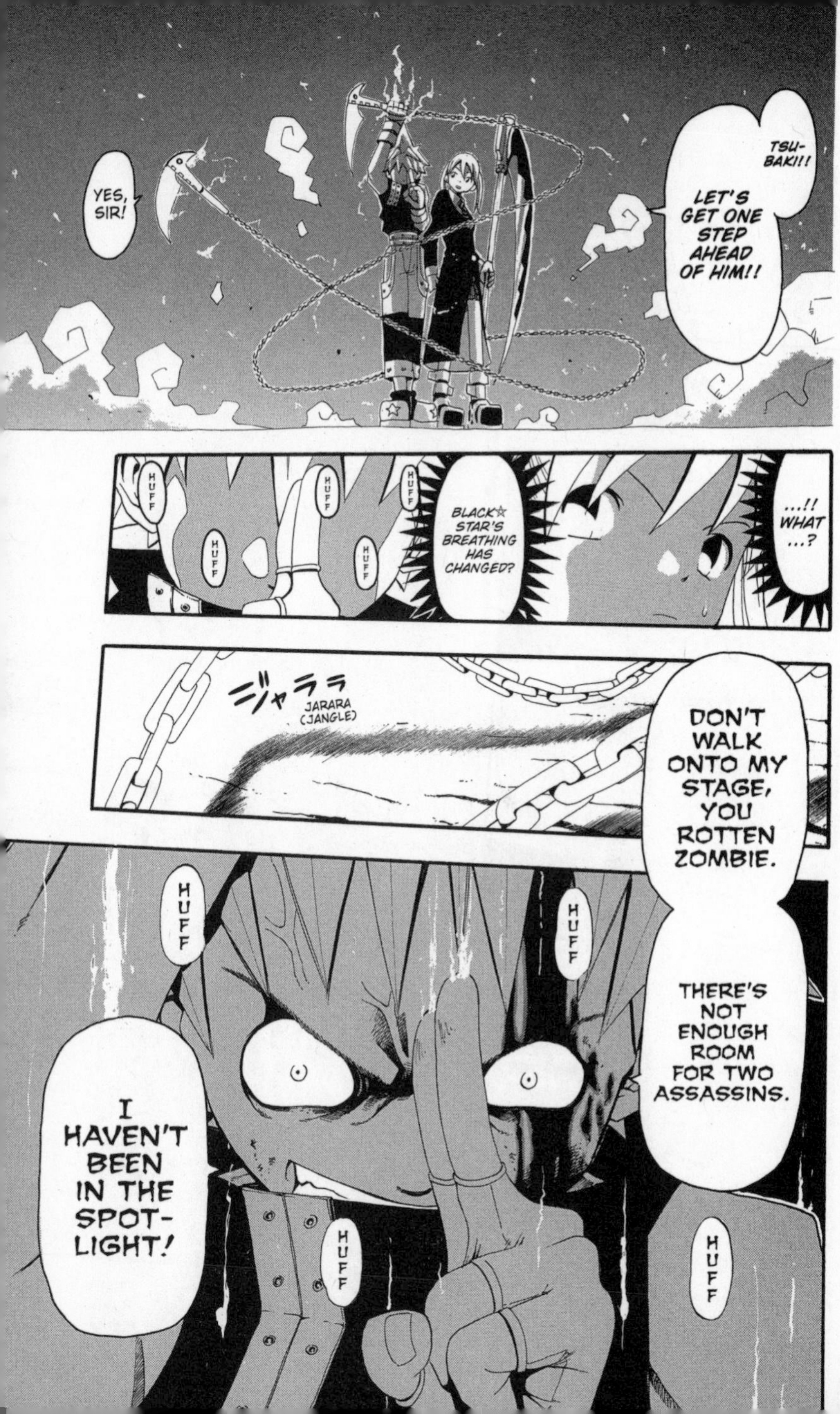
TSU-BAKI!!
LET'S GET ONE STEP AHEAD OF HIM!!
YES, SIR!
...!! WHAT ...?
BLACK☆STAR'S BREATHING HAS CHANGED?
HUFF
HUFF
HUFF
HUFF
HUFF
DON'T WALK ONTO MY STAGE, YOU ROTTEN ZOMBIE.
ジャララ
JARARA (JANGLE)
THERE'S NOT ENOUGH ROOM FOR TWO ASSASSINS.
HUFF
HUFF
I HAVEN'T BEEN IN THE SPOT-LIGHT!
HUFF
HUFF

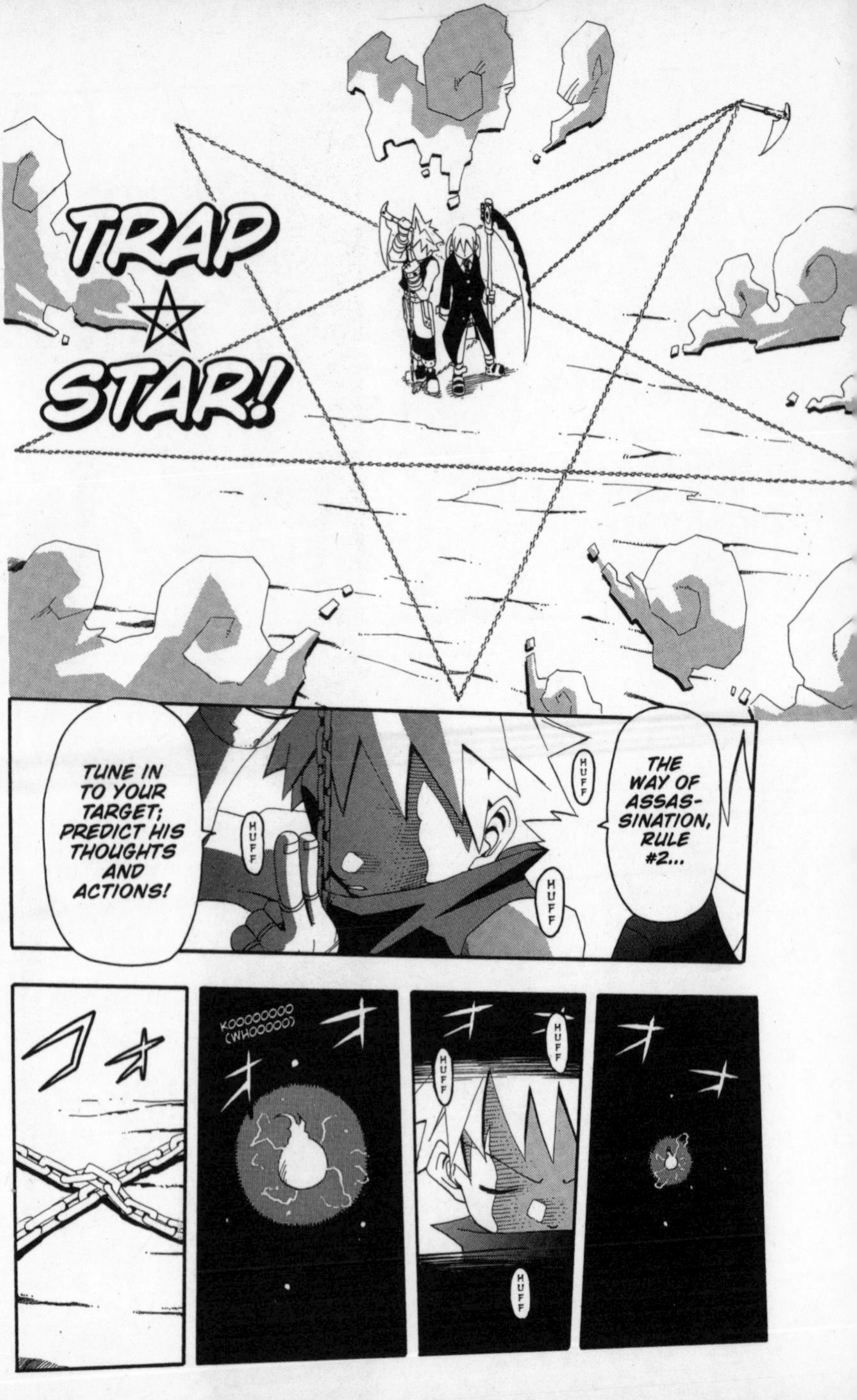
TRAP ☆ STAR!
THE WAY OF ASSASSINATION, RULE #2...
HUFF
HUFF
HUFF
TUNE IN TO YOUR TARGET; PREDICT HIS THOUGHTS AND ACTIONS!
HUFF
HUFF
HUFF
KOOOOOOOO (WHOOOOO)
コォ

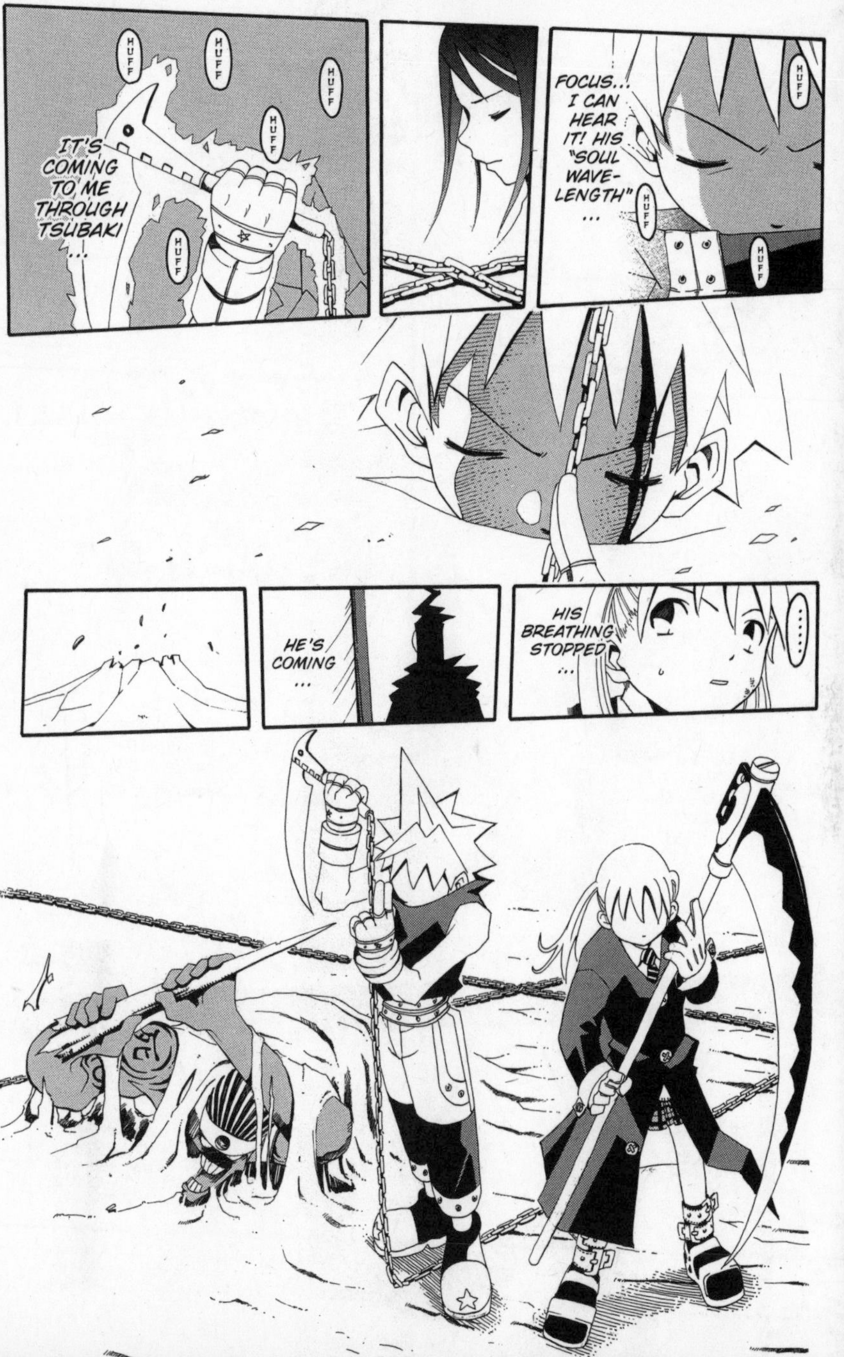
HUFF
FOCUS... I CAN HEAR IT! HIS "SOUL WAVE-LENGTH"...
HUFF
HUFF
HUFF
HUFF
HUFF
HUFF
IT'S COMING TO ME THROUGH TSUBAKI...
HUFF
......
HIS BREATHING STOPPED...
HE'S COMING...

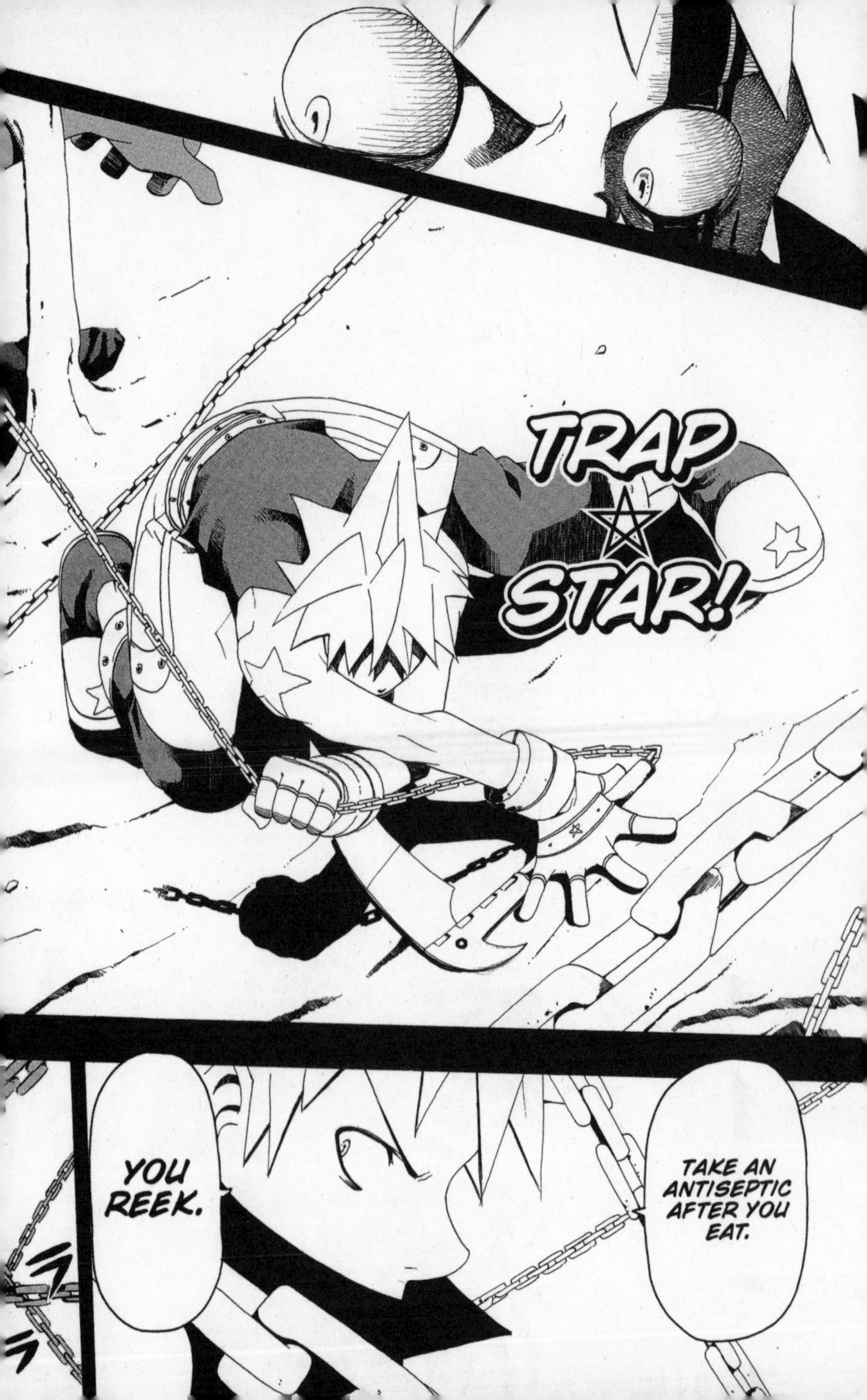
TRAP ☆ STAR!
TAKE AN ANTISEPTIC AFTER YOU EAT.
YOU REEK.

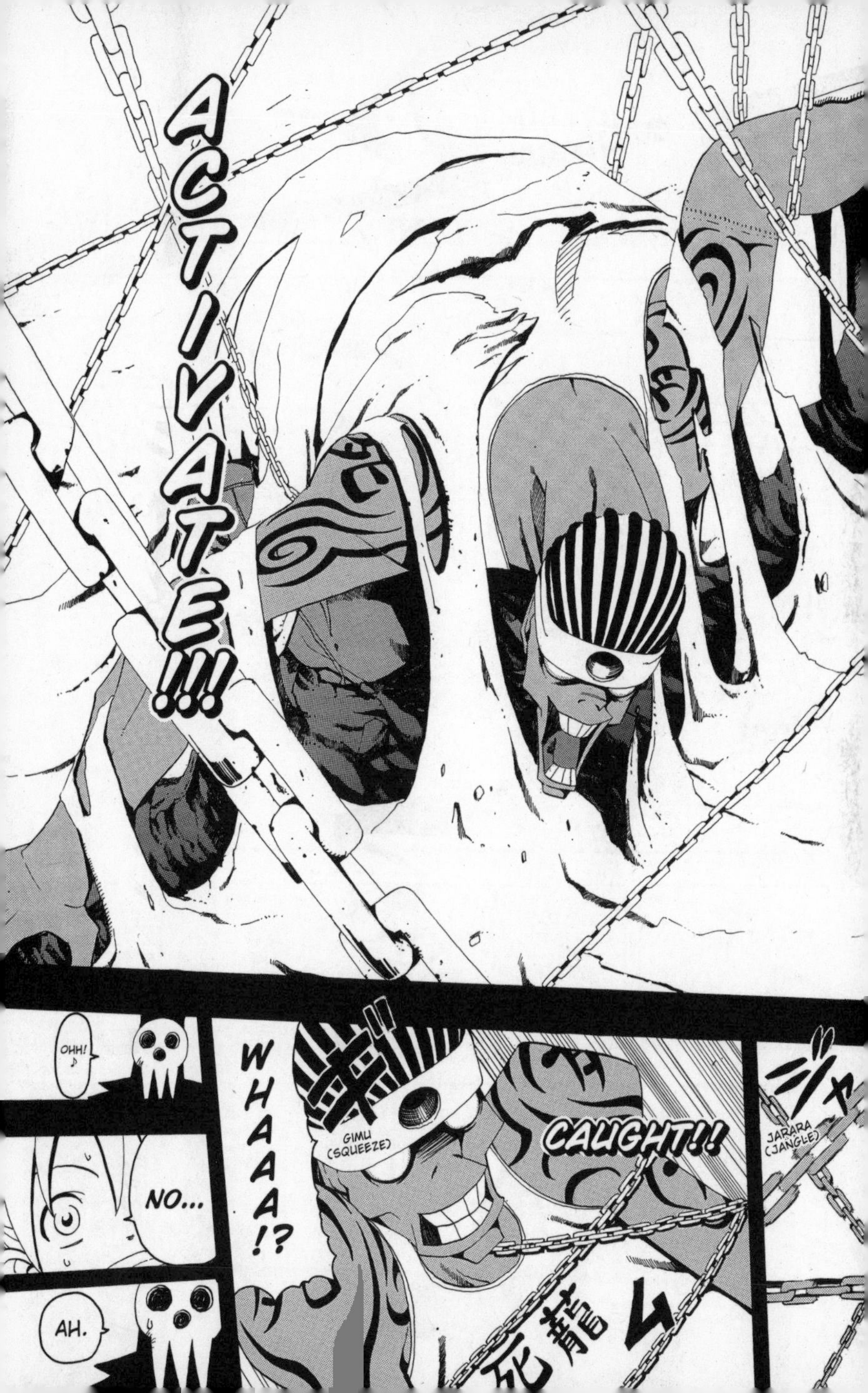
ACTIVATE!!!
ジャ
JARARA (JANGLE)
CAUGHT!!
GIMU (SQUEEZE)
WHAAAA!?
OHH! ♪
NO...
AH.

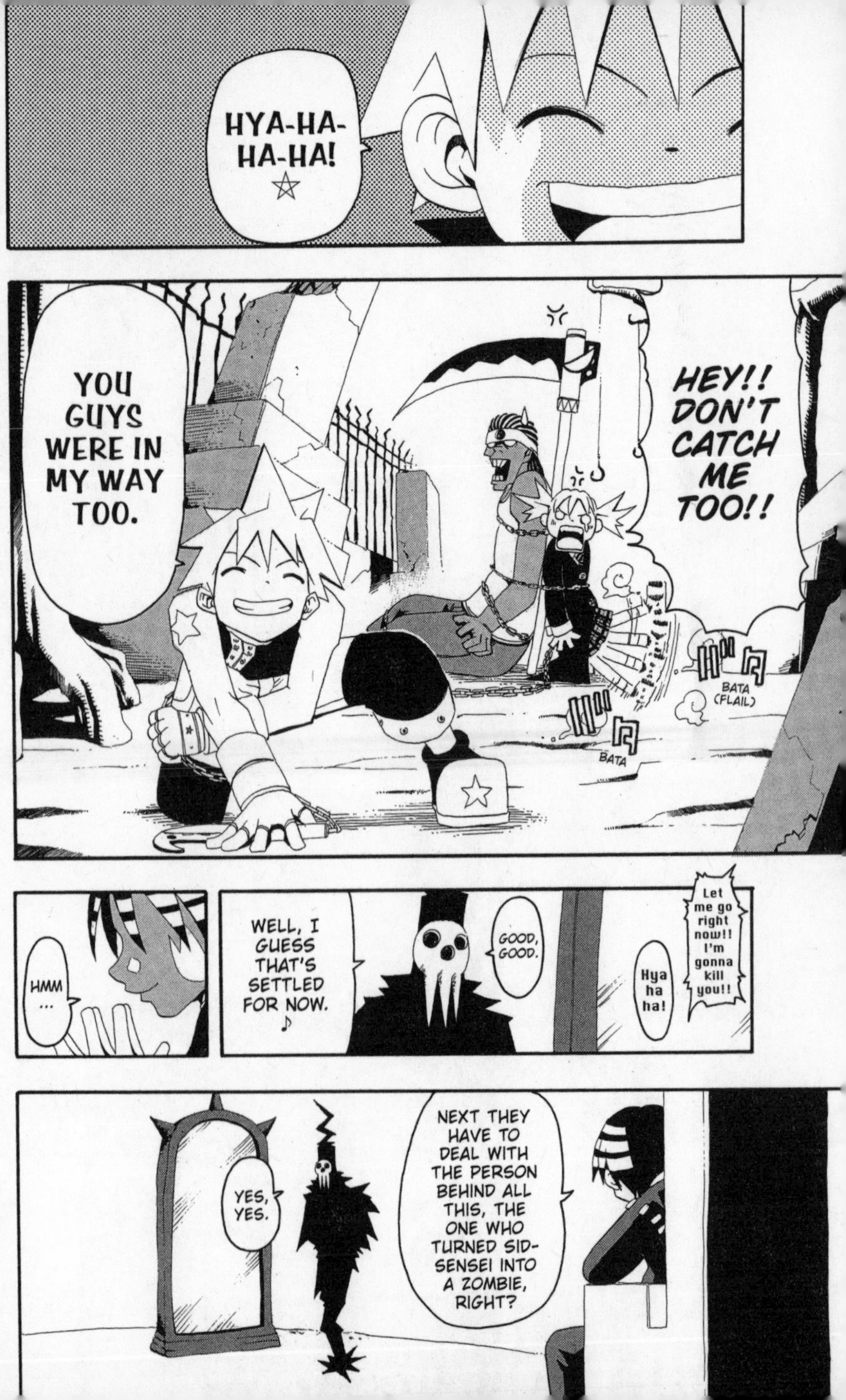
HYA-HA-HA-HA! ☆
HEY!! DON'T CATCH ME TOO!!
YOU GUYS WERE IN MY WAY TOO.
BATA (FLAIL)
BATA
Let me go right now!! I'm gonna kill you!!
Hya ha ha!
GOOD, GOOD.
WELL, I GUESS THAT'S SETTLED FOR NOW. ♪
HMM ...
NEXT THEY HAVE TO DEAL WITH THE PERSON BEHIND ALL THIS, THE ONE WHO TURNED SID-SENSEI INTO A ZOMBIE, RIGHT?
YES, YES.

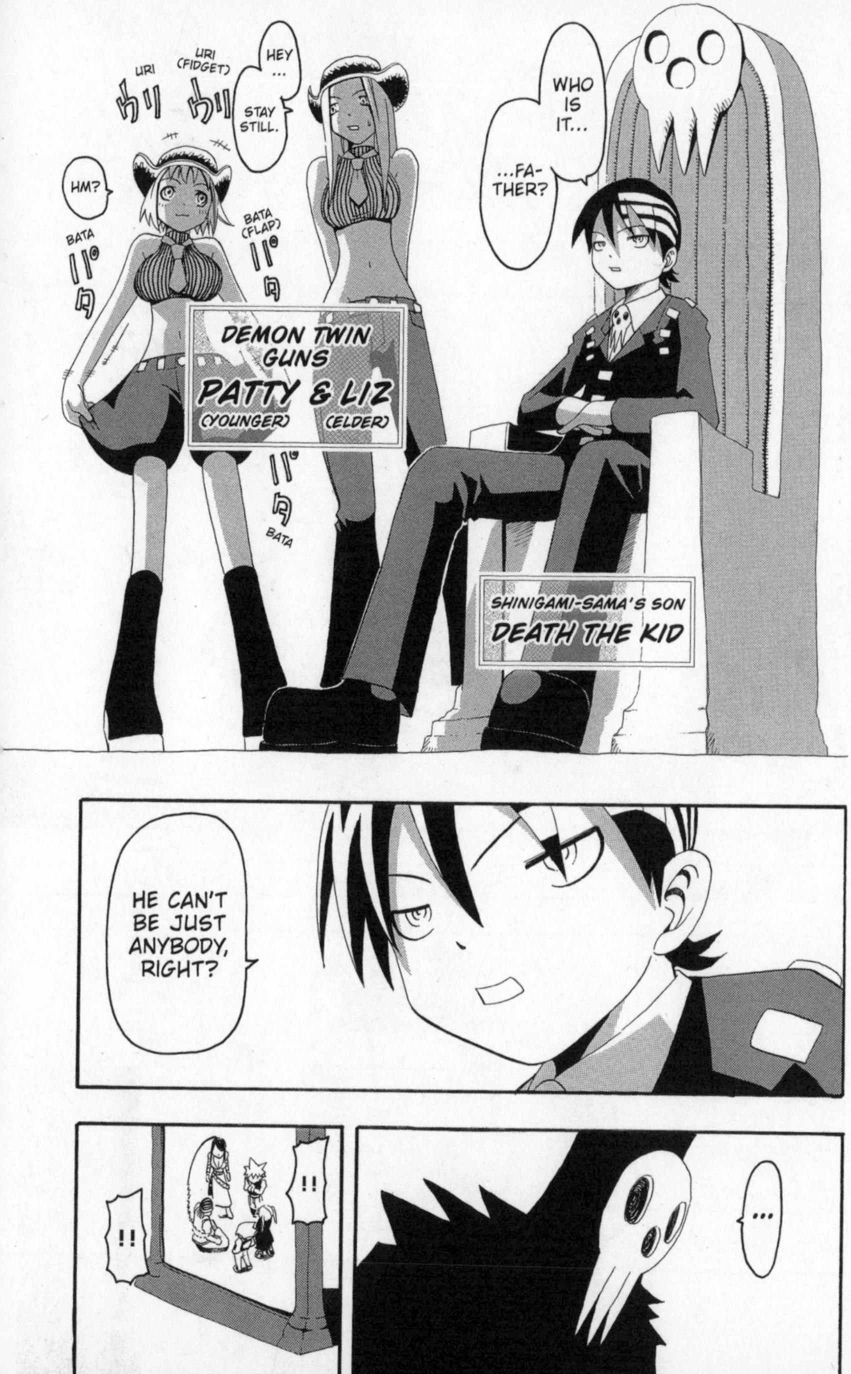
WHO IS IT... ...FA- THER?
HEY... STAY STILL.
URI (FIDGET)
ウリ
URI
ウリ
HM?
BATA (FLAP)
パタ
BATA
パタ
パタ
BATA
DEMON TWIN GUNS
PATTY & LIZ
(YOUNGER) (ELDER)
SHINIGAMI-SAMA'S SON
DEATH THE KID
HE CAN'T BE JUST ANYBODY, RIGHT?
...
!!
!!

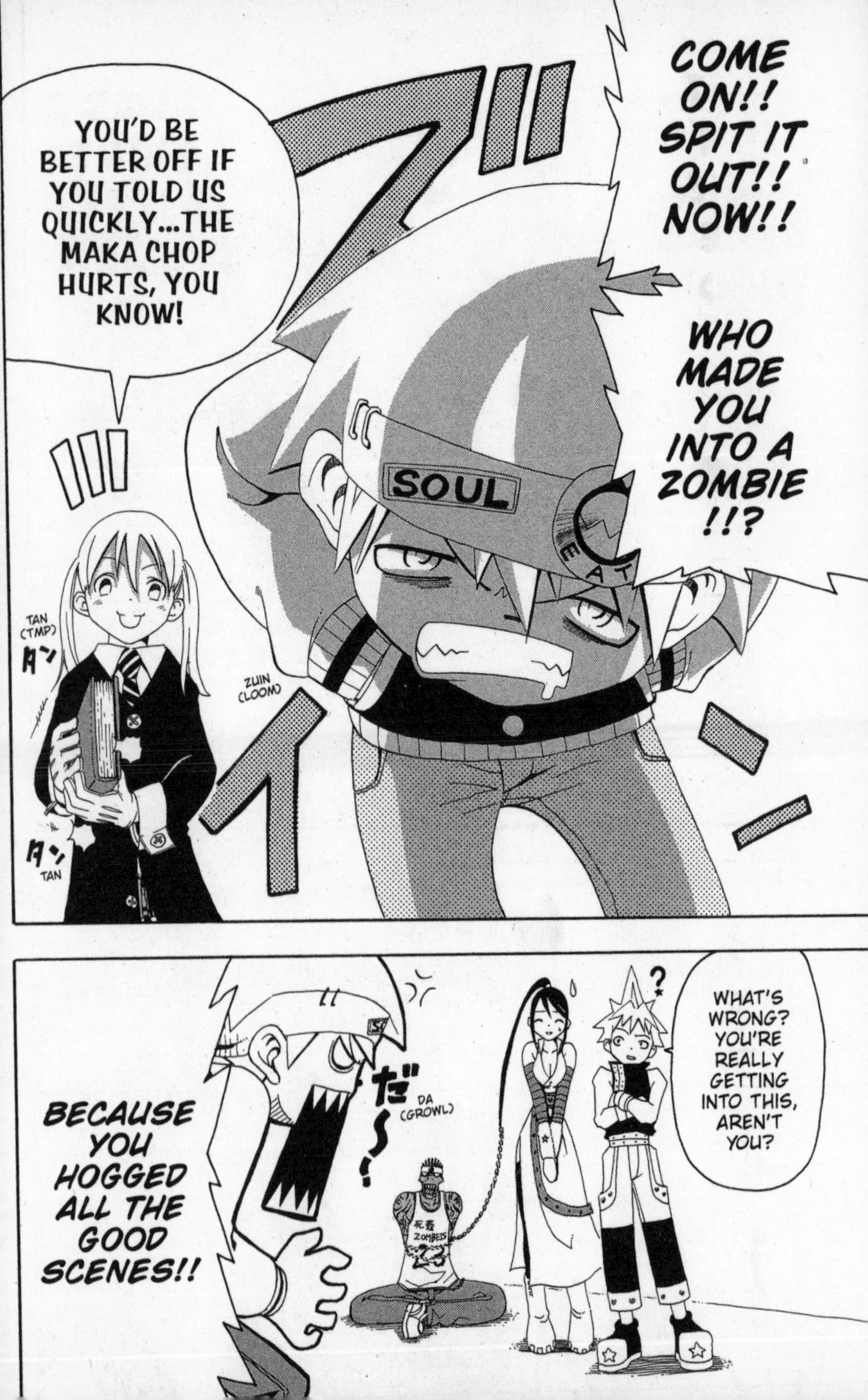
COME ON!! SPIT IT OUT!! NOW!!
WHO MADE YOU INTO A ZOMBIE!!?
ZUIN (LOOM)
YOU'D BE BETTER OFF IF YOU TOLD US QUICKLY...THE MAKA CHOP HURTS, YOU KNOW!
TAN (TMP)
TAN
WHAT'S WRONG? YOU'RE REALLY GETTING INTO THIS, AREN'T YOU?
DA (GROWL)
BECAUSE YOU HOGGED ALL THE GOOD SCENES!!

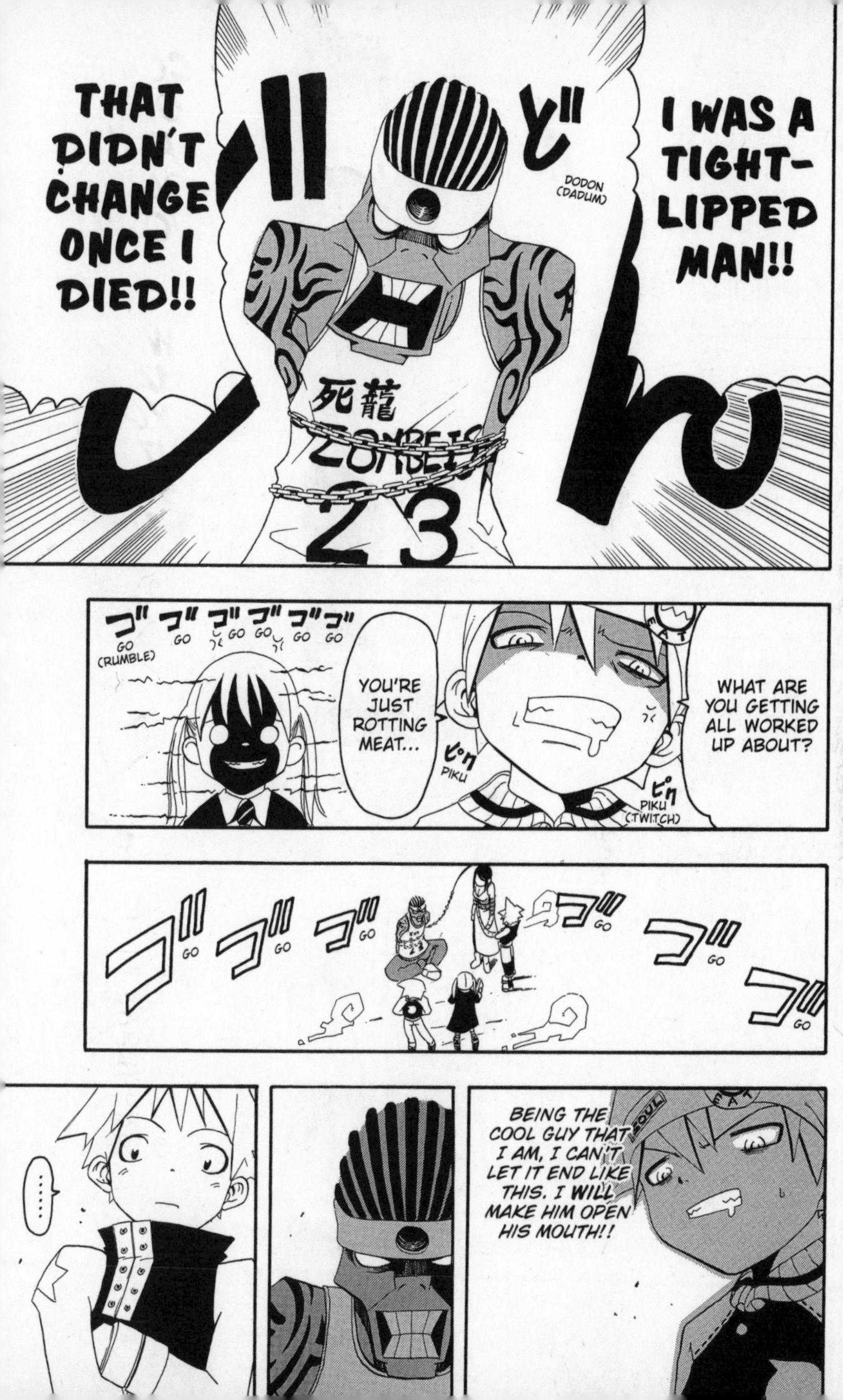
I WAS A TIGHT-LIPPED MAN!!
DODON (DADUM)
THAT DIDN'T CHANGE ONCE I DIED!!
WHAT ARE YOU GETTING ALL WORKED UP ABOUT?
PIKU (TWITCH)
YOU'RE JUST ROTTING MEAT...
PIKU
GO (RUMBLE) GO GO GO GO GO
GO GO GO
GO GO GO
BEING THE COOL GUY THAT I AM, I CAN'T LET IT END LIKE THIS. I WILL MAKE HIM OPEN HIS MOUTH!!
......

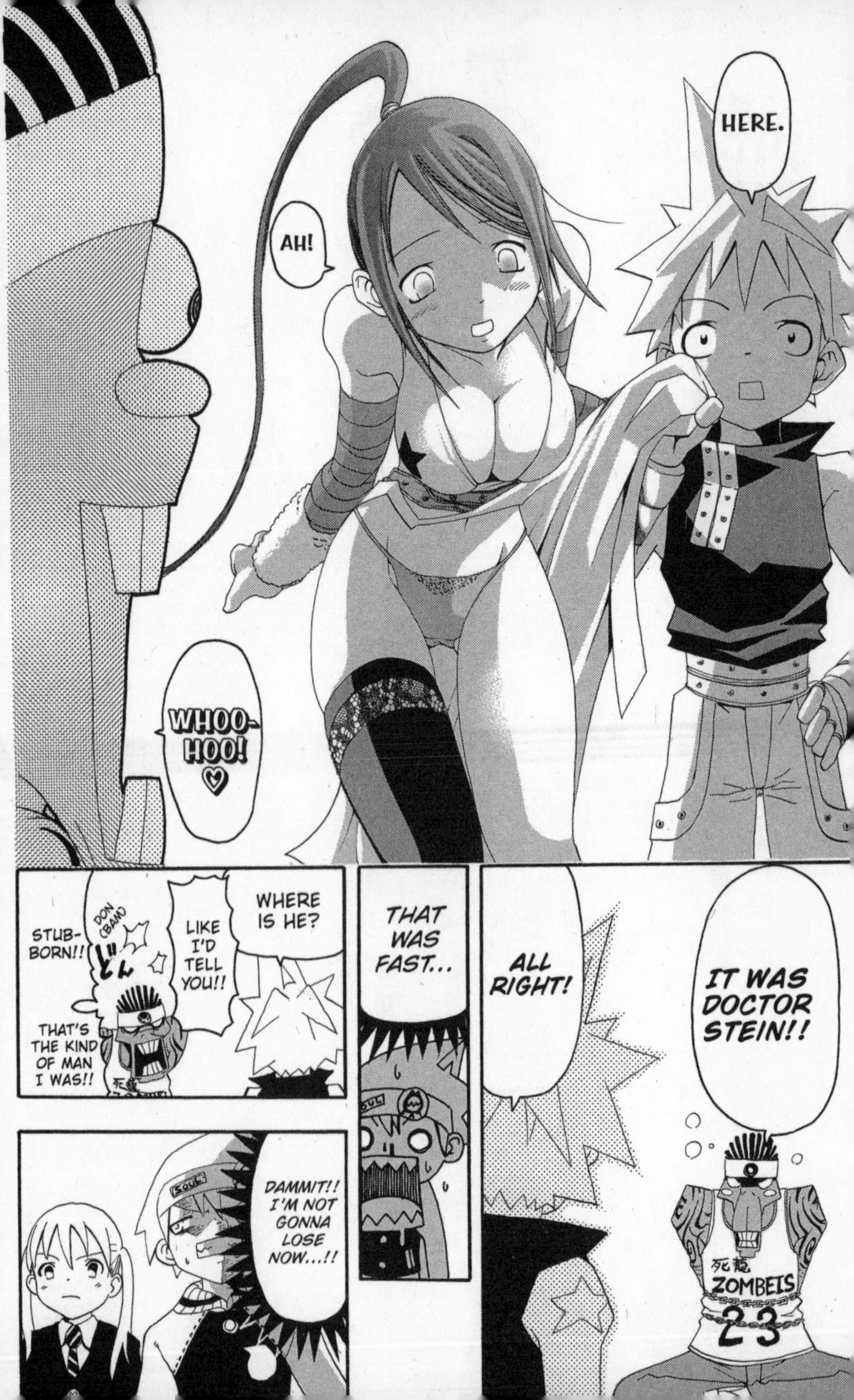
HERE.
AH!
WHOO-HOO! ♡
IT WAS DOCTOR STEIN!!
死龍 ZOMBEIS 23
ALL RIGHT!
THAT WAS FAST...
WHERE IS HE?
LIKE I'D TELL YOU!!
DON (BAM)
どん
STUB-BORN!!
THAT'S THE KIND OF MAN I WAS!!
DAMMIT!! I'M NOT GONNA LOSE NOW...!!

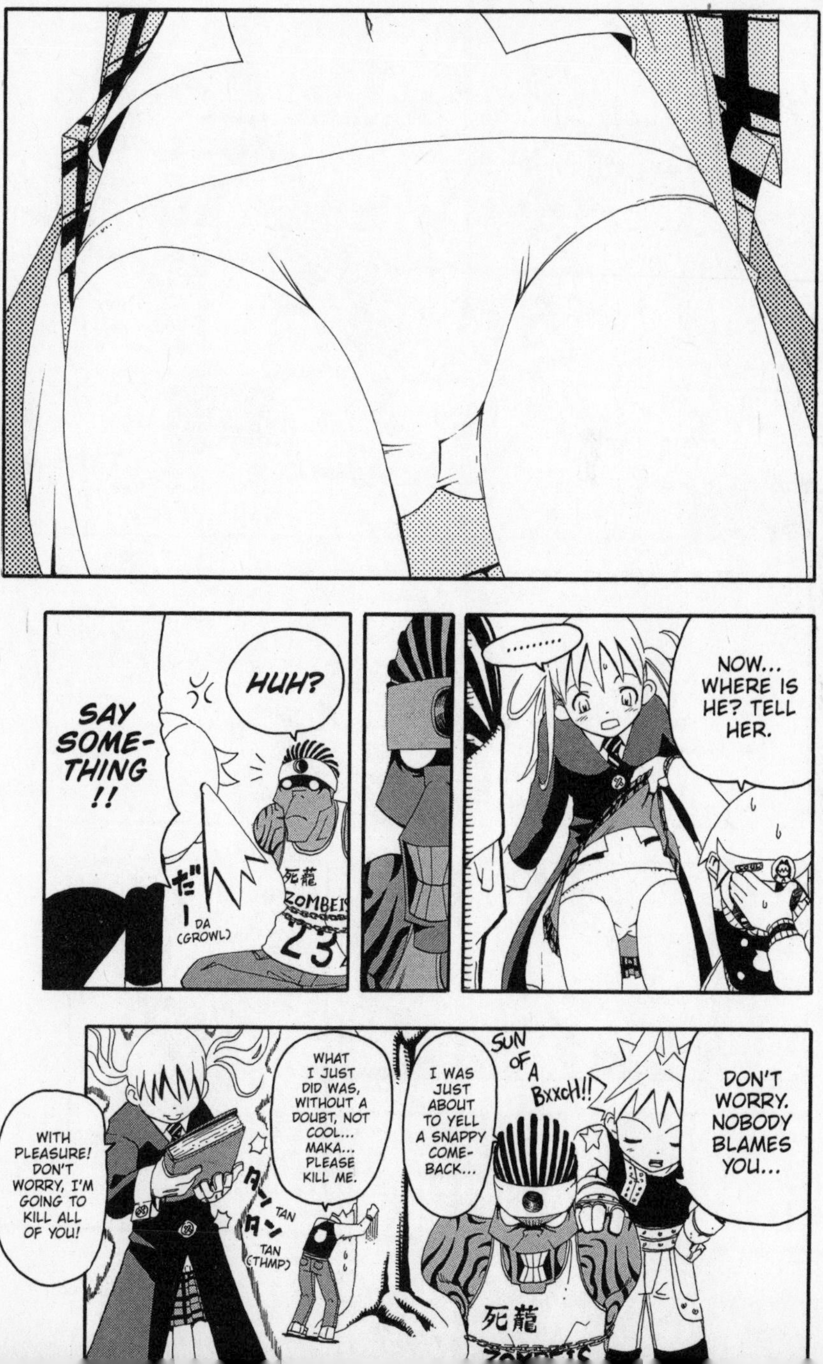
NOW... WHERE IS HE? TELL HER.
....
HUH?
SAY SOME-THING!!
だー DA (GROWL)
DON'T WORRY. NOBODY BLAMES YOU...
SUN OF A BxxCH!!
I WAS JUST ABOUT TO YELL A SNAPPY COME-BACK...
WHAT I JUST DID WAS, WITHOUT A DOUBT, NOT COOL... MAKA... PLEASE KILL ME.
タン TAN
タン TAN (THMP)
WITH PLEASURE! DON'T WORRY, I'M GOING TO KILL ALL OF YOU!

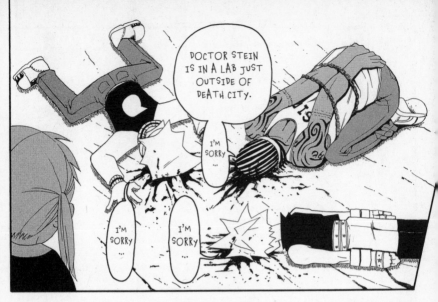

DOCTOR STEIN IS IN A LAB JUST OUTSIDE OF DEATH CITY.

I'M SORRY...

I'M SORRY...

I'M SORRY...

A LAB JUST OUTSIDE OF DEATH CITY...

I'M SORRY...
I'M SORRY...
I'M SORRY...
MY QUEEN...

...WHO IS HE ...!?

DOCTOR STEIN...

AH-HA! NOW WE KNOW THE CULPRIT! ♪

PUN (CLICK)

プツン

IT ENDED WITH A WEIRD FADE-OUT, THOUGH...

...VERY TOUGH...

HE IS...

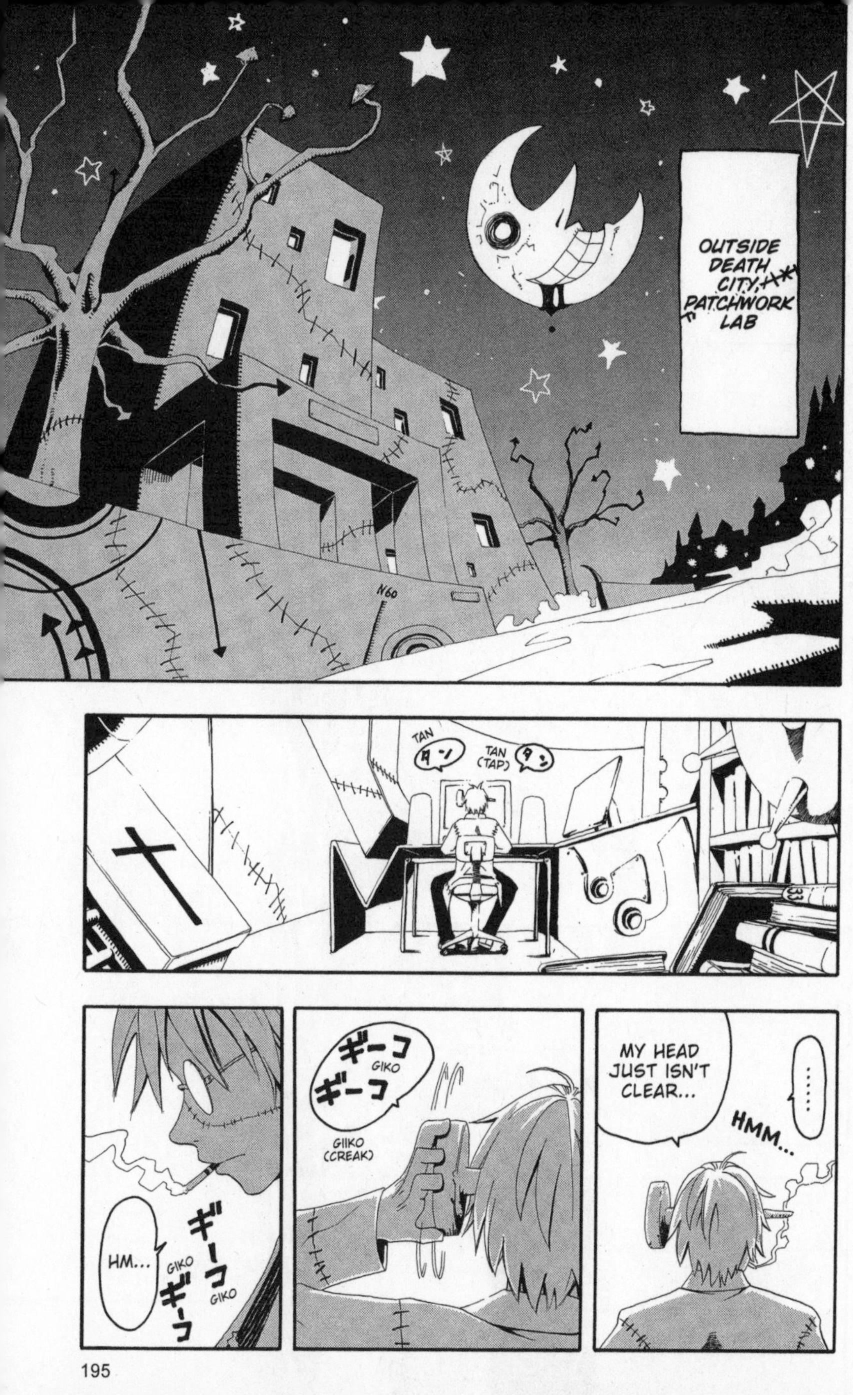
OUTSIDE DEATH CITY, PATCHWORK LAB
タン TAN (TAP)
タン TAN
......
MY HEAD JUST ISN'T CLEAR...
HMM...
ギーコ GIKO
ギーコ GIIKO (CREAK)
ギーコ GIKO
ギーコ GIKO
HM...

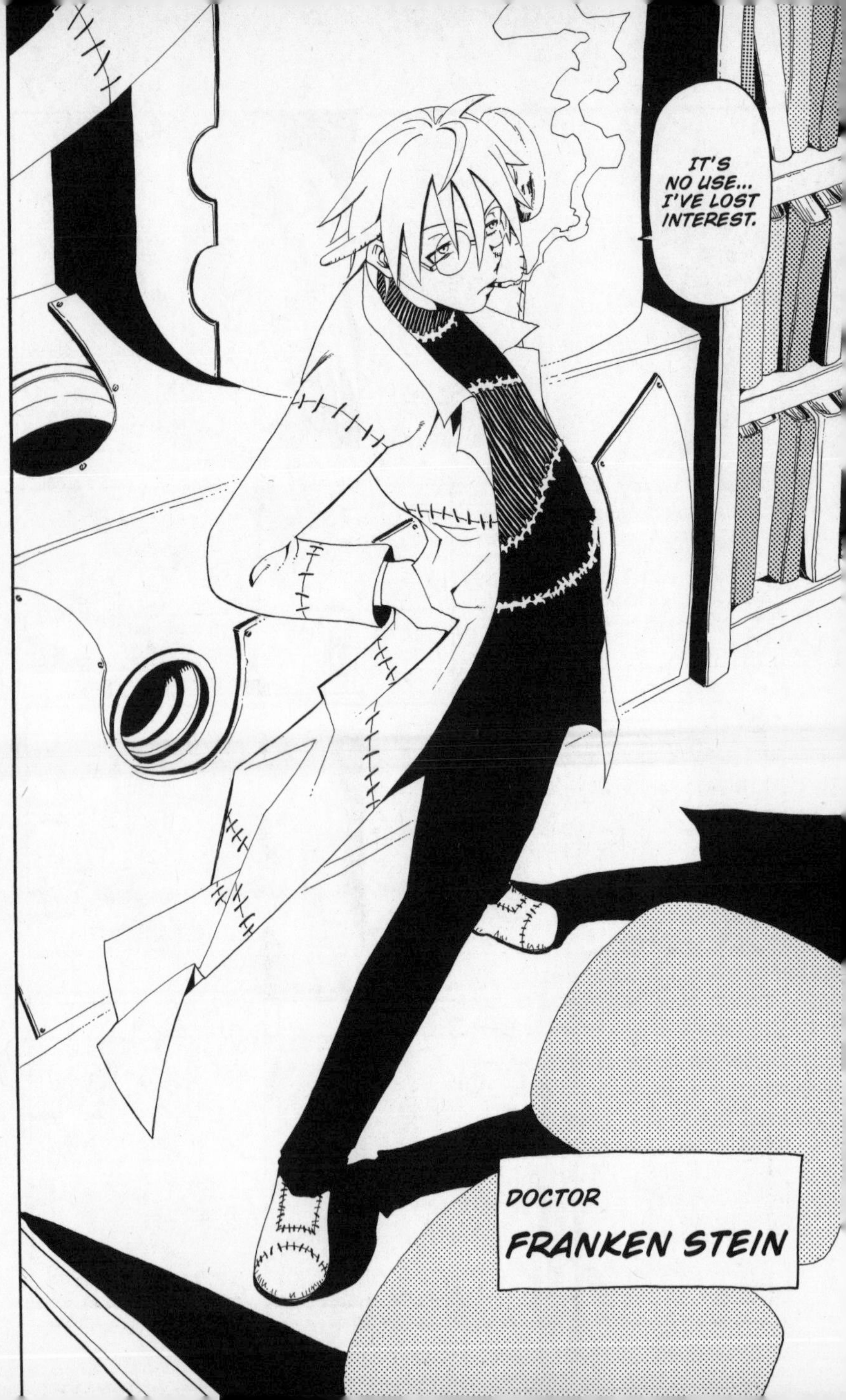
IT'S NO USE... I'VE LOST INTEREST.
DOCTOR FRANKEN STEIN

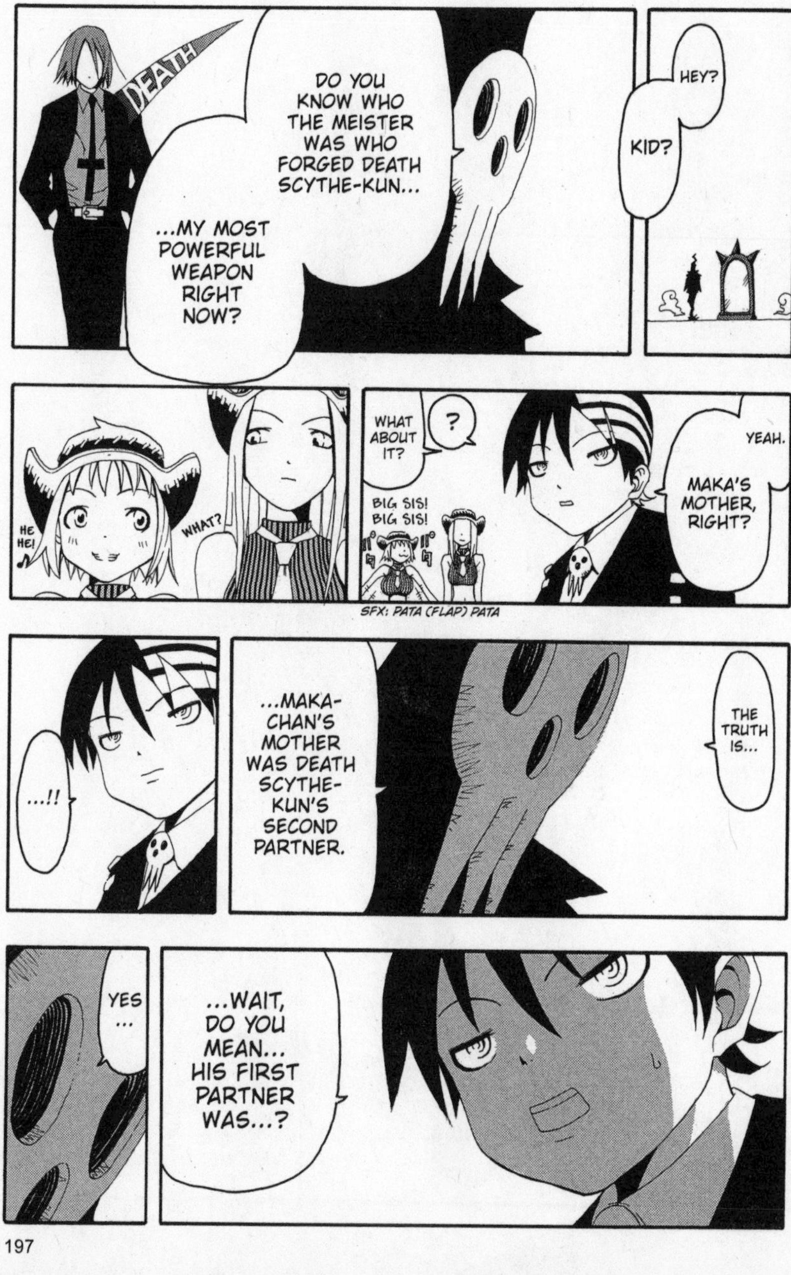
HEY?
KID?
DEATH
DO YOU KNOW WHO THE MEISTER WAS WHO FORGED DEATH SCYTHE-KUN...
...MY MOST POWERFUL WEAPON RIGHT NOW?
YEAH.
MAKA'S MOTHER, RIGHT?
?
WHAT ABOUT IT?
BIG SIS! BIG SIS!
SFX: PATA (FLAP) PATA
WHAT?
HE HE!
THE TRUTH IS...
...MAKA-CHAN'S MOTHER WAS DEATH SCYTHE-KUN'S SECOND PARTNER.
...!!
...WAIT, DO YOU MEAN... HIS FIRST PARTNER WAS...?
YES ...

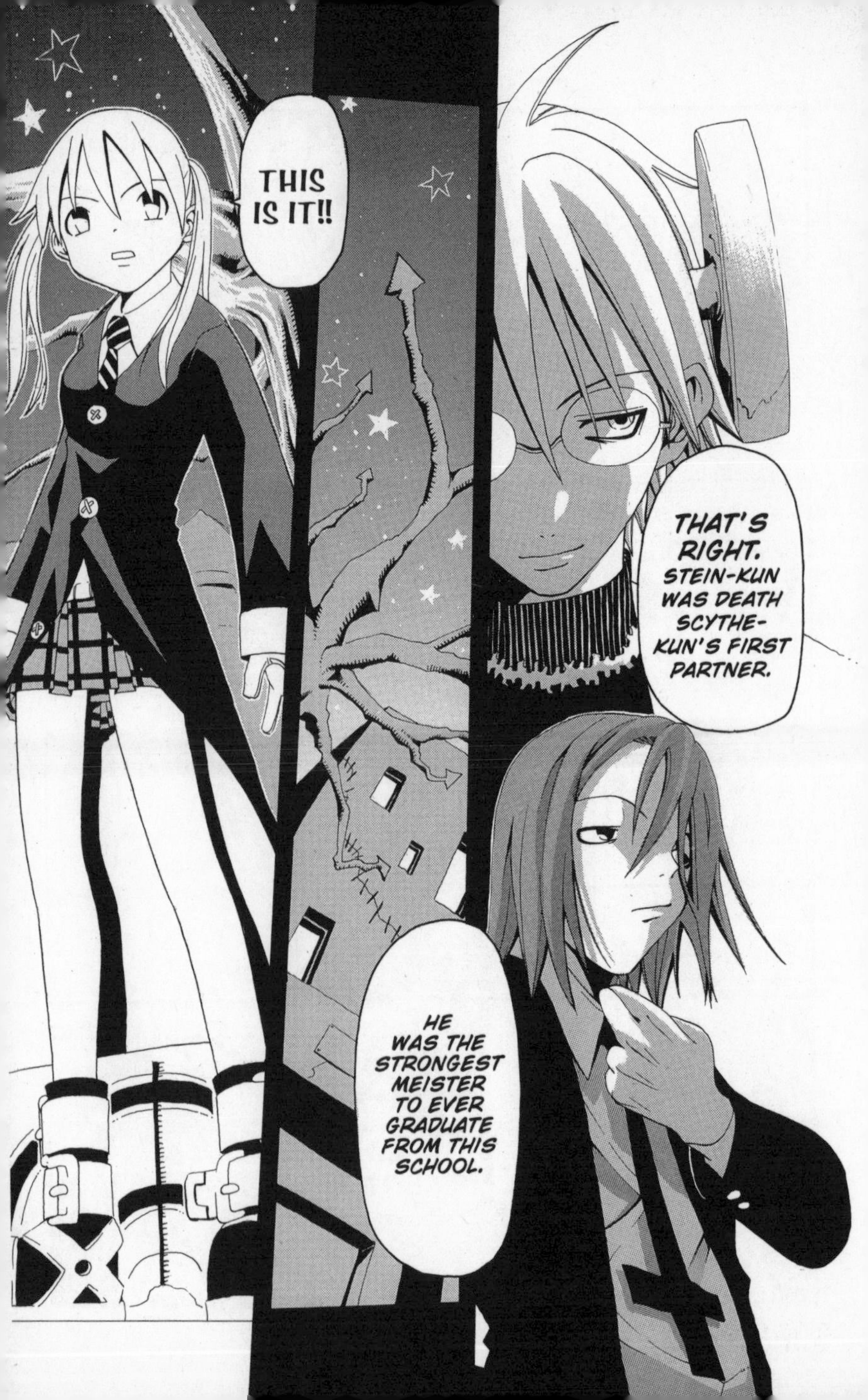
THAT'S RIGHT. STEIN-KUN WAS DEATH SCYTHE-KUN'S FIRST PARTNER.
HE WAS THE STRONGEST MEISTER TO EVER GRADUATE FROM THIS SCHOOL.
THIS IS IT!!

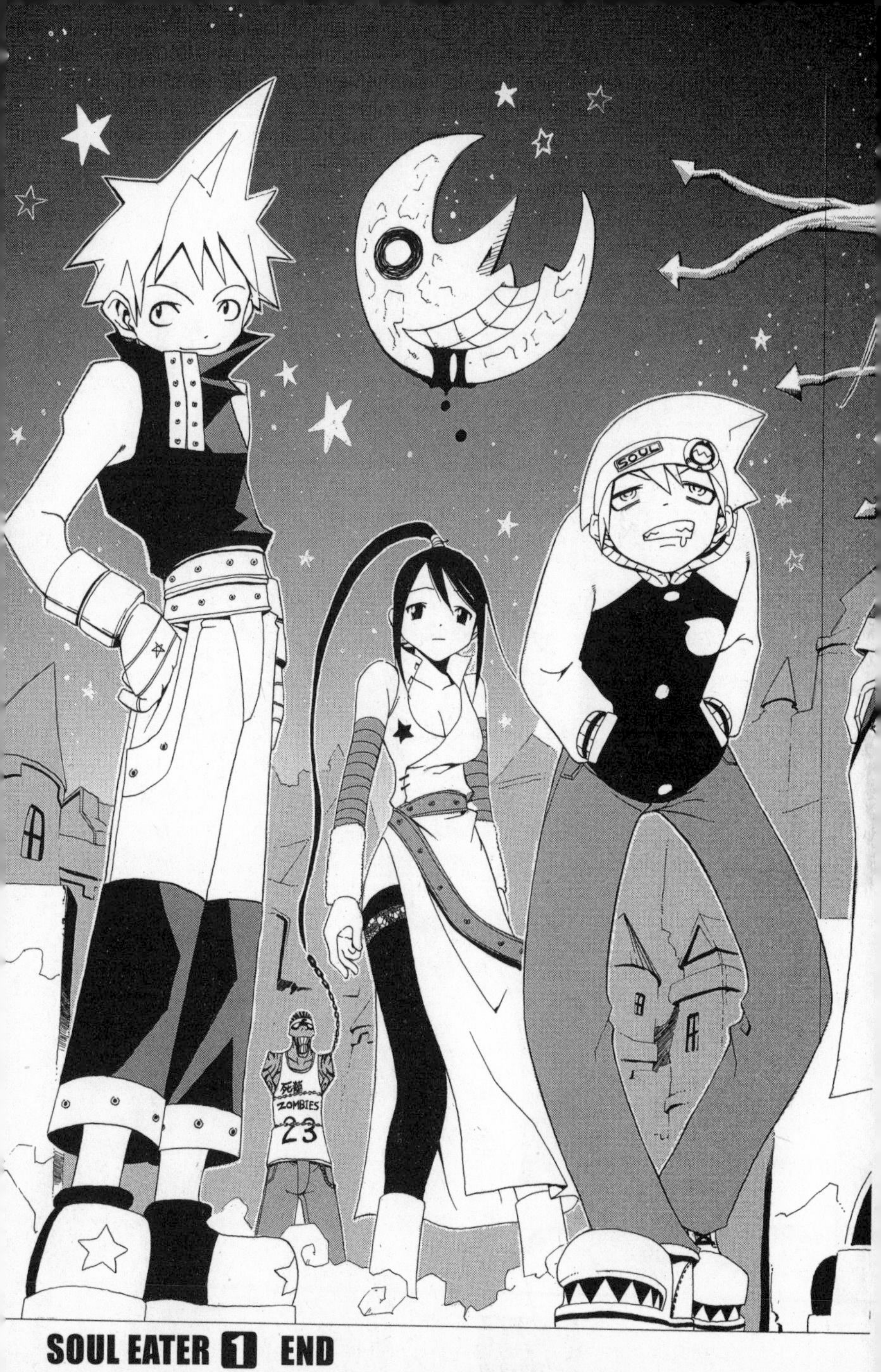
SOUL
ZOMBIES
23

SOUL EATER 1 END

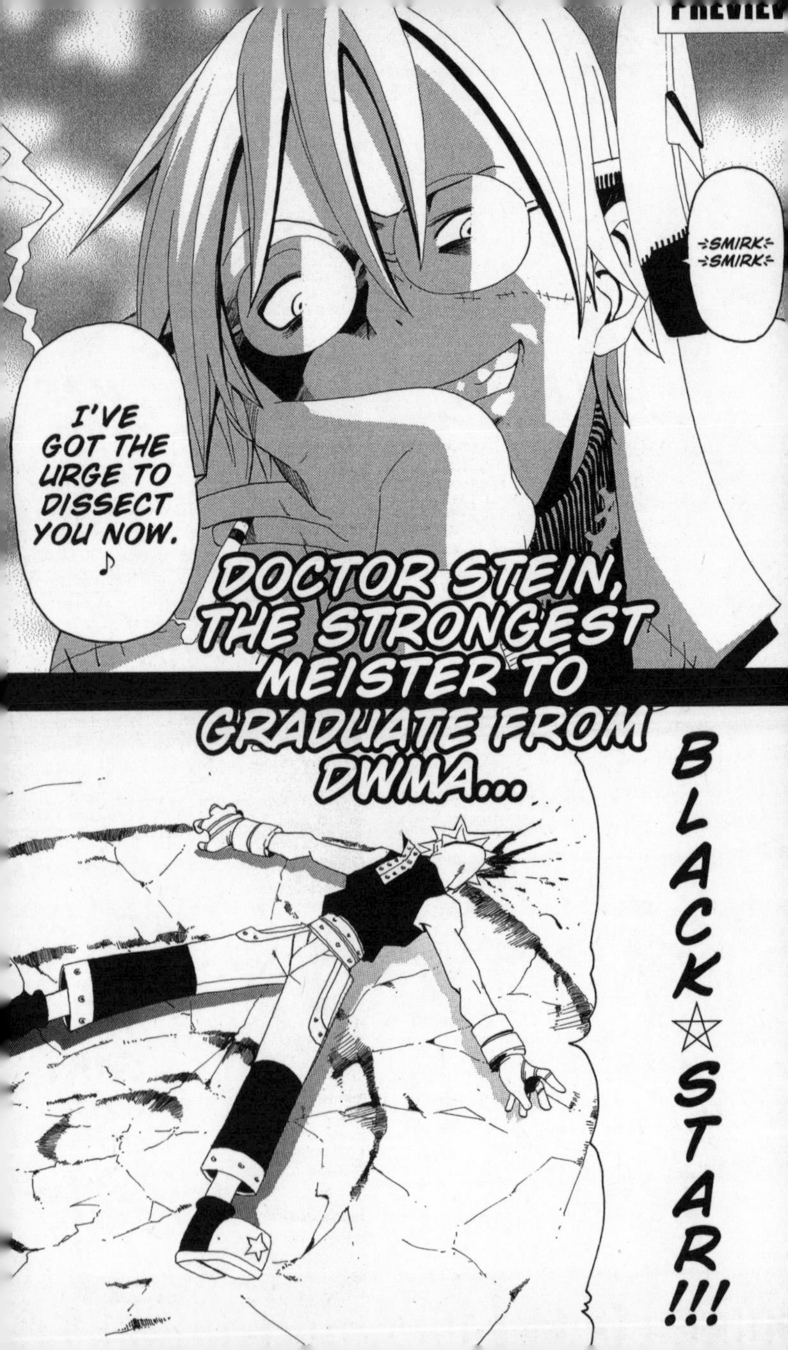
PREVIEW
SMIRK SMIRK
I'VE GOT THE URGE TO DISSECT YOU NOW. ♪
DOCTOR STEIN, THE STRONGEST MEISTER TO GRADUATE FROM DWMA...
BLACK☆STAR!!!

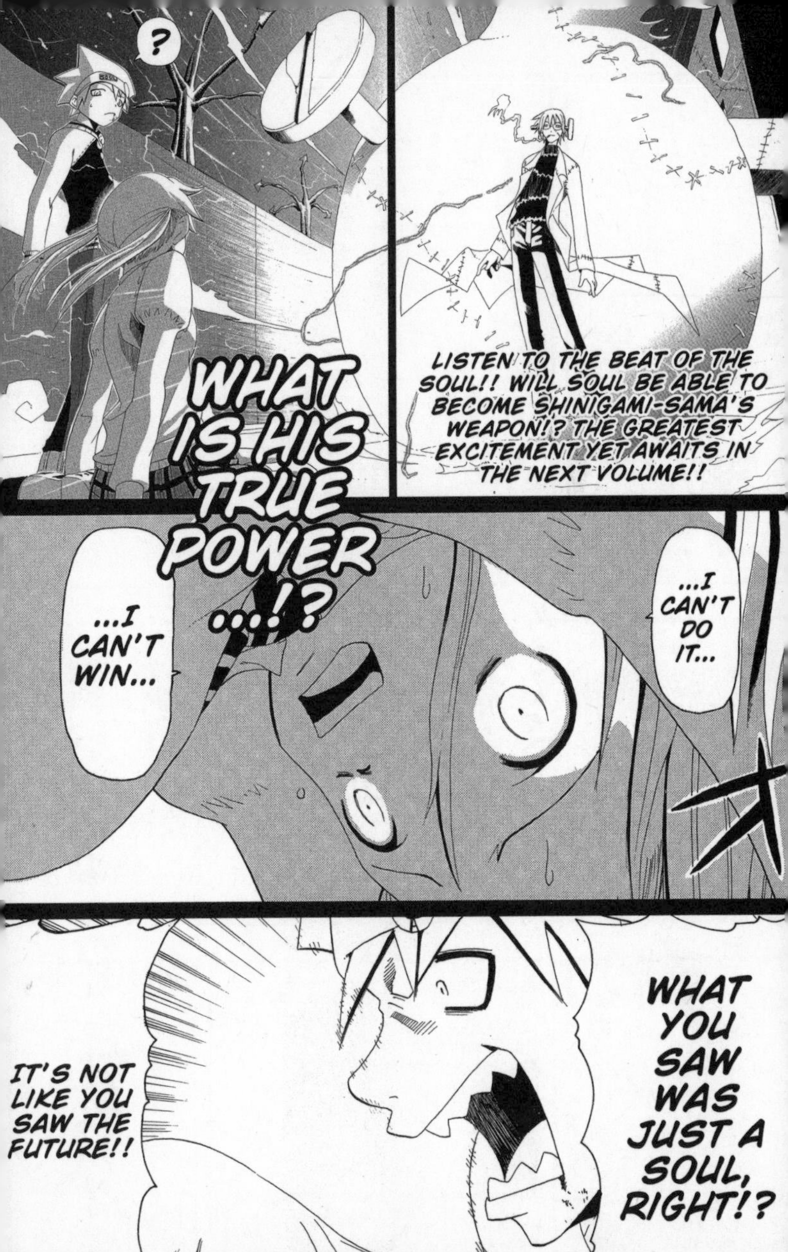
LISTEN TO THE BEAT OF THE SOUL!! WILL SOUL BE ABLE TO BECOME SHINIGAMI-SAMA'S WEAPON!? THE GREATEST EXCITEMENT YET AWAITS IN THE NEXT VOLUME!!
?
WHAT IS HIS TRUE POWER ...!?
...I CAN'T DO IT...
...I CAN'T WIN...
WHAT YOU SAW WAS JUST A SOUL, RIGHT!?
IT'S NOT LIKE YOU SAW THE FUTURE!!

Continued in Soul Eater Volume 2!!

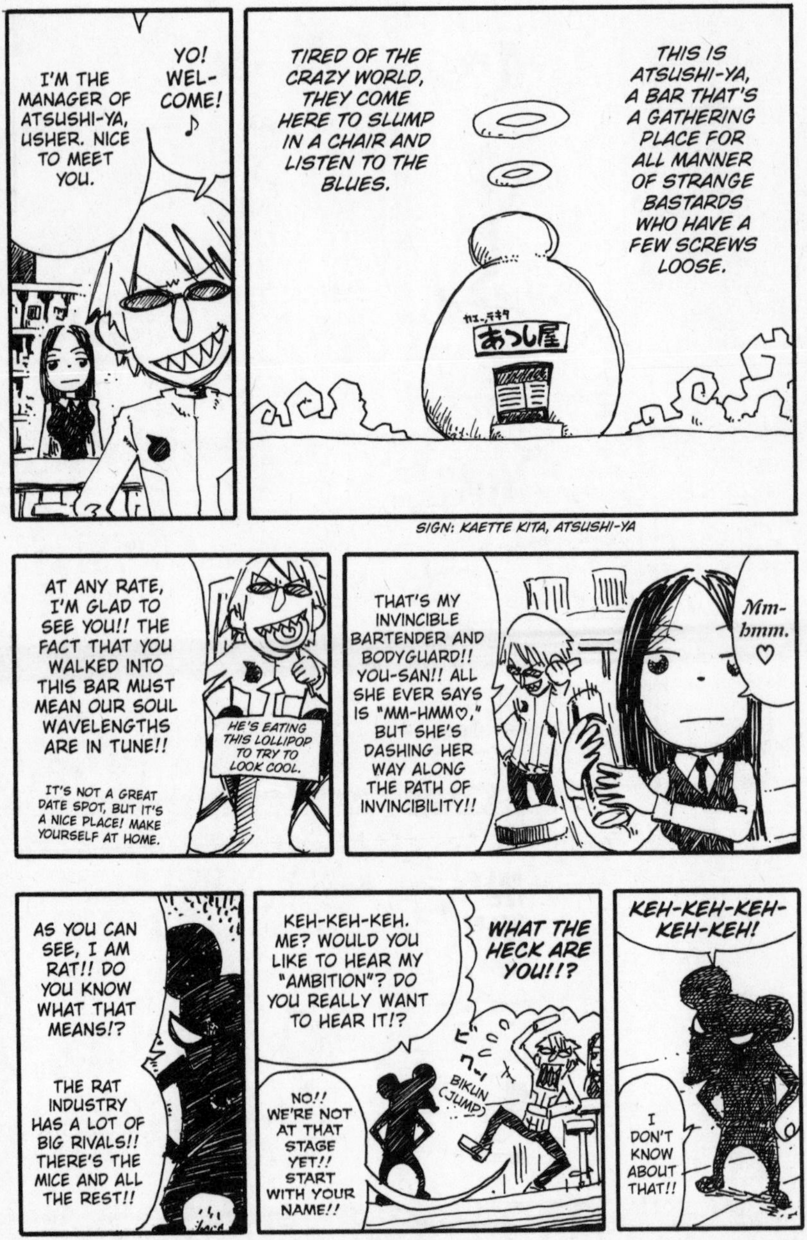

THIS IS ATSUSHI-YA, A BAR THAT'S A GATHERING PLACE FOR ALL MANNER OF STRANGE BASTARDS WHO HAVE A FEW SCREWS LOOSE.
TIRED OF THE CRAZY WORLD, THEY COME HERE TO SLUMP IN A CHAIR AND LISTEN TO THE BLUES.
あつし屋
YO! WELCOME! ♪
I'M THE MANAGER OF ATSUSHI-YA, USHER. NICE TO MEET YOU.
SIGN: KAETTE KITA, ATSUSHI-YA
Mm-hmm. ♡
THAT'S MY INVINCIBLE BARTENDER AND BODYGUARD!! YOU-SAN!! ALL SHE EVER SAYS IS "MM-HMM♡," BUT SHE'S DASHING HER WAY ALONG THE PATH OF INVINCIBILITY!!
AT ANY RATE, I'M GLAD TO SEE YOU!! THE FACT THAT YOU WALKED INTO THIS BAR MUST MEAN OUR SOUL WAVELENGTHS ARE IN TUNE!!
HE'S EATING THIS LOLLIPOP TO TRY TO LOOK COOL.
IT'S NOT A GREAT DATE SPOT, BUT IT'S A NICE PLACE! MAKE YOURSELF AT HOME.
KEH-KEH-KEH-KEH-KEH!
I DON'T KNOW ABOUT THAT!!
WHAT THE HECK ARE YOU!!?
KEH-KEH-KEH. ME? WOULD YOU LIKE TO HEAR MY "AMBITION"? DO YOU REALLY WANT TO HEAR IT!?
BIKUN (JUMP)
NO!! WE'RE NOT AT THAT STAGE YET!! START WITH YOUR NAME!!
AS YOU CAN SEE, I AM RAT!! DO YOU KNOW WHAT THAT MEANS!?
THE RAT INDUSTRY HAS A LOT OF BIG RIVALS!! THERE'S THE MICE AND ALL THE REST!!

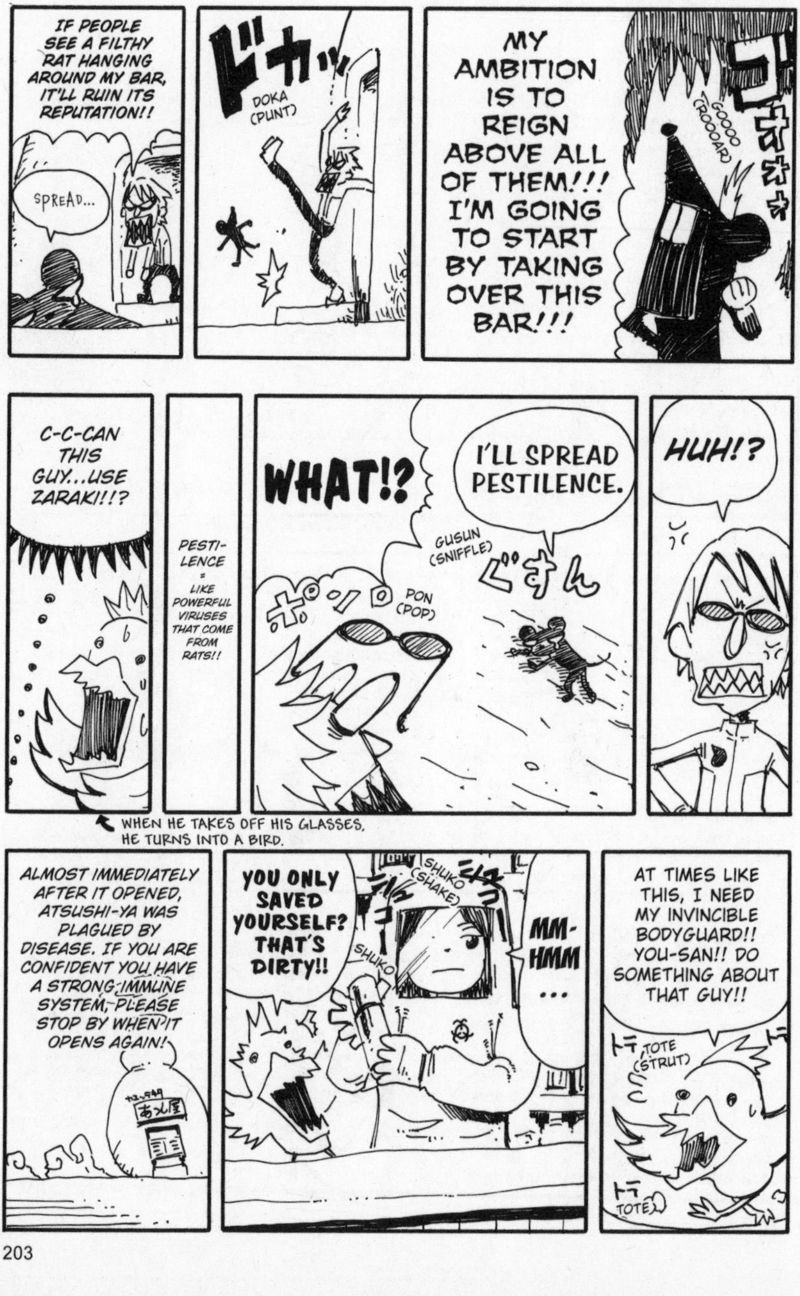
MY AMBITION IS TO REIGN ABOVE ALL OF THEM!!! I'M GOING TO START BY TAKING OVER THIS BAR!!!
GOOOO (ROOOAR)
DOKA (PUNT)
IF PEOPLE SEE A FILTHY RAT HANGING AROUND MY BAR, IT'LL RUIN ITS REPUTATION!!
SPREAD...
HUH!?
I'LL SPREAD PESTILENCE.
GUSUN (SNIFFLE)
WHAT!?
PON (POP)
PESTI-LENCE = LIKE POWERFUL VIRUSES THAT COME FROM RATS!!
C-C-CAN THIS GUY...USE ZARAKI!!?
WHEN HE TAKES OFF HIS GLASSES, HE TURNS INTO A BIRD.
AT TIMES LIKE THIS, I NEED MY INVINCIBLE BODYGUARD!! YOU-SAN!! DO SOMETHING ABOUT THAT GUY!!
TOTE (STRUT)
TOTE
MM-HMM...
SHUKO (SHAKE)
SHUKO
YOU ONLY SAVED YOURSELF? THAT'S DIRTY!!
ALMOST IMMEDIATELY AFTER IT OPENED, ATSUSHI-YA WAS PLAGUED BY DISEASE. IF YOU ARE CONFIDENT YOU HAVE A STRONG IMMUNE SYSTEM, PLEASE STOP BY WHEN IT OPENS AGAIN!

Translation Notes

Common Honorifics

no honorific: Indicates familiarity or closeness; if used without permission or reason, addresssing someone in this manner would constitute an insult.

-san: The Japanese equivalent of Mr./Mrs./Miss. If a situation calls for politeness, this is the fail-safe honorific.

-sama: Conveys great respect; may also indicate that the social status of the speaker is lower than that of the addressee.

-kun: Used most often when referring to boys, this indicates affection or familiarity. Occasionally used by older men among their peers, but it may also be used by anyone referring to a person of lower standing.

-chan: An affectionate honorific indicating familiarity used mostly in reference to girls; also used in reference to cute persons or animals of either gender.

-sensei: A respectful term for teachers, artists, or high-level professionals.

Page 11
A **shinigami** (literally "death god") is Japan's rough equivalent to the Grim Reaper in Western culture.

When spoken aloud in Japanese, Shinigami-sama's mirror number, **42-42-564**, becomes *shini shini koroshi*, which translates to "death, death, murder."

Page 18
"But your nose is gushing blood." When a guy gets a nosebleed in manga, it's an indication of sexual excitement.

Page 22
Chupa Cabra's is a reference to the Chupacabra, the legendary monster reportedly seen in Puerto Rico, Mexico, and parts of the United States. It supposedly attacks livestock (especially goats) and sucks their blood.

Page 24
Maka's Blair Witch Project is parodying *The Blair Witch Project*, a low-budget American horror film released in 1999.

Page 48
Al Capone was an infamous organized-crime boss most active during the 1920s. He was often seen wearing a hat like the one shown and smoking a cigar. He was involved in smuggling and the bootlegging of liquor and was also in control of a prostitution ring. He was eventually convicted of tax evasion.

Page 50
One of the major activities of Al Capone's gang was the bootlegging and sale of alcohol, which is why **"alcohol"** is written on his hat. At the time, America was in the midst of Prohibition, which meant the production and sale of alcohol was banned.

Page 52
"I'm going to start jumping at shadows instead of blending into them." In the original Japanese, Tsubaki uses the term *gishinanki*, which means to be suspicious of everything, to be paranoid — to jump at shadows. This is a play on *anki* (literally "dark tool"), which is what Tsubaki is.

Page 53
"Stop with the weird jokes, you bloke!!" In the original Japanese, he says "*Hen na share wa yamen shai*" (Stop the weird jokes). The "joke" here is that he slurs "*yamenasai*" (please stop) into "*yamen shai*," in order to make the end part, "*shai*," sound kind of like "*share*" (joke).

Page 56
The name **Mifune** is a reference to Toshiro Mifune, a famous Japanese actor who often played samurai characters. He appeared in many of legendary director Akira Kurosawa's films, including *Yojimbo* ("The Bodyguard").

Page 57
In Japanese, the "cinder" in **Demon Cinder Castle** is written *shinderu*, which can also mean "dead." In this case, the word *shinderu* is written in katakana (a form of Japanese writing often used for transliterating words from non-Japanese languages), so it could also be a a reference to Cinderella, the shortened, transliterated version of which is also *Shinderu* (from *Shinderura*).

Page 93
Lupin is a reference to Arsène Lupin, the gentleman thief who appears in a series of detective/crime novels by French author Maurice LeBlanc. He was also the inspiration for the manga and anime character Lupin the Third.

Page 105
You'll notice that when Liz gets licked by the mummy, she crosses her fingers. This is supposed to be a way to ward off "dirt."

Page 146
Sid-sensei's name is written "Sid" in English, but in Japanese it's written "Shido," spelled with the characters meaning "dead" and "person." Quite an appropriate name for this particular character.

Page 158
Sid-Sensei is saying **"Ohisashiburi-desu,"** a common phrase in Japanese that is roughly translated into "long time, no see." However, to make the term polite (as he insists he is), he adds *-desu* at the end, which sounds like "death" in English. He is using a pun by saying "*death*" where he should say "*desu*."

Page 162
Ding dong, DEAD dong. In the original Japanese, Sid-sensei says "*KILL (kiru) koon kaan koon.*" "*Kiin koon kaan koon*" is a fairly standard way to represent the sound of school bells in Japanese. But Sid-sensei replaced "*kiin*" with "*kiru*" (kill).

Page 169
Sid-sensei calls his attack **"Living End,"** but written next to the words "Living End" is the phrase "*juuji otoshi,*" which means "cross slam."

Page 202
Kaette Kita, which means "Returned" in Japanese, is a reference to *Kaette Kita Ultraman* ("The Return of Ultraman"), a short live-action film made by Daicon Films — a company that would eventually develop into Gainax, a major anime production company.

Usher
When written in Japanese, "Usher" is *Asshaa*, which contains the same letters as Atsushi-ya.

Page 203
Zaraki is the name of an attack spell in the *Dragon Quest* game series.